T0305895

Developing the Digital Economy in ASEAN

This book advances the international debate on the development of e-commerce with focus on emerging ASEAN economies. It provides readers insights on Asia's needs and efforts to improve the regional legal and economic conditions to support e-commerce. This book looks at the rules and regulations on e-commerce, and e-commerce for inclusive growth. It provides insights from several ASEAN member states and discovers the requirements for Asian countries to better grasp the new juncture of growth associated with economic digitalization, which also have deep implications on continuous regional integration and community-building.

Lurong Chen is Economist at the Economic Research Institute for ASEAN and East Asia (ERIA). He obtained his PhD in International Economics from the Graduate Institute in Geneva, Switzerland. His recent book, *Emerging Global Trade Governance: Mega Free Trade Agreements and Implications for ASEAN*, was published by Routledge in 2018.

Fukunari Kimura is Chief Economist at the Economic Research Institute for ASEAN and East Asia (ERIA) and Professor at the Faculty of Economics, Keio University, Japan. He obtained his PhD in economics from the University of Wisconsin-Madison, USA. His research interests include international trade and development, economic growth, applied microeconomics, and Japanese and Asian economies. His previous book, *Production Networks in Southeast Asia*, was published by Routledge in 2017.

Routledge-ERIA Studies in Development Economics

Age Related Pension Expenditure and Fiscal Space
Modelling techniques and case studies from East Asia
Edited by Mukul G. Asher and Fauziah Zen

Production Networks in Southeast Asia
Edited by Lili Yan Ing and Fukunari Kimura

The Indonesian Economy
Trade and Industrial Policies
Edited by Lili Yan Ing, Gordon H. Hanson and Sri Mulyani Indrawati

Social Protection Goals in East Asia
Strategies and Methods to Generate Fiscal Space
Edited by Mukul G. Asher, Fauziah Zen and Astrid Dita

World Trade Evolution
Growth, Productivity and Employment
Edited by Lili Yan Ing and Miaojie Yu

Emerging Global Trade Governance
Mega Free Trade Agreements and Implications for ASEAN
Edited by Lurong Chen, Shujiro Urata, Junji Nakagawa and Masahito Ambashi

East Asian Integration
Goods, Services and Investment
Edited by Lili Yan Ing, Martin Richardson and Shujiro Urata

Developing the Digital Economy in ASEAN
Edited by Lurong Chen and Fukunari Kimura

For more information about this series, please visit www.routledge.com/Routledge-ERIA-Studies-in-Development-Economics/book-series/ERIA

Developing the Digital Economy in ASEAN

Edited by Lurong Chen
and Fukunari Kimura

Routledge
Taylor & Francis Group

LONDON AND NEW YORK

Economic Research Institute
for ASEAN and East Asia

First published 2019
by Routledge
2 Park Square, Milton Park, Abingdon, Oxon OX14 4RN

and by Routledge
52 Vanderbilt Avenue, New York, NY 10017

Routledge is an imprint of the Taylor & Francis Group, an informa business

First issued in paperback 2021

British Library Cataloguing-in-Publication Data
A catalogue record for this book is available from the British Library

Library of Congress Cataloging-in-Publication Data
Names: Chen, Lurong, editor. | Kimura, Fukunari, editor.
Title: Developing the digital economy in ASEAN / edited by Lurong
Chen and Fukunari Kimura.
Description: Abingdon, Oxon ; New York, NY : Routledge, 2019. |
Series: Routledge-ERIA studies in development economics | Includes
bibliographical references and index.
Identifiers: LCCN 2018060326 | ISBN 9781138586062 (hardback) |
ISBN 9780429504853 (ebook)
Subjects: LCSH: Electronic commerce—Southeast Asia. | Information
technology—Economic aspects—Southeast Asia. | Economic
development—Southeast Asia
Classification: LCC HF5548.325.A785 D48 2019 | DDC
381/.1420959—dc23
LC record available at https://lccn.loc.gov/2018060326

ISBN: 978-1-138-58606-2 (hbk)
ISBN: 978-1-03-209287-4 (pbk)
ISBN: 978-0-429-50485-3 (ebk)

Typeset in Galliard
by Apex CoVantage, LLC

Contents

Figures

Tables

Acknowledgements

The idea for this book emerged from an ERIA research project on "Digital Economy, Innovation and Asia's Competitiveness in Global Value Chains (GVCs)". The project brought together economists, lawyers, officials, and trade negotiators to study Asian development in the era of digital economy. As a stage achievement of the study, this editorial volume, *Developing the Digital Economy in ASEAN*, brings together twelve articles into a major statement on the requirements for ASEAN to better grasp the new juncture of growth associated with economic digitalisation and e-commerce development.

We are very grateful to Hank Lim of Singapore Institute of International Affairs for providing his very insightful suggestions and comments.

Support from ERIA colleagues, in particular, Hidetoshi Nishimura, Izuru Kobayashi, Shujiro Urata, Anita Prakash, Ponciano Intal, Shigeki Kamiyama, Maria Rosario, Stefan Wesiak, Lydia Ruddy, Fany Trianingsih, Chrestella Budyanto, Yuanita Suhud, Tyagita Silka Hapsari, Meilawati and Handayani is gratefully acknowledged.

Throughout the compilation of the book, we also received great support from Yongling Lam and Samantha Phua of Routledge. Their encouragement and patience have been critical to the completion of this project.

Last but not least, we are indebted to all contributors to this book: their enthusiasm has been unwavering, from the involvement in the initial research project and through the subsequent dialogues to complete this book.

Lurong Chen and Fukunari Kimura

Contributors

Keon-Hyung Ahn is Assistant Professor at the Department of International Commerce, Daejeon University, Daejeon, Korea. He obtained a PhD in Business Administration from Graduate School of SungKyunKwan University, Seoul, Republic of Korea.

Lurong Chen is Economist at the Economic Research Institute for ASEAN and East Asia (ERIA). He obtained his PhD in International Economics from the Graduate Institute in Geneva, Switzerland.

Inkyo Cheong is Professor of International Trade at the Inha University, Incheon, Republic of Korea. He also serves as Director of FTA Research Forum.

Ramon L. Clarete is Professor at the University of the Philippines School of Economics. He obtained his doctoral degree from the University of Hawaii at Manoa.

Ludo Cuyvers is Professor Emeritus of International Economics, Faculty of Applied Economics, and Director of Centre for ASEAN Studies (CAS), University of Antwerp, Belgium and Professor Extraordinary, Faculty of Economics and Management Sciences, North-West University, Potchefstroom Campus, South Africa.

Noor Azina Ismail is Professor at the Faculty of Economics and Administration, University of Malaya. She received her PhD from Queensland University of Technology, Australia.

Fukunari Kimura is Chief Economist at the Economic Research Institute for ASEAN and East Asia (ERIA) and Professor at the Faculty of Economics, Keio University, Japan. He obtained his PhD in Economics from the University of Wisconsin-Madison, USA.

Jane Kelsey is Professor of Law at the University of Auckland, New Zealand. She has law degrees from Victoria University of Wellington, Oxford University, Cambridge University and the University Auckland.

Muhammad Mehedi Masud is Senior Lecturer at the Faculty of Economics and Administration, University of Malaya. He received his PhD from University of Malaya.

Michitaka Nakatomi is Consulting Fellow at the Research Institute of Economy, Trade and Industry (RIETI) and a Special Advisor to the Japan External Trade Organization (JETRO). He was Principal Trade Negotiator of the Ministry of Economy, Trade and Industry (METI) of the government of Japan in 2011–2012.

Kalamullah Ramli is Professor and Chairman, at the Center for Science and Technology Research (CSTR), Universitas Indonesia. He received his doctoral degree from Universitaet Duisburg-Essen, NRW, Germany.

Siriluck Rotchanakitumnuai is Professor of Management Information Systems and Distinguished Professor of Thammasat University, Thailand. She was the Former Dean of Thammasat Business School, Thailand.

Reth Soeng is Adjunct Professor of Economics at the American University of Phnom Penh and the Royal School of Administration, Cambodia. He holds a PhD in economics from the University of Antwerp, Belgium.

Morarith Soeung is Chief Executive Office of Chief (Cambodia) Commercial Bank Plc, Phnom Penh, Cambodia. He holds DBA from the National University of Management, Singapore.

John Walsh is Lecturer in International Business at the Hanoi Campus of RMIT Viet Nam. He received his doctorate from Oxford University, UK.

Kar-yiu Wong is Professor of Economics at the University of Washington, USA. He received his PhD from Columbia University, USA.

Part I

Understanding e-commerce

Introduction

ASEAN development in the digital economy

Lurong Chen and Fukunari Kimura

1. Background

Digitalisation is delivering an unprecedented set of tools to bolster growth and productivity. Economic activities that depend on the Internet or new information and communications technology (ICT) to purchase goods or services or to do business online are rapidly expanding. Electronic commerce (e-commerce) has been increasingly important in the international economy. It typically involves fewer intermediate links between sellers and buyers, but has higher demand on services, especially information, payment, and logistics. Cross-border business-to-business (B2B) e-commerce has been steadily growing since the 1990s. The growth has accelerated with the spread and deepening of global value chains in the 21st century. Since around 2014–2015, the radical growth of business-to-consumer (B2C) and customer-to-customer (C2C) markets has attracted increasing public attention to global e-commerce. Various factors have laid a solid foundation for the boom in cross-border e-commerce, such as the use of smartphones, high-speed Internet, the maturity of online payment systems, the changes in consumer behaviours, services sector liberalisation, and so on.

This has introduced new dynamics to international trade with global retail e-commerce sales growing faster than traditional retail sales. Global revenue from cross-border e-commerce was estimated to be more than US$600 billion in 2018, twice as much as that in 2012. E-commerce in many Asian markets will see double-digit growth in the next 5–10 years. India, Indonesia, and Malaysia are among the world fastest-expanding retail e-commerce markets, growing at a rate of over 20 percent per year. From 2015–2021, the region's total market revenue from e-commerce will increase from around US$320 billion to over US$900 billion. The Chinese market will contribute over 90 percent of this growth. China's share in the world e-commerce market will increase from about 30 percent in 2015 to nearly 40 percent in 2021, while India and the 10 member states of the Association of Southeast Asian Nations (ASEAN) will increase their combined share in the global market from 2.5 percent to 4 percent (Statista, 2016).

Globally, the share of e-commerce in total retail sales increased by 12 percentage points between 2015 and 2016. By mid-2016, the scale of online shoppers in China had reached 448 million, and the online shopping usage rate had reached 63 percent (CNNIC, 2016). Singapore (60 percent), Malaysia (52 percent), and Thailand (51 percent) are among the world's top markets with the highest online shopping penetration rates. In the next five years, an increasing share of the increment in private consumption will come from global e-commerce growth. Sustained growth of online shoppers provides a solid base for e-commerce consumption. Overall, the scale of the digital economy in ASEAN is projected to increase by 5.5 times by 2025 (Think with Google, 2017). With growth like this, Asia is likely to be the global epicentre of e-commerce in the next decade.

However, the radical growth of e-commerce could be a double-edged sword. On one side, economic digitalisation tends to facilitate international trade since consumers and producers can obtain information from a wide range of geographical locations at low cost within a short time. This injects new dynamics into the global market. With new entrants, new products, new services, and new business models, as well as changes in innovation and technology diffusion processes, the price level is lowered, the variety of supply increases, and market competition intensifies.

On the other side, the region needs to face more intensive competition, either within or outside the region. Technological progress may widen development gaps among countries, if those latecomers cannot manage to grasp the opportunities to accelerate the growth. Equally, there is no guarantee that front runners in the past will still be able to perform well in the future. In the digital world, one should continuously adjust in response to technology and market changes to remain competitive. In this regard, Asia will have to maximise the e-commerce-related benefits but minimise or eliminate the associated risks to turn the region's potential into a real engine of growth.

2. ASEAN's potentials: adaptiveness, market gravitation, and readiness

To promote e-commerce development, ASEAN needs to increase efforts and make progress in areas such as connectivity, services, rules and regulations, and human capital development. Above all, one should have more comprehensive and in-depth understanding about the region's potentials, needs, and actions in developing its digital economy.

More precisely, strategic plans and policy prescriptions will draw considerations from three layers. First, adaptiveness: economic digitalisation is a worldwide phenomenon. From the economic aspect, the information revolution is associated with the emergence of new market conditions and dynamics in the global business environment. This requires the regional economy in Asia, both the public and private sectors, to respond to these changes quickly. Second, market gravitation: despite those new features of the digital economy, the development of e-commerce also depends on some 'classic' conditions for economic development such as market size, trade facilitation, and investment freedom. Third, readiness: e-commerce development needs support from technology, market, and policy. Countries' preparation and readiness to develop the digital economy will determine the performance of their business in e-commerce.

2.1. Adaptiveness

The information revolution is associated with the emergence of new market conditions and dynamics in a global business environment. Simply put, the region's adaptiveness to global economic digitalisation comes from its capacity in at least two aspects: (i) technology adoption and (ii) incremental innovation. First, deep involvement in global value chains (GVCs) opens new windows for ASEAN member states (AMS) to access the latest technologies and also facilitates their learning. Second, the countries' capacity in incremental innovation allows them to benefit from second-mover advantages to grow faster and even leap forward to the front of the market – the popular use of e-payments in China and the success of the Alibaba Group are typical examples.

In ASEAN, facilitation of the growth of e-commerce is one of the six main areas covered by the e-ASEAN Framework Agreement, whilst at the national level, developing a digital economy and e-commerce have already been part of most Asian countries' national strategies and action plans. AMS have put great effort into accelerating their learning processes and adopting new technologies. According to the World Economic Forum (2017), businesses in ASEAN have managed to adopt the last ICTs to link with the global market. In comparison, the speed of firm-level technology adoption in the region is higher than the world average. When the same report asked companies to rank the use of ICT in business transactions, both B2B and B2C, the results show that most AMS get higher scores than the world average level. Considering the region's overall stage of development, it is evident that the business sector in ASEAN has been catching up quickly with the new dynamics of the global economy and actively promoting digitalisation. Government efforts in promoting digitalisation, measured by the index of e-participation, are also worth noting. In 2016, the scores of most AMS' e-participation of government were higher than the world average. The scores of Cambodia, Lao PDR, and Myanmar were still relatively low, but they have made progress significantly since 2012.

In the long run, economic digitalisation tends to improve the adaptability of Asian countries to the world economy and to facilitate countries' integration into GVCs. There are efficiency gains associated with the application of digital technologies. For instance, producers or service providers can create/enlarge their markets, lower operating costs, facilitate transactions, and improve competitiveness.[1] For consumers, it offers them more information, more choice, easier ways to purchase, and higher quality of services. Moreover, digitalisation has been introducing new business/organisational models to the region, generating more knowledge-intensive activities, and creating more job opportunities. The International Labour Organization (2016) estimated that in 2016, more than 50 million employees in ASEAN had knowledge-intensive jobs, representing over 13 percent of the total workforce in the region.[2]

2.2. Market gravitation

Despite the new features of the digital economy, the development of e-commerce is still influenced by traditional factors such as market size, trade facilitation, investment freedom, and so on. ASEAN, as a group, is the world's third most populous market, following China and India. Two-thirds of the population in ASEAN is aged between 15 and 64 years, representing a large potential market on the consumption side and an abundant labour force on the supply side. By the end of 2016, ASEAN had 260 million Internet users, representing two-fifths of the total population in the region. Most of them are aged younger than 40 years. About half of the Internet users had started shopping online. By 2021, e-commerce users in ASEAN are projected to number more than 170 million.

The existing large pool of young Internet users not only represents consumers directly linked to the e-commerce market, but also suggests they may have higher purchasing power in society. In the case of ASEAN, Internet use has been very popular in Singapore and Malaysia, playing an important role in those economies. Nearly 90 percent of households in Singapore are Internet users. Internet-related economy accounted for 4.1 percent of Malaysian gross domestic product in 2012 (MGI, 2012). By the end of 2015, four out of every ten Malaysians had already used e-commerce (Statista, 2016). Malay has been ranked as the seventh most widely used language on the Internet. Moreover, less-developed countries – Cambodia, Lao PDR, Myanmar, and Viet Nam (CLMV countries) – are quickly catching up. For instance, the share of Internet users in the total population of Viet Nam increased from 1.3 percent to 52.7 percent between 2001 and 2015, whereas the number of Internet users grew at 34.7 percent in Cambodia and 32.4 percent in Myanmar per year.

2.3. E-commerce readiness

E-commerce development needs support from technology, market, and government policy. A country's preparation and readiness to support the digital economy will determine the level of success of businesses involved in e-commerce. Widespread Internet use is the first step. Technically, ICT drives the development of e-commerce by expanding the volume and capacity of online communication, especially the use of fibre-optic cables and commercial satellites. Moreover, physical infrastructure that provides stable and fast Internet connectivity is a precondition for doing business online.

In particular, Asian countries have made great progress in developing mobile broadband. By the end of 2014, mobile broadband covered over 43 percent of the region. The relative cost of data usage, as measured by its share in gross national income, decreased from 37 percent in 2010 to 6.2 percent in 2013. This positively impacted regional connectivity, as more people living in rural areas or the countryside can now access the Internet using their smartphones.

At least two-thirds of users in ASEAN use a smartphone to access the Internet. CLMV countries have the highest growth rates of mobile subscriptions per

100 inhabitants. Specifically, the compounded annual growth rate ranges from 36 percent in Cambodia to 70 percent in Myanmar. Indian users are expected to catch up with the country's smartphone penetration rate, projected to increase from 58 percent in 2015 to 74 percent in 2021. With the expansion of mobile broadband, the popularisation of smartphones, the reduction in the cost of data usage, and the richness of online shopping and payment tools available on portable devices and platforms, a new wave of e-commerce growth is underway. A survey[3] of 30,000 owners of mobile devices across the world in 2016 shows that 46 percent of respondents in Asia-Pacific use their mobile devices to purchase products and services online, mainly with mobile apps. This share is higher than that of Europe (32 percent) or North America (28 percent).

3. Structure and chapter synopsis

Literature on e-commerce development and governance in Asia is still under development. This book advances the international debate on the development of e-commerce with a focus on emerging ASEAN economies. It highlights the importance of and provides insights on ASEAN and AMS efforts to promote digital economy from the aspects of rules and regulations, inclusive growth, and regional cooperation.

In addition to this introductory chapter, the book consists of 12 chapters containing analyses conducted at industrial, national, and regional levels, as well as viewpoints from legal, economic, and policymaking perspectives. All these studies combined deliver a positive message regarding the e-commerce development in the region. That is, ASEAN will be able to better grasp the new opportunities of growth that come along with economic digitalisation and become part of the global epicentre of e-commerce activities with more efforts on (i) rules and regulations on e-commerce-related activities and market, (ii) policy action plans to let new technologies and business models serve for inclusiveness, and (iii) the combination of countries' national strategies and regional cooperation.

Chapter 1 by Kar-yiu Wong, 'E-commerce and international trade', examines the nature and features of cross-border e-commerce in combination with the theory of international trade. It investigates how digitalisation affects resource allocation, prices, and international trade, and the consequent effect on market equilibrium. By modelling the cost-savings effect resulting from digital platforms' facilitation of e-commerce, the study demonstrates how digitalisation can lead to lower transaction costs, larger market size, and higher degree of market competition.

Wong's chapter further explores the trade price-volume dynamics. Under the model, a higher degree of digitalisation tends to (i) encourage more business (increasing the quantity of sale and purchase) in a closed economy, and (ii) increase the market autarkic price if and only if the elasticity of demand for digitalisation is larger than that of supply of digitalisation. In an open economy, economic digitalisation will increase the volume of international trade, but cannot guarantee that the free trade price will decrease, unless digitalisation encourages the exporting countries to sell more than that the importing countries will buy.

3.1. Rules and regulations

E-commerce calls for new rules and regulations to improve trust, security, and facility in the online marketplace. Chapters 2–5 of the book discuss the rules and regulations on cross-border e-commerce from different aspects.

In Chapter 2, 'Cross-border digital trade, e-commerce governance, and necessary actions ahead', Michitaka Nakatomi analyses the importance of digital trade and e-commerce in the global and regional economies. He states that international discipline on digital trade is necessary to guard against national restrictions and regulations on e-commerce that would impede the development of a digital economy. Above all, digital protectionism has raised concerns, asking for greater global effort to define the boundaries of allowable regulations to balance regulation and market freedom.

Nakatomi then explores a solution for global governance on e-commerce in the multilateral framework but with consideration of other fora and methods. He proposes to launch negotiations for a 'digital-only agreement' by like-minded countries along the structure of the Trade in Services Agreement (TiSA). Ensuring that such an agreement is consistent with World Trade Organization rules will accelerate the process of rule-making on e-commerce, not only of trade in goods but also trade in services. In addition to the legally binding approaches, soft law approaches, such as guidelines and best practices, should also be actively promoted.

Chapter 3, 'The risks for ASEAN of new mega-agreements that promote the wrong model of e-commerce' by Jane Kelsey, examines how a systematic strategy of norm creation through mega-agreements on trade and investment could embed the current asymmetries for the future. Based on her analyses of the legal obligations of cross-border e-commerce and advanced economies' demand for regulation in the mega-agreements, Kelsey suggests that developing countries, including ASEAN, should be the 'rule makers' rather than the 'rule takers' in the naissance of the new agreement(s) in order to prevent the normative regime from being systematically developed to entrench the first movers' dominant power over source codes, data and digital technologies, and facilities.

Kelsey further highlights the importance of collective commitment to local investment and shared knowledge in achieving a development dividend through digitalisation. For ASEAN, it is crucial to identify and develop appropriate national and regional frameworks that can effectively regulate (i) technology transfer and disclosure of source codes, (ii) data localisation, (iii) skills upgrade, and (iv) financial assistance to bridge the digital divide and facilitate e-commerce.

Chapters 4 and 5 dig deeper into two specific issues: data privacy and consumer protection. Data as a key driving factor of the digital economy has been increasingly prominent with the advance of new technologies such as big data, cloud computing, and artificial intelligence. In Chapter 4, 'E-commerce in free trade agreements and the trans-pacific Partnership', Inkyo Cheong deals with the issue of free data flows and privacy protection in e-commerce, and to what extent free trade agreements can help involved parties enhance their cooperation in this area.

Cheong reviews what the Organisation for Economic Co-operation and Development (OECD), Asia-Pacific Economic Cooperation (APEC), and the European Union (EU) have done in regulating privacy. He examines the e-commerce chapter in the Trans-Pacific Partnership (TPP) agreement, which requires member states to support an open Internet and not to obligate data localisation; and asks them to commit to protecting personal data through national laws. This has twofold implications for the ongoing negotiation of the e-commerce chapter in the Regional Comprehensive Economic Partnership (RCEP) agreement. First, the RCEP e-commerce chapter should also cover a wide range of topics. And second, sensitive issues such as data localisation and regulating the cross-border transfer of personal data are important, but difficult to agree on. The negotiations will run more smoothly if the participating countries are given flexibility in making commitments.[4]

In Chapter 5, 'An online dispute resolution scheme to resolve e-commerce disputes in ASEAN', Keon-Hyung Ahn explores a solution for ASEAN to improve online consumer protection in supporting e-commerce. AMS have realised that the lack of consumer rights protection could be a barrier to further e-commerce development. Establishing a regional online dispute resolution (ODR) scheme could be an effective measure to protect online consumers.

The chapter starts with an overview of the e-commerce and consumer protection laws in ASEAN countries. With reference to international rules and practices on consumer protection, especially the EU's ODR platform, Ahn proposes a roadmap for ASEAN to adopt an effective ODR system in three steps: (i) establish a national ODR system, (ii) create an ASEAN ODR network, and (iii) launch a regional dispute settlement mechanism dealing with cross-border e-commerce complaints. In this process, AMS need to ensure compatibility of national, regional, and global consumer protection laws, and at the same time enhance consumer awareness and conduct campaigns. Extensively, it will also be in ASEAN's interest to include in the RCEP e-commerce chapter the establishment of a regional ODR in the ASEAN Plus Six framework.

3.2. E-commerce for inclusive growth

Advances in ICT, typically the development of the Internet, have been the backbone of the wide spread of GVCs. The unbundling of globalisation (Baldwin, 2016; Kimura, 2018) provides countries, both developing and developed, new fuel for development. For ASEAN, a big concern is to unleash digitalisation's potential as a driver for inclusive growth. Chapters 6–11 analyse actions and plans to grasp the new growth opportunity in the digital age in individual AMS.

Indonesia, the most populous country in ASEAN, has its vision as the 'digital energy of Asia'. In Chapter 6, 'Indonesia's preparation for the digital economy and e-commerce: infrastructure, regulatory, and policy development', Kalamullah Ramli presents how Indonesia is getting ready to face the emergence of e-commerce that has found a quick-booming market in the country. He investigates three dimensions: (i) the development of infrastructure, (ii) efforts on the national legal and regulatory framework, and (iii) the industry and market responses to the government's policy initiatives.

The chapter shows that Indonesia has been progressively developing ICT infrastructure driven by the Indonesia Broadband Plan via the Palapa Ring Project and Spectrum Refarming. Indonesia has adopted a three-layer governance model for Internet regulation: infrastructure, services, and content. The national e-commerce roadmap consists of strategic priorities in areas such as taxation, consumer protection, human skills development, logistics, infrastructure, and cybersecurity. Digitalising micro, small, and medium-sized enterprises (MSMEs) remains on top of the list of priorities. There have been efforts to make MSMEs aware and capable of participating in online business, but more effort will be needed to help them take more advantage of the booming e-commerce sector.

Looking forward, Ramli points out the need for the government, local communities, and all stakeholders to move in synergy to further improve Indonesia's digital ecosystem, especially in the fields of e-payment readiness and technology and service affordability.

Noor Azina Ismail and Muhammad Mehedi Masud analyse domestic and international challenges faced by Malaysian small and medium-sized enterprises (SMEs) in adopting e-commerce in Chapter 7, 'E-commerce adoption by ASEAN SMEs and its domestic challenges: evidence from Malaysia'.

Their interviews with Malaysian SME entrepreneurs reveal factors that have hindered the country's e-commerce adoption compared to other AMS. These include: (i) superficial understanding of e-commerce, (ii) lack of information about latest available e-commerce tools and applications, (iii) inadequate technical skills in using new tools, and (iv) low awareness of the benefits of e-commerce and online transactions. Many Malaysian SMEs also highlighted the importance of a digital platform in promoting online business.

To solve these problems, Ismail and Masud's prescription includes three aspects of improvement: (i) rules and regulations to improve the credibility of the online marketplace, (ii) skill upgrading and awareness-raising campaigns on the digital economy, and (iii) e-payment and microfinancing to facilitate SMEs participation.

For ASEAN emerging economies, the two main factors that hinder their e-commerce inclusiveness are underdeveloped e-payment systems and inefficient connectivity. Chapters 8 and 9 provide insights into these two areas, combined with the experience of digitalisation in Cambodia and the Philippines, respectively.

Chapter 8, 'E-commerce development and Internet banking adoption in Cambodia', by Reth Soeng, Ludo Cuyvers, and Morarith Soeung, investigates the adoption of Internet and mobile banking services in Cambodia. Although, in general, e-commerce in Cambodia is in its infancy, Internet banking has been increasingly popular among local consumers. After reviewing the footprints of

ICT development and the government's efforts to establish its ICT-related legal framework, the chapter summarises some stylised facts concerning e-commerce development in Cambodia.

Soeng, Cuyvers, and Soeung further examine the potential factors that affect Internet banking adoption using econometric models and firm-level data. The results of their empirical work show that perceived benefits have a larger impact on whether a consumer will adopt Internet banking compared to the effect of social influence. For that reason, a critical step of promoting the use of online banking – and in turn, e-commerce – will be to increase awareness of the potential benefits. In the long run, however, Cambodia will require more effort on legislation and infrastructure to develop its ICT sector to sustain economic growth and achieve more equitable development.

In Chapter 9, 'E-commerce in the Philippines: gains and challenges', Ramon L. Clarete assesses the country's digital economy readiness, before looking into the question of why the Philippines lags behind others. Although the Philippine e-commerce market has been growing fast, when compared to other AMS, Internet connection is slow, and the market is still small in size and not efficient enough in facilitating online business. The country's poor connectivity, caused by not only inadequate ICT infrastructure but also immature legal and institution building, has hindered Philippine firms' involvement in the digital economy.

Clarete's prescription highlights the role of competition, breaking down the monopoly or oligopoly in the Philippine ICT industry and introducing competition is a straightforward solution. Furthermore, the government will need to make continuous efforts to develop laws, regulations, and policy to support market competition.

In the case of Thailand, Siriluck Rotchanakitumnuai concerns about how to accelerate the country's pace in digitalisation. Chapter 10, 'Measuring e-readiness of Thailand in ASEAN: macro and micro e-commerce perspectives', assesses Thailand's digital readiness compared to that of other AMS using various indicators. The results show that Thailand has yet to unleash fully its digital economy potential. Rotchanakitumnuai urges the country to develop faster, with the government playing the leading role at both the macro and micro levels. To promote cross-border B2C e-commerce, Thailand needs to make further progress in logistics, trust, legislative protection, consumer protection, and e-payment.

Chapter 11, 'Internet services and the potential for market access for rural agricultural households in Myanmar and Viet Nam', casts attention on the links between digitalisation and poverty reduction. John Walsh conducted a survey covering over 600 rural households living in Myanmar and Viet Nam. It is evident from the results that, in both countries, using mobile phones and the Internet improves access to information and markets – and therefore household prospects in terms of income and opportunities for better business.

Walsh's study re-emphasises two important issues when considering inclusive digitalisation: education and connectivity. In rural areas of Myanmar and Viet Nam, using the Internet for commercial purposes has not yet reached a mature phase. It is critical to educate people to use digital tools more profitably. Regarding connectivity, however, feedback received from different countries and sites varies significantly. The findings suggest that the need for connectivity depends on the pattern of the local economy and society. Given such variability, no single plan or strategy can promote connectivity through ICT and market access.

4. Policy suggestion for the way forward

Chapter 12, 'ASEAN in the digital era: enabling cross-border e-commerce', serves as the concluding chapter of this book. It investigates and discusses some common challenges that ASEAN as a whole and its member states face in developing their digital economy, primarily in connectivity, services, rules and regulations, and labour skills. The chapter further suggests policy efforts in supporting market mechanisms to improve performance in these areas.

First of all, creating an e-commerce-enabling ecosystem. Since value chains of e-commerce cover both the physical world and cyberspace, there are needs for rules, regulations, and legislation in both spaces of the market to increase trust, ensure security, and facilitate doing business online.

Second, improving connectivity. For this, e-commerce requires free information flow, efficient logistics, free cash flow, and seamless links among networks. The corresponding actions include (i) increasing the supply of public goods to improve infrastructure and ICT connectivity, (ii) establishing rules and regulations to ensure dynamics and competition in the online marketplace, (iii) promoting connectivity-required services to improve the quality of connectivity, (iv) collaborating in building the regionwide e-commerce ecosystem, and (v) seeking new technologies that can provide new solutions to improve regional connectivity, such as smartphone economy and e-payment and e-finance innovation.

Third, encouraging e-commerce-derived services. Service sector development has extensive implications on the economy. It can generate more value-added and create more jobs to absorb labour and, more importantly, give SMEs more opportunities to join GVCs.

Fourth, e-commerce rule setting. Continuous effort is required to form rules and regulations to ensure free data flow and consumer protection, as well as fair competition and cybersecurity. In this regard, the conclusion the ASEAN Agreement on E-commerce is a milestone. However, its significance still depends on how effectively the agreement will be implemented.

Last, but most important, improving labour skills. Human capital and innovation determine the fundamental competitiveness – and therefore the long-term success – of e-commerce. AMS are urged not only to increase the coverage but also to improve the quality of their education and training systems. Furthermore, it calls for regionwide service liberalisation to accelerate knowledge diffusion.

Notes

1 Chapter 1 of this book provides more insights using the model illustration.
2 Here the aggregate data of ASEAN do not include Lao PDR and Myanmar, due to the lack of data for these two countries.
3 Statista online database. Available at www.statista.com/statistics/418393/mcommer cepenetration- worldwide-region/
4 For instance, the ASEAN Agreement on E-commerce requires each AMS to 'provide protection for consumers using e-commerce that affords a similar level of protection to that provided for consumers of other forms of commerce under its relevant laws, regulations and policies', but at the same time allows Cambodia, Lao PDR and Myanmar not to be obliged to implement this commitment for a period of five years after the agreement enters into force (Government of Singapore, 2018).

Bibliography

Baldwin, R. (2016), *The Great Convergence: Information Technology and the New Globalization*. Cambridge, MA: The Belknap Press of Harvard University.
China Internet Network Information Center (CNNIC) (2016), 'The 38th Report of China Internet Development Statistics'. Available at www.cnnic.cn/hlwfzyj/ hlwxzbg/hlwtjbg/201608/t20160803_54392.htm
Government of Singapore (2018), 'Factsheet ASEAN Agreement on Electronic Commerce'. Available at https://www.gov.sg/~/sgpcmedia/media_releases/mti/ press_release/P-20181112-1/attachment/Annex%20A%20Factsheet %20on%20ASEAN%20Agreement%20on%20e-Commerce.pdfInternational Labour Organization (2016), 'ASEAN in Transformation'. Available at www.ilo.org/ public/english/dialogue/actemp/downloads/publications/2016/asean_in_ transf_2016_r3_persp.pdf
Kimura, F. (2018), ' "Unbundlings" and Development Strategies in ASEAN: Old Issues and New Challenges', *Journal of Southeast Asian Economies*, 35(1): 13–21.
McKinsey Global Institute (MGI) (2012), 'Online and Upcoming: The Internet's Impact on Aspiring Countries'. Available at www.mckinsey.com/industries/ high-tech/our-insights/impact-of-the-internet-on-aspiring-countries
Statista (2016), 'Digital Market Outlook'. Available at www.statista.com/statistics/ 220177/b2c-commerce-sales-cagr-forecast-for-selected-countries/
Think with Google (2017), 'E-Economy SEA, Unlocking the 200 Billion Digital Opportunity in Southeast Asia'. Available at http://apac.thinkwithgoogle.com/ research-studies/e-conomy-sea-unlocking-200b-digital-opportunity.html
World Economic Forum (2017), 'The Global Competitiveness Report 2016–2017'. Available at www.weforum.org/reports/the-global-competitiveness-report-2016- 2017-1

1 E-commerce and international trade

Kar-yiu Wong

1. Introduction

The rapid development of the Internet and digital technology in many countries such as the United States and China has led to the rise of a new form of marketing, transactions, and payment: electronic commerce (e-commerce). This system has drastically changed the way of doing business for firms and consumers. Instead of window shopping in a traditional market like a shopping mall or retail shop, customers can browse online. Instead of placing an order personally in a shop, paying with cash or a credit/debit card, and receiving the product on the spot or shortly after, customers can place the order online, transfer the purchase money online, and receive the item via postal or express delivery or via Internet transmission. This new form of business and transactions affects not only the costs of selling and buying, but also the volumes of sales, the prices of products, local and international trade, and resource allocation.

This new form of business is responsible for only a small fraction of the retail transactions in most countries. For example, the online transaction volume of total retail sales in 2016 was 0.03 percent for Brazil, 0.60 percent for China, 0.05 percent for France, 0.13 percent for Germany (revenue), 0.03 percent for India, 0.02 percent for Indonesia, 0.12 percent for the Republic of Korea (henceforth, Korea), 0.17 percent for the United Kingdom, and 0.05 percent (2015) for the United States (US). However, the growth rates of online business are astonishing in many countries. In 2017, global business-to-consumers (B2C) e-commerce was estimated to have grown at a rate of 17 percent, totalling US$1.84 trillion in sales. Regionally, the Asia-Pacific region has the biggest e-commerce turnover volume and the fastest growth rate. For example, in 2015, the Asia-Pacific region recorded an e-commerce turnover volume of US$1.06 trillion, about 46.5 percent of the total volume in the world, representing a growth of 28.4 percent over the 2014 volume (Ecommerce Foundation, 2016).

This new system of doing business has brought a lot of changes to both sellers and buyers, and has important impacts on the market equilibrium. E-commerce has become a very attractive and convenient way of doing business because the costs of selling and buying products through electronic platforms (e-platforms) are generally lower than what people have to pay in the traditional markets. This has been made possible by rapid advances in technologies such as the Internet and electronic equipment, including computers and mobile phones.

China had the largest B2C e-commerce market in 2016 and 2017. Its B2C e-commerce sales totalled US$976 billion in 2017, which is about 150 percent of that of the next ranked country, the US (US$648.6 billion) (Statista 2018). China's market also recorded the highest growth rate from 2016 to 2017. The Asia-Pacific region is very receptive to this new technology and new approach to doing business.

With the improvement in and falling costs of necessary technologies, sellers and buyers in one country can easily access e-platforms in other countries. Such access allows sellers to sell products and buyers to purchase products on e-platforms in other countries. In other words, e-platforms encourage international trade, which is also called cross-border e-commerce.

This chapter analyses the effects of e-platforms on cross-border sales, including the impacts on foreign sellers offering products to local buyers and on foreign buyers purchasing products from local sellers. It examines how the establishment of e-platforms affects market prices and transaction volumes, and analyses the effect of a new electronic platform on foreign trade in products.

Because e-commerce is a relatively new system of doing business, and its volumes and values are still small relative to those of total retail sales, research on e-commerce is still rare. Terzi (2011) and Zhang (2014) are a few earlier papers, but much more work needs to be done, particularly on how the emergence of e-commerce may affect resource allocation, trade, employment, and market equilibrium. This chapter examines some of these issues and tries to provide analysis and answers.

The next section examines and describes the main characteristics of e-commerce. Interactions between sellers and buyers are explored with the aid of diagrams. Section 3 focuses on e-commerce and international trade, which happens when an e-commerce market is open not only to domestic sellers and buyers but also to sellers and buyers in other countries. Section 4 investigates the effects of digitalization on online sales. Section 5 examines the relationship between e-platforms and foreign trade more closely. It shows that digitalization may affect foreign sellers and foreign buyers differently. Section 6 concludes.

2. The main characteristics of e-commerce

E-commerce is business that is carried out online. It has two major types: (i) *e-transactions* (buying and selling) online, and (ii) *e-transmission* of business-related information online (e.g. e-payments, online interviews, or electronic transmission of business-related documents). E-transactions usually involve the e-transmission of relevant information such as e-payments (using credit cards, debit cards, e-payments, or other forms of money transfer), but e-payment does not have to be part of an e-transaction; e.g. a purchase is made in a regular shop, and it is paid for using e-payment. Furthermore, online interviews or e-transmission of a document may or may not be related to business transactions.

E-transactions are the main form of e-commerce and are what people think of when e-commerce is mentioned. Each transaction involves a buyer and a seller. A seller can be a business enterprise or consumer that or who offers to sell something, with information about the product available online. A buyer can be a business enterprise, consumer, or the government. Depending on the entities involved, an online transaction can be identified as business to business (B2B), B2C, business to government (B2G), consumer to business (C2B), or consumer to consumer (C2C).

Most online transactions are B2C and C2C, but B2B transactions are becoming more important. In China, only one-quarter of online retail sales were B2C in 2011 while the rest were C2C. In 2015, the share of B2C transactions had risen to more than half (52 percent) of online retail sales. The importance of B2C transactions is expected to continue to rise, and more than 68 percent of online retail sales are projected to be B2C in 2018 (Deloitte, 2017).

Transactions, whether regular or e-commerce, have strong implications on resource allocations, but e-transmissions of business-related information generally have little such effect. Therefore, this chapter focuses mainly on e-transactions and examines how they affect resource allocation, international trade, and employment.

To illustrate how e-commerce is carried out and examine its implications, let us begin the discussion with a more traditional type of transaction. Consider a shopping mall, a grocery store, a car dealer, a night market, or a shop where many types of commodities are displayed, with their prices listed. Consumers visit the mall, browse the displayed commodities, and eventually buy the ones they like. For the time being, the economy is assumed to be closed to foreign trade. This means that both sellers and buyers are local residents.

The shopping mall way of retail sale is costly for both sellers and buyers. Sellers (producers or retailers) have to rent a space to display their products, and there is a time lag between when the products leave the factories and when they are sold. Buyers have to browse and shop, possibly going from one mall to another. This process involves time and transportation costs, which are paid for by the buyers. Because of the rental costs involved, the shopping mall has to limit the number of products on display. On the other hand, because of the costs of time and transportation, a buyer has to limit the number of mall visits and the number of commodities to browse before making a purchase decision.

This is illustrated by Figure 1.1, which shows the case of a traditional market like a shopping mall or a grocery store. The sellers display the products and the buyers come and browse the products, and eventually may purchase them. However, the existence of costs on both sides of the transactions limits the number of sellers that can display their products in the market and the number of potential buyers.

We now consider an alternative market platform: the electronic platform. Recent rapid advances in relevant technologies allow the electronic display of products, online browsing of products, and electronic transactions, including

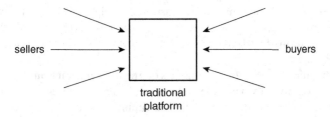

Figure 1.1 A Diagrammatical Representation of a Traditional Platform
Source: The author.

electronic payment (e-payment). E-platforms are assumed to have the following properties:

i   The costs of displaying a product are very small for the sellers. They usually include the cost of registration with the vendor, the cost of writing and publishing the product description, and the cost of setting up an e-payment system (which may be included in the registration). These costs are much less than the cost of building a shopping mall/centre, renting space to display the products, hiring employees to greet the buyers, promoting the products to potential buyers, and completing the transaction if an order is made.

ii   The costs of browsing products and making payments are very small for the buyers. Browsing requires some electronic equipment, such as a computer or a smartphone, and access to the Internet. Many people already own these conditions, and what they have to do to shop online is to visit an e-platform.

iii   There is virtually no limit on the number of sellers that can display their products, the number of products that can be displayed, or the number of buyers that can browse the platform and make transactions.

These characteristics of e-commerce imply the following effects, as compared with a traditional market:

i   For both sellers and buyers, the costs of transactions are much smaller using an electronic platform than in a traditional market.

ii   Because of the lower transaction costs and because of the unlimited nature of e-commerce, the number of sellers, buyers, and products displayed are much greater than in a traditional market.

iii   The much higher numbers of sellers and buyers, and the nearly instantaneous and costless transmission of information, greatly increase the degree of competition among sellers and buyers. In other words, an electronic platform generally has a much higher degree of competition than a traditional market.

An electronic platform is a place where sellers and buyers meet before transactions are made. Its functions can be illustrated in Figure 1.2, which reveals that (i) an electronic platform has many more sellers and buyers, and (ii) the use of the Internet means that buyers do not have to meet face-to-face with sellers or their representatives.

An electronic platform also has impacts on the market equilibrium and resource allocation. To find out what these impacts are, let us first examine how the supply of the product may be affected. A normal supply is assumed here, which means that, other things being equal, the quantity supplied depends positively on the market price. The effect of setting up a new electronic platform is represented by a new parameter, α, which describes the degree of digitalization of the market. This parameter is defined so that a higher value of α means a higher degree of digitalization. Furthermore, $\alpha = 1$ in the presence of the traditional platform and is $\alpha = \alpha_1 > 1$ if an electronic platform is set up. For convenience, α is assumed to be a continuous variable.

The supply of the product can be described by the following function, $S = S(p, \alpha)$. Based on the preceding discussion, the supply function is assumed to satisfy the following properties:

(a) $S_p > 0$, $S_\alpha > 0$, and $S_{p\alpha} > 0$, where a subscript represents a partial derivative;
(b) If $\underline{p}$ is the minimum price for the firms to be willing to produce a positive output, then $d\underline{p} / d\alpha < 0$.

In (a), $S_p > 0$ means that the supply curve is positively sloped, and $S_\alpha > 0$ and $S_{p\alpha} > 0$ imply that an increase in the degree of digitalization will shift the curve to the right and the new curve is less steep than the old one at the same price level.[1] That the curve is less steep is due to the assumption that digitalization will increase the degree of competition of the market. For assumption (b), note that $\underline{p}$ is the vertical intercept of the supply curve. A drop in the cost of displaying and advertisement will mean that the firms are willing to produce a positive output, even if the market price is lower. Possible effects of the market digitalization on the supply curve are shown in Figure 1.3. The solid curve labelled S is the supply

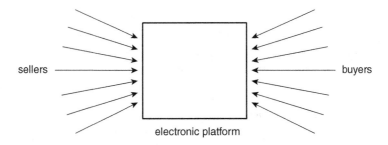

sellers ⟶   buyers

electronic platform

Figure 1.2 A Diagrammatical Representation of an Electronic Platform

Source: The author.

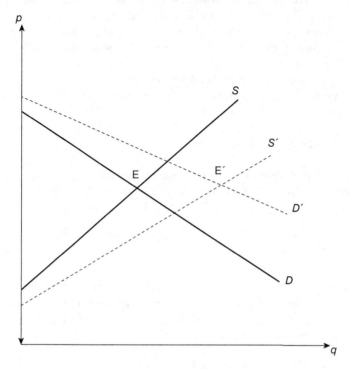

Figure 1.3 Impact of Digitalization on Market Equilibrium
Source: The author.

curve under a traditional market platform, while the dotted curve S' is the supply curve with a higher degree of market digitalization.

Demand for the product can be explained as follows. First, it is assumed to be negatively dependent on the price. Second, an increase in the degree of market digitalization increases the demand for the product. Third, market digitalization also increases the degree of competition. This is reflected by a drop in the steepness of the demand curve at any given level of consumption. Fourth, market digitalization lowers the costs of obtaining product information. Based on this description, the demand function is assumed to be $D = D(p, \alpha)$, which satisfies the following properties:

(a) $D_p < 0$, $D_\alpha > 0$, and $D_{p\alpha} < 0$;
(b) If $\bar{p}$ is the maximum price for consumers to be willing to buy a positive quantity of the product, then $d\bar{p} / d\alpha > 0$.[2]

In (a), the signs of D_p and D_α directly follow the preceding description. The assumption of $D_{p\alpha} < 0$ implies that an increase in market digitalization will make the demand curve less steep (but still negatively sloped).[3] Condition (b) means that with an increase in the degree of digitalization, consumers' willingness to purchase a small quantity of the product is higher. The effects of digitalization on the demand curve are illustrated in Figure 1.3. The solid curve labelled D is the demand curve before market digitalization, while the dotted curved labelled D' is that with a higher level of market digitalization.

Given a particular platform (the value of α), the equilibrium of the market is described by:

$$S(p,\alpha) = D(p,\alpha). \tag{1}$$

The equation is solved to give the autarkic equilibrium price for a particular platform, $p^a = p^a(\alpha)$, which depends on the degree of digitalization of the platform. Differentiate (1) totally and rearrange the terms to give:

$$\frac{dp^a}{d\alpha} = \frac{D_\alpha - S_\alpha}{S_p - D_p}. \tag{2}$$

Because $S_p > 0$ and $D_p < 0$, condition (2) implies that an increase in market digitalization would raise the equilibrium price if and only if $D_\alpha > S_\alpha$, i.e., if and only if, at the initial market price, digitalization creates more demand than supply. The effect on the equilibrium quantity is:

$$\frac{dS}{d\alpha} = \frac{\partial S}{\partial p}\frac{dp}{d\alpha} + \frac{\partial S}{\partial \alpha} = \frac{S_p D_\alpha - S_\alpha D_p}{S_p - D_p}, \tag{3}$$

where condition (2) has been used. Applying the assumed signs of the variables, the expression in (3) is positive, implying that an increase in market digitalization raises the quantity of sale and purchase.

Proposition 1: An increase in market digitalization in a closed economy (i) raises the quantity of sale and purchase, and (ii) increases the market autarkic price if and only if $D_\alpha > S_\alpha$ at the autarkic price.

The change in the market equilibrium because of digitalization is shown in Figure 1.3. With the shift of the supply and demand curves, the equilibrium point shifts from E to E'. Note that with market digitalization, while the change in the market price is ambiguous, the equilibrium quantity clearly increases.

3. E-commerce and international trade

We now examine the implications of e-commerce on international trade. In terms of the platform described in Figure 1.2, this means that some foreign sellers and buyers can enter and offer sales or make purchases. The economy is an exporter of a product if the volume of sales made by foreign sellers is greater than the volume of purchases made by foreign buyers.

To examine trade, the export supply of the product is first derived and analysed.

3.1. *Export supply function*

The export supply function is defined as $E = E(p, \alpha) = S(p, \alpha) - D(p, \alpha)$. Using the analysis in the previous section, we can obtain $E_p > 0$ and $E_{p\alpha} > 0$. The sign of E_α, however, is ambiguous, as analysed earlier because it depends on how sellers and buyers are attracted to the electronic platform. The effect of market digitalization on the export supply function is shown in Figure 1.4. The solid curve labelled E represents the original export supply function, which is positively sloped and passes through the vertical axis at the autarkic price, p^a. Because the sign of E_α is ambiguous, how the curve shifts when an electronic platform is set up is not clear. For the sake of analysis, we assume that both the supply and the demand are equally affected at the autarkic point by market digitalization, i.e., $S_\alpha(p^a, \alpha) = D_\alpha(p^a, \alpha)$. Graphically, this means that in Figure 1.4, the export supply function corresponding to a higher degree of market digitalization remains passing through the same vertical intercept. The diagram also shows the case in which $E_{p\alpha} > 0$, i.e., the new export supply function is less steep at the autarkic point.

3.2. *Free trade equilibrium*

To analyse international trade, let us turn to a two-economy case. Call the economy introduced earlier the home country and label the other economy the foreign country. Free trade is allowed between the two countries. Denote the foreign import demand function for the product by $M^* = M^*(p^*, \alpha)$, where an asterisk represents a variable of the foreign country. Note that the present analysis

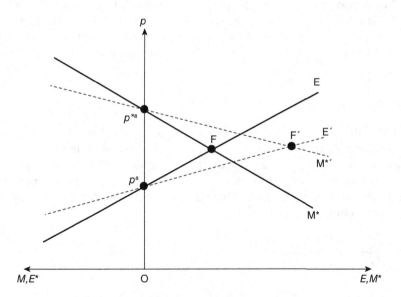

Figure 1.4 Impact of Digitalization on a Trade Equilibrium

Source: The author.

focuses on the effects of market digitalization in the home country, meaning that we use the same digitalization parameter α in both the home export supply and the foreign import demand functions.[4] Based on the preceding analysis, the foreign import demand function is assumed to have the following properties: (i) $M^*_{p'} < 0$, and (ii) The sign of M^*_α is in general ambiguous. As was done earlier, it is assumed that $M^*_\alpha = 0$ at the foreign autarkic price. At the autarkic price, digitalization attracts equal quantities of supply and demand.

Figure 1.4 shows the foreign import demand curve before (the solid curve labelled M^*) and after (the dotted curve labelled $M^{*'}$) market digitalization. By assumption, the two curves pass through the same vertical intercept, with the post-digitalization curve less steep than the pre-digitalization curve.

We now allow free trade between the two countries and assume the traditional market for the time being, $\alpha = 1$. For convenience, transport costs are assumed to be negligible. Free trade leads to equalization of commodity prices in equilibrium, i.e., $p = p^*$. The equilibrium condition is:

$$E(p^f, \alpha) = M^*(p^f, \alpha), \tag{4}$$

where p^f is the free trade equilibrium price. Figure 1.4 shows both the home country's export supply curve E and the foreign country's import demand curve M^*. The free trade equilibrium is represented by the point of intersection between the two curves. The free trade equilibrium price can be expressed as a function of the degree of digitalization, $p^f = p^f(\alpha)$. For the present analysis, assume that the product is exported by the home country, i.e., $E(p^f, \alpha) > 0$.

Suppose now that an electronic platform is established. Then curves E and M^* will shift out to, say, E' and $M^{*'}$, respectively. The new equilibrium is represented by point F. To evaluate how the free trade price is affected by market digitalization, differentiate (4) totally and rearrange the terms to give:

$$\frac{dp^f}{d\alpha} = \frac{M^*_\alpha - E_\alpha}{E_p - M^*_{p'}}. \tag{5}$$

Using the preceding analysis, the denominator on the right-hand side of (5) is negative. The condition thus implies that market digitalization lowers the free trade price if and only if $E_\alpha > M^*_\alpha$, i.e., under the initial free trade price, digitalization leads to an increase in the home country's export greater than the increase in the foreign country's import demand. The effect of market digitalization on the trade volume is:

$$\frac{dE}{d\alpha} = \frac{E_p M^*_\alpha - E_\alpha M^*_{p'}}{E_p - M^*_{p'}} > 0. \tag{6}$$

The results are summarized by the following proposition:

Proposition 2: Consider a product being exported by a country. An increase in the degree of market digitalization will (a) increase the free trade price if and only if $M^*_\alpha > E_\alpha$, and (b) will increase the volume of trade.

4. Further implications of e-commerce on foreign trade

The previous section develops a general theory of e-commerce and international trade. To get more information, let us now consider some special cases and issues that demonstrate some of the characteristics of e-commerce.

4.1. Asymmetric impacts of e-commerce on different industries

When the buyers are consumers, as in the cases of B2C and C2C, most commodities in transactions via e-platforms are small and light items or finished and non-perishable products[5] This is understandable because the purchased items are mostly delivered via postal services, electronic transfer, or direct express delivery. The result is that e-platforms generally have different impacts on the sale and purchase of different products. Furthermore, since e-platforms do not allow consumers to inspect products physically, these platforms have greater impacts on the sale of standardized products that do not require much inspection by consumers before placing orders, e.g. electronic products such as computers, cellular phones, books, and videos.[6]

Table 1.1 shows the online sales of various products by industry in Korea in 2016. The numbers indicate that the two most popular items for online purchases that year were clothing and household goods, both with values close to W70 trillion. The third industry with the most online sales was travel arrangements and reservation services, but it was a distant third because the sale value was only one sixth of that of the top-ranked industry.

Market digitalization has different impacts on the sale of products from different industries, creating resource allocation implications. Thus, the development of e-commerce will encourage the production of products that are more suitable

Table 1.1 Online Sales of the Republic of Korea by Industry, 2016 (in Billion Won)

Category	Value
Clothing	68,995
Household goods	66,502
Travel arrangements	11,352
Home electronic appliances	7,170
Food and beverages	6,289
Cosmetics	5,162
Computer and computer-related appliances	4,020
Goods for infants and children	2,935
Miscellaneous services and others	2,783
Sports and leisure appliances	2,518
Agricultural, livestock, and fisheries	1,727
Furniture	1,669
Books	1,335
Footwear	1,058

Source: Statista (2017)

to be advertised and sold on e-platforms. Resources are then drawn to these industries, raising the output levels of these industries.

4.2. E-commerce and comparative advantage

Could the establishment of an electronic platform affect, or even reverse, the comparative advantage of an economy? For example, consider again the two-country model introduced in the previous section. Suppose that traditionally, the home country exports the product. Now let a new electronic platform be set up. Would the home country become an importer of the product?

In practice, the chance of trade pattern reversal is small because the online transaction volume is still only a very small part of the total retail sale volume. Therefore, the impact of an electronic platform on the trade pattern is not likely. However, assuming that online sales become more important, would trade pattern reversal be possible?

To examine such a possibility, refer again to Figure 1.4, which shows the export supply curve of a product of the home country. It is well known that the vertical intercept of the curve represents the autarkic price of the product, p^a. The effect of digitalization on the autarkic price is given by equation (2).

Suppose that the foreign country's autarkic price is equal to p^{*a}. Since the product is exported by the home country before digitalization, $p^{*a} > p^a$. Digitalization in the home country will affect both autarkic prices. Denote the new autarkic prices of the home country and the foreign country by $\tilde{p}^a$ and $\tilde{p}^{*a}$, respectively. Under what conditions would $\tilde{p}^a$ be greater than $\tilde{p}^{*a}$?

From equation (2), a necessary condition is that:

$$\frac{dp^a}{d\alpha} > \frac{dp^{*a}}{d\alpha}, \tag{7}$$

i.e., digitalization will raise the home country's autarkic price relative to that of the foreign country. If we take the common case that digitalization in the home country will affect the home economy more than the foreign economy, we can assume that $dp^{*a}/d\alpha$ is very small or even negligible. Then equation (7) reduces to:

$$\frac{dp^a}{d\alpha} > 0. \tag{8}$$

In other words, the necessary condition for reverting a product for the home country from being exported to being imported, under the condition that the foreign country's autarkic price does not change, is that digitalization will cause an increase in the home country's autarkic price. Using equation (2), condition (8) can be written as:

$$D_\alpha > S_\alpha, \tag{9}$$

where the condition that $S_p - D_p > 0$ has been used.

Note that condition (9) is only a necessary condition (assuming that the change in the foreign country's autarkic price is negligible). To have a trade pattern reversal, the home country's autarkic price needs to increase substantially.

Proposition 3: A necessary condition for a reversal of comparative advantage caused by an increase in digitalization is that it raises the autarkic price of a product more in the exporting country than in the importing country. If the autarkic price in the importing country is not much affected by digitalization, then a necessary condition for a reversal of comparative advantage is that digitalization increases the quantity demanded more than the quantity supplied at the autarkic price in the exporting country.

5. Foreign trade through e-platforms

For countries that have Internet facilities, e-platforms allow some of their sellers to offer products to buyers in other countries, and to allow sellers in other countries to offer their products to local buyers. However, because different countries have different development levels of their Internet facilities, and because producers and consumers in different countries have different degrees of receptiveness to the Internet, a new e-platform in a country may affect the export and import sides to different extents.

5.1. Overseas sales

First, let us consider the export side of e-platforms. Table 1.2 shows the transaction value of the direct online overseas sales of major types of goods of Korea in the third quarter of 2017. Cosmetics were the most popular items for overseas online shoppers (Row 2). The online overseas sales in that quarter reached

Table 1.2 Direct Online Overseas Sales of the Republic of Korea, Third Quarter 2017 (in Billion Won)

Category	Value	RCA	HS Code
Cosmetics	569.65	0.57	3304
Fashion goods	104.18	(0.52)	61
Electronic goods and home appliances	19.13	0.28	85
CDs, videos, and musical instruments	11.11	0.11	8523
Household items and car accessories	10.42	0.7	8708
Grocery	6.94	(0.14)	21
Books	6.56	(0.18)	4901
Baby and children's products	4.23	(0.65)	95
Sports and leisure	3.71	(0.65)	95
Stationery	2.21	0.22	48
Computers	2.02	(0.11)	8471

Notes:
() = negative.
RCA = revealed comparative advantage.
Source: Statista (2017).

W569.65 billion, which was more than five times that of the second category, fashion goods. The other products had much smaller sales volumes. For example, the online sales of either electronic goods and home appliances; or CDs, videos, and musical instruments; were only slightly more than W10 billion, but those of each of the following types of products were well below W10 billion in the same quarter: grocery, books, baby and children's products, sports and leisure products, stationery, and computers.

Table 1.2 (direct online overseas sales) can be compared with Table 1.1 (online sales). Both tables include similar products, e.g., cosmetics, fashion goods, electronic goods and home appliances, books, food, and computers. This suggests that sellers which are good at selling their products to domestic buyers are also good at selling their products to overseas buyers. The tables also suggest that for products that are suitable for e-commerce sales, both domestic and overseas buyers can have similar access to the e-platforms and make purchases.

Are these overseas sales related to the comparative advantage of the home country? To answer this question, we refer again to Table 1.2. Column 3 of the table presents the revealed comparative advantages (RCAs) of comparable industries (with the corresponding Harmonized Commodity Description and Coding System [HS] codes given in column 4).[7] The figures show that overseas sales have little relation to the RCAs. For example, the biggest overseas sales item in the third quarter of 2017 was cosmetics. The RCA of the industry (3304: cosmetic and toilet preparations) is 0.57. The second biggest overseas sales item is fashion goods, but the RCA of a comparable industry (61: apparel and clothing accessories) is –0.52, meaning that Korea is revealed to have a strong comparative disadvantage.[8] Several other overseas sales items also show negative RCAs, suggesting that overseas sales may not have a strong relation to the country's RCAs.

Why are overseas sales so weakly related to RCAs? A very simple reason is the existence of differentiated products and intra-industry trade. An electronic platform facilitates the sales of local products, which not have much to do with the RCAs of the industries. For example, Korea had strong overseas sales of fashion goods. While the country has a revealed comparative disadvantage in clothing because it is labour-intensive and because of the high labour costs in Korea, local firms may be competitive in producing high-end fashion clothing and goods. The e-platforms allow the sales of these products to overseas buyers. Another example is books. It is possible that Korea has a negative RCA in books, but it is competitive in selling certain types of books, e.g., books in Korean.

5.2. Foreign products sold locally

Evidence suggests that e-platforms tend to attract foreign buyers more than foreign sellers, at least shortly after the setup of the platforms. This is likely because it is easier and less costly for foreign buyers to gain access to the platforms, browse the products, and place orders, since all they need is Internet access plus an e-payment system such as a credit or debit card. For sellers overseas, it may be more difficult and costly to place their products on the platform, as they need to set up systems for display, delivery, payment, and refunding. However, given time, e-platforms will gradually attract sellers from other countries. Moreover, governments in some countries encourage some domestic firms to sell on e-platforms in other countries. This allows buyers in one country to order products in other countries, creating what is called cross-border sales.

One example is that Jack Ma, CEO of Alibaba, announced in early 2017 that he planned to create more than 1 million jobs in the US. His plan is to encourage small and medium-sized firms in the US to list their products online and purchased by consumers in China. Jack Ma's plan suggests that small and medium-sized firms in the US may not have the expertise or experience to sell their products through an electronic platform. Alibaba offers to provide the start-up capital, guidance, and experience.

6. Concluding remarks

This chapter explains and analyses some of the characteristics and properties of e-commerce, which is a new way of doing business between sellers and buyers. For nearly all countries, it is still a small section of the economy, but its growth rates in the past years had been very impressive. It may not be too long before e-commerce will be a dominant way of carrying out business transactions, especially for consumers.

Because e-commerce is still an emerging form of economic activity, there had not been much research or publications in the literature. This chapter is an attempt to examine and analyse the fundamental features and impacts of e-commerce.

Looking forward, e-commerce is expected to be a more dominant means of transactions, both domestically and internationally, as the Internet, communication and transportation facilities become more developed and less costly. Obviously, more research on the properties and impacts of e-platforms will grow, together with the rising importance of e-commerce. However, statistical data collected and provided by the governments are very limited right now. More reliable and extensive data will be needed for more research in the future.

Notes

1 Note that the slope of the supply curve is equal to $1 / S_p$.
2 The condition here assumes that $\bar{p}$ is positive and finite. If it is infinite, then we assume that the demand curve shifts to the right.
3 Note that the slope of the demand curve is equal to $1 / D_p$ and is negative.
4 Digitalization in both countries can easily be handled by introducing one more digitalization parameter.
5 Exceptions include aircraft, which have been sold (very rarely) through an electronic platform, and food, which is also available on some e-platforms.
6 Since these products usually have brand names and model numbers, consumers unsure of the physical appearance of the products can inspect them in a retail shop and then place an order via an electronic platform. Some e-platforms allow buyers to return the product for a refund under certain conditions if they are not satisfied. Buyers can buy a product, inspect and use it for a limited amount of time, and return it if it is not satisfactory.

7 The industry chosen for each category of goods is based on the description of the industry, and may not be the same as the type of goods used in Statista (2017). The RCA of an industry is defined as the ratio of the trade balance to the trade volume, ranging from +1 to –1. A positive (or negative) RCA means that the industry has a revealed comparative advantage (disadvantage).

8 Industry 61 covers all apparel and clothing products, while Statista (2017) may refer to high-quality clothes and products, in which Korea's RCA may be higher than –0.52.

Bibliography

Deloitte (2017), *China E-Retail Market Report 2016*. Beijing: China Chain Store and Franchise Association.

Ecommerce Foundation (2016), 'Global B2C E-Commerce Report 2016'. Available at www.ecommercefoundation.org/download-free-reports

Statista (2017), 'E-Commerce in South Korea'. Available at www.statista.com/topics/2529/e-commerce-in-south-korea/

Statista (2018), 'E-Commerce in China'. Available at www.statista.com/topics/1007/e-commerce-in-china/

Terzi, N. (2011), 'The Impact of E-Commerce on International Trade and Employment', *Procedia – Social and Behavioral Sciences*, 24: 745–753.

Zhang, Y. (2014), 'Under the Condition of E-Commerce, the New Characteristics of International Trade and the Countermeasures of Enterprises', *Journal of Chemical and Pharmaceutical Research*, 6(6): 2229–2232.

Part II
Rules and regulations

2 Cross-border digital trade, e-commerce governance, and necessary actions ahead

Michitaka Nakatomi

1. Introduction

The Internet has remarkably developed and is now the infrastructure of all economic activities and the basis of development of the manufacturing and services industries. It has created enormous economic values. The coming era of robotics, Internet of Things (IoT), and the Fourth Industrial Revolution (Industry 4.0)[1] rely very much on the Internet.

From an economic viewpoint, the Internet is the basis of the development of global value chains and fragmentation of manufacturing processes across the world. It has dramatically decreased communication costs globally, leading to the second unbundling of manufacturing processes and global fragmentation of the manufacturing industry (Baldwin, 2011a). The Internet has a huge potential as an enabler and as the basis for inclusive growth. In particular, it enables developing countries and small and medium-sized enterprises to access global value chains. Meanwhile, the introduction of various restrictions and regulations on e-commerce and digital trade on different grounds by national authorities are becoming serious impediments for their further development (ICTSD, 2016; Meltzer, 2016). 'Digital protectionism' has become an imminent concern for e-commerce and digital trade. For developing countries, the possible digital divide among different players is a serious problem. Therefore, making necessary trade rules for the smooth and healthy development of digital trade is an urgent task – and new digital trade rules should pursue inclusive solutions for all.

However, regulations and restrictions imposed by national authorities are in many circumstances based on necessary public purposes such as privacy and national security. To define the boundaries of allowable regulations and balance, the need for regulations and freedom of digital trade are imminent issues for all stakeholders. ASEAN and the East Asia region is not only a huge market for digital trade, but also where many players from China and Japan, among others, exist and compete. It is essential and logical for the countries in the region to work together for future digital trade rules in view of the further development of digital trade and the inclusive growth of economies. If the region does not take the initiative now, the result will either be (i) there will be no rules or certain rule will be forced on the members by others, or (ii) neither the global or regional economy will benefit.

This chapter analyses the importance of digital trade and e-commerce in global trade (hereinafter digital trade) and emphasizes the necessity of international rules and disciplines on digital trade. It analyses the possible framework for developing digital trade disciplines in such relevant agreements as those of the World Trade Organization (WTO), free trade agreements (FTAs) including bilateral and regional FTAs such as the Trans-Pacific Partnership (TPP), Trade in Services Agreement (TiSA), possible 'digital trade FTA', plurilateral agreements, and mutual recognition agreements. It also recommends governance of digital trade and necessary actions ahead for ASEAN and East Asia in view of the importance of digital trade and need for global and regional disciplines on it.

2. The need for disciplines on digital trade

To start with, this section overviews the current status of rules on digital trade where rules and understanding among the countries are not clear, which can be the impediment to the further development of digital trade. Generally speaking, the scopes of necessary rules, and therefore the definition of digital trade and e-commerce,[2] are closely linked to policy options and decisions adopted by the individual countries. Moreover, digital trade is an area where many institutional and technical issues are related. To achieve meaningful results, rule-makers must select and concentrate on important issues related to trade and have an overall perspective at the same time.

2.1. Basis for developing rules on digital trade

Five issues are worth highlighting. First, global rules are the basis for digital trade rules. Digital trade, by nature, adjusts to the global regime. The need to prevent different rules and regulations to proliferate comes from the global nature of digital trade. At the same time, in digital trade, benefits from external economies through collaboration of countries are very large (Meltzer, 2016). In order to develop digital trade that is conducive to inclusive growth, proliferation of regulations should be controlled and the scope of appropriate regulations defined (ICTSD, 2016; Bauer et al., 2016).

Second, digital trade requires connected physical and institutional flow. Even one barrier in the flow can easily damage and kill its function. An overall view of this nature of digital trade is required.

Third, to avoid the 'spaghetti bowl' in rule setting,[3] countries should move quickly to establish common digital trade rules before it is too late (Nakatomi, 2013a, 2013b; Baldwin and Nakatomi, 2015).

Fourth, digital trade has potential for inclusive, win-win growth. It can benefit both developed and developing countries, enterprises, and consumers, leading to inclusive growth (ICTSD, 2016). All actions should take place to maximize its potential and realize externalities through close and quick collaborations. It is also essential to introduce technical assistance and capacity building for developing countries and small and medium-sized enterprises.

Fifth, it needs collaboration among governments, business, academia, and non-governmental organizations to realize the maximum benefits of digital trade. To avoid digital divide, all stakeholders will have to get involved in creating digital trade rules.

2.2. The WTO and digital trade

The WTO is the only international organization that stipulates trade rules comprehensively and enforces their implementation through the organization's dispute settlement mechanism. It has more than 160 members, and includes almost all the important trading players in the world. Therefore, rule-making on digital trade under the WTO framework is very desirable, provided that multilateralism has widest coverage and most effective functionality. As this chapter elaborates later in detail, the issues to be dealt with include tariffs, standards, discrimination (most-favoured-nation, or MFN, status and national treatment), cross-border data flow, localization, and forced disclosure of source codes.

The existing rules of the WTO, however, can cover just part of these issues. Even where there are disciplines, ambiguities in their coverage and application to digital trade still exist. Historically, the Uruguay Round was substantially concluded in 1993 and the WTO was established in 1995, when the Internet was just beginning to develop, and WTO rules were negotiated before its full development.

Even though the WTO and the General Agreement on Trade in Services (GATS) foresaw technological development and institutional changes in their framework, paces of innovation and economy digitalization in the recent years have been much faster than that were expected. In comparison, the framework of progressive liberalization and consecutive rounds – the strongest tool and safeguards for the WTO to accommodate further changes implied by technological and institutional innovation – did not seem to be functioning as efficiently as it was supposed to.

Regarding digital trade, a most recent achievement by the WTO in creating new rules and liberalization occurred almost two decades ago when the Information Technology Agreement (ITA), telecommunication and financial services agreements, were concluded in 1997. Since then, its rule-making has been on stalemate. The Doha Round, launched in 2001, is still continuing, with no prospect for its conclusion.

Stalemate in rule-making is not limited to GATS. The Agreement on Trade-Related Aspects of Intellectual Property Rights (TRIPS) and technical barriers to trade (TBT), which are relevant to digital trade, for example, are no exception. As far as the written disciplines are concerned, the agreement in 1993 still prevails in the WTO. Though there have been certain important precedents in dispute settlement cases which give guidelines on the application of WTO rules on digital trade (e.g. Internet gambling cases), and soft rules are developed by WTO committees, they are not enough to respond to the need for clear rules on digital trade. Digital trade requires rules in multiple areas and in multifaceted ways. But the existing WTO rules related to digital trade are rudimentary and ambiguous. For example, dichotomy clearly exists between disciplines on goods and services related to digital trade, and there are gaps and tension in necessary disciplines in the WTO regime (Table 2.1). It is not clear, for example, how the existing rules of the WTO – such as on the imposition of customs duty, application of GATS Article 14, interpretation of market access and national treatment commitment and MFN exemption, services classification, and the applicability of technological neutrality – will be applied to market access, MFN, national treatment, and standards related to digital trade.

2.3. Areas where rules on digital trade need to be further developed

Regarding the creation and application of trade rules to digital trade, the following issues have been discussed extensively and rules governing them should be developed or clarified further (ICTSD, 2016; Meltzer, 2016). This list is just to illustrate major issues.

i   Customs duties and market access – This is the issue first discussed in the WTO in the 1990s. Typically, the issue of customs duty imposition on e-commerce is in question.
ii Standards and regulations – Negotiations on domestic regulation in GATS Article 6 are ongoing, but disciplines comparable to TBT have not been developed.
iii Discrimination – This relates to the issue of discrimination in digital trade, since the principles of the General Agreement on Tariffs and Trade (GATT) and GATS on discrimination (MFN and national treatment) are very different (Tables 2.1 and 2.2).
iv Cross-border data flow – Whether cross-border data flow is protected by trade rules is at issue. The WTO already has many existing rules supporting cross-border data flow. This is one core issue for deliberation in digital trade rules.[4]
v   Localization requirement of servers (Crosby, 2016; Drake, 2016) – Whether localization requirement of servers by regulatory reasons is allowed or not is a big issue for consideration.
vi Forced disclosure of source codes – Whether a country can force disclosure of source code by national security or other public reasons is also an important issue which requires clarification and rule-making.
vii Protection of intellectual property rights.

2.4. Status quo of WTO rules and limitations

Despite discussions on various rules on digital trade, we still do not have a clear picture. This section looks at the present status and limitation of WTO rules that are applicable to digital trade. It especially focuses on the limitation of the GATS rules on digital trade, which need to be developed and further clarified.

Table 2.1 A Comparison of Goods and Services Disciplines

	Goods	Services
Most-favoured nation treatment	Most-favoured nation treatment is the principle (GATT Article I).	Most-favoured nation treatment is the principle (GATS Article II), but exceptions can be registered on the annex on exemptions.
Market access	Each country ordinarily binds tariff rates (GATT Article II) based on the harmonized system (HS) classification table formulated by the WCO. The developed countries have bound almost all products.	It is standard practice to offer commitments regarding market access only in specified sectors (GATS Article XVI). Commitments will not necessarily be made for the entire 155 services sectors covered by the W120 services sectors list based on the Provisional Central Product Classification. The scope of commitments is limited.
National treatment	National treatment is the principle (GATT Article III).	As in the case of market access, it is standard practice to offer commitments only in specified sectors (GATS Article XVII). In the sectors in which commitments have been made, national treatment is guaranteed only within the scope of the commitments.
TBT	TBT Agreement exists in the WTO. It defines procedures for the introduction of regulations for goods, transparency, standards, and conformity assessment.	Negotiations are proceeding regarding domestic regulations (related to GATS Article VI), but there is not much progress. As the importance of BBM increases in the future, rules on domestic regulations will be extremely important to the development of services disciplines.
Subsidies	An agreement concerning subsidies exists in the WTO. Detailed disciplines exist related to elements including prohibited subsidies and countervailing duties.	Discussions concerning disciplines related to subsidies in the services sector are underway (GATS Article XV), but progress is not being made. The fact that no frameworks exist for countermeasures against the overseas expansion of services protected by subsidies, corresponding to countervailing duties in the case of goods, may become a significant issue in the future.

(Continued)

Table 2.1 Continued

	Goods	Services
Safeguards	There is an agreement concerning safeguards in the WTO. The agreement provides disciplines for elements including conditions for the application of safeguard measures and the details of safeguard measures.	There are provisions for negotiations in GATS Article X, and discussions are underway, but progress is not being made. On the one hand, the fact that there are no provisions for safeguards has the effect of preventing members from withdrawing commitments; but on the other, because it closes off the possibility of withdrawing or suspending commitments that have been made, it may make countries cautious to make commitments.
Anti-dumping	An anti-dumping agreement exists in the WTO. Detailed disciplines exist for elements such as the definition of dumping and the conditions for application of anti-dumping duties. Negotiations in the area of rules (anti-dumping, subsidies) are ongoing in the Doha Round, under the leadership of Japan.	No disciplines exist. There is also no provision for negotiations. In the goods sector, anti-dumping duties are frequently used improperly in a protectionist fashion, and it is therefore to be hoped that there will be no progress in discussions concerning dumping-related disciplines in the services sector. Availability of data in services sector also significantly differs from the goods sector, and it is difficult to obtain objective cost and trade data in services. At the same time, the fact that no countermeasures can be applied when services dumping occurs in the sectors covered by commitments may cause countries to become cautious in making commitments in the future.
Government procurement	The Agreement on Government Procurement (an Annex 4 agreement), a plurilateral agreement, exists. The transparency of government procurement fell off the agenda of the Doha Round negotiations. No agreements exist that discipline all WTO members. Increasing the number of participants in the Agreement on Government Procurement is therefore an important issue.	As at left.

		As at left.
Competition rules	No disciplines exist in the WTO. Trade and competition (Singapore issues) fell off the agenda in the Doha Round. These will be important issues in the future for both goods and services.	As at left.
Investment rules	With the exception of TRIM, there are no standard disciplines that function as investment rules in either GATT or GATS. Trade and investment (Singapore issues) fell off the agenda in the Doha Round. Investment disciplines will be important issues in the future for both goods and services.	As at left. Mode 3 has the character of investment-related rules (NT, MA) within its scope, but there is a fundamental limitation due to the scope of commitments.
FTA exemption	A discipline exists in GATT Article XXIV. There is a long history of discussion of this discipline. 'Substantially all trade in goods' is the basis. It allows for significant exceptions to MFN and MA rule in the WTO. On NT, because NT is a principle on goods, FTA does not produce significant difference.	A discipline exists in GATS Article V. 'Substantial sectoral coverage' is the basis. There is almost no history of discussion of this discipline. The fact that exceptions to MFN treatment are allowed (there are numerous cases of registration of exceptions to MFN treatment in the areas of marine transportation and AV) and that the application of NT and MA commences from the obligations within the scope of commitments represent significant differences with GATT. (The discipline commences from GATS and allows further preferential treatment to the participants in the FTA.)

Source: The Author.

Table 2.2 Legal Structure of Exceptions to MFN Treatment

	GATT	GATS
Basic principle	Prohibited (GATT Article I).	Prohibited (GATS Article II).
Registration of exceptions	Not possible	Possible (Annex on Article II Exemptions) (Note: Japan has not registered exceptions).
Exceptions in FTA	GATT Article XXIV (Substantially all trade standard) 1) Sufficient discussion regarding interpretation. 2) The basic principle is elimination of tariffs on approximately 90% of trade within 10 years. (Unclear points exist in the details.)	GATS Article V (Substantial sectoral coverage standard). 1) Insufficient discussion regarding interpretation. 2) No consensus regarding how far the coverage of commitments should extend in FTA in excess of GATS commitments, or the depth of commitments, in relation to 155 categories and four modes of market access and national treatment. In addition, the period for elimination of discrimination in relation to national treatment among participating countries is defined only as 'a reasonable time-frame' (Article V[1b]).
Market access		
Commitments	Tariff rates lower than bound rates are allowed for participants in the FTA	Higher-level commitments than GATS commitments are allowed in relation to participating countries (However, MFN treatment can also be applied).
No commitments		New commitments are allowed in relation to participating countries (However, MFN treatment can also be applied).
National treatment		
Commitments	National treatment is a principle of GATT (Article III)	Conditions for commitments (GATS) are relaxed for participating countries (However, MFN treatment can also be applied).
No commitments		New commitments are allowed in relation to participating countries (However, MFN treatment can also be applied).

Rules of origin	With regard to FTA, disciplined by preferential rules of origin (No relevant rules in WTO)	Existing juridical persons conducting substantive business operations in the territory of a party to the FTA can share the benefits of the FTA (GATS Article V[6]).
Ease of discrimination by country	Discrimination in the areas of border measures and tariffs is easy	Regulations concerning foreign investment can be applied as regulations on market entry, but uniform application is standard for domestic measures (It is not easy to discriminate by country).
Extension of the benefits on MFN basis		
Towards participants in the FTA	Classified into those (i) with clauses specifying MFN extension, (ii) with clauses specifying efforts towards MFN extension, and (iii) without such clauses	As at left. (However, discrimination by country with regard to domestic disciplines is generally difficult.)
Towards non-participants in the FTA	As a general rule, no MFN extension	Can be implemented with or without MFN extension. However, discrimination by country is generally difficult with regard to domestic disciplines.

Source: The Author.

First, there are difference in GATT and GATS disciplines and their applicability to digital trade (Table 2.1). Because of the differences of GATT and GATS disciplines on market access, discrimination (MFN, national treatment) and domestic regulations, the application of relevant rules to digital trade needs to be further discussed and clarified.

Second, there are several limitations of GATS. Digital trade is the area where GATS rules will have very important implications. On GATS disciplines, the limitations include the following:

i   Insufficient commitments – With respect to market access and national treatment, commitments in GATS will bind the country only in the area and the extent of the commitments. The commitments are limited both in coverage and depth. Also, these basically reflect the status of the economy in 1995 and have not reflected the changes in the economy and institutions since then.

ii   Positive list – Together with insufficient commitments, the so-called positive list approach limits the application of commitments to new areas.[5]

iii Obsolete classification – GATS commitments were made based on W/120 classification, which consists of 155 areas. These, however, have not been regularly updated unlike the regular adjustment of Harmonized System in GATT. This makes the interpretation of commitments ambiguous and difficult, irrespective of the changes of economies and technological development. For example, online data storage service is not listed in CPC844 in W/120.

iv   MFN exemption – MFN exemption is allowed in GATS in so far as it was listed by the members at the entry into force of the agreement and new exemption cannot be added to the exemption list (Table 2.2). This limits the flexibility of the members in making new commitments in case they have concerns of free riding by certain members.[6]

v   Lack of clarity on general exceptions (Article 14) and security exceptions (Article 14–2) – Article 14 of GATS stipulates general exceptions allowed for members. However, the conditions are not clear enough, thus leading to abuses of the provision by members. It is the same for national security exceptions in Article 14–2.

vi   Lack of adaptation to technological changes – GATS provisions have not been updated since 1997, when the telecommunication and financial services agreements were concluded. GATS commitments have not been updated reflecting technological and economic changes since GATS came into force in 1995.

vii Stalemate in progressive liberalization and additional commitments – The progressive liberalization expected when GATS came into force in 1995 did not proceed. The framework of additional commitments has not been utilized due to the reciprocal approach and fear of free riding.

3. Development and history of digital trade disciplines

Rule-making in digital trade is rooted in the establishment of the WTO and entry into force of GATS and TRIPS agreement in 1995. Based on W/120 services classification, WTO members made commitments in GATS. These commitments were made based on the institution of each member at that time, expecting additional commitments on progressive liberalization. With members strongly supporting the newly born WTO, the telecommunication services agreement (and financial services agreement) and ITA were signed in 1997 in time for the Singapore Ministerial Meeting. In 1998, WTO members discussed the work programme on e-commerce,[7] and agreed on a moratorium on customs duty on e-commerce. After the debacle at the 1999 Seattle Ministerial Conference, a new round of talks was launched in Doha in 2001. The speed and development of the round were, however, very slow, and the main focus of rule-making and liberalization shifted from the WTO to the arena of FTAs.

Digital trade was no exception. In 2005, the US-Australia FTA introduced an e-commerce chapter, and the US-Korea FTA in 2012 further developed the e-commerce chapter. These are trials for rule-making on e-commerce and digital trade in the framework of FTAs. Japan introduced an e-commerce chapter in the Japan-Switzerland FTA in 2009 and also in the Japan-Mongolia FTA, concluded in 2016, with provision on free cross-border data flow. On top of these developments, the TPP agreement in 2016 introduced the most comprehensive provisions in FTAs by far.

In addition to these developments on digital trade in FTAs, the stalemate of services negotiation in the Doha Round brought about the TiSA initiative covering substantial services sectors. TiSA also intends to cover digital trade disciplines. In 2015, negotiation for the addition of products to ITA was concluded, paving the way for promoting digital trade by eliminating tariffs on information technology products. In this situation, active discussion on e-commerce began in the WTO in 2016. Table 2.3 shows the progress in digital trade rule settings in various international agreements since 1995, when the WTO was born.

In particular, the TPP/Comprehensive and Progressive Agreement for Trans-Pacific (CPTPP) has developed a framework that can be a benchmark for future digital trade/e-commerce disciplines.[8] It will not only affect its signatories,

Table 2.3 Digital Trade Rule Settings

Year	Development
1995	Establishment of the WTO; GATS (binding based on W/120), TRIPS agreement
1997	Telecommunication services agreement; Information Technology Agreement (ITA)
1998	Moratorium on Customs Duties; Work programme on e-commerce
2005	US-Australia FTA (e-commerce chapter)
2009	Japan-Switzerland FTA (e-commerce chapter; first trial by Japan)
2012	US-Korea FTA (e-commerce chapter)
2013	Initiation of TiSA negotiation
2015	ITA II (extension of ITA product coverage)
2016	TPP (signed by 12 members); Japan-Mongolia FTA (e-commerce chapter); Various proposals in WTO on digital trade and e-commerce
2017	CPTPP (signed by 11 members)
2018	Japan-EU EPA

Source: The Author.

but also give non-participating members the reference points for consideration (WEF, 2016b).

The e-commerce chapter in the agreement provides the most comprehensive coverage and disciplines among existing FTAs by far (WEF, 2016a). It has, among other things, such provisions as (i) prohibition of customs duties, (ii) non-discriminatory treatment of digital products, (iii) prohibition of localization, (iv) prohibition of forced sharing of source code, (v) free flow of data, etc. It is also flexible in considering and responding to the difficulties of members, including developing and future members, by going around the dichotomy of GATT and GATS provisions and allowing certain deviations based on public needs.

Even with the withdrawal of the United States (US), the e-commerce chapter of the CPTPP is still relevant and can be a reference point for developing rules on digital trade because of the following:

i   The rules were agreed by the 11 (and also by the 12) members. The rules on digital trade were strongly promoted by member states. US withdrawal from TPP does not necessarily mean that US will not support its digital provisions.
ii The e-commerce chapter in the TPP was clearly anticipated to be applied to the European Union (EU) and China in the future.
iii It has flexibility necessary to be the basis for global rules in terms of development consideration and regulatory needs for public purposes. It includes as members developing economies, such as Brunei Darussalam, Chile, Malaysia, Peru, and Viet Nam.
iv No other framework so far (including the Japan-EU EPA) stipulates disciplines on digital trade in a comprehensive manner. If countries seriously try to develop rules on digital trade, it is natural to refer to the TPP/CPTAPP as a reference.

4. Ways ahead and options for creating a global solution for digital trade rules

It is worth exploring necessary actions and the framework ahead for developing disciplines on e-commerce and digital trade to deal with the reality of e-commerce and business needs that are conducive to inclusive growth, avoid anomalies, and protect private, public, and social infrastructure. This section looks at the WTO, FTA, TiSA, and plurilateral frameworks, and discuss options ahead for the global trade regime as well as for ASEAN and East Asia where digital trade is developing fast and many key players (both governments and businesses) exist.

4.1. The WTO

The WTO stipulates trade rules with a comprehensive coverage, including GATS and TRIPS. The rules are applied to all WTO members, including developing ones, and are enforced by its strong dispute settlement mechanism with retaliatory measures in case of violations.

Digital trade rules are related to many areas of the WTO; among others, GATS disciplines. GATS rules and members' commitments in GATS have various limitations covering digital trade. In light of the global nature of digital trade and the need for unified rules and prevention of spaghetti bowls in digital trade disciplines, the ideal framework for rule-making on digital trade will be multilateral negotiation in the WTO of relevant agreements, including GATS, and new commitments by the members.

In GATS, for example, complementing its rules in view of digital trade, clarifying and complementing commitments of the members and revision of the telecommunication services agreement will be necessary to meet the development and reality of digital trade since 1995. In other areas, revision of the Trade Facilitation Agreement and TRIPS will be necessary. The need to suspend customs duties permanently may also be the issue for negotiation in the WTO (ICTSD, 2016).

Although the WTO is the best framework for creating a global framework, provided that its legislative function works, its legislative function is far from the expectation. The scope is too narrow, and the speed is too slow.

The fact that the only multilateral agreement under the WTO since its establishment is the Trade Facilitation Agreement speaks for itself. The paralysis comes from its decision-making system based on consensus and single undertaking principle (that is, all rules will bind all members) with strong enforcement of the dispute settlement mechanism (Baldwin and Nakatomi, 2015; Baldwin, 2011b). Stalemate in the WTO's legislative function has been partially complemented by the dispute settlement.

In the case of digital trade, WTO panels and appellate body have brought about certain important precedents in interpreting WTO agreements.[9] However, the evolutionary interpretation of the agreements without legislative changes has its limitations. The application of 'technological neutrality' in interpreting the commitments made by the members was also useful; likewise, it has limitations.

The rules applied to digital trade need to be negotiated and stipulated to reflect the rapid development of technologies, and economic and business environment and institutions. The time has come for WTO members to seriously discuss its decision-making mechanism recognizing 'variable geometry'[10] of members and the problems with consensus decision-making and single undertaking. In this regard, a plurilateral approach is one possible way out, as the study discusses later. ITA and the telecommunication and financial services agreements are in essence 'plurilateral agreements'.

On the other side, lack of (or scarce) collaboration with business is another problem the WTO is facing. WTO negotiations and the Doha Round are too narrow in scope and too slow in development. Unfortunately, paralysis in decision-making is expected to continue. For the time being, we cannot expect a lot on the WTO and the Round in developing digital trade rules, though we need to support the WTO as the core of the global trade system.

As for digital trade rules and e-commerce, it is very important to continue discussion and studies in the WTO as mandated by the work programme on e-commerce, and by the wider agenda to deepen understanding of the issues by the members.[11] First, consistency with WTO principles, especially MFN and non-discrimination, will be essential. Second, in case the rule setting is under FTAs and plurilateral framework, all efforts should be made to realize global rules in the WTO in the future.

4.2. The digital trade and commerce chapter of FTAs

FTAs have been the main framework in creating digital trade rules in the stalemate of the WTO and the Doha Round. The trend will most likely continue because the process is relatively fast and easy compared with the WTO negotiation.

Generally speaking, FTAs are in essence bilateral frameworks and will not directly create a global solution in digital trade. Simply accumulating bilateral deals may never realize global rules, but only create spaghetti bowls of rules on digital trade (Nakatomi, 2013a, 2013b). Mega FTAs such as the TPP, which harmonize rules covering a certain region and many countries may alleviate the problems of FTAs. Even Mega FTAs, however, should be treated as a step towards global rules in the WTO in the future.

The TPP/CPTPP can be a reference point for future digital trade rules. To globalize the solution, the disciplines applied in the TPP/CPTPP should accommodate the needs and difficulties of more members, particularly developing member countries. Further flexibility, technical assistance and capacity building, and special and differential treatment may be required.

Among mega FTAs, the Japan-EU EPA and RCEP will have serious implications for the development of digital trade rules. For ASEAN and East Asia, it is very important to have holistic discussions and comprehensive rules on digital trade in RCEP with necessary flexibilities, technical assistance, and capacity building for developing members. Japan's role is very important since it is a member of these two mega FTAs, as well as the TPP/CPTPP.

Apparently, TiSA is also categorized as an FTA based on Article 5 of GATS. TiSA as an FTA, if realized, will definitely affect the development of digital trade rules (ICTSD, 2016). It may also be categorized as a mega FTA in the services area.

Therefore, FTAs can be a building block for future global rules, but there is no automatic mechanism for FTAs, including mega FTAs, to lead to global rules. Digital trade rules are not exceptions. It is a myth that mega FTAs will automatically lead to global rules (Nakatomi, 2013a). For FTAs to pave the way for global rules on digital trade, the members should have strong will and collaboration in setting up future global rules in the WTO.

In addition, digital trade is closely related to the rules and commitments in GATS. Unlike market access in goods in FTAs, which is covered by Article 24 of GATT and has many precedents and a long history of discussion on its interpretation, services in FTAs, which is covered by Article 5 of GATS, have fewer precedents and scarce history of discussion on its interpretation. This will probably further complicate the situation.

4.3. Trade in Services Agreement

Recognizing that progress was not being made through traditional negotiating methods, the 2011 WTO Ministerial Conference acknowledged the possibility of advancing negotiations in different areas at different speeds to overcome the stagnation of the Doha Round, and the idea of TiSA was introduced, with the US as its driving force. TiSA is an initiative for services liberalization and rule-making discussed originally by 23 members, amongst a coalition called 'Really Good Friends of Services' (RGF). Preliminary discussions between participating members commenced in 2012, and on 28 June 2013, the RGF issued a joint declaration saying that discussions on TiSA had advanced, and that the participating members had moved to the stage of full-fledged negotiations.

Marchetti and Roy (2013) considered four possibilities in terms of the legal structure of TiSA[12]:

i   A GATS protocol approach, on an MFN basis, like the previous agreements on financial services and basic telecommunications.
ii A method in which the members participating in the negotiations would voluntarily improve their commitments on an MFN basis.
iii A plurilateral agreement within the WTO, based on consensus among all members.
iv A plurilateral agreement outside the WTO or, in other words, a services FTA based on Article 5 of GATS.

The US-proposed TiSA as an FTA based on GATS Article 5; the negotiations are now taking place as such (Hufbauer et al., 2012). The FTA approach based on GATS Article 5, however, also involves considerable risks (Bosworth, 2014). There is a risk of an arbitrary interpretation of requirements such as 'substantial sectoral coverage' under GATS Article 5. Surprisingly, there has been almost no discussion concerning the interpretation of these exceptions to the MFN principle (Nakatomi, 2015). In general, TiSA is reported to tackle digital trade rules in its coverage. Though the negotiation is currently suspended, serious efforts have been made to find a common solution reflecting diverse interests and different positions of members (among others, the US and the EU).

4.4. Digital trade FTAs

If TiSA can be structured as an FTA consistent with the legal requirements of Article 5 of GATS, what about creating a 'digital-only FTA'? More concretely, is it possible to structure a 'digital trade rules agreement' by like-minded countries as an FTA that is consistent with Article 5 of GATS, fulfilling inter alia the requirements of 'substantial sectoral coverage' and 'all modes'? The flexibility requirement for developing countries also needs to be satisfied. If the answer is yes, in addition to individual FTAs (bilateral or regional FTAs) and TiSA (horizontal services agreement as an FTA), the third type of FTA becomes an option to develop digital trade rules by like-minded countries.

A digital-only agreement could be justified as an FTA similar to the way that TiSA is. The 'substantial sectoral coverage' requirement may be satisfied as far as the digital-only agreement pursues digital disciplines in all areas horizontally (covering 155 areas by W/120). The requirements of all modes may also be satisfied if all modes 1–4 are somehow covered by the agreement or at least no mode is 'a priori' excluded from the scope of the negotiation. The negotiation, of course, aims at lowering the barriers and further liberalizing and giving necessary flexibilities to developing members.

There are enough reasons to pursue an idea of having a 'digital-only FTA'. First of all, individual FTAs (bilateral or regional) have limitations, as discussed. They will not directly lead to global rules. Such issue-specific and horizontal FTAs can be a strong tool for global rule-making on digital trade.

Second, considering the importance of digital trade and the necessity for governing its rules, speed is a top priority. But the future of TiSA is not clear. The negotiation is suspended, and there are no clear time frame and prospect for the conclusion of the negotiation.[13] Negotiations of a 'digital-only FTA' can concentrate on digital trade issues solely, which tends to make it easier and faster to reach the agreement.

Third, TiSA is a multiple issues agreement covering 'substantially all sectors' and not focussed on digital trade issues per se, though a part of digital trade issues may be covered. TiSA members are different from possible digital trade FTA members. This makes it possible to set a negotiation agenda and schedule separately from TiSA. Promoting a 'digital-only FTA' will increase the flexibility of the rule setting process.

Fourth, compared to TiSA, a 'digital-only FTA' would make the collaboration between governments as well as that of business and academia become easier. For instance, telecommunication services and financial services agreements and ITA were realized by concentrating on specific issues with the help of specific industries.

It is worth noting that since e-commerce and digital trade rules dealt with by the FTAs relate not only to GATS (Article 5) but also to GATT (Article 24), holistic analyses will be required if members introduce rules discriminatory to non-members of such FTAs. Consistency with the WTO rules is essential. However, if it is possible for a 'digital-only FTA' to be consistent with Article 5 of GATS, it will be a very strong tool for rule-making in the services-related aspects of digital trade. In reality, the scope of digital trade issues covered by Article 5 of GATS can be extensive.

4.5. Plurilateral agreement on digital trade and e-commerce

Table 2.4 summarizes the historical development of plurilateral agreements in GATT and the WTO. Opinions on who to develop disciplines in the areas covered by the WTO based on the plurilateral approach vary.[14] Here are three typical ones.

Table 2.4 GATT/WTO and Changes in the Treatment of Plurilateral Agreements

	1947	1979 –introduction of Tokyo Round codes	1995 –establishment of WTO	Incorporation of future plurilateral agreements
GATT	GATT 1947 Participation of all members	GATT 1947 Participation of all members	GATT 1994 Participation of all members	
Codes		Agreement on Subsidies and Countervailing Measures, Anti-dumping Agreement, TBT Agreement, Agreement on Import Licensing Procedures, Customs Valuation Agreement, Agreement on Trade in Civil Aircraft, Agreement on Government Procurement, International Dairy Agreement, International Bovine Meat Agreement. >> Non-MFN based agreements Participation of some members	Agreement on Subsidies and Countervailing Measures, Anti-dumping Agreement, TBT Agreement, Agreement on Import Licensing Procedures, and Customs Valuation Agreement were turned into Annex 1a agreements under the WTO (participated by all members). >> Participation of all members.	
WTO Annex 1A agreements on trade in goods			Participation of all members	Introduction of schedules of concessions approach? Amendments by critical mass plus MFN-based distribution of benefits?

(Continued)

Table 2.4 Continued

	1947	1979 –introduction of Tokyo Round codes	1995 –establishment of WTO	Incorporation of future plurilateral agreements
WTO Annex 4 agreements			Agreement on Trade in Civil Aircraft, Agreement on Government Procurement, International Dairy Agreement International Bovine Meat Agreement (Only first two agreements are in effect today). >> Non-MFN-based agreements. Participation of some members.	Easing procedural requirements for establishing new agreements? (e.g., Critical mass + MFN-based distribution of benefits)
WTO Annex 1B agreements on trade in services			Participation of all members Introduction of schedules of commitments approach	Additional sectoral agreements by same approach as those used for Financial Services Agreement and Basic Telecommunication Agreement? (Amendments to schedules of commitments)
WTO Annex 1C agreements on trade-related aspects of intellectual property rights			Participation of all members	Introduction of schedule of concessions/commitments approach? Amendments by critical mass plus MFN-based distribution of benefits?

Source: The Author.

4.5.1. WTO Annex 4 agreement (equivalent to the plurilateral agreement in the WTO in a narrow sense)

One way is to create an Annex 4 agreement which will be binding only to the participating members as the Government Procurement Agreement. However, such Annex 4 agreement can be created only by consensus and the hurdle for the decision-making process is very high.

4.5.2. Critical mass and MFN extension approach (Low, 2011; Nakatomi, 2013b)

The second approach to introduce a WTO-consistent agreement based on the plurilateral approach is to utilize the method taken in the telecommunications and financial services agreements (also in ITA) in 1997. These are based on the formation of agreements by 'critical mass' and 'MFN extension of the benefits of the agreement to non-members'. This becomes a standard approach in market access of goods as in the case of ITA1 (1997) and ITA2 (2015). If the critical mass is big enough, the possibility of realizing a global agreement will be high since MFN extension becomes easier. The biggest difficulty in realizing this approach is a concern for free riding by non-members. Such concern is excessively high in major countries, including the US.

Why then was the situation different in market access in goods, and why was ITA2 (extension of product coverage) realized? There are various reasons, but the author believes that strict MFN principle in GATT – Article 1, on no mechanism for registering exemption – and strict conditions for MFN exemption in Article 24 for FTAs have contributed (the 'substantially all trade' criterion is stringent for having market access solution in FTA).

However, in services, registering MFN exemption was possible and conditions for MFN exemption in Article 5 of GATS for FTAs are loose, allowing WTO members to pursue sectoral liberalization bilaterally in FTAs.

In addition, there are doubts as to the extent to which a non-MFN approach is actually feasible, given the horizontal nature of services regulations. In fact, in many cases, services regulations are implemented domestically on an MFN basis (Mattoo, 1999; Nakatomi, 2015). However, free riding is a politically sensitive issue, and reciprocity is always emphasized in services negotiation. Otherwise, there is no reason to structure TiSA as an FTA on non-MFN basis. How the free-riding issue is handled is a very important challenge for developing services negotiation, including the digital trade agenda.

4.5.3. Self-binding approach (Hoekman and Mavroidis, 2015, 2016).

Alternatively, another approach consistent with GATS that has recently attracted serious attention is the self-binding approach using the additional commitments framework in GATS. Hoekman and Mavroidis (2015) have developed the idea in place since the Warwick Report (The University of Warwick, 2007), which corresponds to 'going alone, on MFN basis' approach in Table 2.5. This is one relevant approach that can detour the consensus requirement to modify GATS, utilizing the additional commitments framework on an MFN basis. Whether this type of additional commitment is carried out will most likely depend on political will as it is not a legal issue.

It is logically possible to not apply the benefits on MFN basis within the limits of the MFN exemption list. But even the US and the EU did not reserve extensive items in the list.[15] But how far members can stick to the MFN principle is a serious issue for consideration since the concern for free ride is in many cases exaggerated and domestic rules are normally applied on an MFN basis.

Some discriminatory (non-MFN) regulations may also be explainable based on the interpretation of Article 14 or 14–2. These provisions, however, should not be interpreted as allowing for arbitrary or unjustifiable discrimination. Therefore, measures allowed under these provisions must be carefully identified.

4.6. *Mutual recognition (GATS Article 7)*

GATS stipulates as an exemption to the MFN the framework of mutual recognition in Article 7, as well as FTAs in Article 5. Since free riding and MFN application are serious bottlenecks for the further development of GATS and new commitments by members, while also a root cause of proliferation of services FTAs, appropriate attention should also be given to mutual recognition agreements, though they are not fully utilized. Normally, mutual recognition is bilateral, but it is also possible to apply it plurilaterally.

In developing and applying digital trade rules, the framework of mutual recognition can be useful. Since mutual recognition is among members and therefore not applied on an MFN basis, if utilized carefully and consistent with the requirement under Article 7 of GATS and other provisions, it will provide a workable framework for like-minded members to promote harmonization of institutions and enforcement of digital trade rules. In addition, unlike Article 5, Article 7 does not require 'substantial sectoral coverage' and 'all modes'.

Though mutual recognition is not commonly used since it requires high-level confidence among the regulatory authorities of members, it provides us with a tool for developing rules bilaterally or plurilaterally in digital trade areas (e.g., privacy shield between the US and the EU may be explained in Articles 14 and 7.)

4.7. *Waiver*

To allow for bilateral deals on a non-MFN basis, a waiver may be provided. A waiver is, however, normally used for provisional and exceptional measures and not appropriate for permanent rules. It is not a sustainable solution for digital trade rules (Table 2.5).

Table 2.5 Perspectives on the Legal Form of TiSA

	Overview	Precedents	Level of difficulty	WTO conflict resolution procedures	Other
A GATS protocol approach, on an MFN basis	Participation of sufficient nations to constitute critical mass is obtained, and the content of the agreements is multilateralized to WTO members via the MFN principle. The agreements are protocol-based, and are positioned at the upper level of the WTO.	Agreements on Financial Services and Basic Telecommunications	If the participation of enough nations to constitute critical mass cannot be secured, concerns over free riders make multilateralization via MFN difficult.	Can be used	Can be considered to be the most desirable approach from the perspective of global rule-making. Multilateralization via MFN is the key to the creation of a protocol based on the agreement of WTO members.
Going alone, on an MFN basis	Participants in the negotiations voluntarily revise their commitments, and the details are multilateralized to WTO members via the MFN principle.	It is not a method of plurilateral implementation of agreements, but there are numerous precedents for individual initiatives.	Difficult. There is no guarantee that all participants in the negotiations will revise their commitments in accordance with the agreement.	Can be used	A high-level relationship of trust between participating nations is a precondition.
A plurilateral agreement within the WTO	Establishment of a WTO Annex 4 agreement	Agreement on Trade in Civil Aircraft, Agreement on Government Procurement	Extremely difficult. A consensus among WTO member nations is necessary for the establishment of an Annex 4 agreement	Can be used	Relationships of rights and obligations exist only between participants in the agreement.
A plurilateral agreement outside the WTO	FTA based on GATS Article V	Many examples of integration with goods FTA based on GATT Article 24. There are no examples of services-only FTA.	According to GATS Article V, an FTA is formed on the basis of agreement between the participating nations. (In this sense, it is easy.)	Cannot be used	Fulfilment of the requirements of GATS Article V is an essential condition.
Waiver	According to Article IX(3) of the Marrakesh Agreement, a waiver can be obtained with the agreement of three-fourths of WTO member nations.		Agreement of three-fourths of WTO member nations is a challenging condition.	Able to be used? (Dependent on content of waiver)	Waivers are not suitable as ongoing exception measures. Periodic updating of the waiver is necessary.

Source: The author.

4.8. Guidelines and best practices

Rule-making on digital trade is an important and pressing task; yet the tools to realize it – such as the WTO, FTAs, TiSA, plurilateral approach, and so on — have pros and cons. Choosing among available tools is not easy.

In case a legally binding solution cannot be readily achievable, discussing and sharing guidelines and best practices, and involving not only governments but business and related parties, are very important.[16] Even when the negotiation on certain formats for digital trade rules kicks off, continuous dialogue and sharing guidelines and best practices need to continue.

For digital trade to be conducive to inclusive growth of developing countries and small and medium-sized enterprises, dialogues and dissemination of guidelines and best practices are a 'must' to prepare for a legally binding solution. Bilateral guidelines such as Japan-US Trade Principles for ICT Services are useful in moving ahead to share best practices in paving the way forward for rules in digital trade. These soft law approaches, in addition to the legally binding approaches of this study, should also be actively promoted.

In short, to formulate relevant digital trade rules, active discussion and deliberation on methods and tools need to take place to pursue the most appropriate and pragmatic way forward. The WTO Doha Round is not matching the speed necessary to fix digital trade rules. Other fora and methods need to be pursued for rule-making in this evolving field, with a view to creating global rules as WTO rules at a later stage. If we just continue discussions in the WTO, nothing may happen in the coming 20 years as in the case of trade and investment and trade and competition, judging from the track record of the WTO on new issues. With decision-making paralyzed in the WTO, we need to continue the serious quest for finding the best framework for rule-making in such complicated and important issues as digital trade and launching holistic negotiations. Otherwise, rule-making on digital trade is destined to be deadlocked.

5. Conclusion

E-commerce and digital trade are developing rapidly and paving the way for global economic activities and trade. At the same time, the introduction of various restrictions and regulations by national authorities are becoming serious impediments for the further development of global economic activities and trade.

Digital protectionism has become an imminent concern for e-commerce and digital trade. At the same time, from the viewpoint of protecting developing countries and less endowed people, the possibility of a digital divide among different players is also a serious problem. New digital trade rules should pursue inclusive solutions for all. On the other hand, regulations and restrictions imposed by national authorities are in many circumstances based on necessary public purposes, such as privacy and national security. Defining the boundaries of allowable regulations and balancing the need for regulations and freedom of digital trade are an imminent issue for all stakeholders.

This chapter study highlights six points as the basis for consideration: (i) global rules as the basis for digital trade rules, (ii) proliferation of regulations and danger of digital protectionism, (iii) one barrier can stifle digital trade, (iv) avoidance of spaghetti bowls in rules, (v) potential for inclusive, win-win growth, and (vi) collaboration among government, business, academia, and non-governmental organizations.

Accordingly, it highlights the significance to develop rules in (i) customs duties and market access, (ii) standards and regulations, (iii) discrimination, (iv) cross-border data flow, (v) localization requirement of servers, (vi) forced disclosure of source codes, and (vii) protection of intellectual property rights.

To prepare relevant digital trade rules, there are needs for active discussion and deliberation on methods and tools that are most appropriate and pragmatic to move forward. As a forum for global rule-making, the WTO is ideally the best, but the reality of the organization is far from the dream. Although the Doha Round is not matching the speed necessary to set digital trade rules, further effort in WTO is still necessary, and other fora and methods will also need to be pursued for rule-making in this evolving field.

In particular, ASEAN and East Asia should and can contribute to rule-making in digital trade given the importance of speed, appropriate selection of issues, adjustment of ambition levels, and strategic choice of framework.

Notes

1 The Fourth Industrial Revolution is characterized by a fusion of technologies that is blurring the lines between the physical, digital, and biological spheres.
2 See, for example, the definition of e-commerce by the World Trade Organization work programme adopted on September 1998. Available at www.wto.org/english/tratop_e/ecom_e/wkprog_e.htm
3 The 'spaghetti bowl' refers to co-existence of different rules in a disharmonized manner, given the fact that there exist over 500 regional trade agreements (RTAs) and 3000 bilateral investment treaties (BITs) in the world.
4 See, for example, Meltzer (2013) and ICTSD (2016).
5 In many FTAs, the negative list approach has been applied to enhance commitments.
6 If a country does not want to apply a new services commitment on an MFN basis, it may end up giving up making a commitment at all (Mattoo, 1999).
7 See www.wto.org/english/tratop_e/ecom_e/wkprog_e.htm
8 In the dimension of developing e-commerce chapters in FTAs, the WTO document, WTO JOB/GC/100 (25 July 2016), summarizes specific provisions in key FTAs with an e-commerce chapter.
9 See the Internet gambling and China electronic payment services cases (WTO DS285, DS413.)
10 In GATT, Tokyo Round 'codes' allowed differential treatment of members in rule-making and its application. Tokyo Round codes were applied only to participating members on condition that the rights of other members not be undermined. This was one way of accommodating the needs of 'variable geometry' of member economies.
11 The trade policy review mechanism is a useful mechanism to deepen understanding of the practices of WTO members and share common views on digital trade rules.

12 On the legal nature of TiSA, see also Table 2.5.
13 Even if TiSA moves forward, it is worth pursuing a separate digital-only agenda.
14 See Hoekman and Mavroidis (2015), WEF (2010), Harbinson and De Meester (2012).
15 In the case of Japan, there is no exemption.
16 In the WTO, utilizing the TPR mechanism for digital trade issues is a good idea for enhancing understanding of practices by WTO members without prejudice to negotiation positions.

Bibliography

Baldwin, R. (2011a), 'Trade and Industrialisation After Globalisation's 2nd Unbundling: How Building and Joining a Supply Chain Are Different and Why It Matters', *NBER Working Paper*, No. 17716, Cambridge, MA: NBER.

Baldwin, R. (2011b), '21st Century Regionalism: Filling the Gap between 21st Century Trade and 20th Century Trade Rules,' *WTO Staff Working Paper* ERSD-2011–08, Geneva: WTO.

Baldwin, R. and M. Nakatomi (2015), 'A World Without the WTO: What's at Stake?' *CEPR Policy Insight*, No. 84. Available at http://voxeu.org/epubs/cepr-reports/world-without-wto-what-s-stake

Bauer, M., M.F. Ferracane, H. Lee-Makiyama and E. van der Marel (2016), 'Unleashing Internal Data Flows in the EU: An Economic Assessment of Data Localisation Measures in the EU Member States', *ECIPE Policy Brief*, No. 03/2016, Brussels, Belgium: ECIPE.

Bosworth, M. (2014), 'The Proposed Non-MFN Trade in Services Agreement: Bad for Unilateralism, the WTO and the Multilateral Trading System', *NCCR Trade Regulation Working Paper*, No. 2014/05, World Trade Institute, pp. 24, 35.

Crosby, D. (2016), 'Analysis of Data Localization Measures Under WTO Services Trade Rules and Commitments', *ICTSD Policy Brief*. Available at http://e15initiative.org/wp-content/uploads/2015/09/E15-Policy-Brief-Crosby-Final.pdf

Drake, W.J. (2016), 'Background Paper for the workshop on Data Localization and Barriers to Transborder Data Flows', 14–15 September, World Economic Forum. Available at http://www3.weforum.org/docs/Background_Paper_Forum_workshop%2009.2016.pdf

Harbinson, S. and B. De Meester (2012), 'A 21st Century Work Program for the Multilateral Trading System', Prepared for the National Foreign Trade Council. Available at www.nftc.org/default/trade/WTO/NFTC21stCenturyTradeAgenda2012.pdf

Hoekman, B. and P. Mavroidis (2015), 'WTO "à la carte" or WTO "menu du jour"? Assessing the Case for More Plurilateral Agreements', *The European Journal of International Law*, 26(2): 319–343.

Hoekman, B. and P. Mavroidis (2016), 'Clubs and the WTO Post-Nairobi: What Is Feasible? What Is Desirable?' *Vox EU Column*, 3 February. Available at http://voxeu.org/article/clubs-and-wto-post-nairobi (accessed 11 August 2017)

Hufbauer, G.C., J.B. Jensen and S. Stephenson (2012), 'Framework for the International Services Agreement,' Peterson Institute for International Economics, *Policy Brief*, No. PB12–10.

ICTSD (2016), 'Maximizing the Opportunities of the Internet for International Trade', *Policy Options Paper*, The E15 Initiative. Available at http://www3.weforum.org/docs/E15/WEF_Digital_Trade_report_2015_1401.pdf

Low, P. (2011), 'WTO Decision Making for the Future,' *World Trade Organization Staff Working Paper* ERSD-2011-05, Geneva: WTO.

Marchetti, J.A. and M. Roy (2013), 'The TISA Initiative: An Overview of Market Access Issues,' *World Trade Organization Staff Working Paper* ERSD-2013-11, Geneva: WTO.

Mattoo, A. (1999), 'MFN and the GATS', presented at the World Trade Forum Conference on Trade in Services in the Asia Pacific Region. Available at www.iatp.org/files/MFN_and_the_GATS.htm

Meltzer, J. (2013), 'The Internet, Cross-Border Data Flows and International Trade', *Issues in Technology Innovation*, Number 22, Washington, DC: The Brookings Institution.

Meltzer, J. (2016), 'The Internet and International Data Flows in the Global Economy', Blog, *ICTSD*. Available at www.ictsd.org/opinion/the-internet-and-international-data-flows-in-the-global-economy

Nakatomi, M. (2012), 'Exploring Future Application of Plurilateral Trade Rules: Lessons from the ITA and the ACTA,' *Research Institute of Economy, Trade and Industry, RIETI Policy Discussion Paper Series* (12-P-009).

Nakatomi, M. (2013a), 'Global Value Chain Governance in the Era of Mega FTAs and a Proposal of an International Supply-Chain Agreement,' *Vox CEPR Policy Portal.* Available at http://voxeu.org/article/it-time-international-supply-chain-agreement

Nakatomi, M. (2013b), 'Plurilateral Agreements: A Viable Alternative to the World Trade Organization?' *ADBI Working Paper Series*, No. 439.

Nakatomi, M. (2015), 'Sectoral and Plurilateral Approaches in Services Negotiations: Before and After TISA', *ECIPE Policy Brief*, No. 02/2015, Brussels: European Centre for International Political Economy.

The University of Warwick (2007), *The Multilateral Trade Regime: Which Way Forward? Report of the First Warwick Commission*. Coventry, UK: The University of Warwick.

World Economic Forum (WEF) (2010), *A Plurilateral "Club-of-Clubs" Approach to World Trade Organization Reform and New Issues*. Geneva: Global Agenda Council on Trade.

World Economic Forum (WEF) (2016a), 'Will the Trans-Pacific Partnership Agreement Reshape the Global Trade and Investment System? What's in and What's New: Issues and Options', Global Agenda Council on Trade and FDI. Available at http://www3.weforum.org/docs/WEF_White_Paper_Whats_in_and_whats_new.pdf

World Economic Forum (WEF) (2016b), 'Will the Trans-Pacific Partnership Agreement Reshape the Global Trade and Investment System? Regional and Systemic Implications: Issues and Options', Global Agenda Council on Trade and FDI. Available at http://www3.weforum.org/docs/WEF_White_Paper_Regional_and_Systemic_Implications.pdf

World Trade Organization (WTO) (2016), 'Work Programme on Electronic Commerce Non-Paper for the Discussions on Electronic Commerce/Digital Trade from Japan', WTO JOB/GC/100, 25 July. Geneva: WTO.

3 The risks for ASEAN of new mega-agreements that promote the wrong model of e-commerce

Jane Kelsey

1. Introduction

The world of digital economies, innovation and global value chains is changing extremely rapidly. Every day, there are stories about new technologies, services and products that present unexpected possibilities and unforeseen challenges. There is potential to harness these innovations to revolutionise development across ASEAN, especially through regional initiatives that support its small and poorer members. If ASEAN countries are to maximise these opportunities, they will need international, regional and national rules that facilitate digital industrialisation, close the digital divide and correct the development asymmetries that currently favour developed countries and their corporations. The wrong rules will deny them those benefits.

This chapter examines how a systematic strategy of norm-creation through new generation mega trade and investment agreements could embed the current asymmetries for the indefinite future. The novel chapter on electronic commerce in the Trans-Pacific Partnership agreement (TPP) (now the Comprehensive and Progressive Agreement for Trans-Pacific Partnership [CPTPP])[1] is largely mirrored in the draft e-commerce annex of the Trade in Services Agreement (TiSA), the terms of reference for the Regional Comprehensive Economic Partnership (RCEP) and Japan's new bilateral free trade agreements (FTAs), including with the European Union (EU).[2] The EU and Japan have taken over from the United States (US) in driving the multilateralisation of that template, pushing for a negotiating mandate on electronic commerce at the 11th ministerial conference of the World Trade Organization (WTO) in Buenos Aires in December 2017 (MC11).

The new e-commerce regime is not about 'free trade' and barely about real commerce. As with the WTO's Agreement on Trade-Related Aspects of Intellectual Property Rights (TRIPS), it aims to protect and entrench the oligopoly of first movers. Achieving a development dividend through digital industrialisation, especially for small and poor countries, requires a collective commitment to local investment and shared knowledge. Instead, the proposed new global norms would consolidate the dominance of the technology giants over digital technologies, infrastructure, services and above all data, the new oil of the 21st century.

ASEAN economies risk being locked into a state of dependency that some are describing as digital colonialism (Knowledge Commons, 2014; Choudhary and Moglen, 2017).

There are fiscal consequences, too: a permanent ban on customs duties for economic transmissions could seriously deplete government revenues, while deterritorialisation will foster the tax avoidance practices of multinational companies. Restrictions on the ability to regulate the digital domain also threatens non-economic imperatives of consumer welfare, economic stability, national security, privacy and other citizens' rights. There is no special and differential treatment in these agreements, nor any genuine development flexibilities that might redress their imbalances, aside perhaps from the RCEP.

The chapter begins by outlining the demands of the US digital industry that the Office of the United States Trade Representative (USTR) has adopted in its 'Digital2Dozen' agenda, and subsequently in the TPP. Their promotion of binding international rules appears to be in response to developing countries' moves to regulate the unregulated digital domain, and a growing competitive challenge from China. The third section outlines some of the development concerns arising from these rules. The fourth section outlines the potential for ASEAN members to be exposed to these proposed new norms through agreements they are currently negotiating. That is followed by a more detailed review of the legal obligations on cross-border services and e-commerce in the mega-agreements, and the weakness of protections for consumers, citizen rights, privacy and national security. The final section reflects on the implications of these mega-agreements for ASEAN members who want to advance their national and regional development through digital industrialisation. As of 2018, they are still in a position to adopt such strategies, individually and collectively. However, the study warns that they will need to vigorously defend that policy space in their current and future negotiations.

2. The US demand for rules

Since its genesis in the US in the 1970s, the US government has insisted that the Internet remains a regulation-free zone. Discussions on Internet governance in the International Telecommunications Union (ITU) and the United Nations have been strongly resisted (Singh, 2017: 11).[3] Instead, the international regime has developed to reflect US domestic law, which regulates telecommunications and protects the Internet from regulation.[4] A private informal system of global Internet 'stakeholder' governance has emerged that is dominated by the major players (Singh, 2017: 8–10).[5] Far from creating a level playing field, this has allowed giant American firms (symbolised by the acronym GAFA – Google, Apple, Facebook and Amazon) to establish control over the digital technologies that will drive the world's economies and societies in the coming decades – at least until some new technology that they do not control makes them redundant or obsolete.

2.1. The digital industry's demands

Ten years ago, the world's five largest companies by market capitalisation were Microsoft, Exxon Mobil, General Electric, Citigroup and Shell Oil. In 2017, they were Apple, Alphabet (parent company of Google), Amazon, Microsoft and Facebook (PWC, 2017). The world's top three Internet companies at the time – Amazon (e-commerce), Google (search engine) and Facebook (social media) – were American, although the next two largest were from China: Tencent (social media) and Alibaba (e-commerce) (Deutsche Welle, 2016).

Specific segments of the market are highly monopolistic: in 2017, Google had an 88 percent market share in search advertising, Facebook controlled 77 percent of mobile social traffic and Amazon had a 74 percent share of the e-book market (Taplin, 2017). Their priority has been to increase their global market share. Sometimes they achieve this through loss-leading behaviour that undercuts competitors in the short term, as Amazon has attempted in India (Peermohamed, 2016). Sometimes they buy up competitors and rising stars. The technology is the driver, not the sector, as major tech companies branch out into driverless cars and drone delivery systems.

These and other first movers who own the intellectual property (IP) and data, control the platforms and markets, and dominate the multi-stakeholder fora of Internet governance hold a massive advantage. Their industry groups have intensively lobbied the Obama administration, and later the Trump administration, to secure global rules that prevent national governments from regulating digital technologies, services and products in the future (Internet Association, 2017).[6] A revolving door between the industry and the Office of the USTR has helped them.[7]

The priority for the major tech corporations is their right to control data, decide where in the world it is held and under what laws. Data is immensely valuable, financially and strategically. It can earn vast sums from advertising and be sold to private interests for commercial or personal purposes. It is the raw material used to analyse and influence social trends and shape public opinion by manipulating the content that individuals can see. Control over data can be abused by corporations and secured by the state to invade privacy, conduct surveillance or cause tangible harm to individuals, businesses and other governments. Equally, it can be censored by providers or governments for commercial or political reasons. Offshoring of data makes it extremely difficult to monitor compliance with privacy, consumer or tax laws, let alone to enforce them. The status of financial data is especially sensitive, as regulators require immediate access at a time of financial crisis or institutional collapse.[8]

Other industry demands include unrestricted rights to supply services across the border and a ban on requirements that cross-border suppliers have a local presence or that firms who are present in the country use local content or computer facilities. Technology transfer requirements should be prohibited, including obligations to disclose source codes for algorithms, apps or 'smart' products.

2.2. The US 'Digital2Dozen'

Since 2010, the US has promoted the industry's agenda in multiple international fora (OECD, 2014; G7, 2016; EU, 2017). In 2016, the USTR encapsulated them in what it called the 'Digital2Dozen' principles (USTR, 2016a), which are carefully couched in the language of freedom and choice versus barriers, discrimination and forced technology transfers or location.

These principles formed the basis for the first comprehensive chapter on electronic commerce and new restrictions on a government's ability to regulate cross-border, financial and telecommunications services in the TPP. The USTR described it as 'the most ambitious and visionary Internet trade agreement ever attempted' (USTR, 2016b). The TPP text set the template for TiSA, which was well advanced before negotiations were suspended in November 2016.[9] The same demands informed the US 'non-paper' tabled in the WTO in July 2016 (WTO, 2016a).

2.3. Digital colonialism

The US initiative gained momentum as developing countries began to regulate Internet activities (ITIC, 2016). The US strategy follows a familiar historical pattern: rich and powerful countries make 'global' rules that are presented to the developing world as a *fait accompli*. Trade agreements are co-opted as vehicles through which to develop binding rules that benefit the first movers. The digital industrialisation strategies of later adaptors, and regulations designed to protect their strategic and social interests, are decried as 'market access barriers', 'discrimination', 'forced localisation' or 'digital protectionism' (ITIC, 2016). In a paper prepared for the South Centre, Parminder Singh observes how:

> In the emerging global digital order, developing countries, with the exception of China, are pushed to the periphery even more than in the traditional geo-economic arenas. A handful of nodes or centres, almost all of them in the US, control global networks of digital intelligence. Going by current trends, the level of structural dependency of developing countries in the digital society context is evidently going to be higher than ever. The phenomenon has also been called digital colonisation.
>
> (Singh, 2017: 6)

This reality belies the notion that ASEAN countries and their firms, let alone their SMEs, might leapfrog the industrial development process and become significant players in the global cross-border commerce (South Centre, 2017a). The barriers they face are set to intensify, unless they can develop effective national, regional and global regulation. The US tech industry is pushing for global rules to pre-empt such regulation.

2.4. The China challenge

The other main impetus for the US to develop these rules was the challenge to its ascendancy from China, whose outreach into Asia and Africa threatens the US's strategic and commercial objectives and the continued dominance of the US tech industry.

China has embarked on a systematic programme of digital catch-up. It has developed local platforms and markets by strategically blocking its competitors, supported by requirements for joint ventures and technology transfer (Dragoo, 2017). Government agencies are required to use national cloud services. The 'Made in China 2025' strategy aims to create the world's largest industrial robot market (Ma, 2016).

China's vision for cross-border e-commerce and Internet regulation is integral to the Belt and Road Initiative (BRI) strategy to re-establish its historical trade routes (Greiger, 2016). The 'Digital Silk Road' component of BRI is closely tied to the internationalisation of its largest digital operator, Alibaba. Alibaba's founder and executive chair Jack Ma describes his strategy as creating an 'ecosystem' that builds 'the fundamental digital and physical infrastructure for the future of commerce, which includes marketplaces, payments, logistics, cloud computing, big data and a host of other fields'. Ma's idea for an Electronic World Trade Platform (eWTP) centres on the establishment of digital free trade zones within and outside China (EUSME Centre, 2016). Alibaba's first offshore venture is a Digital Free Trade Zone in Malaysia in collaboration with the state-owned Malaysia Digital Economy Corporation, announced in March 2017 (Alibaba, 2017). Ma claims this model will facilitate small businesses and there is some evidence of that; he contrasts this to 'pure-commerce players' whom he predicts will face major challenges (Ma, 2016). However, Alibaba retains strategic control of the platform and data in its 'eco-system', which is where the real value lies (Transport Intelligence, 2016). In that sense, China's strategy is as self-interested and anti-competitive as is that of the US.

There are additional tensions around the extent of state regulation. China's digital industrialisation initiatives have been accompanied by a goal, announced in the 12th Five Year Plan in 2011, to strengthen regulation of the Internet (Dragoo, 2017). The new Cybersecurity Law passed in November 2016 includes mandatory data storage inside China and data retention regulations. As Dragoo points out, China has framed Internet regulation as a matter of national security. That law effectively neutralises competing considerations of consumer rights and privacy. The US has lodged and won several disputes at the WTO relating to censorship (e.g. WTO, 2016b), but these were driven by commercial interests, not by principles. The US industry has complained vociferously over China's new cybersecurity law, again on commercial grounds (ITIF, 2017: 8–9). Yet the Chinese market is sufficiently attractive for big players to comply; for example, Apple has built an iCloud data centre in a joint venture with a local company (Dragoo, 2017) and agreed to remove from its hardware the VPN apps that are used to disguise the location of the user (Al Jazeera, 2017).

China is not averse to international rules on digital trade; it chaired the G20 when it adopted a broad list of principles on digital trade in 2016 (G20, 2016). But it does not support the US-led model. In the WTO, China has argued for a gradual approach within the existing mandate of the working group on electronic commerce, which was set up in 1998 to discuss the issue (WTO, 2016b). To avoid polarisation, it urged WTO members to prioritise the 'easy issues' of promotion and facilitation of cross-border trade in goods and support services like payment and logistics services.

China's approach is clearly distinct from the US-led model, and it presents as pro-development and supportive of SMEs (Shuiyu et al., 2017). But it carries a parallel risk for ASEAN that Alibaba and its affiliates will control Asia's regional infrastructure, platforms and data, and become the gatekeeper for ASEAN countries wanting to harness new technologies and value chains for development.

3. Development implications of this model

Concerns about the potential development implications of the US-led agenda have grown since the draft e-commerce annex for TiSA was first leaked (Our World Is Not for Sale, 2014), followed by the release of the final TPP text in November 2015. While the main focus has been on the economic development implications, sensitive questions of government constraints on freedom of speech and inadequate protections for privacy and consumer rights also need to be addressed.

3.1. Digital industrialisation policies

Latecomer developing economies require coherent digital industrialisation strategies. Catch-up policies include targeted investment in domestic infrastructure, technology and R&D, domestic preferences in public procurement and technology transfer and joint ventures as a quid pro quo for market access and foreign investment. Domestic capabilities can be enhanced by requiring digital firms to have a local presence, store and process data locally, and use local computing facilities and infrastructure once they have been developed. Small and least-developed countries that cannot become self-sufficient may look to regional and cross-border collaborations for support that is not driven by purely commercial imperatives.

Various ASEAN members have already adopted one or more of these strategies. Many of those strategies would be unlawful under the mega-agreements. The US Information Technology Industry Council (ITIC) presents an annual catalogue of complaints to the USTR. Its 2016 submission targeted the practices of four ASEAN countries: Viet Nam, Indonesia, Malaysia and the Philippines, especially on requirements to maintain some local servers and data in the country, disclose source codes, use some local content, maintain a local presence alongside government procurement preferences, and licensing and regulatory requirements (ITIC, 2016). ITIC argues that these rules damage the interests of the

host countries as well as their own businesses by restricting state-of-the-art technology and services, cost efficiencies and consumer choice. Moreover, foreign
firms might bypass those countries if such regulations were imposed. However,
the self-interest of ITIC needs to be separated from genuine development arguments. Doing so requires a systematic and independent assessment that balances
the anticipated benefits against the costs and risks, such as those outlined ahead.

3.2. Anti-competitive practices

'Competition' was among the new issues proposed and rejected at the WTO ministerial conferences in Singapore in 1996 and Cancun in 2003. The developed
country proponents wanted rules requiring domestic competition. Developing
countries said the real problem was the oligopolistic dominance and cartel-like
behaviour of transnational corporations, which requires competition rules at the
global level (Khor, 1996).

The same arguments have resurfaced with the digital economy. The demand
for a level playing field within countries belies the global concentration of corporate power. Competition may appear to occur at the retailer or consumer end, but
there is a near monopoly or cartel among those who control the digital platforms
and outlets. Reflecting on the 'problem of bigness' from a development perspective, Sabeel Rahman observes that 'Users are locked into a single platform, which
then leverages this user base and vast store of underlying data to grow even bigger, colonize adjacent markets, and eventually, once other competitors are no
longer a threat, raise prices' (Rahman, 2016: 7).

The concern that dominant ISP providers can block access by others, prioritise content and lower the speed for – or extract rent from – competitors
is central to the net neutrality debate. In 2015, the US Federal Communications Commission (FCC) recognised that ISP providers were so dominant that
consumers had no real choice, and it reclassified the providers as telecom firms
that are subject to common carrier requirements. The Trump administration
has sought to reverse that decision (Romano, 2018). In mega-agreements, net
neutrality is subject to 'reasonable network management',[10] which the providers
are left to define.

Rahman suggests three options that, in theory, could counter these anti-
competitive practices. All options would be difficult for many ASEAN countries,
and some would be unlawful under the mega-agreements:

i   Some governments, notably the EU, have tried to impose their *internal com-
     petition law* on the big players. In June 2017, Google was fined 2.4 billion
     Euros by the EU Competition Commission for a complaint that the com-
     pany was unfairly promoting its own in-house services. Google was given
     90 days to comply or face a significant additional fine of 5 percent of global
     daily revenues (EC, 2017a). However, such inquiries are long and costly; the
     Google complaint dated back to 2010. Most ASEAN countries would have
     to depend on developed states with more sophisticated competition regimes

and more resources to challenge such behaviours, and hope that successful outcomes applied globally.

ii   Competition law might also be used to impose restrictions on predatory behaviour (Peermohamed, 2016) and the consolidation of market power through mergers and acquisitions (Sen, 2017). However, even if that challenge succeeded, the size and resources of the major players mean that only other large players could compete in the long term, especially on a cross-border scale.

iii   The dominant players could be treated as natural monopolies in their market segments and *regulated as public utilities*, as telecommunications usually are. They could then be required to share technologies, and license out search algorithms, advertising exchanges and other key innovations for a nominal fee (Taplin, 2017). The mega-agreements would prohibit such measures.

iv   Governments could conclude that market competition is insufficient incentive for competitors to build infrastructure, and establish a *government-chartered entity* to provide the service directly to the public. This presumes a country (or regional arrangement) has the necessary funding; technological capacity; access to proprietary knowledge, including source codes; and trained local personnel – none of which can be required under the mega-agreements. This option might also fall foul of new disciplines on state-owned enterprises (SOEs).[11]

3.3. *Foregoing benefits of foreign direct investment (FDI)*

There are various development rationales for FDI, although they are not always achieved. Governments expect to improve access to and transfer of technology, strengthen domestic firms and SOEs through joint ventures, develop shared R&D, build managerial skills and train workers. They also aim to secure new export channels and efficiency gains through competitive pressures on local companies. Those opportunities are largely lost by requirements to allow foreign firms to supply services across the border, and prohibitions on requiring them to have a local presence, use the local facilities the country has invested in establishing, employ local people if they would gain access to proprietary knowledge, or transfer technology. While cross-border services might provide better quality, providers lack the commitment to maintain supply that would come with sunk investment, and the country's long-term dependency would intensify.

3.4. *Global value chains (GVCs)*

Research suggests that most integration of developing countries into GVCs since the ICT revolution of the 1990s is through cost-driven outsourcing, which does little to reduce the under-development of host countries (Azarhoushang, 2015: 164). The value-add usually stays in the parent country, with locally earned profits repatriated through complex legal and accounting arrangements. In recent times, procurement sources in GVCs have become more fluid. That can benefit ASEAN economies, and even SMEs, provided that they can compete. At the same time, the constant churning of commercial relationships also creates unpredictability and instability. Those seeking to access international platforms or e-marketplaces to sell products must also negotiate with the aggregator, such as Google or Amazon. Sellers lack negotiating power and remedies.

As part of its anti-trust inquiries, the EU found increased use of contract restrictions to control product distribution (Fioretti, 2017). Big manufacturers are using selective distribution systems whereby products can only be sold by pre-authorised sellers, which gives the manufacturers more control over distribution, price and brand image. Almost half the manufacturers using selective distribution systems blocked pure online retailers like eBay from selling their products, while eBay has complained that such bans prevent small businesses from selling products on online marketplaces. There are no tools in the agreements to constrain these practices, and moves to create such tools could breach the disciplines on domestic regulation of technical standards for services or the administration of general regulations (discussed ahead).

3.5. Artificial intelligence (AI)

Rapid advances in AI have economic, social and political implications. China-based Taiwanese venture capitalist Kai-Fu Lee predicts intense concentrations of wealth in the relatively few hands of those who control the complex AI technology (Lee, 2017). A multiplicity of rules in the mega-agreements – from source code secrecy and bans on technology transfer to unrestricted cross-border supply of services and financial flows – would constrain the development of local AI and its regulation.

Lee observes that 'strength begets strength'. He predicts that dominant players will move to capture AI in other countries, with the US dominating developed markets and China dominating the developing markets. Many jobs will be eliminated and not replaced, especially low-wage jobs that are currently created through offshoring of production and services. That is especially problematic for developing countries that will have growing populations, but fewer jobs and less revenue as money made from AI will be transferred to the US and China.

3.6. Digital products

The scope of e-commerce has expanded from the delivery of tangible goods ordered through the Internet to electronically transmitted products and production through remote additive manufacturing (RAM), such as 3D printing. Rashmi Banga calculates that six countries have captured more than 85 percent of the e-services market that would deliver these digital products: China (40 percent), US (20 percent), UK (9 percent), Japan (5 percent), Germany (4 percent) and France (4 percent) (Banga, 2017: 10). Unrestricted rights to supply services across the border would entrench the dominance of, and structural dependency on, those suppliers, and make it extremely difficult for firms in developing and small countries to participate meaningfully in international markets.

There would also be significant impacts on traditional manufacturing. The huge reduction in manufacturing costs and the ease of relocation means the competitive advantage will shift from high-volume low-cost manufacturers to owners of customer networks. Banga suggests the future for SMEs may be especially bleak. She argues for a digital industrialisation strategy and regulatory framework that can realistically address these challenges. That needs to be accompanied by improved Internet penetration, strengthening of national trade portals, improving the capacity of postal services and strategic action plans to boost cross-border e-commerce. These steps require ASEAN countries to retain their policy space.

3.7. Fiscal and tax impacts

Tax authorities already struggle with the tech giants' complex global corporate structures. It is even more problematic to tax cross-border transactions and profits earned in a country when there is no local presence in that country. Tax exceptions in the mega-agreements are complex and variable.[12]

The new rules pose a second fiscal challenge. A temporary moratorium on customs duties on electronic transmissions at the WTO is renewed every two years. It was first agreed in 1998, when the current scale of coverage was unforeseen by most Members (WTO, 1998). New agreements like TPP ban those duties permanently. Banga conducted a tariff simulation analysis that projects serious revenue impacts for ASEAN countries as net importers of electronically transmitted products, especially for Viet Nam, Thailand, the Philippines, Indonesia and Cambodia (Banga, 2017).

Governments could eventually lose customs duties for most non-agricultural manufactured products if the ban extends to cross-border transmissions of RAM; for example, the cross-border transfer of 3D printing specifications for products that are then printed inside the country. The loss of tariff revenues and/or damage to domestic competitors would be huge. Developed countries that already have minimal or zero tariffs would be unaffected. Falling revenue would deprive ASEAN countries of the investment required for effective digital industrialisation strategies and to address the impacts on local businesses, employment and communities.

An additional concern is the link between the customs duty moratorium and a moratorium on non-violation nullification and impairment disputes under TRIPS, which the US demands as a quid pro quo (Patnaik, 2015). If the current trade-off goes, developing countries may have to concede something else to secure renewal of the TRIPS moratorium.

3.8. Safety, security and citizens' rights

Businesses, households, communities and governments are already heavily reliant on Internet search engines, digital platforms, websites, apps and social media.

That carries significant risks from an ISP outage, faulty software or technical maintenance, or the installing of malware that can bring to a halt banking and payment systems, transportation or entire supply chains. Safety and security risks associated with the applications of artificial intelligence, such as drones, robots and driverless vehicles, will also intensify as other, as-yet-unimaginable technologies evolve.

Foreign states and private actors have even intervened in other nations' electoral processes and created mayhem through politically motivated cyberattacks (Hern, 2018). There is greater awareness of the scope for commercial and political espionage and sabotage, including by foreign governments. Citizens of other countries could be subject to legalised corporate and state surveillance, depending on where their data is located – something over which they have no control. Fundamental human rights are at risk from censorship of providers, sites and content by the user's home or host state, or by ISP and platform operators (UNGAHRC, 2016). These restrictions can also nullify the economic and social benefits of widespread connectivity (Khan, 2009).

The mega-agreements subordinate these considerations to the commercial interests of the industry and, as a later section explains, the protections and exceptions are ineffectual where they are provided.

4. Negotiating challenges for ASEAN

No ASEAN countries are currently subject to these rules, although Brunei Darussalam, Malaysia, Viet Nam and Singapore will be if the TPP comes into force in the form of the CPTPP. However, all ASEAN members are parties to several negotiations in which similar proposals have been tabled.

4.1. RCEP

In February 2015, the Trade Negotiation Committee (TNC) of RCEP endorsed a proposal to establish an e-commerce working group:

> [T]he TNC reiterated the importance and potential of e-commerce to economic development and enhanced global value chains (GVCs), including for the Small and Medium Enterprises (SMEs). The TNC also highlighted the need to seek balance between commercial interests and legitimate public policy and regulatory objectives. Further, the TNC noted the different levels of regulatory capacity and readiness among the RPCs [RCEP participating countries] with regard to e-commerce. Most RPCs welcomed the recommendation to establish a Working Group on e-commerce while a few RPCs were of the view that domestic consultation is required.
>
> (TNC of RCEP, 2015)

As Table 3.1 shows, the headings in the terms of reference for negotiations on e-commerce largely follow the TPP and TiSA template. The author's discussions

Table 3.1 Comparison of TPP with Proposed Elements for RCEP Terms of Reference for E-commerce

TPP		RCEP proposed elements for terms of reference	
Article	Provision	Article (if yes)	Provision
14.9	Paperless trading	II	Paperless trading
14.6	Electronic authentication and electronic signatures	II	Electronic signatures and digital certification
14.7	Online consumer protection	III	Online consumer protection
14.8	Personal information protection	III	Online personal data protection
14.14	Unsolicited commercial electronic messages	III	Unsolicited commercial e-mail
14.5	Domestic electronic transactions framework	III	Domestic regulatory frameworks
14.3	Customs duties	III	Customs duties
14.4	Non-discriminatory treatment of digital products	III	Non-discriminatory treatment of digital products
14.13	Location of computing facilities	IV	Prohibition on requirements concerning the location of computing facilities
14.17	Source code	IV	Prohibition on requirements concerning the disclosure of source code
14.11	Cross-border transfer of information by electronic means	IV	Cross-border transfer of information by electronic means

Source: Adapted from a table prepared by Sanya Reid Smith from Third World Network.

with negotiators confirm that an e-commerce text has been tabled in RCEP that largely mirrors the TPP, with Japan the principal proponent. However, no information on the state of negotiations in this chapter is publicly available.

4.2. ASEAN negotiations with the EU

ASEAN and a number of its members have been or are negotiating FTAs with the EU, which is the world's largest exporter of digitally delivered services (Council of the European Union, 2017).[13] Until recently, the EU was not a strong proponent of e-commerce rules in its agreements. Chapter 8 on Services, Establishment and Electronic Commerce in the Singapore EU FTA focuses on cross-border services.[14] The preliminary text of the EU Viet Nam FTA, released in February 2016, has two significant obligations: it adopts the EU's Understanding on Computer and Related Services (CRS), and Chapter VI on Electronic Commerce imposes a permanent prohibition on customs duties on electronic transmissions. Otherwise, the chapter just establishes a regulatory dialogue. Chapter 16 on e-commerce in the Comprehensive Economic and Trade Agreement between Canada and the EU (CETA) also has limited scope and obligations. There is no public information on the EU's approach to e-commerce in the FTA negotiations with Indonesia (European Commission, 2017a).[15]

The text of the EU Japan Economic Partnership Agreement, released in July 2017, signals a significant shift for the EU. The chapter goes beyond the TPP in several respects,[16] although the sensitive matter of cross-border data flows was deferred for three years, pending Japan's compliance with the new EU data privacy requirements.[17]

4.3. Electronic commerce at the WTO

The EU has also taken the lead in pressing for e-commerce negotiations in the WTO. In 1998 the WTO General Council agreed to a Work Programme on Electronic Commerce with a limited mandate to discuss the issues. The preamble recorded that the General Council would establish a comprehensive work programme to examine all trade-related issues relating to global electronic commerce, including those issues identified by members. The work programme would involve the relevant WTO bodies; take into account the economic, financial and development needs of developing countries; and recognise that work is also being undertaken in other international fora. The General Council should submit a progress report and any recommendations for action at the Third Session of the Ministerial Conference (WTO, 1998). E-commerce was defined for the purposes of these discussions as 'the production, distribution, marketing, sale or delivery of goods and services by electronic means' (WTO, 1998: para 1.3).

Discussions took place across the Council for Trade in Goods, Council for Trade in Services, TRIPS Council and the Committee on Trade for Development. Various reviews and reports were made, including to ministerial conferences.[18] But there was little momentum until July 2016 when the US tabled a 'non-paper' setting out 16 demands, based on its 'Digital2Dozen' principles (USTR, 2016a). Since then, the US has left the heavy lifting to the EU (WTO, 2017a, 2017b) and Japan (WTO, 2016c, 2017c), who – with others – sought a negotiating mandate on e-commerce at the MC11.

They faced strong push-back from many developing countries (South Centre, 2017b). Some least developed countries (LDCs) called for conclusion of the Doha Round before negotiating on any new issues, along with the African Group, who objected that the e-commerce proposals would undermine their regional development strategy for socio-economic transformation 'Agenda 2063' (WTO, 2017d: para 5.36). A group of Friends of E-commerce for Development, including three ASEAN countries,[19] supported negotiations in the hope that it facilitates economic growth and development, especially for MSMEs (WTO, 2017e). China's paper from November 2016 did not support a new WTO mandate, arguing for a consensus approach to address a more limited agenda of customs duties and facilitation (WTO, 2016d), which is consistent with its BRI digital initiative.

ASEAN as a group did not take a firm position on a WTO mandate to negotiate, although it had already set up a coordinating committee on e-commerce and was itself working towards an e-commerce agreement. A communication in April 2017 noted that e-commerce was not new to the WTO, and there was room for clarifying how new concepts fit (WTO, 2017f). There were opportunities for MSMEs from lower cost barriers and greater inclusion, but there were also challenges from a lack of infrastructure and knowledge, limited e-payment options, regulatory barriers and uncertainty, limited access to enabling services, online privacy and security issues, gaining consumer confidence and ongoing digital divides. The paper observed that facilitative trade rules could be supportive if that reduced regulatory uncertainty, and there was a role for international organisations and donor partners.

The MC11 ended in a stalemate, with a continuation of the 1998 Work Programme. In one of several plurilateral moves, ministers from 70 countries announced exploratory work towards future negotiations (WTO, 2017g). Signatories included Brunei Darussalam, Cambodia, Lao PDR, Malaysia, Myanmar and Singapore, making it even more important for ASEAN to assess the implications of pursuing a TPP-based model of e-commerce rules in multiple fora.

5. The new legal texts

Every agreement has idiosyncrasies that reflect the parties and the power dynamics between them. Despite that, a common core of text is populating the contemporary mega-agreements. It has a chameleon-like presence: the same provisions may appear in chapters on cross-border services, investment, e-commerce, intellectual property and transparency. Most were re-categorised as services rules for the purposes of TiSA. The following elements therefore need to be viewed as a whole:

i   cross-border services, whether committed in positive list schedules or subject to negative list annexes of non-conforming measures;
ii   electronic commerce;
iii   financial services;
iv   telecommunications services;
v   intellectual property;
vi   investment performance requirements;
vii   localisation requirements;
viii state-owned enterprises;
ix   customs duties on electronic transmissions;
x   payments and transfers;
xi   balance of payments and prudential exceptions;
xii   the general exception; and
xiii the security exception.

A thorough discussion of all these elements is beyond the capacity of this chapter. The following analysis centres on the cross-border services and electronic commerce chapters.

The digital era has given services a new significance. The 'servicification' of economies dates back to the early 1970s when agricultural, mining, fisheries and manufacturing production began splintering into chains of discrete services activities. Today, digital technologies have enabled those services to be supplied across the border in ways that were previously unimaginable. New services have also emerged, such as leasing cloud storage. The Internet of Things has integrated digital services into physical goods, such as smart cars and household appliances. 3D printers render production itself an IT service. Automated services like robots and artificial intelligence are replacing human labour on production lines, stores and transportation.

A major goal of the mega-agreements is to future-proof services and technologies from regulation. Several complementary ways are used to achieve this.

5.1. Classification of services

The list used for classification of services that dates back to 1991,[20] about the time the World Wide Web was invented. The descriptions that accompany the 160-plus sub-sectors are sometimes specific and sometimes vague. The application of categories like computer and related services, telecommunications, business services and financial services has expanded dramatically since 1991. There is an unresolved debate as to whether and which new services may be captured by the old list, and some agreements adopt later classifications, making it difficult to compare agreements.

The EU promotes CRS (WTO, 2002) that is now a standard requirement in its FTAs. Making full commitments for all those CRS would potentially pre-commit governments to allow unrestricted cross-border provision of all digital-enabled services and never to impose measures such as preferences for locals, requirements for joint ventures or restrictions on the volume or market share of certain services.[21]

5.2. Expanding the scope of commitments

Uncertainty about the classification of services is compounded by the unanticipated expansion of their cross-border delivery (known as mode 1). When the GATS schedules were drafted in the early 1990s most WTO members limited their exposure in mode 1, although acceding countries were required to make more commitments 'out of uncertainty of the legal implications and perceived constraints on their ability to intervene later for regulatory purposes or employment-related and other strategic policy reasons ... or to encourage delivery of services through investment in the country' (Adlung and Roy, 2005: 12). That caution now seems justified with the exponential growth of cross-border services for the infrastructure of the digital economy, such as CRS, telecommunications, financial, transport and distribution services, and for specific sectors like audio-visual, tourism, education and the professions.

Parties in the mega-agreements are under pressure to increase their commitments on cross-border services, which may combine mode 1 and mode 2. At the same time, new provisions seek to ban requirements for cross-border service suppliers to have a local presence inside the country.[22] That poses serious obstacles to the host country's ability to vet qualifications and assess compliance with technical and professional standards and consumer protections, as well as to monitor and enforce the labour standards of workers who are delivering the service. Effective oversight and enforcement may depend on the laws of the country from which the services are supplied, the cooperation of their regulators, affordable access to their legal systems and their courts' willingness to accept jurisdiction. Lack of a local presence may also pose practical and legal obstacles for the state's ability to tax transactions and local earnings.

A further expansion of obligations would occur if the concept of 'technological neutrality' is applied. Commitments to allow the supply of a particular service would apply, regardless of the technology used to deliver that service – even if the technology (such as drones and driverless vehicles) was inconceivable when the schedule was drafted and the government would not have made the commitment had it known. If accepted, the concept would consolidate the dominance of first movers, especially in sectors where governments have made unlimited commitments on the cross-border supply of services.

Developed countries treat the application of technological neutrality as a settled question, and the WTO Secretariat has described it as 'the general view' of members (WTO, 1999: para 4). However, technological neutrality is not referred to in the GATS text, or mentioned in the scheduling guidelines (WTO, 2001), and its application in the WTO has been repeatedly and vehemently rejected by many developing countries, including Malaysia and the Philippines (Kelsey, 2018). Some later agreements make explicit reference to technological neutrality,[23] which reinforces the view that it is not implicit in countries' commitments.

5.3. Scheduling of commitments

Parties to agreements can determine their exposure to certain rules through country-specific schedules. These, too, are being reframed to expand the scale and scope of obligations and restrict future regulatory and policy space. Most ASEAN countries have traditionally insisted on a positive list approach to schedules to maximise their control over their commitments. That records each party's commitments not to use proscribed market access measures and not to discriminate in favour of domestic services and suppliers (national treatment) for specific services sub-sectors, differentiating between modes of supplying the service, and allowing limitations on any commitment in any mode. The major services exporting countries and their commercial lobbies object that this result in limited, partial and fragmented coverage of their services operations. They have developed three techniques to secure more extensive commitments and restrict the existing and future regulation of services, including services not yet created.

i.   A negative list approach to scheduling fully commits governments to all the relevant rules[24] for all services and measures they do not expressly reserve. Reservations are usually listed in two annexes of non-conforming measures (NCMs). One annex allows a party to specify existing measures that will not be subject to certain of the rules, but these measures cannot be made less conforming (more restrictive) in the future (a 'standstill'). In some agreements, that annex is also subject to a 'ratchet', which automatically locks in any future liberalisation. A second annex allows governments to explicitly preserve the right to maintain and adopt measures for specific sectors or activities that would otherwise contravene specified rules ('policy space' reservations). Both schedules must be negotiated with the other parties.

The negative list forecloses the ability of a government to address policy, regulatory, social or political failures, unless it had the foresight and negotiating strength to preserve the necessary policy space or can successfully invoke one of the agreement's exceptions (discussed ahead). This approach is high risky in legal and political terms, even for governments with a long experience of liberalisation, privatisation, de-regulation and market-based regulation, and which have well-resourced bureaucracies and experienced negotiators.

ii.   The hybrid approach combines positive and negative lists. TiSA uses a hybrid of a positive list for market access and a negative list for national treatment and other 'anti-localisation' rules, including local presence requirements. The Indonesia-Japan FTA required the parties to identify services sub-sectors in their positive list schedule that would be subject to a standstill, meaning no more restrictive measure could be adopted in the future for those sub-sectors.[25]

Some agreements that have investment chapters leave the commercial establishment of services (mode 3) in the positive list services schedule, while non-services investment is covered in a negative list NCMs. Drafting and interpreting these schedules is technically complex, especially as the boundary between services and non-services investment is unclear and different classifications systems may be used. Alternatively, all forms of investment might be covered by the negative list annexes, which makes it difficult to compare a country's mode 3 services commitments in its positive list agreements.

The RCEP allows parties to use either a positive or negative list; apparently only Australia has chosen the latter.[26] However, additional requirements are proposed for RCEP's positive lists. The parties would have to apply a standstill and ratchet to their limitations for a minimum number of those sub-sectors on which they have made commitments with limitations. They must also *either* identify sectors in their schedules to which they will apply the most-favoured-nation (MFN) rule to future FTAs ('MFN forward')[27] *or* draw up a 'transparency list' that describes the current measures that are protected in their schedules. The author understands that RCEP parties have agreed to shift to a negative list in a specified number of years, with LDCs having several years longer.

iii.   Sectoral chapters or annexes may require full, or a minimum level of, commitments on particular sectors, sub-sectors or modes (especially mode 1). Financial services and telecommunications have always been a priority for developed countries in trade in services agreements.

Most US and EU FTAs either require the parties to adopt the voluntary GATS Reference Paper on Basic Telecommunications or incorporate the provisions of an extended version of the Reference Paper into a chapter or annex on telecommunications. The TPP and TiSA impose special obligations on major public telecommunications providers, which are implicitly targeted at public monopolies in developing countries (Kelsey, 2017). Specific obligations on inter-connection, access to unbundled services, rights of resale, and limits on universal service obligations all advantage large foreign telecommunication and digital providers.

Digitisation has also re-ordered financial services priorities. E-commerce requires secure and fast payment systems. Traditional banking transactions are cumbersome and costly. Most e-commerce is now conducted through electronic payment systems that use the major international credit cards, Visa and MasterCard, and specialist online exchanges such as PayPal, Poli and Alipay. Digitally enabled cross-border financial services are highly lucrative in their own right, and present serious regulatory challenges as the finance industry finds ever more creative and non-transparent ways to circumvent national regulations. Product and qualification standards, ethical codes and the company's employment practices can become impossible to monitor effectively or enforce when, for example, insurance companies operate from offshore through call centres or online. Financial and tax regulation may be rendered impotent if offshore financial firms are not required to have any local presence or store data locally.

Many ASEAN countries have already taken commitments on financial services for consumption abroad (mode 2), but fewer for cross-border supply (mode 1). That creates additional uncertainty about the extent of obligations: for instance, cross-border financial transactions are mode 1, but the offshore bank account involved in those transactions is mode 2.

The mega-agreements may also require a country to allow the sale of any new financial service or product that is not currently provided in its territory, but is available in the territory of another party. This is drawn from the voluntary Understanding on Commitments in Financial Services among some WTO members.[28] Some agreements say the provider of the new service or product must be established in the receiving country;[29] that presumably increases the financial regulators' ability to apply prudential measures, although the standard exception is weak and its meaning is contested (Lang and Amarasekara, 2016: 30). Other agreements require the financial service or product to be permitted under the country's existing law;[30] yet innovative financial products are usually designed to circumvent existing regulations. These pre-commitments not to regulate as-yet-unknown services and products pose especially high risks in an era when electronic trading in toxic financial products has contributed to contagious financial crises.

5.4. *Domestic regulation*

In addition to standard market access and national treatment rules, there is pressure for new disciplines on how governments can regulate licensing requirements and procedures,[31] qualification requirements and procedures,[32] and technical standards.[33] All three forms of regulation are crucial for digitally provided services, and are especially difficult to apply when services are operated across the border. *Technical standards* are particularly important for the digital economy, as they include the rules on how and where data is stored or used; quality and operating standards and practices for the Internet, telecommunications and e-finance; conflicts of interest and ethical codes; universal service obligations; and consumer protections and privacy rules.

Developing countries have successfully resisted demands for such disciplines in the GATS. The TPP and TiSA texts are also limited because the US cannot restrict the regulatory authority of its states. However, there is a major push to include sweeping disciplines on these forms of domestic regulation in the RCEP and recent EU FTAs,[34] and renewed pressure in the WTO.[35] The proposed restrictions could apply to central, regional and local governments, as well as delegated bodies, such as professional associations.

The author understands that New Zealand and Australia are pressing for strong disciplines in RCEP across all these areas of domestic regulation. That includes a requirement for governments to ensure that measures do not constitute 'unnecessary barriers to trade in services', which means choosing the regulatory option that imposes the least burden on commercial interests to achieve permitted objectives.

These provisions use bland terminology, such as 'reasonable', 'objective', 'impartial' and 'transparent', which obscures the extent to which current and future regulatory approaches would become open to challenge. They would also impose significant administrative and budgetary burdens on all levels of government, even where application of the obligations is limited by a party's schedule or negative list of reservations.

The proposals also require that measures of general application that affect services transactions are *administered* in a reasonable, objective and impartial manner, regardless of whether the sector has been committed. These open-ended words invite disputes over the administration of a wide range of services, especially services delivered across the border (mode 1). They could apply, for example, to a decision not to grant a license or authorisation to operate a service, processes for proving the authenticity of an offshore supplier's qualifications, disclosure and reporting requirements, procedures to assess compliance with consumer protection laws or disciplinary actions and penalties imposed for a regulatory breach. This provision might also apply to tax measures, leaving countries to rely on the increasingly complex taxation exceptions.

5.5. Transparency

'Transparency' provisions in the GATS required governments to make their laws, regulations, criteria and procedures publicly available, and provide applicants with information on the progress and outcomes of licensing applications and authorisations. The mega-agreements extend this by providing rights for governments and their corporations to be informed of proposed new regulations in advance. Many developed countries already provide such opportunities in the name of 'best practice regulation'. An EU-led proposal on transparency in domestic regulation (WTO, 2017g) promoted the same obligations in the WTO.

The transparency obligation may be couched as a 'best endeavour'.[36] The wording is usually neutral, referring to 'interested persons'. In reality, major commercial interests and industry groups have superior resources to generate reports and submissions, and lobby governments (Azmeh and Foster, 2016). This entitlement can therefore skew the balance of interests in the lawmaking process, and increase the potential chilling effect if foreign corporations threaten to withdraw their investment or bring an investment dispute if the government proceeds. There are already examples of tech corporations making such threats over new taxes and stricter regulation (Australian Financial Review, 2017).

6. E-commerce rules

The electronic commerce chapters or annexes in the mega-agreements embody virtually all the US tech industry's demands. As noted earlier, the label e-commerce is misleading; very few of the rules are about commercial transactions per se. They embed the power of incumbents and erect barriers to digital industrialisation by developing countries and their affordable and reliable access to global value chains. The TPP, TiSA, RCEP, EU-Japan FTA and WTO proposals share three substantive elements, although individual agreements vary:[37]

i   Prohibitions on national requirements to: store or process data locally, transfer or provide access to source code, use local computer facilities, include local content in electronic transmissions and transfer technology as a condition of foreign investment;
ii Weak provisions on: the protection of consumers and personal information, restrictions on censorship, unsolicited commercial electronic messages (spam) and access to and use of the Internet and open networks; and
iii Promoting actual cross-border commerce: by eliminating customs duties on electronic transmissions, streamlining transactions through electronic authentication and e-signatures, and international cooperation.

6.1. *Unrestricted movement of data*

A government cannot stop a service supplier from another party operating in its country from transferring or processing data offshore, including personal or commercial information. While the rules do not explicitly refer to 'storage' of data offshore, such a restriction would be covered as a 'measure that affects trade by electronic means'.[38] Governments are not allowed even to specify a list of acceptable countries to which the data can be transferred and processed.

Under TiSA, the operator would simply have to establish a need to transfer the data offshore 'in connection with' the conduct of its business.[39] In other agreements it is 'for the conduct of the business',[40] which would protect the export of data by operators of search engines and digital market-places, as well as sectors like insurance, tourism, online education, and mining. Some agreements exclude government data from the rule; others may not.[41] In practical terms, an Australian private hospital operator in Thailand could not be prevented from transferring Thai patients' health data outside the country. The Indonesian government could not require a US-owned mining operator to hold data, such as safety records or inventory, within Indonesia. Uber could not be required to store financial records of local transactions in Malaysia for tax purposes.

When personal and commercial information is held offshore, including 'in the cloud', it is beyond the subject's control. The company that holds the data will choose the repository, but the company may not know which country the server is located in and whose privacy and consumer regimes apply. Once the data is offshore, the government may lose the ability to regulate its use, abuse or sale, unless it can impose effective licensing or technical standards, within whatever domestic regulation disciplines apply in the agreement.

A government might be allowed to keep or adopt a measure that restricts the movement of information to achieve a 'legitimate public policy objective'. What qualifies as a legitimate objective would ultimately be decided by a panel of trade experts. If its scope was limited to objectives that are widely recognised internationally, it would be difficult for governments to be proactive or take precautionary approaches to emerging problems. A measure that was considered legitimate might still be disallowed if it was applied in a way that constitutes 'arbitrary or unjustified discrimination' (even though the measures might be especially pertinent to foreign suppliers), or was a disguised restriction on 'trade', broadly defined.[42] The latter would rule out digital industrialisation measures.

Rules that prohibit so-called 'data localisation' need to be read alongside a country's commitments on cross-border services. A government might already be prohibited from requiring data to be held locally through commitments in a positive list schedule for data processing or database services, or a negative list that has no relevant reservations. A requirement to hold data in the country might also be problematic as a 'measure affecting the supply' of a committed sector, such as tourism, or if it was a condition of licensing or a technical standard for supplying the service or an aspect of administering regulations of general application. The uncertainty, and the constantly expanding scope, of these rules deepen the legal risk that local policy makers face.

There are special sensitivities about the transfer and location of financial data, especially at times of financial crisis or insolvency of individual firms. The finance industry argues that data location regulations are costly, inefficient and unnecessary, and degrade financial institutions' ability to provide services in a seamless way to customers across countries and regions (Kaplan and Rowshankish, 2015). The US Treasury blocked the inclusion of financial data in the movement of information provision in the TPP. Under pressure from the industry, the USTR later proposed its inclusion in the TiSA negotiations (Kelsey, 2018). The EU-Viet Nam agreement required the parties to allow the financial service provider to transfer information in electronic or other form into or out of the country for data processing in the ordinary course of business from two years after its entry into force. Each party is required to adopt or maintain 'appropriate safeguards' to protect privacy and personal data, including personal records and accounts.[43]

6.2. *Location of computer facilities*

A government cannot require the use or location of computing facilities inside the country as a condition of supplying a service in that country.[44] 'Computing facilities' means 'computer servers and storage devices for the processing or storing information for commercial use'.[45] This ban is a major disincentive for governments to invest in upgrading their local infrastructure for domestic use in the hope of attracting foreign firms. Lack of such investment reinforces the country's long-term dependency on foreign-owned and located infrastructure. A similar provision on legitimate public policy objectives to that on data transfers may apply. However, the TPP imposed an additional and contestable constraint that restrictions relating to local computer facilities must be no greater than needed to achieve the public policy objective (a necessity test).[46]

6.3. *Prohibited performance requirements*

The WTO's Agreement on Trade-Related Investment Measures (TRIMS) prohibits the imposition of certain goods-related performance requirements on foreign investors. Recent agreements have expanded TRIMS to services. These provisions may be located in the investment, services or e-commerce chapters.[47] The list of prohibitions has expanded in recent agreements and may ban requirements to use local content (even in return for a subsidy), transfer technology and proprietary knowledge, use local or a particular technology, employ and train local personnel if that involves transfer of proprietary knowledge and trade balance considerations. These are all common elements of a digital industrialisation strategy. Governments are usually allowed to schedule reservations to these rules, subject to the difficulties noted earlier.

6.4. No local content requirements on e-supply

The US promotes a further rule that content supplied electronically must not receive more favourable treatment because it was created, produced, published, contracted for, commissioned or first made available on commercial terms locally, or where the creator, producer, developer or owner is local.[48] That rule would prevent central or local governments from using preferences to support local firms to develop content or requiring use of local knowledge and cultural content to enhance the quality of the service provided. This restriction is most obviously targeted at the entertainment industry, apps and games. But it applies equally to services like education, consultancy and research and development. It would not apply to subsidies or grants, government-supported loans, guarantees and insurance.[49]

6.5. Keeping source codes secret

A source code is the formula for a computer programme that humans can read, which is then converted into an object code or machine code that can be read by the computer. It can encompass anything from software in smart products to translation of the algorithms used to run Google's search engines and Amazon's digital marketplace. Open source means it is accessible to everyone to use, copy, check, alter or correct. Protected source codes could be described as trade secrets, which most countries protect under their competition, intellectual property or contract law.

6.5.1. The rule of non-disclosure

The basic rule on source codes says a government cannot require a person (firm or individual) of another party who owns software to transfer or provide access to the source code for that software as a condition for being allowed to supply the service.[50] The EU-Japan FTA goes further; it bans disclosure requirements that would affect 'trade by electronic means'.[51] The ban includes transfer of source codes to a government. There is no ability to schedule a reservation on the source code provision. A 'legitimate public policy' defence might apply, similar to the prohibition on restricting movements of data. But the measure must be accepted as 'legitimate', not involve 'arbitrary' or 'unjustified discrimination' against the owner of source code, and not be a disguised restriction on trade – again, excluding its use for digital industry policy. If it failed that test the government would have to rely on the general or security exception (discussed ahead).

As with the rule on data transfers, a requirement for disclosure of source code could also be a licensing condition or a technical standard for the delivery of certain services. That could bring it under the 'disciplines' on domestic regulation proposed for the WTO and RCEP.

6.5.2. Economic implications

Monopoly rights over source codes have significant economic implications. Source codes are essential to competition, and developing countries' participation in the smart economy. Without such access, they are competing on an un-level playing field. There are parallels to the previous era of industrialisation when intellectual property rights were used to shut the door on developing countries' ability to catch-up. At least with patents, the disclosure requirement makes it possible for competitors to enter the market once the patent expires, as generic medicine producers do. The source code monopoly has no such disclosure requirement.

Relying on expensive imported technology makes domestic production uncompetitive, and reverse engineering is extremely difficult. Without compulsory disclosure of source codes, the secondary industry of component manufacturers and servicers of smart products would also be unable to supply the necessary information.

6.5.3. Non-economic implications

Secrecy of source codes also poses non-economic risks.[52]

i   *Corporate non-compliance:* Computer programmes are now embedded in smart products, from household appliances to motor vehicles to sports shoes. Non-disclosure of source codes makes it impossible to monitor compliance with product standards. Volkswagen's fraudulent software for monitoring emissions, which was discovered fortuitously by researchers (Hotten, 2015), shows the importance of disclosure for consumer protection, enforcing environmental standards, and prosecuting criminal acts.

ii   *Judicial proceedings:* Disclosure is a crucial evidential tool in civil proceedings, such as determining responsibility for faulty software or identifying algorithms used to manipulate financial trades or engage in anti-competitive practices, as in the case of Google. While the EU-Japan FTA allows governments to require disclosure of source codes to *remedy* a violation of competition laws;[53] it does not cover disclosure to *prove* a violation.

iii   *Security and safety:* As well as errors and design faults in software, there are growing risks from hacking and installing of malware. Those risks will intensify with the rapid expansion of artificial intelligence and use of drones, robots and driverless vehicles. Attacks on individuals or premises may also be routed indirectly through less secure software.

iv   *Financial risk and fraud:* Complex algorithms are used to engineer financial products, conduct automated trading in currency, shares and derivatives, allocate ratings to financial products and assess risk for insurance. If the e-commerce annex applies to financial services, the secrecy of source code will fetter financial regulators and enable destabilising and/or unlawful financial practices associated with fraud,[54] company collapses and financial crises.

v   *Manipulation of information:* Algorithms may be used for profiling based on race or ethnicity, nationality, religion, gender or income, which violate consumer, labour, religious or human rights protections. Without access to the code, it may be impossible to verify – let alone successfully prosecute – a breach.

6.6. Legal protections

There are various possible protections from the e-commerce rules, but they are very restricted.

6.6.1. Schedules

Parties cannot schedule limitations on the most significant obligations, which deal with movement of information, location of computing facilities, source codes and local content (except as a performance requirement).

6.6.2. Consumer protection

Consumers are likely to presume that their domestic laws, dispute mechanisms and remedies apply to e-commerce transactions. Where the service is provided from offshore, they may become reliant on a foreign jurisdiction, without knowing it. Some agreements contain no consumer protection obligations. The EU-Japan FTA merely recognises the importance of consumer protection measures.[55] The TPP requires countries to adopt consumer protection laws, but does not set any level, and restricts their scope to laws that 'proscribe fraudulent and deceptive commercial practices that cause harm or potential harm to consumers engaged in online commercial activities'.[56] Other anti-consumer practices, such as re-routing, geo-blocking and price discrimination, are not mentioned.

These flexibilities might reduce the compliance burden on ASEAN countries that do not yet have robust consumer protection regimes.[57] But they presumably will want to improve those protections in the future. The trade in services disciplines on licensing requirements and procedures, technical standards and administration of general regulations could restrict the quality of measures they can adopt. The transparency rules would also guarantee foreign states and foreign firms the right to lobby against effective new consumer protection laws.

6.6.3. Privacy protection

The TPP adopts a similar provision on 'protection of personal information' as for consumers, although it suggests parties 'should take into account' principles and guidelines of international bodies. This hands-off approach protects the weak US privacy regime. The US proposal in TiSA would allow private firms to decide how to reconcile the different privacy regimes that apply to a cross-border transaction.[58] The EU has not yet disclosed how it will balance provisions on offshore data flows with the new General Data Protection Regulation, which became operative in May 2018.

6.6.4. The general exception

The general exception offers a defence when a measure has otherwise breached a party's obligations. Most new agreements apply the GATS general exception to e-commerce.[59] However, some include additional provisions on protection of personal information and of consumers that use similar but not identical wording.[60] That implies that the general exception is considered too narrow or too weak.

The general exception provides less protection for consumers and privacy than for health, environment, public order and public morals. First, the measure must relate to one of two narrowly defined matters:

i   fraud or default on services contracts (no other forms of consumer protection); or
ii   processing and dissemination of an individual's data and confidentiality (but not, for example, for use or storage of data).

Next, the measure must be adopted to *secure compliance with a law or regulation that is not inconsistent with the agreement*. A government might, for example, impose a local data processing requirement as part of implementing its privacy law. That measure would breach the data localisation rule in the e-commerce chapter. The government could only rely on the exception if the privacy law itself was not inconsistent with the agreement. The exception would not be available, for example, if the privacy law itself required data to be held in the country or required disclosure of source code, or if it was discriminatory in its treatment of foreign operators and therefore breached the government's national treatment obligation.

Third, the measure must be 'necessary' to implement that law, meaning there was no less burdensome approach reasonably available to do so.

Finally, the measure must not involve arbitrary or unjustifiable discrimination between the countries where 'like' conditions prevail or be a disguised trade restriction that favours domestic suppliers or services.

6.6.5. Censorship

States are legitimately concerned about protecting their regulatory sovereignty from binding and enforceable guarantees to foreign corporations. Yet corporations are not the only threats to citizens' rights in the rapidly expanding digital domain. All states have some capacity to manipulate and censor information in ways that violate free speech and citizens' rights in their own and other countries in violation of the right to freedom of opinion and expression under Article 19 of the Universal Declaration of Human Rights.

The mega-agreements make no genuine attempts to protect the interests of digital users as consumers, let alone as citizens who have fundamental human rights. The general exception includes a category of measures to protect public order or morals, which is subject to a necessity test. China was allowed to invoke the public morals justification as a defence in the WTO dispute brought by the US over restrictions on the importation and distribution of goods and services with 'cultural content', but it failed to satisfy the necessity test because there were less restrictive alternatives (Pauwelyn, 2010). However, aggrieved citizens cannot bring a dispute challenging a measure for violation of their rights. They require another state party to do so, and its decisions will be driven by its own commercial and strategic interests. This dilemma highlights the inappropriateness of a trade agreement as the vehicle through which to devise an Internet governance regime that requires a balancing of diverse international and domestic obligations.

6.6.6. Security exception

The standard security exception applies across the new agreements. A state can judge for itself whether a measure is 'necessary' in its 'essential security interests'. However, the defence is only available in limited circumstances, the most relevant being an 'emergency in international relations'. That seems to exclude longer-term measures that are precautionary or general, such as for cybersecurity.

The US and secured a broader security exception in the TPP that allows a government to define its 'essential security interests' and what action it considers is necessary to protect them.[61] Japan asked for more clarity on what 'essential security interests' meant in a similar proposal on e-commerce in TiSA.[62] This approach would allow governments to exploit the elastic, self-defined concept of 'security' in an era of 'terrorism' and 'cyberthreats' to their own purposes. If governments are nervous about security consequences, it makes more sense not to adopt the e-commerce obligations.

7. The challenge for ASEAN

This chapter shows the risks for developing countries, including ASEAN, as rule takers – not rule makers – in the new generation agreements. A normative regime is systematically being developed that aims to guarantee the continued monopoly of already dominant, mainly US, companies over source codes, data and digital technologies and facilities. Parminder Singh warns of:

> a significant mismatch between the most important geo-economic and geo-political implications of the digital phenomenon and the way developing countries have been viewing it at the global level. This has resulted in developing countries getting trapped in new extractive global economic relationships, and also excluded from processes shaping the global digital norms and policies.

> (Singh, 2017: 6)

Of the large, well-resourced developing countries, only China seems equipped to compete, and that prospect carries its own risks of dependency for ASEAN.

It is crucial that ASEAN members have the time and flexibility to identify and develop appropriate national and regional regulatory frameworks that can advance their digital industrialisation, individually and in solidarity. These frameworks might include rules on:

i   binding technology transfer and mandating disclosure of source code to encourage the development of infrastructure and domestic suppliers;
ii   requiring data localisation, joint ventures and use of local facilities for the development of domestic capacities;
iii training of a skilled IT workforce; and
iv   commitments to financial assistance for technology development and infrastructure in order to bridge the digital divide and facilitate e-commerce.

The template developed in the mega-agreements, especially the TPP, RCEP, the WTO and EU FTAs, would foreclose those options in ways that are practically impossible to undo. ASEAN members will need to resist those proposals if they are to maintain their regulatory sovereignty and the policy space to capitalise on the 21st century digital revolution.

Notes

1 The CPTPP was signed by the remaining eleven countries in March 2018 after the US withdrew from the TPP.
2 The notable difference is the failure of the parties yet to agree on rules relating to cross-border movement of data.
3 Singh reports that India proposed to the UN General Assembly the creation of a Committee for Internet Related Policies, with a mandate similar to the OECD committee, but that was rejected by the US and other countries as a move towards governmental control of Internet.
4 The stated goals of the US Telecommunications Act of 1996 (Code 47 U.S.C.230[b]) were to 'promote competition and reduce regulation in order to secure lower prices and higher quality services for American telecommunications consumers and encourage the rapid deployment of telecommunications technologies' but to 'preserve the vibrant and competitive free market that presently exists for the Internet and other interactive computer services, unfettered by Federal or State regulation'.
5 The Internet Corporation for Assigned Names and Numbers (ICANN).
6 An open letter to the USTR, October 2016, from seven groups that encompass all the major players: (1) Internet Association, (2) Computer and Communications Industry Association, (3) Information Technology Industry Council, (4) BSA/Software Alliance, (5) ACT, (6) The App Association, and (7) the Consumer Technology Association. The industry also wanted a chief digital trade negotiator appointed in Office of USTR and to expand USTR's Digital Trade Working Group established in 2016 (USTR, 2016c).
7 Robert Holleyman, deputy USTR from 2014–2017, had spent 23 years as President and CEO of BSA/Software Alliance (Crowell Moring, 2017).
8 Financial data was not covered in the TPP. The e-commerce chapter in the EU-Japan FTA does not exclude financial services, but Article 6 in the Financial Services Chapter has square brackets, meaning the related content is not essential.
9 TiSA, Annex on Electronic Commerce, undated (November 2016), www.bilaterals.org/?tisa-draft-annex-on-electronic-32465
10 TPP, Article 14.10(a).

11 TPP, Article 17.4: Non-discriminatory treatment and commercial considerations, and Article 17.6: Non-commercial assistance.
12 For example, Article 14.3 of the TPP preserves the right to impose internal taxes on electronically transmitted content, provided they are imposed in a manner consistent with the agreement. Article 29.4 is a complex provision that excludes tax from the agreement, subject to various carve-ins.
13 The EU estimates the global market in e-commerce is worth over 12 trillion euros.
14 EU-Singapore Free Trade Agreement, signed in June 2015, Sub-Section 3, Article 8.21 commits the parties to adopt the EU's Understanding on Computer and Related Services.
15 The report of the second round of negotiations in January 2017 does not refer to e-commerce.
16 For example, Chapter VI, Article 3 bans customs duties on electronic transmissions.
17 The EU General Data Protection Regulation (Regulation (EU) 2016/679) came into force on 25 May 2018.
18 These are accessible at: www.wto.org/english/tratop_e/ecom_e/ecom_e.htm
19 Brunei Darussalam, Malaysia and Singapore
20 GATT Services Sectoral Classification List, MTN/GNS/W/120, 10 July 1991.
21 The rules of trade in services agreements apply to 'measures that affect the supply of a service'.
22 That may be located in the services or e-commerce chapter; e.g. TPP, Chapter 10: Cross border services, Article 10.6; TiSA, Localization Provisions, November 2016, Art X.1
23 For example, Korea US FTA 2012, Article 15.2.
24 These may include national treatment, local presence, performance requirements, senior managers and boards of directors.
25 Agreement between Japan and Republic of Indonesia for an Economic Partnership Agreement 2007, Articles 81.3 and 81.4.
26 RCEP, Text proposal from Australia, New Zealand and Korea, Article [X], Schedule of Specific Commitments, undated.
27 Requiring RCEP parties to receive any better treatment provided in future FTAs.
28 Understanding on Commitments in Financial Services, Article A and Article B.3–6.
29 For example, EU-Japan FTA, Article 3.
30 For example, TPP, Article 11.7.
31 The authorisation of a company and/or personnel to supply a service and the procedures to gain a license.
32 The competence of a person to supply a service, and which they need to show before they are authorised to supply that service, and the administrative and procedural rules to show they comply.
33 Measures that lay down the characteristics of a service or the manner in which it is supplied.
34 For example, CETA Chapter 12.
35 Joint Ministerial Statement on Services Domestic Regulation, WT/MIN(17)/61, 13 December 2017.
36 For example, TPP, Article 26.2.
37 For example, some rules in Chapter 9: E-Commerce of the Agreement between Japan and Mongolia for an Economic Partnership go beyond the TPP: an indefinite extension of the temporary moratorium on customs duties on electronic transmissions (Article 9.3), and a necessity test is imposed on Domestic Regulation (Article 9.9), but there is no formal prohibition on data localisation requirements. In the e-commerce chapter of the EU-Japan FTA, both Japan and the EU

agreed to TPP-plus rules, but deferred the question of data transfers for three years after entry into force.
38 For example, TPP, Article 14.2.2.
39 Proposal in TiSA, Article 2.2, Annex on Electronic Commerce, undated (November 2016).
40 TPP, Article 14.11.
41 This has not been decided, for example, in TiSA.
42 Proposed in TiSA, Article 2.3, Annex on Electronic Commerce, undated (November 2016). The US has not agreed to this.
43 EU-Vietnam FTA, Article (. . .) [sic]: Data processing.
44 For example, TPP, Article 14.13.
45 For example, TPP, Article 14.1.
46 TPP, Article 14.11.3(b).
47 For example, in TPP, Article 9.10 Performance Requirements is in the investment chapter.
48 TiSA, Article 10.3, Annex on Electronic Commerce, undated (November 2016), proposed by the US.
49 TiSA, Article 10.5, Annex on Electronic Commerce, undated (November 2016).
50 TPP, Article 14.7.
51 EU-Japan FTA, Article 4 and Article 1.4.
52 Based on research by Sanya Reid Smith, Third World Network, Malaysia, 2017.
53 EU-Japan FTA, Article 4.2(a).
54 For example, the London Interbank Offer Rate (LIBOR) that provides the benchmark for interest rates from the City of London was subject to fraudulent manipulation by bankers from 2012–2014.
55 EU-Japan FTA, Article 9, Chapter VI: Electronic commerce.
56 TPP, Article 14.7.
57 This gap is common across developing countries. Despite India's promotion of free data flows in the WTO, as part of its Trade Facilitation in Services proposal, the Indian government only announced in April 2017 that it would develop a regulatory regime for data protection (PTI, 2017).
58 TiSA, Article 4.3, Annex on Electronic Commerce, undated (November 2016).
59 For example, GATS Article XIV is imported into TPP, Article 29.1.3.
60 EU-Japan FTA, Article VI.4 Source Code.
61 TPP, Article 29.2 Security Exceptions.
62 TiSA, Article 13, Annex on Electronic Commerce, undated (November 2016).

Bibliography

Adlung, R. and M. Roy (2005), 'Turning Hills into Mountains? Current Commitments Under the GATS and Prospects for Change', *WTO Staff Working Paper*, ERSD 2005-01, March.

Alibaba (2017), 'Alibaba Turns eWTP into Reality with the Creation of the First Overseas E-Hub', 22 March. Available at www.alibabagroup.com/en/news/article?news=p170322

Al Jazeera (2017), 'The Great Firewall Update: Clamping Down on VPNs', *Al Jazeera*, 12 August. Available at www.aljazeera.com/programmes/listeningpost/2017/08/great-firewall-update-clamping-vpns-170812090721781.html

Australian Financial Review (2017), 'Esty, Amazon, Alibaba Join eBay in Threat to Block Australian Consumers in GST War', *Australian Financial Review*, 21 April. Available at www.afr.com/news/politics/etsy-ebay-and-alibaba-join-amazon-in-threat-to-block-australian-consumers-in-gst-war-20170420-gvp951

Azarhoushang, B., A. Bramucci, H. Herr and B.B. Ruoff (2015), 'Value Chains, Underdevelopment and Union Strategy', *International Journal of Labour Research*, 7(1–2): 153–175.

Azmeh, S. and C. Foster (2016), 'The TPP and the Digital Trade Agenda: Digital Industry Policy and Silicon Valley's Influence on New Trade Agreements', *London School of Economics and Political Science International Development Working Paper Series*, No. 16–175.

Banga, R. (2017), 'Rising Product Digitalisation and Losing Trade Competitiveness', Centre for WTO Studies, New Delhi, *CWS Working Paper*, No. 39, June.

Behsudi, A. (2017), 'Amazon Snatches up Punke', *Politico*, 21 February. Available at www.politico.com/tipsheets/morning-trade/2017/02/china-among-pacific-nations-confirmed-for-chile-meeting-218838

Choudhary, M. and E. Moglen (2017), 'Head Off Digital Colonialism: How Indian IT Can Compete with Google and Facebook and Show the World a Better Way', *India Times*, 29 May. Available at http://blogs.timesofindia.indiatimes.com/toi-edit-page/head-off-digital-colonialism-how-indian-it-can-compete-with-google-and-facebook-and-show-the-world-a-better-way/

Council of the European Union (2017), 'Concept Paper on Data Flows in Trade Agreements', 27 January, WK 959/2017 INIT.

Crowell Moring (2017), 'Robert Holleyman'. Available at www.crowell.com/Professionals/Robert-Holleyman

Deutsche Welle (2016), 'The World's Biggest Internet Based Companies', 4 August. Available at www.dw.com/en/the-worlds-biggest-internet-based-companies/g-19446253

Dragoo, H. (2017), 'China's Cybersecurity Law: The Impact on Digital Trade', 7 August. Available at www.internetgovernance.org/2017/08/07/chinas-cybersecurity-law-the-impact-on-digital-trade/

European Commission (2017a), 'Antitrust: Commission Fines Google €2.42 Billion for Abusing Dominance as Search Engine by Giving Illegal Advantage to Own Comparison Shopping Service', 27 June. Available at http://europa.eu/rapid/press-release_IP-17-1784_en.htm

European Commission (2017b), 'Report of the Second Round of Negotiations for a Free Trade Agreement Between the European Union and Indonesia', 24–27 January. Available at trade.ec.europa.eu/doclib/html/155297.htms

European Union (2017), 'Communication from the Commission to the European Parliament and the Council', *Exchanging and Protecting Personal Data in a Globalised World*, COM(2017)-7-final. Available at https://eur-lex.europa.eu/legal-content/EN/TXT/?uri=COM%3A2017%3A7%3AFIN

EUSME Centre (2016), 'China to Establish New Cross-Border E-Commerce Pilot Zones in 12 Cities', EUSME Centre, 10 January. Available at www.eusmecentre.org.cn/article/china-establish-new-cross-border-e-commerce-pilot-zones-12-cities

Fioretti, J. (2017), 'EU to Launch More E-Commerce Antitrust Investigations', *Reuters Technology News*, 10 May. Available at www.reuters.com/article/eu-competition-geoblocking-idUSL1N1IC22B

G7 (2016), 'Principles and Actions on Cyber'. Available at www.mofa.go.jp/files/000160279.pdf

G20 (2016), 'Digital Economy Development and Cooperation Initiative'. Available at www.mofa.go.jp/files/000185874.pdf

Greiger, G. (2016), 'One Belt, One Road (OBOR): China's Regional Integration Initiative', *Briefing to the European Parliament*, July. Available at www.europarl.europa.eu/RegData/etudes/BRIE/2016/586608/EPRS_BRI(2016)586608_EN.pdf

Hern, A. (2018), 'Cambridge Analytica: How Did It Turn Clicks into Votes?' *The Guardian*, 6 May. Available at www.theguardian.com/news/2018/may/06/cambridge-analytica-how-turn-clicks-into-votes-christopher-wylie

Hotten, R. (2015), 'Volkswagen: The Scandal Explained', *BBC*, 10 December. Available at www.bbc.com/news/business-34324772

Information Technology Industry Council (ITIC) (2016), 'USTR Request for Public Comments to Compile the National Trade Estimate Report (NTE) on Foreign Trade Barriers'. Available at www.trade.gov/td/standards/Standards%20Notes/Request%20for%20Public%20Comments%20To%20Compile%20the%20National%20Trade.pdf

Information Technology & Innovation Foundation (ITIF) (2017), 'The Worst Innovation Mercantilist Policies of 2016'. Available at www2.itif.org/2017-worst-innovation-mercantilist-policies.pdf

Inside US Trade (2017), 'EU Decision on Data Flow Language in TiSA Not Expected Until Fall; U.S. Position Still Unknown', *Inside US Trade*, 13 February.

Internet Association (2017), 'Letter to Hon Robert Lighthizer', 16 May. Available at https://cdn1.internetassociation.org/wp-content/uploads/2017/05/Lighthizer-Letter-5.16.pdf

Kaplan, J. and K. Rowshankish (2015), 'Addressing the Impact of Data Location Regulation in Financial Services', *Global Commission on Internet Governance Paper Series*, No. 14, May.

Kelsey, J. (2017), 'TiSA – Foul Play', *UNI Global Union*, 111–124.

Kelsey, J. (2018), 'How a TPP-Style E-Commerce Outcome in the WTO Would Endanger the Development Dimension of the GATS Acquis (and Potentially the WTO)', *Journal of International Economic Law*, 1–24.

Khan, A.W. (2009), 'Universal Access to Knowledge as a Global Public Good', *Global Policy Forum*, June. Available at www.globalpolicy.org/social-and-economic-policy/global-public-goods-1-101/50437-universal-access-to-knowledge-as-a-global-public-good.html

Khor, M. (1996), 'Will WTO Competition End Oligopolies?' *SunsOnLine*, 18 December. Available at www.sunsonline.org/trade/process/followup/1996/12180096.htm

Knowledge Commons (2014), 'Digital Colonialism and the Internet as a Tool of Cultural Hegemony'. Available at www.knowledgecommons.in/brasil/en/whats-wrong-with-current-internet-governance/digital-colonialism-the-internet-as-a-tool-of-cultural-hegemony/

Lang, A. and L. Amarasekara (2016), 'Financial Services Liberalisation and TiSA: Implications for EU Free Trade Agreements, Report to the European Parliament', July.

Lee, K.F. (2017), 'The Real Threat of Artificial Intelligence', *New York Times*, 24 June. Available at www.nytimes.com/2017/06/24/opinion/sunday/artificial-intelligence-economic-inequality.html

Levy, N. (2017), 'Amazon Patents Shipping Label with Built-In Parachute for Dropping Packages from Drones', *Geekwire*, 30 May. Available at www.geekwire.com/2017/amazon-patents-shipping-label-built-parachute-dropping-packages-drones/

Ma, J. (2016), 'Letter to Shareholders from Executive Chairman Jack Ma', 13 October. Available at www.alizila.com/letter-to-shareholders-from-executive-chairman-jack-ma/

OECD (2014), *Principles for Internet Policy Making*. Paris: OECD.

OECD (2016), *Economic and Social Benefits of Internet Openness*. Paris: OECD.

Our World Is Not for Sale (2014), 'Leaked TiSA Text Exposes US Threat to Privacy, Data Security and Net Neutrality', 17 December. Available at http://notforsale.mayfirst.org/es/node/24452

Patnaik, P. (2015), 'Away from the Glare, a Push for More Stringent IPR Protection at the WTO', *The Wire*, 2 November. Available at https://thewire.in/14593/away-from-the-glare-a-push-for-more-stringent-ipr-protection-at-the-wto/

Pauwelyn, J. (2010), 'Squaring Free Trade in Culture with Chinese Censorship: The WTO Appellate Body Report on China – Audiovisuals', *Melbourne Journal of International Law*, 11(1): 119.

Peermohamed, A. (2016), 'India E-Commerce Industry Losses May Swell Amazon's $1 Billion Loss This Year', *Business Standard*, 23 November. Available at www.business-standard.com/article/companies/indian-e-commerce-industry-s-losses-may-swell-on-amazon-s-1-billion-loss-this-year-116112200265_1.html

PTI (2017), 'Will Have Regulatory Regime on Data Protection: Government to Supreme Court', *The Economic Times*, 27 April.

PWC (2017), 'Global Top 100 Companies by Market Capitalization', 31 March. Available at www.pwc.com/gx/en/audit-services/assets/pdf/global-top-100-companies-2017-final.pdf

Rahman, S. (2016), 'Challenging the New Curse of Bigness', *The American Prospect*, 29 November. Available at http://prospect.org/article/challenging-new-curse-bigness

Reuters (2017), 'Hackers Hit Russian Bank Customers, Planned International Cyber Raids', *Fortune*, 22 May. Available at http://fortune.com/2017/05/22/hackers-russian-bank-customers/

Romano, A. (2018), 'Senate Votes to Save Net Neutrality – But the Fight Is Far from Over', *Vox*, 16 May. Available at www.vox.com/2018/5/16/17360318/net-neutrality-senate-vote-result

Sen, S. (2017), 'Flipkart Raises $1.4bn from Tencent, eBay, Microsoft', *Hindustan Times*, 10 April. Available at www.hindustantimes.com/business-news/flipkart-raises-1-4-bn-from-tencent-others-buys-ebay-to-take-on-amazon/story-hw59Dl3ixaxzG08dJFdxSN.html

Shuiyu, J., Q. Xin and H. Wei (2017), 'AliBaba bringing Belt, Road Benefits to SMEs', *China Daily*, 24 April. Available at www.chinadaily.com.cn/business/2017-04/24/content_29051117.htm

Singh, P.J. (2017), 'Developing Countries in the Emerging Global Digital Order – A Critical Geopolitical Challenge to Which the Global South Must Respond', *Background Paper to South Centre Presentation*, January.

Sood, V. (2017), '7 Top IT Firms Lay Off 56,000 This Year, New Tech and Trump's Policies Blamed', *Hindustan Times*, 19 July. Available at www.hindustantimes.com/business-news/seven-top-it-firms-to-lay-off-56-000-this-year-new-tech-and-trump-s-policies-blamed/story-nDPfhZ3taX0WkE3sJotVwM.html

South Centre (2017a), 'Micro, Small and Medium-Sized Enterprises', SC/AN/TDP/2017/4, July.

South Centre (2017b), 'The WTO's Discussions on Electronic Commerce', SC/AN/TDP/2017/2, January.

Taplin, J. (2017), 'Is It Time to Break Up Google?' *New York Times*, 22 April. Available at www.nytimes.com/2017/04/22/opinion/sunday/is-it-time-to-break-up-google.html

Trade Negotiation Committee (TNC) of RCEP (2015), 'Terms of Reference: Working Group on Electronic Commerce'. Available at www.bilaterals.org/IMG/pdf/ecommerce_draft_terms_of_reference.pdf

Transport Intelligence (2016), 'Global E-Commerce Logistics: E-Commerce Supply Chain Profiles – Alibaba – Fulfilment'. Available at www.ti-insight.com/product/global-e-commerce-logistics-2016

United Nations General Assembly Human Rights Council (UNGAHRC) (2016), *Resolution on the Promotion, Protection and Enjoyment of Human Rights on the Internet*, A/HRC/32/L.20. Geneva: UNGAHRC.

USTR (2016a), 'The Digital2Dozen'. Available at https://ustr.gov/sites/default/files/Digital-2-Dozen-Final.pdf

USTR (2016b), 'Ensuring a Free and Open Internet'. Available at https://ustr.gov/sites/default/files/TPP-Ensuring-a-Free-and-Open-Internet-Fact-Sheet.pdf

USTR (2016c), 'Ambassador Froman Announced New Digital Trade Working Group'. Available at https://ustr.gov/about-us/policy-offices/press-office/press-releases/2016/july/ambassador-froman-announces-new

Vaughan, L. and G. Finch (2017), 'Libor Scandal: The Bankers Who Fixed the World's Most Important Number', *The Guardian*, 18 January. Available at www.theguardian.com/business/2017/jan/18/libor-scandal-the-bankers-who-fixed-the-worlds-most-important-number

World Trade Organization (WTO) (1998), 'Electronic Commerce and the Role of WTO', WTO Special Studies, No. 2. Available at www.wto.org/english/res_e/publications_e/special_studies2_e.htm

WTO (1999), *Progress Report to General Council, Work Programme on Electronic Commerce*, S/L/74. Geneva: WTO.

WTO (2001), *Guidelines for the Scheduling of Specific Commitments under the General Agreement on Trade in Services*, S/L/92, Geneva: WTO.

WTO (2002), *Communication from the European Communities and their Member States, Coverage of CPC 84 – Computer and Related Services*, TN/S/W/6, S/CSC/W/35, 24 October. Geneva: WTO.

WTO (2016a), *Work Programme on Electronic Commerce: Non-paper from the United States*, JOB/GC/94. Geneva: WTO.

WTO (2016b), *Work Programme on Electronic Commerce: Aiming at the 11th Ministerial Conference. Communication from the People's Republic of China and Pakistan*, JOB/GC/110/Rev.1. Geneva: WTO.

WTO (2016c), Proposal by Japan and others, *Reinvigorating Discussions on Electronic Commerce*, JOB/GC/96/Rev.1. Geneva: WTO.

WTO (2016d), *Aiming at the 11th Ministerial Conference*, JOB/GC/110/Rev.1, JOB/CTG/2/Rev.1, JOB/SERV/243/Rev.1, JOB/DEV/39/Rev.1. Geneva: WTO.

WTO (2017a), *Communication from Canada, Chile, Colombia, Cote d'Ivoire, the European Union, the Republic of Korea, Mexico, Montenegro, Paraguay, Singapore, and Turkey*, Work Programme on Electronic Commerce. Trade Policy, the WTO, and the Digital Economy, 13 January, JOB/GC/116, JOB/CTG/4, JOB/SERV/248, JOB/IP/21, JOB/DEV/42. Geneva: WTO.

WTO (2017b), Communication from the European Union, *An Enabling Environment to Facilitate Online Transactions*, TN/S/W/64. Geneva: WTO.

WTO (2017c), Proposal by Japan, *Possible Way Forward on Electronic Commerce*, JOB/GC/130. Geneva: WTO.

WTO (2017d), *Council for Trade in Services.* Report of the Meeting held on 16–17 March, S/C/M/130. Geneva: WTO.

WTO (2017e), Communication from Brunei Darussalam, Colombia, Costa Rica, Hong Kong, China, Israel, Malaysia, Mexico, Nigeria, Pakistan; Panama, Qatar, Seychelles, Singapore and Turkey, *Electronic Commerce and Development*, JOB/GC/117, JOB/CTG/5, JOB/SERV/249, JOB/IP/22, JOB/DEV/43. Geneva: WTO.

WTO (2017f), *ASEAN Reflections on Lunch Panel on "Can e-commerce Trade Rules Help MSMEs from Developing Countries"*. Held During the UNCTAD e-commerce Week, 27 April, JOB/GC/126. Geneva: WTO.

WTO (2017g), Communication from Australia, Colombia, the European Union, Japan, Republic of Korea and Mexico, *Domestic Regulation – Transparency*, JOB/SERV/251. Geneva: WTO.

4 E-commerce in free trade agreements and the Trans-Pacific Partnership

Inkyo Cheong

1. Introduction

E-commerce has been a major contributor to global economic development. Its dynamism has been one of the core business platforms in the digital economy, and its importance is increasing due to the fast-growing trend of Internet users in the world. E-commerce involved the transmission of personal data. For example, when you order a shirt from Amazon, open an account in Gmail, or purchase an airline ticket online, you provide your name, address, phone number, and credit card number. During the process, your personal data will be saved in the server of the vendor and could be transferred across countries depending on where the server is located. If your vital information falls into the wrong hands, information may be misused and you risk being harmed. Here, the issue is how to protect personal data. It involves issues concerning legal obligations, regulations, and/or guidelines.

Collected data can be processed as part of big data, and big data makes money through business analytics solutions. E-commerce provides a channel for collecting consumer data, and companies can utilise the data for enhancing the competitiveness of their businesses. With the development of data processing and artificial intelligence (AI), big data has become a key driving factor in improving the quality of services for customer satisfaction.

As a global issue, the concern over privacy protection was first raised by the Organisation for Economic Co-operation and Development (OECD) in 1980, and this was underlined by the World Trade Organization (WTO) in 1998 with the expansion of e-commerce. The perception arose that promoting corporate use of personal data may create economic benefits as well as cause the breach of privacy. This was globally recognised in the case of 'PRISM Backdoor'[1] involving Amazon Simple Notification Service messages from Edward Snowden in 2013, as well as in the case of Maximilian Schrems in the same year. As a result of these cases, the Data Protection Directive of the European Union (EU) strengthened its regulations regarding personal data and safeguards in order to protect privacy in 2016. More restrictive regulations for the transnational transfer of personal data were introduced by the EU, based on the concept of 'guarantee adequate protection'.

Considering the importance of e-commerce in the digital economy, international organisations and international trade agreements have adopted e-commerce rules and regulations. Although no country objects to the protection of personal data, different views exist regarding the commitment levels for protecting personal data and cross-border transfer of data, which is related to regulations concerning the location of data servers.

This chapter reviews and compares the guidelines, rules, and regulations that affect data and privacy protection in e-commerce, proposed by various international organisations. It analyses in detail the related provisions in the e-commerce chapter of the Trans-Pacific Partnership (TPP)/the Comprehensive and Progressive Agreement for Trans-Pacific Partnership (CPTPP), and provides insight how to regulate data and privacy protection to promote e-commerce. Following the introduction, Section 2 illustrates the role of data in promoting e-commerce growth. Section 3 introduces efforts on regulating data and privacy from OECD, APEC, and EU. From the comparative perspective, Section 4 examines the provisions on e-commerce regulation that exist in the TPP/CPTPP agreement, as well as those written some other FTAs. Section 5 concludes.

2. E-commerce and big data

The definition of e-commerce or digital trade ranges from the narrow definition of trade for digitised products to a broad definition of all trades involving digital information and communications technology. As information and communications technology develops, e-commerce is expanding rapidly, and e-commerce is shaping global trade through increasing online transactions. E-commerce is gaining importance in business. For example, online music sales have been growing steadily, accounting for approximately half of the music industry's total revenue in 2014, according to UNCTAD (2016d) (Figure 4.1).

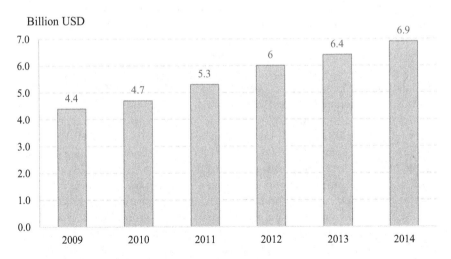

Figure 4.1 Global Digital Revenues of the Music Industry, 2009–2014
Source: UNCTAD (2016d: 8).

The value of global retail e-commerce was US$1.915 trillion (8.7 percent of global retail spending) in 2016, and is expected to reach US$4 trillion in 2020, showing an annual double-digit growth rate (Figure 4.2). The Asia-Pacific region will account for more than half of the global retail e-commerce market (eMarketer, 2016).

Approximately 40 percent of Internet users have bought products or goods via e-commerce, amounting to 1 billion e-commerce consumers. Leading e-commerce platforms include Amazon in the US, Rakuten in Japan, and Alibaba in China. Their shares of the B2C e-commerce market are continually expanding. In addition, mobile e-commerce is growing with the popularity of smartphones. E-commerce ranges from retail services for goods and services to mobile media content and digital payment (Statista, 2017).

E-commerce can be categorised into four types: B2B, B2C, B2G and C2C.[2] Although the digital trade of B2B (business to business) is dominant in current e-commerce,[3] UNCTAD (2016b) reported that B2C e-commerce is increasing faster than B2B transactions, and the e-commerce market in the Asia-Pacific region is growing faster than other regions in the world. Figure 4.3 shows the relative scores of B2C e-commerce readiness of Asia-Pacific countries in terms of capability/infrastructure, as assessed by the United Nations Conference on Trade and Development (UNCTAD). Some countries, such as Japan, the Republic of Korea (henceforth, Korea), New Zealand, Australia, and Singapore, have already invested heavily in e-commerce infrastructure, while many developing Association of Southeast Asian Nations (ASEAN) countries have a lack of infrastructure. E-commerce infrastructure can be a priority sector for regional economic

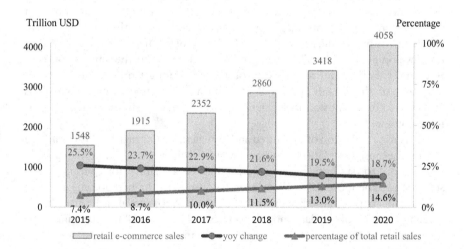

Figure 4.2 Global E-commerce Sales, 2015–2020

Source: eMarketer (2016).

Note: Retail e-commerce sales include products or services ordered using the Internet via any device, regardless of the method of payment or fulfilment; excludes travel and event tickets.

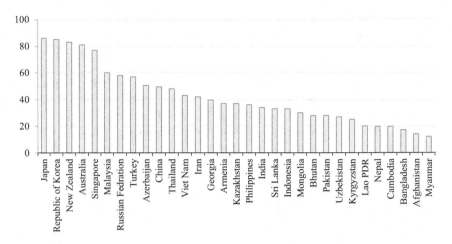

Figure 4.3 UNCTAD B2C E-commerce Readiness, 2016
Source: UNCTAD (2016b).

cooperation (Figure 4.3). As e-commerce infrastructure improves in developing countries, e-commerce sales will grow.

E-commerce involves online transactions utilising digital technologies including Internet marketing, mobile communication, electronic funds transfer, automated data collection systems, and electronic data interchange systems. 'The use of automated data exchange systems, cloud computing, big data and open source operating systems can help businesses run international supply chain management more efficiently' (UN ESCAP, 2016b). This assertion is based on the development of AI. The quality of AI improves with the amount of data. Big data, robotics, and the Internet of Things, amongst others, have become the basis of the fourth industrial revolution in manufacturing. Big data is expected to bring substantial efficiency gains and new business models, including e-commerce.

Big data is a collection of structured and unstructured information.[4] E-commerce can be the business platform to benefit most from the utilisation of big data, since its day-to-day business operations could be a channel for collecting consumer data. The more data collected from consumers, the better companies can tailor products through efficient marketing and advertising in order to enhance revenue. The use of big data and AI analytics will be essential in determining the international competitiveness structure of e-commerce businesses.

Big data processes, such as data collection and the transfer of data across countries, entail several barriers and issues (Table 4.1). First, one of the biggest issues is data localisation, which requires that data be stored and processed within a country's borders. This implies banning the free flow of data across borders, causing efficiency losses for e-commerce companies. Second, personal data protection

Table 4.1 Big Data: Barriers and Issues

Barriers	Issues/Effects
Location of data server	Efficiency of equipment (investment)
Data privacy	Level of protection
Source codes	Protection of intellectual property rights
Online censorship	Cybersecurity

Source: The author.

imposes additional costs, particularly in the case of structured data in which the consumer could be identified. The third and fourth barriers are source codes for the protection of intellectual property rights and online censorship.

These barriers result in big data services being more costly and less efficient. For example, if data is required to be stored only in domestic servers (data localisation), e-commerce companies would be prevented from utilising cheaper facilities in foreign countries. If data will not be moved cross-border, smaller sizes of data will be available for AI analytics than trans-border movement. There are two predominant views concerning data privacy: the utilitarian approach supported by the Chicago school (US) vs. fundamental rights viewpoint held in Europe. The former was theoretically supported by Posner (1978, 1981), Stigler (1980), Varian (1997), and Calzolari and Pavan (2006), while the latter was developed by Hirshleifer (1971), Taylor (2003), and Hermalin and Katz (2006). The compromise between these two camps was the EU-US Safe Harbor Privacy Principle in 2000. The Safe Harbor was rejected by the EU following a claim by Maximilian Schrems, an Austrian lawyer and privacy advocate, against Facebook (see Section 3.3).

Four studies regarding barriers to big data are worth mentioning. The European Center for International Political Economy (ECIPE, 2014) reported that the costs of data localisation in terms of regulation on data flow and privacy protection reduce gross domestic product (GDP) by 0.8–1.3 percent, and reduce international trade by 7 percent. ECIPE (2014) assessed the effects of China's data localisation policies to reduce GDP by 1.1 percent, exports by 1.7 percent, and investment by 1.8 percent. In addition, the EU would face a 0.4 percent decrease of GDP. McKinsey (2014) estimated that data flow increased by 45 times between 2005 and 2014, and this contributed to an expansion of trade in services and GDP growth of 3 percent between 2003 and 2013. This implies that any barriers to data flow would result in substantial loss. The Leviathan Security Group (2016) forecasted that data localisation enforcement would raise operational costs of data hosting companies by 30–60 percent, because such enforcement does not allow scale economies in centralised data storage and cloud computing, and requires extra investment for domestic data servers. In the case of Brazil's 2014 law 'Internet Bill of Rights', Brazilian consumers pay 55 percent more using data hosting from Brazilian servers than from servers outside Brazil.

3. Regulating privacy

No one opposes the promotion of e-commerce in that e-commerce facilitates trade and creates new opportunities for trade. The WTO Ministerial Conference adopted the Declaration on Global Electronic Commerce in 1998, which mandates the General Council to:

> establish a comprehensive work program to examine all trade-related issues relating to global electronic commerce. . . . Without prejudice to the outcome of the work program or the rights and obligations of Members under the WTO Agreements, we also declare that Members will continue their current practice of not imposing customs duties on electronic transmissions.
>
> (WTO, 1998: 1)

Ministers of the WTO member countries have reviewed the reports irregularly since the Doha Round opened in 2001, and have agreed to levying no duties on digital products. However, there has been no progress on data protection. This is predominantly due to the challenges in cross-border transfer of personal data and regulations concerning the location of data centres.

These problems associated with e-commerce were noted at the onset of the Internet. In 1980, the OECD adopted 'Guidelines on the Protection of Privacy and Trans-border Flows of Personal Data', and updated them in 2013. While any rule agreed at the WTO is binding for all member states, the OECD agreements feature guidelines or recommendations that are much easier for members to accept. Non-binding characteristics can be found in Asia-Pacific Economic Cooperation (APEC). Binding commitments are included in FTAs, since member countries tend to support these provisions. Currently, many countries including the US and European countries have enacted laws for the protection of personal data.

3.1. The privacy principles of the OECD

According to the OECD website, the OECD promotes the protection of privacy and adopted a condition for the cross-border flow of personal data.[5] The development of Internet technology and e-commerce enables data transmission across countries within seconds, as well as heightens concern over privacy protection regarding personal data. The OECD considers privacy as one of the fundamental human rights, and recognises that the violations of human rights can happen in 'the unlawful storage of personal data, the storage of inaccurate personal data, or the abuse or unauthorized disclosure of such data'. On the other hand, excessive restrictions on data flow may hamper economic activities such as e-commerce and banking. The OECD (2013) guidelines consider both privacy protection and the disruption of cross-border data flows. It consists of eight privacy principles (Table 4.2).[6] The OECD principles are well defined, but lack of regulations.

Table 4.2 Privacy Principles vis-a-vis APEC Privacy Framework

OECD (2013) Privacy Principles

Principle	Description
Collection Limitation Principle	The collection of personal data should limited, and data should be collected by lawful and appropriate means.
Data Quality Principle	Personal data collected should be accurate, complete, and suitable for the purpose.
Purpose Specification Principle	The purposes for the collection of personal data should be specified when collecting data, and data collected should be used for legitimate purposes.
Use Limitation Principle	Collected personal data should not be used for other purposes except when the data subject agrees or when the law requires such use.
Security Safeguards Principle	Collected personal data should be kept secure in order to prevent various risks such as loss, illegal access, misuse, or disclosure.
Openness Principle	Practices and policies for personal data should be applied with a principle of openness.
Individual Participation Principle	Individuals should have the right to know the status of personal data he provides to a data controller.
Accountability Principle	This principle charges a data controller to be accountable for complying with national policies and measures that affect principles 1–7.

APEC Privacy Framework

Principle	Description
Preventing Harm	Acknowledging the risk of harm from the misuse of personal data. Specific obligations and remedial measures to reduce such risk.
Collection Limitation	Personal data should be collected by lawful and fair means.
Integrity of Personal Information	Similar to Data Quality Principle of the OECD.
Notice	Providing clear statements about the practices and policies about collecting personal data.
Uses of Personal Information	Similar as the Use Limitation Principle of the OECD.
Security Safeguards	Similar to Security Safeguards Principle of the OECD.
Preventing Harm	Acknowledging the risk of harm from the misuse of personal data. Specific obligations and remedial measures to reduce such risk.
Access and Correction	Similar to Individual Participation Principle of the OECD.
Choice	Data subjects should be provided with choice about collection, use and disclosure of their personal information.
Accountability	Similar to Accountability Principle of the OECD.

Source: OECD (2013), APEC (2005).

3.2. APEC privacy framework

The APEC is an Asia – Pacific regional forum involving 21 countries including the US, Japan, China, and ASEAN members, targeting the facilitation of regional economic cooperation since 1989. When APEC adopted the Blueprint for Action on e-commerce in 1998, member countries recognised that:

> the potential of electronic commerce cannot be realized without government and business cooperation to develop and implement technologies and policies, which build trust and confidence in safe, secure and reliable communication, information and delivery systems, and which address issues including privacy. . . . APEC economies recognize the importance of protecting information privacy and maintaining information flows among economies in the Asia – Pacific region and among their trading partners.
>
> (APEC, 2005: 2)

The APEC Privacy Framework overlaps with the 1980 OECD Privacy Principles in terms of the concentration on the negative impacts from disclosing personal information, while the OECD Privacy Principles also focus on individuals' fundamental rights regarding personal information. Since APEC is a non-binding organisation, the APEC Privacy Framework does not include the mechanism of enforcement.

In general, the APEC Privacy Framework aims to promote e-commerce in the region via reaffirming the value of protecting personal data to prevent the misuse and illegal disclosure of such information. The framework was established to suggest specific measures for governments and companies to systemise principles domestically, as well as internationally. For example, to prevent the misuse of personal data and subsequent harm to the subject, the APEC Privacy Framework suggests various measures such as education and awareness campaigns, regulatory efforts, laws/regulations, surveillance mechanisms, and ex-post remedies in case of privacy infringements.

3.3. EU's Data Protection Directive

In 1995, the EU adopted the 'Data Protection Directive', named Directive 95/46/EC, to protect the privacy of personal data concerning EU citizens. Referring to the OECD recommended principles for the protection of personal data, the EU Directive was based on seven principles: (i) Notice of data collection, (ii) The provision of information about collecting such data, (iii) Safety and security of collected personal data from potential misuse or loss, (iv) No disclosure or provision of personal data without consent, (v) Guarantee of access to personal data and correcting any inaccuracies, (vi) Data to be used only for given purpose(s), and (vii) Personal data collectors to abide by all these principles.

It can be said that the EU Directive promotes the protection of personal privacy. Since the EU Directive was complicated for US companies to comply with, the EU and the US negotiated an alternative mechanism for allowing the trans-border transfer of personal data during 1998–2000, and subsequently passed the 'Safe Harbor Privacy Principles'. If a company qualifies under the Safe Harbor Privacy Principles, it is allowed to save personal data in data centres located in foreign countries. The Safe Harbor Privacy Principles (2000) cover the issues of (i) Notice, (ii) Choice, (iii) Onward Transfer, (iv) Security, (v) Data Integrity, (vi) Access, and (vii) Enforcement.

However, many US companies do not store personal data as specified in the Safe Harbor Privacy Principles. Maximilian Schrems recognised that his personal data was improperly handled by Facebook. In 2011, he filed a complaint against Facebook with the European headquarters of the Data Protection Commissioner in Ireland. In 2013, another complaint was filed against Facebook Ireland Ltd, urging the Data Protection Commissioner to prevent Facebook from transferring personal data from the EU (Ireland) to the US. He claimed that Facebook does not handle data with 'adequate protection' under the Safe Harbor Clause and the EU data protection law, and the Data Protection Commissioner should prohibit Facebook from transferring data to the US. (Edwards, 2017) In 2013, Edward Snowden disclosed the PRISM system, which collected personal data without adequate controls. (Greenwald, 2014)

However, the Data Protection Commissioner found in favour of Facebook, and the European Commission argued that personal data could be transferred with 'adequate protection' under the EU-US Safe Harbor Principles.[7] The Austrian lawyer brought the case to the Irish High Court by filing an application for judicial review. The Court referred the Facebook case to the EU's law and regulation/directives on the protection of personal data. In June 2014, the Court concluded that the '2000 European Commission decision should be re-evaluated in light of the subsequent entry into force of Article 8 of the Charter Fundamental Rights of the EU'.[8] In October 2015, the European Court of Justice (ECJ) overturned the EU-US Safe Harbor Principles,[9] ordering US companies that store personal data to abide by EU's privacy protection regulations.

Following the judgement by the ECJ, the European Commission adopted a new directive, which came into effect in May 2016. The directive enforces a higher level of privacy protection and allows EU citizens to enjoy fundamental human rights. Personal data should be collected following strictly defined conditions and for a clear and legitimate purpose. Furthermore, the collector of personal data (organisation, company) is responsible for preventing data misuse and improper disclosure, and guaranteeing the rights of the data subject. The transfer of personal data into a third country is allowed only when data is adequately protected. An exception is permitted when the data collector/controller can guarantee compliance with the protection rules for personal data. Based on the EU's new Directive, the EU and the US formed the 'EU-US Privacy Shield' framework in 2016. One of key requirements for transferring personal data between EU countries and the US is 'adequacy decision' – a set of principles to be equivalent to the level of the protection of personal data.

4. E-commerce chapters in FTAs, the TPP/CPTPP

4.1. E-commerce chapters in recent FTAs

E-commerce is already widely used in business transactions, but the first FTA containing major e-commerce provisions was the Australia-Singapore FTA, which came into effect in 2003. Recent FTAs have included e-commerce provisions with zero tariffs for the importation of digital goods, transparency, cooperation, paperless trading, electronic authentication, consumer protection, and privacy. Examples of FTAs with e-commerce chapters are the Korea-Singapore FTA (2006), the China-New Zealand FTA (2008), the ASEAN-Australia-New Zealand FTA (2009), the US-Korea FTA (2012), the Australia-Japan FTA (2014), and the TPP (not yet effective).[10] Australia, along with the US, has been a leading country in promoting business-friendly e-commerce provisions. The major elements of the e-commerce provisions in the Australian FTAs are presented in Annex 4.1.

Zero-tariffs provisions on digital products are included in most FTAs, including the TPP. A similar exemption had already been adopted by the WTO Ministerial Meeting in 1998. The differences between the WTO Ministerial Meeting of 1998 and the FTAs/TPP are the practice in the former and the binding commitments in the latter. The WTO agreed not to impose tariffs on imported digital products for a certain period, and then renew or extend the practice. Since then, no country has charged tariffs on digital products following the WTO practice or based on FTA commitments.

ASEAN countries have promoted e-commerce through the initiative of the ASEAN Economic Community (AEC), and ASEAN adopted the e-ASEAN Framework Agreement as a part of the AEC. Article 5 of the agreement defines the facilitation of the growth in electronic commerce by stating that 'Member States shall adopt electronic commerce regulatory and legislative frameworks that create trust and confidence for consumers and facilitate the transformation of businesses towards the development of e-ASEAN'.

The E-ASEAN Framework Agreement requires each member country to perform the following tasks to promote e-commerce:

i   match national legal system and policies about e-commerce with international norms;
ii   establish a mutual recognition system for digital authentication;
iii secure transaction security for e-commerce;
iv   protect intellectual property rights (online contents) in the context of e-commerce;
v   protect personal data protection/consumer privacy; and
vi   establish dispute settlement mechanisms for online transactions.

As ASEAN countries promote regional economic integration with a less binding format, the E-ASEAN Framework Agreement seems to be a general format despite the six obligations, since all of these are basic requirements for e-commerce today. Similar chapters in terms of obligations can be found in FTAs concluded by the US. Most of the FTAs involving the US include e-commerce provisions. The North American Free Trade Agreement (NAFTA) is an exception. Table 4.3 shows the US FTAs with e-commerce provisions. When NAFTA was signed in 1992, e-commerce was not yet a business platform deserving international regulations.

However, e-commerce has grown dramatically, and the information technology environment has become a key requirement for business across international borders.

> Some companies argue that new barriers have also emerged, which existing trade rules fail to address. NAFTA parties could consider discussions on issues related to cross-border transfer of information by electronic means or forced localization of data centers. Such provisions could provide North American firms more flexibility in where they process and store data relevant to their business. Some of these issues were addressed in TPP.
>
> (Congressional Research Service, 2017: 28)

The US-Korea FTA and the TPP were agreements in which the US pressured partners to accept proposals on e-commerce provisions. In the US-Korea FTA, soft issues such as customs duties, non-discriminatory treatment of digital products, and electronic authentication and electronic signatures were agreed on, including the obligations of member states in these areas. Korea and the US agreed on close cooperation on several issues such as paperless trading, access to and use of Internet infrastructure, online consumer protection, and cross-border transfer of

Table 4.3 US E-commerce Chapter of FTAs

Agreement	Chapter for e-commerce	Remarks
US-Australia FTA	Chapter 16	Implemented
US-Bahrain FTA	Chapter 13	Implemented
CAFTA-DR FTA	Chapter 14	Implemented
US-Chile FTA	Chapter 15	Implemented
US-Colombia FTA	Chapter 15	Implemented
US-Korea FTA	Chapter 15	Implemented
US-Morocco FTA	Chapter 14	Implemented
US-Oman FTA	Chapter 14	Implemented
US-Panama FTA	Chapter 14	Not approved by Congress
US-Peru FTA	Chapter 15	Implemented
TPP Agreement	Chapter 14	Withdrawn

Source: USTR. Available at https://ustr.gov/issue-areas/services-investment/telecom-e-commerce/e-commerce-fta-chapters

Notes:
CAFTA-DR FTA = Central America-Dominican Republic free trade agreement
TPP = Trans-Pacific Partnership

information. Amongst cooperation sectors, cross-border transfer of information was one of the most sensitive sectors in the negotiation. In the text of the agreement, Article 15.8 (Cross-Border Information Flows) in Chapter 15 (Electronic Commerce) highlights the importance of the cross-border flow of data while protecting personal information, and states that the parties shall endeavour to refrain from imposing or maintaining unnecessary barriers to data flows. However, the two parties had different interpretations of this provision. The US argued that data transfer should be allowed, whereas Korea proposed that the country has the right to restrict the cross-border transfer of sensitive data.[11]

4.2. E-commerce chapter in TPP/CPTPP[12]

USTR (2016a: 1) notes that:

> TPP's Electronic Commerce chapter includes commitments ensuring that companies and consumers can access and move data freely (subject to safeguards, such as for privacy), which will help ensure free flow of the global information and data that drive the Internet and the digital economy. These commitments, along with others on market access and national treatment, combine to help prevent unreasonable restriction, such as the arbitrary blocking of websites.

The e-commerce chapter of the TPP has 18 articles, which can be grouped into three sections including general regulation, obligation, and cooperation. Article 1 defines terms, and Article 2 sets out the scope and general provisions. Several articles (9, 10, 12, 15, and 16) define collaborative areas including paperless trading, principles regarding access to and use of Internet for e-commerce, and cooperation on cybersecurity. The remaining articles set out the obligations of member states.

Parts of the e-commerce chapter are similar to other FTAs. These include facilitating e-commerce, regulating electronic authentication and signatures allowed in commercial transactions, and promoting paperless trading using customised electronic formats. Close cooperation amongst TPP states is required to support small and medium-sized enterprises in utilising e-commerce and overcoming obstacles.

But the TPP also adopts new regulations that are favourable for e-commerce companies. For instance, cross-border transfer of personal data is allowed for the first time via international trade agreement. Paragraph 2 of Article 14.11 (Cross-Border Transfer of Information by Electronic Means) states: 'Each Party shall allow the cross-border transfer of information by electronic means, including personal information, when this activity is for the conduct of the business of a covered person'.[13]

The TPP chapter does not regulate the location of data centres. Paragraph 2 of Article 14.13 (Location of Computing Facilities) notes that: 'No Party shall require a covered person to use or locate computing facilities in that Party's territory as a condition for conducting business in that territory'. Companies can build data centres in the region with low construction and maintenance costs such as electricity. This allows e-commerce companies to enjoy economies of scale, improving their profitability. The chapter prohibits requirements that force suppliers to share valuable software source codes with foreign governments or commercial rivals when entering a TPP market.

Online consumer protection and personal data privacy are defined in Articles 7 and 8, respectively. Article 7 makes consumer protection compulsory in e-commerce through the adoption and enforcement of consumer protection laws. Similar to what the OECD guidelines establish, the TPP agreement includes commitments regarding personal privacy protection. Its e-commerce chapter covers a wide range of topics and takes into account new technologies, tools and models of e-commerce. Most valuable, the TPP agreement requires member states to support an open Internet and not to obligate data localisation and prohibit cross-border data flow. (USTR, 2016a: 3–4)

5. Conclusion

Global Internet infrastructure and data hosting services realise advantages through economies of scale by establishing centralised large-scale data storage centres. When governmental regulations restrict such advantages, the cost of doing business – as well as user fees – rise exponentially. 'Data localization laws, however, threaten this ideal of low-capital-investment, high-availability services' (Leviathan Security Group, 2016: 2). But collecting and processing data entails several problems. The protection of privacy in the process of business transactions was addressed by the OECD (1980) through establishment of guidelines for data treatment. The data privacy issue was extended to the cross-border transfer of data.

ASEAN Plus Six (Australia, China, India, Japan, Korea, and New Zealand) has been negotiating the Regional Comprehensive Economic Partnership (RCEP) since 2013. It aims for a comprehensive and high-quality FTA, and e-commerce is under negotiation. Though the negotiations are still undergoing at the time when this chapter is drafted, it is believed that the RCEP E-commerce chapter will cover most issues that have been included in other FTAs, even though some countries may still be reluctant to make detailed commitments in some areas.

Regarding e-commerce, a key concern is how to ensure the protection of data and whether to allow data to be stored in a third country. These concerns will be critical to determining cross-border transfer, especially when the fundamental human rights are emphasised. However, it seems difficult for RCEP member states to agree on regulating such sensitive issues, either data localisation or the cross-border transfer of personal data.

Notes

1 PRISM is a surveillance programme that allows the US National Security Agency to collect Internet communications across countries.
2 B = business; C = company; G = government
3 The Asian Development Bank (2015) reported that B2B e-commerce accounted for 90 percent of the total online transaction value in Asia.

4 The structured data is consumer information with name and address, while unstructured data is information that cannot identify name and address, and is collected from various types of social media and the Internet.
5 This can be found at: www.oecd.org/internet/ieconomy/privacy-guidelines.htm
6 OECD's 1980 guidelines had seven principles: (i) Notice, (ii) Purpose, (iii) Consent, (iv) Security, (v) Disclosure, (vi) Access, and (vii) Accountability.
7 The Principles were developed to prevent private E-commerce or SNS companies in the EU or US from disclosing or losing personal data.
8 High Court of Ireland Decisions. Available at www.bailii.org/ie/cases/IEHC/2014/H310.html.
9 The EU and the US introduced the EU-US Privacy Shield with a new framework for transnational data transfer on February 2016.
10 A detailed discussion can be found in Weber (2015).
11 The Law of the Protection of Personal Information was enacted on 29 March 2011. The law takes into account the OECD guidelines. Korea Daily (2017) argued that Korea would be left behind other countries in the development of big data business due to strong protection of personal information. It indicated that businesses that cannot operate in Korea or are restricted in their operations due to the law are those in e-commerce, data processing, credit rating, hybrid new businesses, new financial services, and data brokerage.
12 The transition from the TPP to CPTPP, which was signed after the withdrawal of the US from the TPP, does not affect the fundamental and contents of the E-commerce chapter.
13 Special and differentiated treatment was given to developing countries Malaysia and Viet Nam via Dispute Settlement in Article 14.18 of the TPP agreement, as follows:

> Article 14.18: Dispute Settlement

> i With respect to existing measures, Malaysia shall not be subject to dispute settlement under Chapter 28 (Dispute Settlement) regarding its obligations under Article 14.4 (Non-Discriminatory Treatment of Digital Products) and Article 14.11 (Cross-Border Transfer of Information by Electronic Means) for a period of two years after the date of entry into force of this Agreement for Malaysia.
> ii With respect to existing measures, Viet Nam shall not be subject to dispute settlement under Chapter 28 (Dispute Settlement) regarding its obligations under Article 14.4 (Non-Discriminatory Treatment of Digital Products), Article 14.11 (Cross-Border Transfer of Information by Electronic Means) and Article 14.13 (Location of Computing Facilities) for a period of two years after the date of entry into force of this Agreement for Viet Nam.

Bibliography

Asia-Pacific Economic Cooperation (APEC) (2005), *APEC Privacy Framework*. Singapore: APEC.
Asian Development Bank (2015), *Aid for Trade in Asia and the Pacific: Thinking Forward about Trade Costs and the Digital Economy*. Manila: ADB.
Calzolari, G. and A. Pavan (2006), 'On the Optimality of Privacy in Sequential Contracting', *Journal of Economic Theory*, 130: 168–204.
Congressional Research Service (2017), *The North American Free Trade Agreement (NAFTA)*. Washington, DC: CRS.
Department of Foreign Affairs and Trade, the Government of Australia (2017), 'Regional Comprehensive Economic Partnership (RCEP) Negotiations', *Discussion Paper on Electronic Commerce*. Canberra: Department of Foreign Affairs and Trade.

Edwards, E. (2017), 'All You Need to Know in the Max Schrems-Facebook Case', *The Irish Times*, 6 February. Available at www.irishtimes.com/business/technology/all-you-need-to-know-in-the-max-schrems-facebook-case-1.2965482

eMarketer (2016), 'Worldwide Retail Ecommerce Sales Will Reach $1.915 Trillion'. Available at www.emarketer.com/Article/Worldwide-Retail-Ecommerce-Sales-Will-Reach-1915-Trillion-This-Year/1014369

European Center for International Political Economy (ECIPE) (2014), 'The Costs of Data Localization: Friendly Fire on Economic Recovery', *ECIPE Paper*, No. 3/2014, Brussels: ECIPE.

Eurostat (2017), 'E-Commerce Statistics'. Available at http://ec.europa.eu/eurostat/statistics-explained/index.php/E-commerce_statistics

Greenwald, G. (2014), *No Place to Hide: Edward Snowden, the NSA, and the U.S. Surveillance State*. London: Hamish Hamilton.

Hermalin, B.E. and M.L. Katz (2006), 'Privacy, Property Rights and Efficiency: The Economics of Privacy as Secrecy', *Quantitative Marketing and Economics*, 4(3): 209–239.

Hirshleifer, J. (1971), 'The Private and Social Value of Information and the Reward to Inventive Activity', *The American Economic Review*, 61(4): 561–574.

Hirshleifer, J. (1980), 'Privacy: Its Origin, Function, and Future', *Journal of Legal Studies*, 9: 649–666.

Korea Daily (2017), 'Korea Will Be Left Behind Other Countries in Big Data Business Due to the Law of the Protection of Personal Data', *Korea Daily (Chosun Ilbo Newspaper)*, 4 July.

Leviathan Security Group (2016), *Quantifying the Cost of Forced Localization*. Seattle, WA: Leviathan Security Group.

Markle Foundation (2005), 'WTO, E-Commerce and Information Technologies: From the Uruguay Round to Doha Development Agenda – A Report for the United Nations ICT Taskforce'. Available at www.wto.org/english/tratop_e/serv_e/sym_april05_e/wunschvincent_e.pdf

McKinsey Global Institute (2014), *Global Flows in a Digital Age: How Trade, Finance, People, and Data Connect the World Economy*. Brussels, San Francisco, and Shanghai: McKinsey.

National Association of Citizens Advice Bureaux (2015), *Personal Data Empowerment: Time for a Fairer Data Deal?* London: National Association of Citizens Advice Bureaux. Available at http://bit.ly/1XtrIBG

Organisation for Economic Co-operation and Development (OECD) (1980), *Guidelines on the Protection of Privacy and Trans-border Flows of Personal Data*. Paris: OECD.

Organisation for Economic Co-operation and Development (OECD) (2012), *OECD Internet Economy Outlook 2012*. Paris: OECD.

Organisation for Economic Co-operation and Development (OECD) (2013), *OECD Glossary of Statistical Terms*. Paris: OECD.

Posner, R.A. (1978), 'The Right of Privacy', *Georgia Law Review*, 12: 393–422.

Posner, R.A. (1981), 'The Economics of Privacy', *American Economic Review*, 71: 405–409.

Statista (2017), 'Statistics and Market Data about E-Commerce'. Available at www.statista.com/markets/413/e-commerce/

Stigler, G.J. (1980), 'An Introduction to Privacy in Economics and Politics', *Journal of Legal Studies*, 9: 623–644.

Taylor, C.R. (2003), 'Privacy in Competitive Markets', *Duke University Economics Working Paper*, No. 03–10.

United Nations Conference on Trade and Development (UNCTAD) (1999), *Can Electric Commerce Be an Engine for Global Growth? Electric Commerce and the Integration of Developing Countries and Countries with Economies in Transition in International Trade – Note by the UNCTAD Secretariat Trade and Development Board*, TD/B/COM.3/23. Geneva: UNCTAD.

United Nations Conference on Trade and Development (UNCTAD) (2015), *Information Economy Report: Unlocking the Potential of E-Commerce for Developing Countries*. Geneva: UNCTAD.

United Nations Conference on Trade and Development (UNCTAD) (2016a), 'New Initiative to Help Developing Countries Grasp $22 trillion E-commerce Opportunity', *UNCTAD News*, 19 July. Geneva: UNCTAD.

United Nations Conference on Trade and Development (UNCTAD) (2016b), *UNCTAD B2C E-Commerce Index 2016*. Geneva: UNCTAD.

United Nations Conference on Trade and Development (UNCTAD) (2016c), *Data Protection Regulations and International Data Flows: Implications for Trade and Development*. Geneva: UNCTAD.

United Nations Conference on Trade and Development (UNCTAD) (2016d), *UNCTAD B2C E-Commerce Index 2016*. Geneva: UNCTAD.

United Nations Economic and Social Commission for Asia and the Pacific (UN ESCAP) (2016a), 'State of ICT in Asia and the Pacific 2016: Uncovering the Widening Broadband Divide', Technical Paper by the Information and Communications Technology and Disaster Risk Reduction Division. Available at www.unescap.org/resources/state-ict-asia-and-pacific-2016-uncovering-widening-broadband-divide

United Nations Economic and Social Commission for Asia and the Pacific (UN ESCAP) (2016b), *Harnessing Science, Technology and Innovation for Inclusive and Sustainable Development in Asia and the Pacific*, Sales No. E.16.II.F.12. Bangkok: ESCAP.

United States International Trade Commission (USTR) (2013), *Digital Trade in the U.S. and Global Economies, Part 1*. USITC Publication 4415. Washington, DC: USTR.

United States International Trade Commission (USTR) (2016a), 'Electronic Commerce'. Available at https://ustr.gov/sites/default/files/TPP-Chapter-Summary-Electronic-Commerce.pdf

United States International Trade Commission (USTR) (2016b), *Fact Sheet: Key Barriers to Digital Trade*. Washington, DC: USTR.

Varian, H.R. (1997), 'Economic Aspects of Personal Privacy', in *Privacy and Self-Regulation in the Information Age*. Washington, DC: US Department of Commerce, National Telecommunications and Information Administration (NTIA).

Weber, R.H. (2015), 'The Expansion of E-Commerce in Asia – Pacific Trade Agreements'. Available at www.ictsd.org/opinion/the-expansion-of-e-commerce-in-asia-pacific-trade-agreements

World Trade Organization (WTO) (1998), 'Electronic Commerce and the Role of WTO', *WTO Special Studies*, No. 2. Available at www.wto.org/english/res_e/publications_e/special_studies2_e.htm

Annex 4.1

Table 4A.1 Provisions in the E-commerce Chapters of Australia's FTAs

Provision	Description of discipline
Paperless trading	Countries endeavour to provide online availability of import and export documentation and electronic submission of those documents.
Electronic authentication	Except in certain circumstances, countries cannot deny a signature on the basis that it is in electronic form and are required to adopt a flexible approach to authentication technologies.
Online consumer protection	Countries are required to provide the same protections for online consumers as they do for consumers generally.
Online protection of personal information	Countries are required to adopt or maintain a legal framework to protect the personal information of electronic commerce users.
Unsolicited commercial electronic messages (spam)	Countries are required to adopt or maintain measures to reduce the incidences of unwanted commercial messages from various sources (for example, through e-mail and SMS).
Customs Duties on electronic transmissions	Since 1998, WTO members have agreed, biennially, to continue the practice of not charging customs duties on electronic transmissions. This decision will be reviewed at the WTO in December 2017. In FTAs, countries have made this a permanent practice.
Non-discriminatory treatment of digital products	Countries are required to treat all digital products the same, regardless of origin.[i]
Domestic regulatory frameworks/domestic electronic transaction frameworks	Countries required to adopt or maintain legal frameworks consistent with the principles of the United Nations Commission on International Trade Law (UNCITRAL) Model Law on Electronic Commerce (1996).
Localisation of Computing facilities	Countries should not require businesses operating in their territory to locate computing facilities (includes computer servers and storage devices for processing or storing information for commercial use) within the country's borders.[ii]

(*Continued*)

Table 4A.1 Continued

Provision	Description of discipline
Cross-border transfer of information by electronic means	Countries should allow cross-border transfers of information by electronic means, including personal information, when this is required for the conduct of the business of a covered person.
Disclosure of source code	Countries should not require the transfer of or access to mass-market software source code as a condition for the import, distribution, sale or use of such software, or of products containing such software.[iii]

Source: Department of Foreign Affairs and Trade, the Government of Australia (2017).

Note:

SMS = Short Message Service

[i] This discipline does not apply to broadcasting, government subsidies, and grants, or to the extent of any inconsistency with the intellectual property chapter.

[ii] Countries may impose conditions or restrictions required to achieve legitimate public policy objectives, provided that the measures would not constitute a means of arbitrary or unjustifiable discrimination or a disguised restriction on trade.

[iii] This discipline does not include software used for critical infrastructure, and does not apply to patent applications or granted patents.

5 An online dispute resolution scheme to resolve e-commerce disputes in ASEAN

Keon-Hyung Ahn

1. Introduction

E-commerce is radically changing the trade patterns of all economies by establishing international trade through the sale of related goods and services and bringing together in a virtual marketplace traders and consumers from around the world. According to Euromonitor International, global e-commerce is projected to maintain the average annual growth rate of 12 percent until 2020. In contrast, bricks-and-mortar-based retailing, which continues to be the biggest channel by value, will grow by just 2 percent over the same period (Bourlier and Gomez, 2016).

Digitalization of the economy can open entirely new opportunities for developing economies to facilitate job creation, productivity growth, and cross-border e-commerce. It is also expected to enable developing country businesses and consumers to access a wide variety of goods and services at a lower cost; streamline trade operations and logistics; and access new data to create new operational efficiencies, gain in competitiveness, and even productize data as a new revenue stream – all without building their own expensive information technology infrastructures (Suominen, 2017).

However, as digitalization of the economy accelerates, it is likely to generate some critical risks, such as those relating to consumer rights and consumer protection. These risks could become a barrier to further e-commerce development.

A European Commission (2015) survey clearly shows that it is imperative for policymakers and businesses to provide an effective and efficient dispute resolution mechanism to protect consumers and facilitate e-commerce. Regarding cross-border e-commerce, the results of the survey reveal that issues related to delivery receive the most concern (delivery costs were cited by 27 percent of respondents, high return shipping costs by 24 percent, and long delivery times by 23 percent), which are followed by redress (the difficulty solving problems was cited by 23 percent of respondents) and consumer rights (getting a faulty product replaced or repaired was cited by 20 percent of respondents, and returning a product and getting reimbursed by 20 percent). It further reported that among those who had experienced any problem with an online purchase or attempted purchase over the past year, only 16 percent of respondents did not take any action to resolve their most recently experienced problem.[1] Furthermore, almost two-thirds of respondents who took action were satisfied with the way their complaints were handled. Out-of-court dispute resolution institutions – alternative dispute resolution (ADR) – yielded the highest satisfaction rating (68 percent), whilst the court litigation garnered the lowest satisfaction (54 percent).

The ASEAN member states (AMS) have already recognized the importance of consumer protection and an effective and efficient dispute resolution mechanism to ensure a high level of confidence in domestic and cross-border transactions. This is evident in ASEAN's Strategic Action Plan on Consumer Protection, 2016–2025. Strategic Goal 1 of the plan is to strengthen the enforcement capacities of administrative agencies as well as the use of ADR mechanisms for consumer redress, for which two initiatives were proposed: first, developing guidelines for common approaches to ADRs, including consideration of a mechanism for resolving consumer complaints through consumer groups; and second, establishing of national small claim courts or ADR. In parallel, Strategic Goal 3 aims for the ASEAN Regional Online Dispute Resolution (ODR) mechanism, including (i) national ODR systems, (ii) a region-wide ODR network, and (iii) an ASEAN mechanism for cross-border complaints and investigations (ASEAN, 2016).

This chapter investigates the e-commerce-related consumer protection issues in ASEAN from a comparative perspective. It is structured as follows: Section 2 examines the status of the main e-commerce and consumer protection laws in AMS, Section 3 reviews international rules on consumer protection and ODR, and Section 4 provides recommendations on harmonizing the relevant ASEAN regulations and making an effective online dispute resolution platform in ASEAN. Section 5 concludes.

2. Status of e-commerce and consumer protection laws in AMS

2.1. *Principal e-commerce laws*

Governments have a significant role to play in making an efficient legal and regulatory framework for e-commerce to reduce the risk of transacting online and to encourage transparency for all e-commerce stakeholders (UNCTAD, 2015). To promote cross-border e-commerce, it is critical that national legislations in the fields of e-transactions, data protection and privacy, cybercrime, and consumer protection align with those of other AMS and with international legal instruments.

Table 5.1 shows that all AMS except Cambodia have enacted e-transaction laws – the most fundamental laws in the area of cyberlaws – and consumer protection laws. Cambodia, however, is likely to complete its draft consumer protection legislation soon (Redfearn, 2017).[2] Four countries – Brunei Darussalam, Cambodia, Lao PDR, and Myanmar – have yet to enact a privacy and data protection law. Only Cambodia and Lao PDR have not enacted a cybercrime law, although the legislation processes is underway in Cambodia.

Table 5.1 Availability of Legislation or Draft Legislation in Key Areas of Cyber Law

ASEAN Countries	Electronic Transactions		Consumer Protection		Privacy and Data Protection		Cybercrime	
	Legislation	Draft	Legislation	Draft	Legislation	Draft	Legislation	Draft
Brunei Darussalam	✓ [i]		✓		✗	✗	✓	
Cambodia	✗	✓	✗	✓	✗	✗	✗	✓
Indonesia	✓		✓		✓		✓	
Lao PDR	✓		✓		✗	✗	✗	✗
Malaysia	✓		✓		✓		✓	
Myanmar	✓		✓		✗	✗	✓	
Philippines	✓ [i]		✓		✓		✓	
Singapore	✓ [i]		✓		✓		✓	
Thailand	✓		✓		✓		✓	
Viet Nam	✓ [i]		✓		✓		✓	

Source: UNCTAD (2015).

Note:
[i] Countries with e-transaction legislation based on United Nations Commission on International Trade Law texts.

The implementation of cyberlaws in AMS is crucial for their sustainable growth, as a supportive legal framework is vital to create confidence online and to secure electronic interactions between governments, businesses, and consumers to facilitate e-commerce (UNCTAD, 2015).

As the subject of this chapter is ODR schemes to resolve e-commerce disputes in ASEAN, the discussion focuses on mainly on consumer protection law, as this deals directly with dispute resolution mechanisms.

2.2. Consumer protection laws in AMS

This section briefly examines the content of the consumer protection law in the ten AMS in turn. Although these laws embrace consumer dispute resolution mechanisms, their content varies.

2.2.1. Brunei Darussalam

Brunei Darussalam's Consumer Protection (Fair Trading) Order (2011), Art. 6 provides that a consumer has a right to file a suit in a court of competent jurisdiction (Government of Brunei Darussalam, 2011). It also sets forth that a small claims tribunal shall have jurisdiction on a small claim not exceeding B$10,000 in relation to consumer or unfair trading pursuant to Article 7 of the above order.

There is no provision for ADR other than a national court and a small claims tribunal, but general consumer complaints are managed by the Department of Economic Planning and Development, under the Prime Minister's Office (Australian Government Aid Program, 2011a).

2.2.2. Cambodia

The legislation processes for the Consumer Protection Act are underway. At the time this report was written, the consumer complaint handling and publication office of the Cambodia Import-Export Inspection and Fraud Repression Directorate-General accepted complaints from consumers by telephone or letter, although it is said that public awareness of this role is low. Furthermore, there is was institutionalized mechanism for ADR in Cambodia (Australian Government Aid Program, 2011h).

2.2.3. Indonesia

The Indonesian Consumer Protection Act No. 8 (Republic of Indonesia 1999), Chapter X (Settlement of Disputes), Part One (General), Art. 45(1) provides that every consumer may file charges against businesses through the Indonesian Consumers Foundation or through a court under the jurisdiction of the general court. In addition, Art. 49(1) of the act set forth that the government shall establish a consumer dispute settlement body in the Level II administrative regions to settle consumer disputes. According to Article 52, one of the duties and authorities of the consumer dispute settlement body is to handle and settle consumer disputes through mediation, arbitration, or conciliation.

In addition, generally, ADR is interpreted as an alternative to court litigation as it is reflected in the title of the Arbitration and Alternative Dispute Resolution Act No. 30 (Government of Indonesia 1999), which separates ADR in Indonesia (Australian Government Aid Program, 2011b).[3] The Indonesian National Arbitration Body, the Indonesian Institute for Conflict Transformation, and the National Mediation Centre are included in this category (Australian Government Aid Program, 2011b).

2.2.4. Lao PDR

Lao PDR's Law on Consumer Protection No. 2 (2010), Part V (Solution of Disputes between Consumer and Supplier), Chapter 1 (Solution of Disputes), Art. 37 (Process of Solution of Disputes) provides that the disputes regarding the protection of consumers can be solved through (i) compromise (Articles 38–39), (ii) mediation (Articles 40–47), (iii) administrative means by the implementer organizations for consumer protection (Articles 48–52), and (iv) solution of disputes through the Organization of Economic Dispute Arbitration or People Courts (Articles 53–55) (Government of Lao PDR, 2010). Both parties can choose any process for a solution to satisfactory solve the dispute regarding the protection of consumers.

The dispute resolution mechanism provided in the law appears to be well set forth. However, the relevant organizations need to implement an adequate dispute resolution mechanism for consumer protection, including the yet-to-be-formed Consumer Protection Association's mediation service, as soon as possible.

2.2.5. Malaysia

The Malaysian Consumer Protection Act No. 599 (Government of Malaysia 1999), Part XI (The National Consumer Advisory Council), Art. 73(1) (Establishment of the National Consumer Advisory Council) provides that the minister may establish the said council to advise him for implementation of this act and for the protection of consumers among others. In addition, Article 85 of the act requires that a tribunal to be known as the Tribunal for Consumer Claims shall be established to hear and decide on consumer claims not exceeding RM25,000. No mention of ADR, such as mediation or conciliation, was found in the act.

Redress mechanisms available for consumers in Malaysia to resolve disputes include (i) the court system, (ii) the Tribunal for Consumer Claims, (iii) the Tribunal for House-Buyer Claims, and (iv) ADR (Australian Government Aid Program, 2011c). Major leading ADR institutions in Malaysia are (i) the National Consumer Complaints Centre,[4] (ii) Financial Mediation Bureau,[5] (iii) Banking Mediation Bureau,[6] (iv) The Malaysian Mediation Centre,[7] and (v) the Insurance Mediation Bureau (Australian Government Aid Program, 2011c).

2.2.6. Myanmar

Myanmar's Consumer Protection Law No. 10 (2014), Chapter III (Formation of the Central Committee), Art. 4 provides that the government shall make the Consumer Protection Central Committee comprising the Union Minister of the Ministry of Commerce as chair, the deputy ministers from the respective ministries, the heads of respective government departments and organizations, the representatives from the non-governmental organizations, and experts as members and persons assigned duty by the chair as secretary and joint-secretary (Government of Myanmar, 2014). Pursuant to Article 5 of the act, the functions and duties of the committee include deciding the appeal case on administrative penalty passed by the consumer dispute settlement body, which should be formed by the committee in accordance with Article 16 of the act.

2.2.7. Philippines

The Philippines' Republic Act No. 7394 – The Consumer Act of 1992, Title V (The National Consumer Affairs Council), Chapter I (Establishment and Composition), Art. 148 requires the National Consumer Affairs Council be established to improve the management, coordination, and effectiveness of consumer programmes (Republic of the Philippines, 1991). According to Chapter II (Powers and Functions), the concerned department may commence an investigation upon petition or upon letters of complaint from any consumer (Article 159) and the concerned department secretaries shall appoint not more than ten qualified consumer arbitration officers per province, including the National Capital Region (Article 160). It is also provided that these officers shall have original and exclusive jurisdiction to mediate, conciliate, hear, and adjudicate all consumer complaints (Article 162).

The Arbitration Act of the Philippines of 1953 (RA 876) (Republic of the Philippines (1953) and the Alternative Dispute Resolution Act of 2004 (RA 9285) also provide ADR mechanisms including arbitration and mediation (Republic of the Philippines, 2009).

In most cases, the Department of Trade and Industry (DTI) uses ADR to resolve consumer complaints (Australian Government Aid Program, 2011d). According to the Australian Development Cooperation Program Phase II (2011d):

> In 2013, the DTI issued Department Administrative Order (DAO) No. 13–02, Series of 2013 amending certain provisions of therewith, DTI issued DAO No. 5, Series of 2007 providing for the rules on mediation in resolving inquiries, complaints, and/or cases filed with the DTI for violations of RA 7394 or other trade and industry laws supplementing DAO No. 7, Series of 2006 and DAO No. 07, Series of 2006 providing simplified and uniform rules and procedures for administrative cased filed with the DTI. DAO No. 13–02, Series of 2013 specifies definite number of days for the resolution of consumer complaints by either mediation or adjudication (arbitration). For mediation, complaints must be resolved within ten (10) working days while twenty (20) working days by arbitration.

The DTI's Fair Trade Enforcement Bureau, under the Office of the Consumer Protection Group, handles consumer complaints. The DTI has developed a customer relationship management system that records and tracks all complaints and queries (Australian Government Aid Program, 2011d). Consumers residing outside Metro Manila can seek redress through the consumer welfare desks established in the DTI's regional and provincial offices.

2.2.8. Singapore

Singapore's Consumer Protection (Fair Trading) Act 2009, Part I (Preliminary), Arts. 6 and 7, provides that a consumer who has entered a consumer transaction involving an unfair practice may file a suit to the small claims tribunals against the supplier if the amount of the claim does not exceed SG$30,000 or another amount as the minister may, by order in the gazette, prescribe (Republic of Singapore Law Revision Commission, 2009).

The study was unable to find any mention on ADR in the act, but it was found that there are practical ADR channels to resolve consumer disputes, as seen in Table 5.2.

Furthermore, ADR is used extensively in Singapore to solve civil and commercial transaction disputes through the relevant institutions including Community Mediation Centre[8] and Singapore International Arbitration Centre.[9] One point to note is that the Consumer Association of Singapore signed a memorandum of

Table 5.2 Agencies Handling Consumer Complaints in Singapore

Agency	Affiliation	Types of Complaints Handled	Complaints-Filing Mechanism
Consumer Association of Singapore	Independent	Consumer-to-business transaction (goods and services)	General phone hotline; fax; walk-in consultation; online submission
Financial Institution Disputes Resolution Centre	Independent	Banking and finance; insurance; products and services	Fax; post mail; e-mail
Singapore Mediation Centre	Independent	Arrange mediation sessions for dispute resolution between parties	Mediation session in person
Small Claims Tribunal	Government	All consumer goods and services; civil claims regarding all goods and services	Filing a claim personally and by fax
Monetary Authority of Singapore	Government	Civil penalty enforcement action for false trading	Filing a claim personally and by fax

Source: Australian Government Aid Program (2011e).

understanding with the Federation of Malaysian Consumers Association in 2010 for cross-border consumer dispute resolution from both countries, a first for the ASEAN region (Australian Government Aid Program, 2011e).

2.2.9. Thailand

Thailand's Consumer Protection Act, B.E. 2522 (1979), Chapter 1 (Consumer Protection Board), Sections 9–10 prescribe that the government shall establish the Consumer Protection Board to (i) consider the complaints from the consumers, (ii) give recommendations and advice to the ad hoc committees and determine appeals against order of the ad hoc committees, and (iii) institute legal proceedings regarding the infringement of the consumer's right as the Board sees fit or when there is a request from consumers (Government of Thailand, 1979). A person who is not satisfied with the order issued by an ad hoc committee has the right to appeal to the Board (Article 43), and the decision of the Board shall be final (Article 44) in accordance with the act.

There is no mention of ADR in the act. However, ADR has been encouraged since the new Constitution was promulgated in 1997, and the Arbitration Office, Ministry of Justice (now called the Thai Arbitration Institute) is the longest-running and most successful arbitration centre.[10] Other arbitration institutions only exist in their embryonic stage (Australian Government Aid Program, 2011f).

2.2.10. Viet Nam

Viet Nam's Law on Protection of Consumer Rights No. 59/2010/QH12 (Government of Viet Nam 2010), Chapter IV (Settlement of Disputes between Consumers and Goods and Services Traders), Art. 30 provides that a dispute between a consumer and a goods or service trader shall be settled through negotiation, mediation, arbitration, and court. The law further stipulates adequate provisions on negotiation in Section 1 (Articles 31–32), mediation in Section 2 (Articles 33–37), arbitration in Section 3 (Articles 38–40), and dispute settlement by courts (Articles 41–46) in detail.

Regarding mediation, the law expressly allows that a trader and a consumer may agree to select a third party – a person or mediation organization – to mediate their dispute (Article 33), and organizations and individuals satisfying the conditions provided by the government may establish mediation organizations to settle disputes between consumers and goods or service traders (Article 35).

The most remarkable point in the law is that *a goods and service trader, before concluding a contract, shall notify a consumer of the arbitration term which is acceptable to the consumer* and when the trader includes the arbitration term in its model contract or general transaction conditions, *an individual consumer may select another mode for settlement* when a dispute arises according to Article 38 of the law. It is interesting that the law expressly enjoins a duty on traders to notify a consumer of the arbitration term that is acceptable to the consumer, while a consumer can freely choose a dispute resolution method, including arbitration. Considering that some jurisdictions do not allow consumer arbitration arising out of an adhesive contract, this provision may be a good compromise solution to avoid any limitation on consumer arbitration under the pertinent laws in some jurisdictions.[11]

It is said that redress is not popular among consumers, but the Consumers Complaint Bureau run by the Viet Nam Standards and Consumers Association is more popular than the consumer complaints mechanism of the government in Viet Nam, and the bureau receives complaints from consumers by phone, e-mail, and through their website (Australian Government Aid Program, 2011g).

Although all AMS except Cambodia provide consumer redress and dispute resolution mechanisms in their consumer protection laws, their contents differ. AMS are working on harmonizing their laws to facilitate economic integration and regional economic growth. At the same time, the question arises whether those consumer protection laws can provide an adequate dispute resolution mechanism to govern cross-border e-commerce disputes arising from high-volume, low-value transactions. The following sections examine this matter.

3. International rules on consumer protection and online dispute resolution

Business-to-business (B2B) and business-to-consumer (B2C) e-commerce has experienced unforeseen growth since the 2000s due to the increased connectivity provided by the Internet. E-commerce has also become a driving force to expand cross-border trade all over the world because it has removed geographical barriers to international trade and opened new marketplaces (Cupido, 2016). With this increase in Internet activity and interactions comes a rise in the number of domestic and cross-border e-commerce disputes (Cupido, 2016). Disputes arising in the online context can vary significantly and are very difficult for courts to deal with because of (i) the high volume of claims, (ii) the low value of the transaction claims, (iii) questions as to the applicable law (in both e-commerce and consumer protection contexts), and (iv) the difficulty of enforcing foreign judgements (Del Duca et al., 2012).

Consumers should have the right to fair, easy-to-use, transparent, and effective mechanisms to resolve domestic and cross-border e-commerce disputes in a timely manner to obtain redress, as appropriate, without incurring unnecessary cost or burden (OECD, 2016). This is why demand for ADR, especially ODR, is increasing exponentially around the globe.

Despite significant progress in the adoption of cyberlaw, such as e-transaction law, consumer protection law, and privacy and data protection law, consumer protection laws in AMS do not provide adequate redress and dispute resolution mechanisms for the new era of the digital economy. Accordingly, ASEAN must devote further efforts to harmonizing the regulations among member states and aligning their laws with international legal instruments to favour cross-border e-commerce (UNCTAD, 2015). To this end, this study examines consumer protection and ODR instruments enacted at the international level, including in the Organisation for Economic Co-operation and Development (OECD), the United Nations (UN), and the European Union (EU).

3.1. *Organisation for economic co-operation and development*

The Guidelines for Consumer Protection in the Context of Electronic Commerce, approved in December 1999, was enacted to ensure that consumers are given as much protection when shopping online as when they buy from offline marketplaces or order from a catalogue (OECD, 2000). Chapter VI of Part II (General Principles) of the guidelines handles dispute resolution and redress, and expressly requires that business, consumer representatives, and governments work together to provide consumers with the option of ADR mechanisms that enable resolution of the dispute in a fair and timely manner without undue cost and burden to the customer (OECD, 2000). The guidelines do not contain any explicit reference to the term ODR, but it is required that information technology is employed innovatively in implementing them.

OECD also announced a Recommendation on Consumer Resolution and Redress on 12 July 2007 setting out principles for an effective and comprehensive dispute resolution and redress system that would also be applicable to domestic (Chapter II) and cross-border disputes (Chapter III) (OECD, 2007). But reference to ODR remained tacit in the recommendation.

The OECD Recommendation on Consumer Protection in E-Commerce 2016 revised the 1999 guidelines, aiming to address the challenges identified and achieve effective consumer protection whilst stimulating innovation and fair competition in the market (OECD, 2016). The most notable change is that in Article 45, the recommendation expressly refers to ODR as an example of ADR (OECD, 2016; Yun, 2016).

The OECD recommendation may be useful to ASEAN as a source of relevant guidelines to enact and AMS could adopt them through their domestic laws. However, given that its contents lack specific details, the recommendation is too limited for ASEAN or AMS to use as a reference in establishing regional or domestic ODR platforms for consumer protection and redress.

3.2. European Union

3.2.1. The EU's legislation on consumer protection and alternative dispute resolution

The EU has adopted two European Commission recommendations on ADR to solve consumer disputes more effectively in its region, one in 1998 and the other in 2001 (European Commission, 1998, 2001). There are two networks, (i) the European Consumer Centres Network[12] and (ii) the Financial Dispute Resolution Network (FIN-NET),[13] that are supporting the implementation of those recommendations (Yun, 2016).

Nevertheless, the efficiency with which the ADR was implemented has been criticized (Son, 2013; Yun, 2016), and steps have been taken to improve the situation. In 2010, the EU announced a strategy to strengthen the ADR system through A Digital Agenda for Europe (European Commission, 2010). Furthermore, the European Commission included legislation on ADR as a key action in the 2011 Single Market Act (European Commission, 2011), urging countries to establish simple, fast, and affordable out-of-court settlement procedures for consumers and to protect relations between business and their customers (European Commission, 2011). In particular, the legislation noted that the action would also include an e-commerce dimension (Yun, 2016).

In addition, the EU enacted the Directive on ADR for Consumer Disputes and Regulation on Online Dispute Resolution for Consumer Disputes in 2013 (EU, 2013a, 2013b). Eventually, the EU ODR platform was set up and launched by the Commission on 16 February 2016 (Yun, 2016). It is reported that 24,000 consumers used the new ODR platform in its first year of operation (European Commission, 2017).

3.2.2. Analysis of the European Union online dispute resolution platform

If consumers living or based in the EU enter into an e-commerce transaction and eventually end up with a problematic deal, they can use the EU ODR site to try to settle their dispute out of court. In some countries, such as Iceland and Norway, traders can use this site to complain about a consumer over a good or service they sold online.[14]

As of 13 October 2018, there were 394 dispute resolution bodies in 28 EU countries and three EEA/EFTA countries including Norway, Iceland, and Liechtenstein (Table 5.3). All the bodies listed have been checked to make sure that they meet the standards of the EU ODR platform and are registered with their respective national authorities.[15]

Each dispute resolution body has its own rules and procedures. There are four main steps to use the EU ODR site: (i) submitting a complaint, (ii) agreeing on a dispute resolution body, (iii) handling of the complaint by the dispute resolution body, and (iv) outcome and closure of complaint. Table 5.4 shows the procedure in more detail. At each stage, parties to the dispute can contact their national contact points designated and provided by the site if they have question or need help.

3.3. United Nations

During its 43rd session held in New York, US in 2010, the United Nations Commission on International Trade Law (UNCITRAL) agreed to establish a working group to embark on cross-border e-commerce transactions in ODR. Discussion on cross-border electronic transactions, including B2B and B2C low-value, high-volume transactions, commenced at the 22nd meeting of Working Group III in December 2010 (UNCITRAL, 2016).

3.3.1. Package model of online dispute resolution

From the 22nd to the 25th meetings of Working Group III, the members considered a package model for the ODR platform, consisting of three stages: negotiation,

Table 5.3 Dispute Resolution Bodies Listed on the European Union Online Dispute Resolution Platform[i]

Country	Number of Platforms	Country	Number of Platforms	Country	Number of Platforms
Austria	8	Germany	26	Netherlands	4
Belgium	13	Greece	4	Norway	10
Bulgaria	16	Hungary	20	Poland	24
Croatia	8	Iceland	0	Portugal	12
Cyprus	2	Ireland	3	Romania	1
Czech Republic	6	Italy	38	Slovakia	6
Denmark	27	Latvia	7	Slovenia	11
Estonia	4	Lithuania	5	Spain	5
Finland	3	Luxembourg	4	Sweden	7
France	71	Malta	3	United Kingdom	44

Source: The European Union Online Dispute Resolution Platform. Available at https://ec.europa.eu/consumers/odr/main/?event=main.adr.show2

Notes:
[i] Statistics by 13 October 2018.

Table 5.4 Procedure for Dispute Resolution of EU ODR Platform

Step 1: Complaint submitted	*Step 2: Agreement on dispute resolution body*	*Step 3: Dispute handled by the dispute resolution body*	*Step 4: Outcome of the procedure*
The consumer fills out the online complaint form and submits it to this site. The other party will be informed of the complaint.	The consumer has 30 days to agree with the other party on the dispute resolution body that will handle the dispute. Once you do so, this site will automatically send the details of your dispute to that body. If you cannot agree, your complaint will not be processed further.	The case of dispute will be sent to the dispute resolution body. The dispute resolution body has three weeks to decide whether it is competent or not to deal with the case, and inform the consumer thereof. It may contact the consumer for more information.	The dispute resolution body informs the consumer the outcome of resolution.

Source: Author, based on the European Union Online Dispute Resolution Platform webpage. Available at https://ec.europa.eu/consumers/odr/main/?event=main.home.howitworks

Note: In each step, if the consumers need help, they can contact the national contract point.

facilitated settlement, and arbitration (Yun, 2016). According to the package model, the ODR process commences when a claimant submits a notice of claim via the ODR platform to the ODR administrator. The ODR administrator then notifies the respondent of the existence of the claim and the claimant of the response. In this technology-enabled negotiation stage, the claimant and respondent negotiate directly with one another through the ODR platform. If that negotiation fails to result in a settlement, the process may move to a second, 'facilitated settlement' stage. In this stage, the ODR administrator appoints a neutral adjudicator who tries to reach a settlement between the parties. If the facilitated settlement fails, the process moves to the final stage, 'arbitration' (UNCITRAL, 2015).

However, at its 25th meeting of Working Group III, the EU questioned when an arbitration agreement should be made between a consumer and a trader in the package model (Yun, 2016). Under the model, it was envisaged that an agreement on dispute resolution (negotiation, facilitated settlement, arbitration) should be concluded between a consumer and a trader when the e-commerce transaction was agreed.

3.3.2. Two-track model

From the 26th to 29th meetings of Working Group III, discussion on the package model was abandoned and a range of proposals were submitted to lead to a consensus. A two-track model, in which different ODR rules would be applied to two kinds of tracks – Track I comprising three stages (negotiation, facilitated settlement, arbitration), and Track II comprising two stages (negotiation, facilitated settlement) – failed to reach consensus as to which model should be adopted (Nam and Yun, 2016).

3.3.3. Integrated model

A controversial debate on the two-track model during the 30th and 31st meetings of Working Group III established two opinions. The EU took the position that the Track I model should be adopted, and proposed adding an annex to the international instrument[16] (Nam and Yun, 2016) to cover some jurisdictions in which a binding arbitration with consumers is not allowed under their proper laws.[17] However, this approach was also faulted, considering that the annex approach is only suitable for a legally binding international convention or treaty and requires a depository body in the UN Secretariat. Furthermore, it was practically infeasible considering the budget and human resources available in the UN (Yun, 2016).

In contrast, the US insisted that pre-dispute arbitration agreements with consumers in general should be respected. However, states in which a binding arbitration agreement with consumers capable of resulting in an enforceable award requires that the agreement to utilize the Track I Rules take place after the dispute has arisen should be listed and administered by each ODR institute on its website (Yun, 2016).[18]

3.3.4. China's proposal

At the 31st meeting of Working Group III, China made a revised proposal to integrate tracks I and II.

According to China's proposal, parties to an e-commerce transaction must agree to have their prospective dispute resolved pursuant to ODR rules, and if negotiation and facilitated settlement fails, an ODR administrator shall advise the parties on three options: to accept a neutral adjudicator's recommendation, move to arbitration, or choose other modes including litigation. The drawback of China's proposal is that there is no default rule defining when a facilitated settlement process fails.

3.3.5. The EU's proposal

In this circumstance, the EU proposed that a neutral adjudicator's recommendation should be the default rule. The proposed rule becomes applicable after a facilitated settlement fails to result in an amicable solution, and where parties did not choose arbitration after an ODR administrator explained the final options (i.e. to accept a neutral adjudicator's recommendation or use arbitration) (Yun, 2016).

3.3.6. UNCITRAL online dispute resolution

The proposals of the UNCITRAL Draft ODR Rules (Track I), the EU, China, and the US are summarized and compared in more detail in Table 5.5.

The 30th and 31st meetings of Working Group III failed to reach consensus on certain issues regarding ODR, including (i) the validity of a binding pre-arbitration agreement with consumers, (ii) the distinction between B2B and B2C, and (iii) the default rule when a facilitated settlement process fails to bring an amicable solution (Yun, 2016).

Table 5.5 Comparison of Proposals for ODR

Proposer	Time of Arbitration Agreement and its Validity	Features
Draft UNCITRAL Rules (Track I)	If a pre-arbitration agreement was agreed, the process will go through to arbitration automatically.	Without further consideration on different approaches in pre-arbitration agreement among countries. A problem can arise when in deciding on consumer's or buyer's nationality pursuant to a governing law.
European Union	It requires a subsequent arbitration agreement for consumers from a state listed in Annex or a buyer from buyers who are in certain states.	Administer certain states that do not allow pre-arbitration agreement with consumers by annex. Inclusion of concept of 'consumer' Governing law depends on consumer's nationality or buyer's location.
China	If facilitated settlement fails, the online dispute resolution administrator shall advise parties that they have an option to use arbitration, and if they agree on arbitration, the parties can make a binding arbitration agreement.	Arbitration agreement enters into force after a facilitated settlement process concluded, not just after a dispute arose. It does not require any Annex or list to administer states that do not allow a binding pre-arbitration agreement with consumers.
US	It is necessary to make an additional arbitration agreement if a buyer's billing address will be included in the list, which does not allow a binding pre-arbitration agreement with consumers.	Instead of Annex, it is necessary to put on the website a list of countries that do not allow pre-arbitration agreement with consumers. Buyer's nationality is decided based on his/her billing address.

Source: Yun (2015).

Accordingly, UNCITRAL instructed Working Group III to work towards elaborating a non-binding descriptive document reflecting elements of an ODR process, and incorporating elements on which the Working Group III had previously reached consensus, excluding the question of the nature of the final stage of the ODR process (arbitration or non-arbitration) (UNCITRAL, 2016).

This non-binding document entitled 'UNCITRAL Technical Notes on Online Dispute Resolution' (UNCITRAL, 2017) was discussed and finally agreed among participants, and the final draft of the document was submitted to the European Commission, where it was adopted on 5 July 2016 (Yun, 2016)

The UNCITRAL Technical Notes on Online Dispute Resolution consist of 12 sections and 53 articles, as summarized in Table 5.6.

The characteristic features of the Technical Notes on Online Dispute Resolution are that (i) the scope is for cross-border, low-value e-commerce in goods and service transactions, regardless of B2B or B2C; (ii) they are a non-binding instrument; and (iii) there is no conclusive default rule that will apply if the parties to an ODR process fail to reach a consensus on a solution at the facilitated settlement stage.[19]

Table 5.6 Overview of UNCITRAL Technical Notes on ODR

Section	Article	Main Contents
I.	1–6	Overview of ODR (Purpose and Non-Binding Nature of Technical Notes)
II.	7–17	Principles of ODR (Fairness, Transparency, Independence, Expertise, Consent)
III.	18–21	Stages of an ODR Proceeding (Negotiation, Facilitated Settlement, a third [final] stage)
IV.	22–23	Scope of ODR Process (E-Commerce Transaction regarding cross-border, low-value, B2B or B2C, sales and service contracts)
V.	24–32	ODR Definitions, Roles and Responsibilities, and Communications
VI.	33–36	Commencement of ODR Proceedings (Required Elements in Complaint Notice and Response, Commencement Date of ODR Proceedings)
VII.	37–39	Negotiation Proceedings
VIII.	40–45	Facilitated Settlement Proceedings
IX.	46	Final Stage (It recommends that an ODR administrator or neutral informs the parties of the nature of the final stage, and of the form it might take)
X.	47–50	Appointment, Powers and Functions of a Neutral
XI.	51	Language (Even where an ODR agreement or ODR rules specify a language, a party may indicate a certain language which it wishes in the notice or response)
XII.	52–53	Governance (Guidelines and/or Minimum Requirements regarding the Conduct of ODR Platforms and Administrators, Confidentiality and Due Process, etc.)

Source: The author. Based on Yun (2016) and UNCITRAL (2017).

4. ASEAN's way forward to adopt an effective online dispute resolution system

The e-commerce ecosystem continues to impose new challenges on the consumer. A new framework is needed to protect online shopping consumers and to foster consumer confidence in e-commerce, especially cross-border e-commerce (UNCTAD, 2016). As noted in Chapter II, however, AMS do not provide adequate laws and a dispute resolution environment that fully protects online consumers in the region. Accordingly, AMS governments must acknowledge the importance of e-commerce and consumer protection, and allocate sufficient resources towards its development (UNCTAD, 2015). ASEAN needs to provide an efficient and effective dispute resolution model, such as an ODR scheme, which is suitable for cross-border e-commerce disputes arising from high-volume, low-value goods or services transactions, in order to facilitate confidence in the ASEAN marketplace. To this end, the author would like to present the following eight recommendations for an effective framework for consumer protection:

4.1. Align consumer protection laws

Ensuring regional and global compatibility of consumer protection laws can be the first step to developing an effective protection regime in ASEAN. This entails modernizing and harmonizing legislation of relevant provisions of national consumer protection legislation, including unfair contract terms, e-commerce, product liability and safety, and consumer data privacy (ASEAN, 2016).

When revising legislation, ASEAN countries should seek to benefit from international instruments such as the 'Consumer Protection in E-Commerce: OECD Recommendation' (2017) and the 'UN Manual on Consumer Protection' (2016). These two international instruments provide policy advice only, and therefore will not conflict with either national laws or regional frameworks and instruments (UNCTAD, 2015). Furthermore, aligning AMS legislation with the two international instruments will facilitate harmonization of consumer protection legislation and foster consumer confidence in e-commerce in the respective jurisdictions (UNCTAD, 2015).

4.2. Develop alternative dispute resolution and redress schemes

ASEAN needs to develop affordable consumer complaints ADR and redress schemes and easy-to-use dispute resolution handling processes through relevant institutions including consumer protection agencies (UNCTAD, 2015). To this end, it is recommended that ASEAN establishes guidelines on ADR and redress schemes with reference to international instruments such as the EU Directive on ADR for Consumer Disputes (2013).

In addition, some of the most effective schemes in use are the self-regulatory mechanisms employed by most e-commerce companies, law enforcement agencies, ombudsmen, and other bodies (UNCTAD, 2015). Further, the use of trustmarks, such as the eConfianza initiative of the Instituto Latinamericano de Comercio Electrónico (eInstituto) is also notable (UNCTAD, 2015). This non-profit body has enacted a code of good practice to guide businesses on how to deal with consumer needs appropriately when designing their online businesses, and provides an ODR tool called Pactanda (UNCTAD, 2015). Last, given that some AMS have not established or do not operate small claims courts, ASEAN needs to establish national small claims courts that consumers can use as one of the reliable methods to seek the proper remedies.

4.3. Develop a two-track online dispute resolution framework

An ODR framework and platform is not a panacea for protecting consumers against new risks arising from cross-border e-commerce transactions, but it can be the best alternative plan to solve consumer disputes considering the drawbacks of existing dispute resolution modes and the high-volume, low-value nature of online transactions.

The author considers it desirable to operate the ODR framework in two tracks: (i) built-in ODR arrangements by online traders, and (ii) an ASEAN ODR platform. According to Colin Rule, a former ODR director of PayPal, the company's first ODR platform was established and started to be used in 2003. By 2012, the platform was already dealing with 60 million disputes annually, compared with around 300,000 cases dealt with by the US court system per year during the same period (UNCTAD, 2016; Rule, 2012). In the ASEAN context, it is also necessary for policy-makers to set the rule to ensure that large numbers of consumer complaints will be amicably solved through online traders' built-in ODR mechanisms. If the ODR scheme is designed to have the remaining disputes solved by the ASEAN ODR platform, it will be efficient enough to avoid a heavy burden for ASEAN.

4.4. Establish an ASEAN regional ODR platform

As noted in Section 3, the EU's ODR platform, which was launched in 2016, is the best model for ASEAN as it seeks to establish a regional ODR platform. The EU platform was built on the legal basis of the EU Directive on ADR for Consumer Disputes (2013).[20] Accordingly, ASEAN needs to enact similar legislation to provide the legal basis to establish its own ODR platform.

It is not an easy task for ASEAN to establish a regional ODR platform, so it is desirable to develop the platform step by step. The author recommends that ASEAN makes guidelines on ODR with reference to the EU Regulation on Online Dispute Resolution for Consumer Disputes (2013) and the UNCITRAL Technical Notes on Online Dispute Resolution (2017), taking into consideration the status of its member states' legal framework, technical infrastructure, and ADR practice. To this end, ASEAN must encourage its member states to establish a national ODR system, and then create an ASEAN ODR network, and finally launch an ASEAN mechanism for cross-border complaints and investigations (ASEAN, 2016).

4.5. *Feasibility study of consumer arbitration in ASEAN*

As seen in Section 3, UNCITRAL has sought to enact uniform rules on ODR, but has failed to reach an agreement between participating countries. The biggest reason for this failure is countries' different positions on the feasibility of consumer arbitration. Considering this fact, ASEAN needs to closely examine the relevant rules of law, such as the Consumer Protection Law, the ADR Law, the Arbitration Law, and the Act on the Regulation of Terms and Conditions, if any, to determine whether they expressly allow a binding pre-arbitration agreement with consumers and ODR procedures.

For example, Korea's Act on the Regulation of Terms and Conditions (Act No. 14141, 2016, Art. 14) provides that 'a clause in terms and conditions concerning filing, etc. of lawsuits shall be null and void where a clause prohibits customers from filing a lawsuit unreasonably disadvantageous to them or requires customers to agree to jurisdiction.' This means that there is a risk that the recognition and enforcement of an arbitration award arising out of a binding pre-arbitration agreement with consumers can be denied by a pertinent national court.

In comparison, Philippine ODR aims to resolve both B2B and B2C e-commerce disputes. Consumer ADR is currently available in the Philippines through the Department of Trade and Industry (DTI). Although there is no explicit provision that mandates or allows the use of ODR, and the ADR Law does not expressly classify the allowable forms of ADR, it was suggested that Section 2 of Republic Act No. 9285 (ADR Law) encourages the active promotion and the use of ADR. The Implementing Rules and Regulations under the Department of Justice Department Circular 98 of the ADR Law embraces schemes akin to mediation and arbitration. Itaralde (2017) believes that ODR should be readily applied in the Philippines given the fact that Philippine ODR abides by the principles and application of ADR by applying online technology into mediation and arbitration.

4.6. *ODR in the e-commerce chapter of the Regional Comprehensive Economic Partnership*

The proposed terms of reference of the RCEP's Working Group on E-Commerce in the Regional Comprehensive Economic Partnership (RCEP) negotiation includes online consumer protection to create a conducive environment for e-commerce. It will be highly recommended to include an ODR framework in the RCEP's e-commerce chapter that reflects ASEAN's opinions on consumer protection given that it is closer to the position of consumers than that of the big online traders. ASEAN can also take this chance to foster the establishment of its regional ODR network, and the economic growth to be derived from the integration of the e-commerce marketplace in the Asia-Pacific region.

4.7. International financial and technical cooperation

Establishing a regional ODR platform inevitably requires financial and technical resources. ASEAN cannot be expected to implement the task on its own. Accordingly, it is desirable for ASEAN to use public-private partnerships in their region or seek financial and technical assistance from international organizations such as UNCITRAL, UNCTAD, the World Bank, and the Asia Development Bank, as well as bilateral official development assistance agencies including the Korea International Cooperation Agency and the Japan International Cooperation Agency.

Given the fact that UNCITRAL has recently enacted Technical Notes on Online Dispute Resolution and located the UNCITRAL Regional Centre for Asia and the Pacific ('the Regional Centre') in Incheon, Korea, the Regional Centre could be the most qualified organization to assist in establishing the regional ODR platform for ASEAN. If the Regional Centre becomes involved in the project, it would be desirable to collaborate with the Korea International Cooperation Agency, the Ministry of Justice of Korea, the Korean Commercial Arbitration Board, the Korea Consumer Agency, and the Korea Internet & Security Agency to successfully carry it out.

4.8. Enhance consumer and business awareness

ASEAN's consumers and businesses need to be aware of the laws, redress, and dispute resolution schemes of the evolving legal environment for e-commerce, as well as the differences between jurisdictions. Greater awareness is particularly important to build confidence in cross-border e-commerce. National and regional radio and TV campaigns can be a key element of awareness-raising strategies about online consumer protection (UNCTAD, 2015). Training and education by industry associations or consumer protection agencies on consumer rights and the use of consumer dispute resolution modes, especially the ODR platform, can also help build confidence in the e-commerce marketplace in ASEAN.

5. Conclusion

How effectively an ODR platform will be established and implemented in ASEAN will depend on the confluence of people, process, and platform (Itaralde, 2017). This will require that (i) clear regulations, including in the areas of consumer protection laws and ADR laws, including arbitration laws, are established and harmonized among ASEAN countries and aligned with international legal instruments; (ii) a user-friendly platform is available; (iii) Internet connection stability and speed are upgraded; (iv) personnel are well-trained to use the procedure; and (v) the public is educated and made aware of the availability of this remedy (Itaralde, 2017). To this end, and bearing in mind the status of legislation and ADR frameworks summarized in Annex 5.1, the author recommends that ASEAN:

i   develops ADR and redress schemes with reference to international instruments such as the EU Directive on ADR for Consumer Disputes (2013);
ii   develops a two-track ODR framework with (a) built-in ODR arrangements by online traders, and (b) an ASEAN ODR platform;
iii   seeks financial and technical assistance from international organizations, including the UNCITRAL Regional Centre;
iv   utilizes the RCEP by including ODR in the e-commerce chapter to foster the establishment of its regional ODR network and platform;
v   enhances consumer awareness and conducts campaigns for this purpose; and
vi   carries out research on the availability of consumer arbitration in ASEAN countries to (a) harmonize AMS policies for a binding pre-arbitration agreement with consumers, and (b) hold the consistent position in preparation for further negotiations on cross-border e-commerce ODR schemes in a wider scope, especially in the ASEAN Plus Six framework.

Notes

1 The most common reasons given for not taking action were related to the product price being too low (27 percent), a lack of trust in a satisfactory outcome (23 percent), and the fear that problem resolution would take too long (19 percent).
2 The Asian Development Bank provided the Ministry of Commerce of Cambodia with financial and technical assistance for drafting the law (Redfearn, 2017).
3 According to the Australian Government Aid Program (2011b), 'The use of arbitration in the *administrative type ADR* such as in the labor, environment and consumer protection dispute settlement are also prescribed in the Law No. 30/1999' (emphasis added), but the author could not find any provision on that point. Rather, the author could find the provision setting forth 'Only disputes of a commercial nature, or those concerning rights which, under the law and regulations, fall within the full legal authority of the disputing parities, may be settled through arbitration' in Art. 5(1) of the Act.
4 The National Consumer Complaints Centre is an independent ADR institution that handles national and cross-border complaints of not more than RM15,000 without any charge. Claims exceeding this amount are referred to the Tribunal for Consumer Claims.
5 The Financial Mediation Bureau is an independent institution set up to help resolve disputes between consumers and their financial service providers that are members of the bureau.
6 The Banking Mediation Bureau was established in 1996 under the Companies Act (1965) to resolve disputes between consumers and commercial banks, finance companies or merchant banks. Its services are provided free of charge to customers of these bodies and it handles claims involving monetary losses of up to RM25,000.
7 The Malaysian Mediation Centre was established under the auspices of the Bar Council to promote mediation as a means of ADR and provide a proper avenue for successful dispute resolutions.

8 For further information, please refer to the Community Mediation Centre's web-page: www.mlaw.gov.sg/content/cmc/en.html (accessed June 28, 2017).
9 For further information, please refer to Singapore International arbitration Cen-tre's webpage: www.siac.org.sg/ (accessed June 28, 2017).
10 For further information, please refer to Thai Arbitration Institute's webpage: www.adro.coj.go.th/ (accessed June 29, 2017).
11 For example, the Act on the Regulation of Terms and Conditions (Act No. 14141, 2016, Art. 14) of the Republic of Korea (henceforth Korea) provides that a clause in terms and conditions concerning filing, etc. of lawsuits shall be null and void where a clause that prohibits customers from filing a lawsuit is unreason-ably disadvantageous to them or requires customers to agree to jurisdiction. In this regard, there is a risk that arbitration also can be prohibited if the arbitration clause in an adhesive consumer contract is against the stated provision.
12 The European Consumer Centres Network is a network of 30 offices in the 28 EU member states, Norway, and Iceland. The centres are cofinanced by the European Commission and national governments as part of the European policy to help every citizen in Europe to take advantage of the single market. The objective of the network is to provide free help and advice to consumers on their cross-border purchases, whether online or on the spot within these 30 countries. See http://ec.europa.eu/consumers/solving_consumer_disputes/non-judicial_redress/ecc-net/index_en.htm
13 FIN-NET is a network of national organizations responsible for settling consum-ers' complaints in the area of financial services out of court. The network covers the countries of the European Economic Area including the EU, Iceland, Liech-tenstein, and Norway. The network was set up by the European Commission in 2001 to promote cooperation among national ombudsmen in financial services to provide consumers with easy access to ADR procedures in cross-border disputes about provision of financial services. See https://ec.europa.eu/info/business-economy-euro/banking-and-finance/consumer-finance-and-payments/consumer-financial-services/financial-dispute-resolution-network-fin-net_en
14 Information in this subsection is derived from the EU ODR platform webpage. https://ec.europa.eu/consumers/odr/main/?event=main.home.show (accessed July 3, 2017).
15 However, in Iceland, consumers are still not able to use this site to resolve their disputes with traders directly. They need to choose a dispute resolution body to handle their complaints by mutual consent.
16 This would mean that parties to the e-commerce transaction must make a subse-quent arbitration agreement after the facilitated settlement fails if one party to the transaction is from a state specified in the annex to the instrument.
17 If the relevant law in their countries does not allow consumer arbitration, the award may not be recognized or enforced by a national court in the other party's state, even if a party had won the prevailing arbitration award.
18 There was also criticism of the list approach suggested by the US, including the prac-tical question of who would bear the burden of updating the list and ODR bodies.
19 Instead, Article 45 of the Technical Notes provides that it is desirable that an ODR administrator or neutral adjudicator informs the parties of the nature of the final stage and of the form – mostly litigation or arbitration – it might take.
20 Article 11 of the Directive provides that 'Given the increasing importance of online commerce and in particular cross-border trade as a pillar of Union eco-nomic activity, properly functioning ADR infrastructure for consumer disputes and *a properly integrated online dispute resolution (ODR) framework for consumer disputes* arising from online transactions are necessary in order to achieve the Single Market Act's aim of boosting citizens' confidence in the internal market' (emphasis added).

Bibliography

ASEAN (2016), 'The ASEAN Strategic Action Plan for Consumer Protection (ASAPCP) 2016–2025: Meeting the Challenges of a People-Centered ASEAN Beyond 2015'. Available at http://asean.org/storage/2012/05/ASAPCP-UPLOADING-11Nov16-Final.pdf

Australian Government Aid Program (2011a), 'Roadmapping Capacity Building Needs in Consumer Protection in ASEAN (Country Report: Brunei Darussalam)'. Available at www.asean.org/wp-content/uploads/images/2015/february/Consumer_protections_information/BRUNEI-FINAL%20REPORT-rev%2018Jun14.pdf

Australian Government Aid Program (2011b), 'Roadmapping Capacity Building Needs in Consumer Protection in ASEAN (Country Report: Indonesia)'. Available at www.aseanconsumer.org/accp/download/INDONESIA%20FINAL%20REPORT%20-%2025Feb2011.pdf

Australian Government Aid Program (2011c), 'Roadmapping Capacity Building Needs in Consumer Protection in ASEAN (Country Report: Malaysia)'. Available at www.asean.org/wp-content/uploads/images/2015/february/Consumer_protections_information/MALAYSIA%20FINAL%20REPORT%20-%20rev%204Aug14.pdf

Australian Government Aid Program (2011d), 'Roadmapping Capacity Building Needs in Consumer Protection in ASEAN (Country Report: Philippines)'. Available at www.asean.org/storage/images/2015/february/Consumer_protections_information/PHILIPPINES%20FINAL%20REPORT%20-%20rev%2024Jun14.pdf

Australian Government Aid Program (2011e), 'Roadmapping Capacity Building Needs in Consumer Protection in ASEAN (Country Report: Singapore)'. Available at www.asean.org/storage/images/2015/february/Consumer_protections_information/SINGAPORE%20FINAL%20REPORT%20-%20rev%207Jul14.pdf

Australian Government Aid Program (2011f), 'Roadmapping Capacity Building Needs in Consumer Protection in ASEAN (Country Report: Thailand)'. Available at www.asean.org/storage/images/2015/february/Consumer_protections_information/THAILAND-FINAL%20REPORT-%20rev%2023May14.pdf

Australian Government Aid Program (2011g), 'Roadmapping Capacity Building Needs in Consumer Protection in ASEAN (Country Report: Vietnam)'. Available at www.asean.org/storage/images/2015/february/Consumer_protections_information/VIETNAM%20FINAL%20REPORT%20-%20rev%2023May14.pdf

Australian Government Aid Program (2011h), 'Roadmapping Capacity Building Needs in Consumer Protection in ASEAN (Country Report: Cambodia)'. Available at www.asean.org/wp-content/uploads/images/2015/february/Consumer_protections_information/CAMBODIA%20FINAL%20REPORT%20-%20rev%2020Jun14.pdf

Australian Government Aid Program (2011i), 'ASEAN Consumer Protection: Essential Actions Towards a Single Market'. Available at http://aadcp2.org/wp-content/uploads/CPcapbldg_plcbrief.pdf

Bilaterlas.org (2016), 'RCEP – Draft E-Commerce Chapter Terms of Reference', www.bilaterals.org/rcep-draft-e-commerce-chapter?lang=en (accessed 14 July 2017)

Bourlier, A. and G. Gomez (2016), 'Strategies for Expanding into Emerging Markets with E-Commerce, Euromonitor International'. Available at http://unctad.org/meetings/en/Contribution/dtl-eWeek2017c08-euromonitor_en.pdf

Cupido, R. (2016), 'The Growth of E-Commerce and Online Dispute Resolution in Developing Nations: An Analysis', *International Journal of Social, Behavioral, Education, Economic, Business and Industrial Engineering*, 10(10): 3354–3357.

Del Duca, L., C. Rule and Z. Loebl (2012), 'Facilitating Expansion of Cross-Border E-Commerce – Developing a Global Online Dispute Resolution System', *Penn State Journal of Law and International Affairs*, 59: 62–63.

EU (2013a), 'Directive 2013/11/EU of the European Parliament and of the Council of 21 May 2013 on Alternative Dispute Resolution for Consumer Disputes and Amending Regulation (EC) No 2006/2004 and Directive 2009/22/EC'. Available at http://eur-lex.europa.eu/legal-content/EN/TXT/PDF/?uri=CELEX:32013L0011&from=EN

EU (2013b), 'Regulation (EU) No 524/2013 of the European Parliament and of the Council of 21 May 2013 on Online Dispute Resolution for Consumer Disputes and Amending Regulation (EC) No 2006/2004 and Directive 2009/22/EC'. Available at http://eur-lex.europa.eu/legal-content/EN/TXT/PDF/?uri=CELEX:32013R0524&from=EN

European Commission (1998), 'Commission Recommendation of 30 March 1998 on the Principles Applicable to the Bodies Responsible for the Out-of-Court Settlement of Consumer Disputes (98/257/EC)'. Available at http://eur-lex.europa.eu/legal-content/EN/TXT/PDF/?uri=CELEX:31998H0257&from=EN

European Commission (2001), 'Commission Recommendation of 4 April 2001 on the Principles for Out-of-Court Bodies Involved in the Consensual Resolution of Consumer (ADR 2001/310/EC)'. Available at www.synigoroskatanaloti.gr/docs/Rec-EC-2001-310.pdf

European Commission (2010), 'A Digital Agenda for Europe'. Available at www.kowi.de/Portaldata/2/Resources/fp/2010-com-digital-agenda.pdf

European Commission (2011), 'Communication from the European Commission to the European Parliament "Single Market Act" (206)'. Available at http://eur-lex.europa.eu/legal-content/EN/TXT/PDF/?uri=CELEX:52011DC0206&from=EN

European Commission (2015), 'Provision of Two Online Consumer Surveys as Supported and Evidence Base to a Commission Study: Identifying the Main Cross-Border Obstacles to the Digital Single Market and Where They Matter Most'. Available at http://ec.europa.eu/consumers/consumer_evidence/market_studies/obstacles_dsm/docs/21.09_dsm_final_report.pdf

European Commission (2017), *Buying Online and Solving Disputes Online: 24,000 Consumers Used New European Platform in First Year*. Brussels: European Commission. Available at http://europa.eu/rapid/press-release_IP-17-727_en.htm

Government of Brunei Darussalam (2011), 'Consumer Protection (Fair Trading) Order'. Available at www.depd.gov.bn/DEPD%20Documents%20Library/KH/CPFTO/s066Optout.pdf

Government of Indonesia (1999), 'Indonesian Arbitration and Alternative Dispute Resolution Act No. 30'. Available at www.aseanconsumer.org/accp/download/INDONESIA%20FINAL%20REPORT%20-%2025Feb2011.pdf

Government of Lao PDR (2010), 'Law on Consumer Protection No. 2'. Available at www.aseanconsumer.org/accp/download/Lao/Law%20on%20Consumer%20Protection%20-%20English.pdf

Government of Malaysia (1999), 'Malaysian Consumer Protection Act No. 599'. Available at https://mystandard.kpdnkk.gov.my/mystandard_portal2014/document/akta_perlindunganpengguna1999.pdf

Government of Myanmar (2014), 'Consumer Protection Law No. 10, Arts. 4–5, Art. 16'. Available at www.dica.gov.mm/sites/dica.gov.mm/files/document-files/related_law_eng_1.pdf

Government of Thailand, Office of the Consumer Protection Board (1979), 'Consumer Protection Act, B.E. 2522'. Available at www.ocpb.go.th/ewtadmin/ewt/ocpb_eng/ewt_dl_link.php?nid=1

Government of Viet Nam (2010), 'Vietnamese Law on Protection of Consumer Rights No. 59/2010/QH12'. Available at moj.gov.vn/vbpq/en/lists/vn%20bn%20php%20lut/view_detail.aspx?itemid=10489

Itaralde, M.D. (2017), *Sustaining Trust and Fairness in E-Commerce with Online Dispute Resolution* (Unpublished thesis). Manila: Far Eastern University and De La Salle University.

Nam, Y.S. and M.S. Yun (2016), 'Main Contents and Implications of Technical Notes on Online Dispute Resolution in UN', *Chonbuk Law Review*, 49: 441–471.

OECD (2000), *Guidelines for Consumer Protection in the Context of E-Commerce*. Paris: OECD.

OECD (2007), *Recommendation on Consumer Resolution and Redress*. Paris: OECD.

OECD (2016), *Consumer Protection in E-Commerce: OECD Recommendation*. Paris: OECD.

Redfearn, N. (2017), 'New Cambodian Consumer Protection Law', *Rouse (Jakarta)*, 13 June. Available at www.rouse.com/magazine/news/new-cambodian-consumer-protection-law/

Republic of Indonesia (1999), 'Indonesian Consumer Protection Act No. 8'. Available at www.wipo.int/edocs/lexdocs/laws/en/id/id050en.pdf

Republic of the Philippines (1953), 'Republic Act No. 876: The Arbitration Act of the Philippines (1953)'. Available at www.lawphil.net/statutes/repacts/ra1953/ra_876_1953.html

Republic of the Philippines (1991), 'Republic Act No. 7394: The Consumer Act of the Philippines (1992)'. Available at www.fda.gov.ph/issuances/305-others/others-republic-act/29036-republic-act-no-7394

Republic of the Philippines (2009), 'Implementing the Rules and Regulations of the Alternative Dispute Resolution Act of 2004 (Section 52 of Republic Act 9285)'. Available at www.doj.gov.ph/files/irr-of-adr.pdf

Republic of the Philippines, Special Rules on ADR (2009), 'Supreme Court En Banc Resolution No. AM-07–11–08-SC, Special Rules on Alternative Dispute Resolution'. Available at www.lawphil.net/courts/supreme/am/am_07-11-08-sc_2009.html

Republic of Singapore, Law Revision Commission (2009), 'Consumer Protection (Fair Trading) Act (2009)'. Available at http://statutes.agc.gov.sg/aol/download/0/0/pdf/binaryFile/pdfFile.pdf?CompId:7c0af8d9-431a-47b9-8620-684c1682d692

Rule, C. (2012), 'Quantifying the Economic Benefits of Effective Redress: Large E-commerce Data Sets and the Cost-Benefit Case for Investing in Dispute Resolution', *University of Arkansas at Little Rock Law Review*, 34(4): 767–777.

Son, H. (2013), 'Proposals for New Regulations Concerning Consumer ADR and ODR and their Implications in the EU', *Journal of Arbitration Studies*, 23(1): 107–131.

Suominen, K. (2017), 'Private Sector Priorities for Ecommerce Development', Paper presented at *the UNCTAD's E-Commerce Week 2017: Towards Inclusive E-Commerce*. Geneva. Available at http://unctad.org/en/conferences/e-week2017/Pages/MeetingDetails.aspx?meetingid=1311

UNCITRAL (2015), 'Submission by Colombia and the United States of America of Working Group (Online Dispute Resolution) on the Work of Its Thirty-Second Session', Vienna, 30 November – 4 December, A/CN.9/WG./XXX/CRP.3. Available at www.uncitral.org/pdf/english/workinggroups/wg_3/crp3-e.pdf

UNCITRAL (2016), 'Report of Working Group III (Online Dispute Resolution) on the Work of its Thirty-Third Session', A/CN.P/868.2. Available at https://documents-dds-ny.un.org/doc/UNDOC/GEN/V16/014/73/PDF/V1601473.pdf?OpenElement

UNCITRAL (2017), *UNCITRAL Technical Notes on Online Dispute Resolution*. Vienna: United Nations.

United Nations Conference on Trade and Development (UNCTAD) (2015), *Information Economy Report 2015: Unlocking the Potential of E-Commerce for Developing Countries*. Geneva: UNCTAD.

United Nations Conference on Trade and Development (UNCTAD) (2016), *Manual on Consumer Protection*. Geneva: UNCTAD.

Yun, M.S. (2015), 'Trends in the Discussions about the ODR Procedure Rules of UNCITRAL – Focused on the Discussion in the 30th & 31st Session of Working Group', *Chung-Ang Journal of Legal Studies*, 39(2): 43–70.

Yun, M.S. (2016), *A Study on Technical Notes on Online Dispute Resolution of UNCITRAL*. Eumseong: Korea Consumer Agency.

Annex 5.1

Table 5A.1 Comparison of Consumer Redress and ADR Schemes in AMS

Country	Consumer Protection Act	Provisions on Alternative Dispute Resolution	Provisions on Small Claims Tribunal	Main Concerned Ministry	Agencies Handling Consumer Disputes
Brunei Darussalam	Consumer Protection (Fair Trading) Order (2011)	(None)	Cases not exceeding B$10,000 (Art. 7)	Department of Economic Planning and Development	1. Small Claims Tribunal 2. Department of Electrical Services 3. Department of Water Services 4. The Authority for Info-communications Technology Industry of Brunei Darussalam
Cambodia	(Draft in progress)	(None)	(None)	Ministry of Commerce	Cambodia Import – Export Inspection and Fraud Repression Directorate-General
Indonesia	Indonesian Consumer Protection Act No.8 (1999); Indonesian Arbitration and Alternative Dispute Resolution Act No. 30	Mediation or Arbitration or Conciliation (Art. 52)	(None)	Ministry of Trade and Industry	1. National Consumer Protection Agency 2. Consumer Dispute Settlement Body 3. Indonesian Institute Conflict Transformation 4. National Mediation Centre 5. YLKI Indonesia 6. Telecommunication Regulatory Authority 7. Sub Directorate of Consumer Protection 8. Directorate of Electricity 9. Ministry of Energy and Mineral

Country	Law	Dispute Resolution	Monetary Threshold	Ministry/Department	Agencies
Lao PDR	Law on Consumer Protection No. 2 (2010)	1. Compromise (Arts. 38–39) 2. Mediation (Arts. 40–47) 3. Administrative Mean (Arts. 48–52) 4. Arbitration or Court (Arts. 53–55)	(None)	Ministry of Industry and Commerce	1. Ministry of Industry and Commerce 2. Ministry of Health 3. Ministry of Agriculture and Forest 4. Ministry of Science and Technology 5. Consumer Protection Association
Malaysia	Malaysian Consumer Protection Act No. 599 (1999)	(None)	Case not exceeding RM25,000 (Art. 85)	Ministry of Domestic Trade, Cooperatives and Consumerism	1. National Consumer Advisory Council 2. National Consumer Complaints Centre 3. Financial Mediation Bureau, Banking Mediation Bureau 4. Mediation Bureau 5. Insurance Mediation Bureau 6. Malaysian Mediation Centre 7. Tribunal for Consumer Claims 8. Federation of Malaysian Consumers Association
Myanmar	Consumer Protection Law No. 10 (2014)	(None)	(None)	Ministry of Commerce	Consumer Protection Central Committee
Philippines	Republic Act No. 7394 – The Consumer Act (1992); Implementing the Rules and Regulations of the Alternative Dispute Resolution Act of 2004	1. The concerned Department Secretaries shall appoint qualified consumer arbitration officers not more than ten per province (Art. 160) 2. Consumer arbitration officers have exclusive jurisdiction to mediate, conciliate, hear, and adjudicate all consumer complaints (Art. 162)	(None)	Department of Trade and Industry	1. National Consumer Affairs Council 2. DTI's Fair Trade Enforcement Bureau under Consumer Protection Group 3. DTI's Consumer Welfare Desks for consumers residing outside Metro Manila

(Continued)

Table 5A.1 Continued

Country	Consumer Protection Act	Provisions on Alternative Dispute Resolution	Provisions on Small Claims Tribunal	Main Concerned Ministry	Agencies Handling Consumer Disputes
Singapore	Consumer Protection (Fair Trading) Act (2009)	(None)	Case not exceeding S$30,000 (Arts. 6–7)	Monetary Authority of Singapore	1. Consumer Association of Singapore 2. Financial Institution Disputes Resolution Centre 3. Singapore Mediation Centre 4. Small Claims Tribunal 5. Monetary Authority of Singapore
Thailand	Consumer Protection Act, B.E. 2522 (1979)	(None)	(None)	Prime Minister (Sec. 8)	1. Consumer Protection Board 2. CPB's ad hoc committees 3. Arbitration Office, Ministry of Justice (now Thai Arbitration Institute)
Viet Nam	Law on Protection of Consumer Rights No. 59/2010/QH12 (2010)	1. Types of Dispute Settlement (Art. 30) 2. Negotiation (Arts. 31–32) 3. Mediation (Arts. 33–37) 4. Arbitration (Arts. 38–40)[a] 5. Courts (Arts. 41–46)	(None)	Ministry of Industry and Trade	1. Ministry of Trade and Industry's Viet Nam Competition Authority 2. Consumers Complaint Bureau (run by Viet Nam Standards and Consumers Association)

Sources: AMS National Consumer Protection Laws; Australian Government Aid Program (2011a, 2011b, 2011c, 2011d, 2011e, 2011f, 2011g, 2011h).

Note:
[a] Article 38 of the Viet Nam's Law on Protection of Consumer Rights provides that '*a goods and service trader, before concluding a contract, shall notify a consumer of the arbitration term which is acceptable to the consumers*' and where the trader includes the arbitration term in its model contract or general transaction conditions, and '*an individual consumer may select another mode for settlement*' when a dispute arises (emphasis added).

Part III
Inclusive growth

6 Indonesia's preparation for the digital economy and e-commerce

Infrastructure, regulatory, and policy development

Kalamullah Ramli

1. Introduction

Southeast Asia has 260 million Internet users, 70 percent of whom are aged under 40, and this is projected to increase to 480 million by 2020 (Google-Temasek, 2017). The region's Internet economy is forecast to grow sixfold from US$31 billion in 2015 to US$197 billion in 2025 (Russell, 2016).

As the fourth largest population in the world, Indonesia is the most promising market in Southeast Asia. Its Internet penetration continues to grow despite the digital divide.[1] Indonesia has 132.7 million Internet users, of whom 72.8 percent are aged 10–44 years, up from 88.1 million in 2014 (APJII, 2016). According to the same report, 98.6 percent of users recognize that the Internet is a platform to buy and sell products or services, and 63.5 percent of them have performed online transactions.

The Indonesian electronic commerce (e-commerce) industry offers a booming market for online shopping and could become one of the drivers of the national economy by 2020. Indonesia's e-commerce market revenue was US$9.54 billion in 2018 (Statista, 2018). At the 2016 ASEAN-US (Association of Southeast Asian Nations-United States) summit, President Joko Widodo stated his vision of Indonesia as the 'Digital Energy of Asia', targeting the creation of 1,000 technopreneurs[2] with a business valuation of US$10 billion, to reach US$130 billion by 2020. The government of Indonesia announced the National E-commerce Roadmap as one of its national economy packages in November 2016 (Agarwal, 2017).

This chapter is organized as follows. Section 2 describes the development of infrastructure, while section 3 covers the legal and regulatory landscape, including the latest presidential policy direction. Section 4 shows the industry and market response to the government's policy initiatives. Section 5 concludes the report by identifying issues that could hinder Indonesia's ambition to become the largest e-commerce market in the region.

2. Infrastructure development

Almost all countries in the world, including Indonesia, encourage the development of a broadband ecosystem to improve the use of ICT in everyday life. The government has various roles in maximizing the economic benefits of broadband. It helps create the macroeconomic framework conditions for a favourable innovation and investment climate; and plays an important role as a regulator, standard maker, and infrastructure development facilitator, as well as protector of public interests.

ICT and broadband create new ways for companies and people to exploit their creativity and innovation, and open up opportunities for generating new sources of revenue. Broadband enables people to start small businesses from home, contributing to a more dynamic entrepreneurial business sector.

2.1. Indonesia broadband plan

Presidential Decree No. 96 year 2014 on the Indonesia Broadband Plan (IBP, *Rencana Pitalebar Indonesia*) introduced a strategic plan to develop broadband across the archipelago by 2019 (Secretary of the Cabinet, 2014). ICT connectivity is considered meta-infrastructure to maintain the nation's competitive edge and provides significant impetus for a digital economy.

According to the IBP, the government is committed to a neutral technology policy. Broadband is developed using an integrated broadband ecosystem approach – from infrastructure, services, content and national manufacturing, to capacity building. The IBP also highlights the distribution of responsibility between government, private, and community roles. The access target and distribution of tasks is shown in Table 6.1.

The plan has two main agendas, expected to be realized in 2019: (i) enhancement of the Internet's speed and coverage, and (ii) a reduction in service fees.

The IBP targets building broadband infrastructure to reach up to 30 percent of the total population and up to 71 percent of households in urban areas, with a maximum speed of 20 megabits per second (Mbps). For rural areas, the plan aims to reach up to 6 percent of the population and 49 percent of households, with a maximum speed of 10 Mbps. This is depicted in Table 6.2.

Table 6.1 Targets and Tasks in Indonesian Broadband Plan

Year	2013	2014	2015	2016	2017
Fixed	45%	55%	75%	85%	100%
Mobile Broadband	70%	80%	90%	100%	100%
Ministry of Communication and Information Technology	To create regulation for broadband dissemination	To encourage operators to expand networks			
Ministry of Finance	Incentive and capital				
Operator	To provide network				
Local Government	To provide Right of Way (RoW)				
People	– Captive market – Supervisory of quality of service				
Vendor	To provide devices and systems				

Source: Tayyiba (2015).

Table 6.2 Indonesian Broadband Plan Target

	2013	2019	
		Urban	Rural
Fixed broadband	15% HH (1Mbps)	71% HH (20Mbps)	49% HH (10Mbps)
Mobile broadband	12% of population (512 Kbps)	100% of population (1 Mbps)	52% of population (1Mbps)
Broadband service price	Max 5% of average monthly income		
Priority sectors	e-government, e-education, e-health, e-logistics, e-procurement		

Source: The Author. With reference to IBP, and Tayyiba (2015).

The government also promotes mobile broadband infrastructure through the IBP. Everyone in urban areas and 52 percent of the population in rural areas is expected to be able to access mobile broadband with a maximum speed of 1 Mbps. The IBP also aims to lower the cost of Internet service to 5 percent of people's income by 2019 to bring it into line with their willingness to pay for good quality service.

Regulation encourages fair competition among mobile broadband operators and endorses consolidation and reposition to reduce the currently excessive numbers of operators in the field. Budgeted at Rp278 trillion (around US$18.5 billion), the IBP consists of six flagship programs: (i) Palapa Ring project (expansion and financing), (ii) E-government Networks and Data Centre, (iii) Passive Infrastructure and Shared Ducts, (iv) Rural Wireless Terrestrial Broadband, (v) Universal Service Obligation Reform, and (vi) National Digital Literacy. These six flagship programs focus on developing infrastructure, including the establishment of optical fibre in cities and districts, the improvement of the human resource capacity of the national information technology industry, and the establishment of coordinated data centres and private virtual networks for government needs, as well as the institutional and regulatory reforms needed to maximize the program benefits.

2.2. Palapa Ring project

ICT should be developed to allow nations and communities to accelerate the improvement of their competitiveness with a view to promoting economic growth. To do this, it is crucial to encourage business-to-business processes in the private sector to open and interconnect their networks, which in turn would promote the accessibility of local ICT applications to the world.

Global connectivity starts from national people-to-people connectivity. In Indonesia, the Presidential Masterplan for Acceleration and Expansion of Indonesia's Economic Development, abbreviated as MP3EI in Bahasa, acknowledges people-to-people connectivity (Indonesia Investments, 2012). This is reflected in the IBP, which involves all stakeholders including state and private companies, universities, central government, and local governments.

The government of Indonesia, through the Ministry of Communication and Information Technology, is building a nationwide broadband infrastructure program called the Palapa Ring. This program is a network of 35,280 kilometres (km) of submarine fibre-optic cable and 21,807 km of land fibre-optic cable to connect all regencies[3] in Indonesia.

Indonesia has 514 regencies. PT Telkom Indonesia, the state-owned telecommunications company, is committed to building fibre-optic infrastructure in 457 regencies (88.9 percent of all regencies). These regencies are commercially viable. The government will develop the remaining 57 regencies, which are not commercially viable.

The development of the optical backbone through the Palapa Ring project is divided into three regions: Palapa Ring West, Palapa Ring Central, and Palapa Ring East. These will cover the western, central, and western parts of Indonesia. Figure 6.1 illustrates such division.

Palapa Ring West will connect Bengkalis, Meranti, Natuna, Lingga, and Anambas regencies in the provinces of Riau and Riau Islands, using 2,000 km of fibre-optic cable. Palapa Ring Central, with a total cable length of 2,700 km, covers Kalimantan, Sulawesi, and North Maluku. With a cable length of 6,300 km, Palapa Ring East travels across East Nusa Tenggara, West Papua, and Papua provinces.

In January 2016, the government announced the winning bids for the western and central sections of the Palapa Ring project. The Palapa Ring is positive for the development of Indonesia's telecommunications industry, because a fibre-optic-based Internet could cost 30 times less than a satellite network. This will help

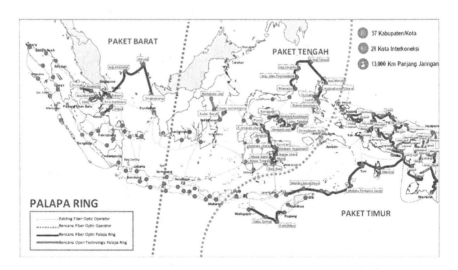

Figure 6.1 Palapa Ring Project Development Plan

to reduce the bandwidth price in remote areas, which may help the Internet to achieve critical mass there. The winning bid for Palapa Ring East was announced later, in July 2016.

The Palapa Ring project was auctioned based on the least-cost subsidy scheme, whereby the winner is the consortium requiring the least amount of government subsidy to build the network. They must also comply with the tight deadline for completion by the end of 2018, to achieve the targets laid out in the IBP.

2.3. Spectrum 'refarming' strategy

'Refarming' is the rearrangement of previously used frequency, to make space for the implementation of new technologies and to optimize its use. The government aims to develop spectrum policy and regulation that will enable investment, innovation, and deployment of wireless communications for all. This would include reformatting of the licencing regime, spectrum reallocation through refarming, auctions, and encouraging shared spectrum. The final target for this policy is to obtain digital dividends that will be used to provide specific spectrum allocation for public protection and disaster recovery communication links and for other means of broadband communications. The strategy for spectrum refarming is shown in Table 6.3.

In November 2015, Indonesia completed assigning or refarming, which permits for high-speed cellular data transmissions and paves the way for the nationwide rollout of 4G Long-Term Evolution (LTE) services. The refarming is for the 1,800-megahertz (MHz) frequency, previously used for the now-obsolete 2G network. Carriers began offering 4G services on the 1,800 MHz band in selected cities in July 2015, migrating from the crowded 900 MHz band, and are upgrading infrastructure to expand coverage nationwide.

LTE is way forwards for high-speed cellular communications. With LTE, anything on the Internet can be performed using a mobile phone as if it were a fixed broadband line. This mobile technology has created an environment in which more innovation can be developed and the growing demand for future applications, as well as digital economic activities can be supported.

Table 6.3 Spectrum Refarming in the Context of Indonesia Broadband Plan

Term	Targets
Short Term	Refarming 450 MHz, 850 MHz, 900 MHz, 1,800 MHz, 2.1 GHz and 2.3 GHz
Medium Term	Digital dividend 700 MHz, extended 850 MHz (trunking band), 2.6 GHz, 3.5 GHz, and other bands identified by ITU IMT band
Unlicensed (Class Licensed) Band	2.4 GHz, 5.1 GHz, 5.8 GHz, 26 GHz, 60 GHz, for traffic offloading

Source: Ministry of Communication and Information Technology (2013).

The remaining task of the government is to reallocate 700 MHz of frequency band which analogue TV transmission currently occupies. Allocating the 700 MHz band for LTE offers many advantages, such as a reduction in the number of towers because of wide spectrum coverage, and saves the cost of LTE network deployment and maintenance. In addition, countries in Asia are committed to the Asia Pacific Telecommunity 700 MHz band for LTE technology, including Brunei Darussalam, China, Japan, Indonesia, Korea, Malaysia, Papua New Guinea, Singapore, Taiwan, and Tonga (Vanston, 2013).

3. Legal and regulatory progress

In Indonesia's legal system, a law is a set of rules established by the House of Representatives with the joint approval of the president. A government regulation is set of rules conveyed by the government to implement the law. A presidential decree refers to the rules set by the president to implement the instruction of higher rules or in the conduct of the law. Ministerial decrees and circulation letters are usually formed by a minister to govern more detailed implementation or operational issues of a regulation.

3.1. Three-layer model of Internet regulation

Internet regulation in Indonesia adopts the three-layer governance model: infrastructure, services, and content. Figure 6.2 depicts these layers. ICT infrastructure is a capital-intensive sector that needs heavy regulation to guarantee a return on investment. It usually has few players. The regulation stipulates that

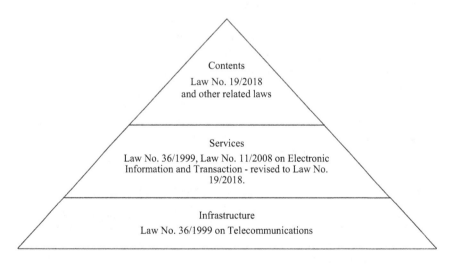

Figure 6.2 Three-Layer Model
Source: The author.

the infrastructure operator should provide open access of its network on a fair, transparent, and non-discriminatory basis to any service or Internet providers that operate above the infrastructure layer.

ICT service providers or Internet operators require mild regulation, with the emphasis on establishing fair competition and giving more options to the public to select their Internet or mobile operator based on the quality of service offered. The number of players is generally greater than that of infrastructure providers.

Content is the most lightly regulated layer, to create a low barrier to entry for new technopreneurs to offer their applications or content. Competition determines the survival of the most innovative content providers, but they must obey content-related laws and regulations.

In Indonesia, Law No. 36/1999 on Telecommunications primarily governs the first layer (infrastructure). This stipulates that the government is responsible for spectrum allocation, industry management (including principle and operational licences, related to industry management), and strategic national standards.

The second layer is jointly regulated by Law No. 36/1999 and Law No. 11/2008 on Electronic Information and Transactions (*Informasi dan Transaksi Elektronik*, ITE). A crucial issue of the ITE law is Article 27 (3), which allegedly impairs the freedom of speech and expression. In October 2016, the House of Representatives passed and enacted an amendment to the law known as the Revision of Electronic Information and Transactions Law No. 19/2016. The amendment includes the obliteration mechanism of electronic information and documents (Article 26), the law interception mechanism (Article 31), and the authorization for the government to block any websites or applications that abuse the law (Article 40 [2a] [2b]).

The content layer is critical, since it is a multisectoral area of interests. The Ministry of Communications and Information Technology (MCIT) is responsible for ICT infrastructure, in addition to issuing licences to operators or providers in the infrastructure and service layers. The e-commerce sector is commonly regulated by three ministries or state bodies: (i) Bank Indonesia, the central bank, which is responsible for regulating technology-based financial transactions; (ii) the Ministry of Trade, which oversees commerce activities; and (iii) the MCIT, which regulates operators' compliance with the related laws and regulations. Applications such as online-based transportation are under the supervision of the Ministry of Transportation in addition to the MCIT.

3.2. *Regulation of applications, content, and electronic transactions*

The amendment to the ITE law in 2016 does not necessarily terminate Government Regulation No. 82/2012 on Electronic System and Transaction Management until a new or revised government regulation is formulated. This government regulation regulates public and non-public electronic transactions and system providers for local and international operators to ensure equal treatment for all.

Three provisions at the Government Regulation No. 82/2012 that are relevant to local and international application and content providers:

i   providers must register their operations with the MCIT;
ii any electronic transactions that take place and system providers that operate in Indonesia must use the '.id' domain address;[4] and
iii public electronic transactions and system providers must place their data centre and disaster management centre in Indonesian territory in the interest of law enforcement and personal data protection (Article 17 [2]).

The current minister of communications and information technology is planning to revise the government regulation that obliges foreign over-the-top (OTT)[5] companies, applications, and content providers to locate their data centres on Indonesia territory[6]

Mobile applications and content delivery via the Internet are growing rapidly. This has provoked concern regarding the lack of regulations governing misuse of personal data protection, content blocking, and taxation of large money flows.

The government is responding to these challenges. MCIT Decree No. 36/2014 on the Registration Procedure for Electronic System Operators regulates public and private electronic transaction and system providers. These include government institutions, state-owned enterprises, independent regulatory bodies, and other public and private institutions or companies which fulfil government duties and/or offer services to the public (Article 4). According to Law No. 25/2009 on Public Services, e-commerce platform providers are considered public service institutions.

MCIT Decree No. 36/2014 stipulates that the taxpayer's registration number is required for registration. Hence, any electronic transactions and system providers (individual or institutions) should be registered taxpayers under Indonesian law.

The MCIT released Circular Letter No. 3/2016 on Internet Content and/or Applications Service Providers in 2016. This states that OTT service providers must:

i   have permanent establishment in Indonesia for taxation purposes, including non-Indonesian companies;
ii use a national payment gateway and Indonesia Internet protocol address;
iii be fully liable for the service they deliver;
iv comply with all applicable laws and regulations in Indonesia, including laws governing anti-monopoly and unfair competition, advertising, trade, film, and broadcasting, consumer protection, intellectual property rights, pornography, and anti-terrorism;
v   make an Indonesian language service available; and
vi provide full access for legal interceptions.

Even though it is not legally binding, it clarifies the regulatory environment for local and global Internet-based applications and content providers. It also reflects the MCIT's position on OTT-related issues in Indonesia. This is important for OTT service providers, since the MCIT has the authority to allow or block the transmission of applications or content in Indonesia.

3.3. Digital economy policy and regulation

In 2016, President Joko Widodo asserted his vision to make Indonesia the 'Digital Energy of Asia'. To achieve this objective, the government established a fast-tracked policy and empowered digital economy driven by small and medium-sized enterprises (SMEs). It also set well-defined and objective-driven plans to achieve rapid digitization of SME market participants by outlining the following milestones:

i   Introducing a strategic plan that is focussed on empowering SMEs and is aimed at encouraging greater participation of SMEs in national economic growth.
ii Developing an e-commerce roadmap that synchronizes strategic initiatives across eight ministries to ensure impactful growth of the technopreneurship sector, destined to reach an estimated US$130 billion in e-commerce transactions in Indonesia by 2020.
iii Establishing friendly foreign direct investment (FDI) policies to attract tech-oriented investment.
iv Facilitating greater access to funding for SMEs and rapid growth of quality start-ups establishments through: (i) subsidized soft loans microcredit for SMEs in digitization, and (ii) reformed venture capital regulations to stimulate greater capital seeding.
v   Providing an attractive and easier exit strategy through strengthening the liquidity of technology-based company listed in the capital market.
vi Adopting pro-innovation policies such as: (i) national agenda to initiate 1,000 digital technopreneurs, and (ii) establishing regulations to protect e-commerce players which store customer data from accidentally disclosing or losing personal information, known globally as safe harbour privacy principles.

The government has introduced a series of economic policy packages since the last quarter of 2015 to improve national industry competitiveness, exports, and investment, and to generate significant economic growth for the country. The economic policy package outlines three main strategies: (i) harmonizing regulation, (ii) simplifying bureaucratic processes, and (iii) ensuring law enforceability. A summary of each economic policy package is shown in Table 6.4.

3.4. Regulatory evolution to support e-commerce

Indonesia is expected to maintain strong economic progress in the coming years. In the first two quarters of 2016, its economic growth was the strongest

Table 6.4 Economic Policy Package, 'To Improve National Industry Competitiveness, Export and Investment to Generate Significant Economic Growth', 2015–2017

Harmonizing Regulations	*Simplifying Bureaucratic Process*	*Ensuring Law Enforceability*
Phase I (9 September 2015) Improving national industry competitiveness *Phase II* (29 September 2015) Easing permit requirement and simplifying export proceeds requirement *Phase III* (7 October 2015) Boosting investment, spurring exports, and maintaining people's purchasing power *Phase IV* (15 October 2015) Simplifying wage formula and expanding loans for small business *Phase V* (22 October 2015) Improving industry and investment climate through tax incentives and deregulation on sharia banking *Phase VI* (5 November 2015) Stimulating economic activities in border areas and facilitating strategic commodities availability *Phase VII* (7 December 2015) Stimulating business activities in labour-intensive industries nationwide through incentives in the form of accelerating land certification process for individuals		*Phase VIII* (21 December 2015) Resolving land acquisition disputes, intensifying domestic oil production, stimulating domestic parts, and aviation industries *Phase IX* (27 January 2016) Accelerating electricity generations, stabilizing meat prices, and improving rural-urban logistics sector *Phase X* (11 February 2016) Revising the Negative Investment List and improving protection for SMEs *Phase XI* (29 March 2016) Stimulating national economy through facilitation of SMEs and industries *Phase XII* (28 April 2016) Improving Indonesia's rank on ease of doing business *Phase XIII* (24 August 2016) Low-cost housing for low-income communities *Phase XIV* (10 November 2016) Roadmap for e-commerce *Phase XV* (15 June 2017) Development of Business and Competitiveness of National Logistics Service Provider

Source: Coordinating Ministry for Economic Affairs (2017).

in Southeast Asia (Asian Development Bank, 2016). During the second quarter of 2016, its gross domestic product increased by 5.18 percent after falling by 4.96 percent in the fourth quarter of 2015. In full-year 2017, the growth Indonesian economy was 5.07 percent year-on-year (Indonesia Investments, 2018). Nevertheless, Indonesia is predicted to increase economic growth to 7 percent by 2025 (Indonesia Investments, 2012).

As Indonesia's e-commerce sector is set to reach US$130 billion in transactions by 2020, a national cybersecurity system is addressing consumer protection and cybersecurity as the foundation for public education on cybercrime and the secure handling of customer data by e-commerce providers. The coordination of regulations as well as persistent monitoring of the initiatives' success are defining factors in achieving targeted amount of transactions.

The government has been drafting the regulation on e-commerce since 2011, led by the Ministry of Trade and supported by several ministries including the MCIT and the Ministry of Finance (Rumata and Sastrosubroto, 2017). Complexity in drafting this government regulation is due to the intersection between multisector interests such as infrastructure, as well as the business process, content, competition environment, investment support, and taxation issues, which require harmonization.

The Ministry of Trade issued Law No. 7/2014 on Trade, which requires the e-commerce service provider to make available relevant data or information, including a detailed description of the product, merchant, payment information, and delivery procedures (Articles 65–66).

The government regulation on e-commerce focuses on transaction issues, such as creating fair trade in the e-commerce ecosystem, as well as establishing customer protection schemes. Other challenges include tax regulations, retained payment, cross-border settlements, and applied sanctions. According to Presidential Regulation No. 44/2016 concerning Lists of Business Fields that are Closed to and Business Fields that are Open with Conditions to Investment, the electronic-based retail marketplace platform, for example, is categorized as business fields that are open under special conditions. FDI for this category should be limited to 49 percent if the investment value is less than Rp100 billion or US$7.5 million; if the investment is greater than that amount, FDI is allowed up to a 100 percent share.

In December 2016, the MCIT initiated Circular Letter No. 5/2016 on the Limitations and Responsibilities of Platform Providers and Merchants who engage in e-commerce while Utilizing User-Generated Content (UGC) Platforms. This circular letter sets out guidelines for e-commerce platforms hosting UGC and for those who upload UGC content. It is part of the safe harbour privacy principles and is intended to foster the growth of local e-commerce players.

According to MCIT Decree No. 36/2014 on the registration procedures of electronic system providers, public electronic transactions and system providers present all the required documents to register their services in Indonesia. These include the registration of taxpayer number, certificate of company registration, certificate of business domicile, and domain name registration.

On 3 August 2017, the President issued Presidential Regulation No. 74/2017 on the Road Map for the National Electronic Commerce System for 2017–2019, which is an important regulation for nurturing the e-commerce industry and known as the 2017–2019 e-commerce roadmap. It aims at coordinating state bodies to support digitally focussed businesses as part of a wider blueprint to transform Indonesia into a digitally focussed economy. Other areas include cooperation with the education sector to ensure a pool of qualified, innovative, entrepreneurial local human resources; and encouragement to the state postal service provider, PT Pos Indonesia, to take on the role of providing a nationwide logistics network for e-commerce deliveries.

To support e-commerce, which has become one of the most promising prospects for Indonesia's economy, the roadmap states eight key strategic priorities:

i   funding schemes to encourage greater investment in digital SMEs and e-commerce start-ups;
ii   easing tax regulations for investors and e-commerce providers;
iii consumer protection;
iv   human resources development;
v   logistics schemes, including the establishment of a national logistics information system;
vi   broadband infrastructure development;
vii cybersecurity regulations, including a national monitoring system for e-commerce transactions and standard procedures for consumer data protection; and
viii an evaluation and monitoring management team to oversee implementation of the roadmap (eight ministries are supporting its implementation).

4. Industry and market response

According to Statista (2018), revenue in Indonesia's e-commerce market reached US$6,963 million in 2017. This is expected to show annual growth (compound annual growth rate [CAGR] 2018–2022) of 13 percent, resulting in a projected market volume of US$15.53 billion in 2022. User penetration was 15.1 percent in 2017, and is expected to reach 21.2 percent in 2021.

According to the Investor Relations Unit of the Republic of Indonesia (2017), Indonesia remains as a top investment destination for 2017 (Figure 6.3).

Following the success of several Indonesian smartphone applications, such as Go-Jek and Traveloka, the latest government policies seek to dismantle hurdles to locally developed smartphone applications moving from concept to the public domain. New smartphone applications are high risk, and new businesses in this arena are often SMEs whose lack of assets makes them unattractive to Indonesia's banking sector, which tends to focus on traditional industries.

The 14th economic policy package mandates the government to play a more active role in supporting digital start-ups, such as distributing subsidized loans and creating business matchmaking fora to connect innovators to venture capital. The crucial component underpinning the success of start-ups in other markets has been the linking of angel investors with nascent start-ups.

Crowdfunding is another avenue to raise the necessary capital for rolling out a new application or digital business. The latest government policies advocate for the state to play an intermediary role between investors and start-up businesses while supporting the development of crowdfunding initiatives.

The following examples of digital start-ups indicate that foreign investors do not undermine Indonesia's potential to become the biggest digital nation in the region. The selected Indonesian unicorn start-ups – unicorn is a title given to a start-up company valued at more than US$1 billion – are among the most

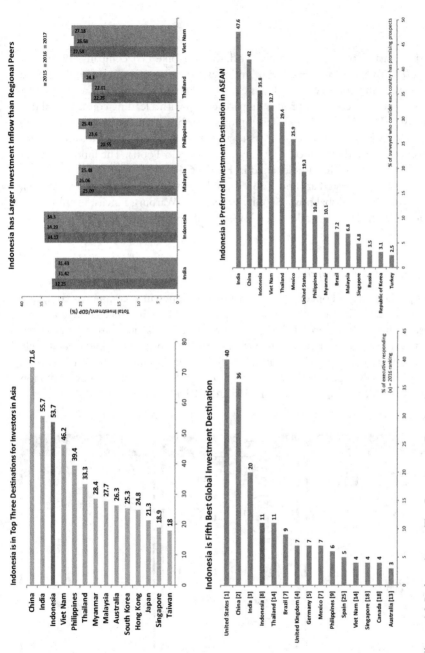

Figure 6.3 Indonesia as a Top Investment Destination

Sources: Investor Relations Unit of the Republic of Indonesia (2017)

promising and notable in the categories of transportation, retail market, and travel and leisure search engine.

4.1. Case study: Go-Jek

Go-Jek started out as a motorcycle ride-hailing bike taxi company. With over 200,000 drivers across 25 cities in Indonesia, it is now the most notable tech company in the country. Go-Jek has expanded its business to Go-Car private car service; and formed a very promising partnership with a leading conventional taxi firm, Blue Bird. Go-Jek is also developing its mobile payment business (Go-Pay) and is innovating to allow customers to access services such as document/packet delivery (Go-Send) and food order and delivery (Go-Food). The innovation services offered by Go-Jek are depicted in Figure 6.4.

Tencent has invested around US$150 million in Go-Jek (Wu and Zhu, 2017). By August 2016, global private equity firms KKR, Warburg Pincus, Farallon, and Capital Group Private Markets had invested US$550 million in Go-Jek (KKR & Co, 2016)

4.2. Case study: Tokopedia

Tokopedia (www.tokopedia.com), a leading Indonesian e-commerce company, is one of Asia's biggest costumer-to-customer (C2C) Internet companies and most promising start-ups. Tokopedia allows individuals and business owners to open and manage their own online stores for free. Founded in 2009, its mobile app has been downloaded at least 10 million times (SimilarWeb, 2017), with a total of 1.3 billion page views per month. Tokopedia also claims to have 1 million registered sellers on its platform (Freischlad, 2016).

Figure 6.4 Go-Jek Innovation and Services

In August 2016, Tokopedia stated that the total number of products sold on the platform increased to 16.5 million per month (Freischlad, 2016). The exponential growth in the period 2013–2016 is shown in Figure 6.5.

Tokopedia announced a US$1.1 billion investment from China's Alibaba Group Holding on 18 August 2017 (Suzuki and Maulia, 2017). Tokopedia's marketplace model is similar to Alibaba's Taobao platform.

4.3. Case study: Traveloka

In October 2015, the International Air Transport Association (IATA) stated that Indonesia can expect an increase of 183 million new passengers by 2034 (Cosseboom, 2015). Indonesia would be one of the five fastest-growing markets for additional passengers per year. This prediction offers a huge opportunity for technology start-ups, particularly travel booking services.

Traveloka (www.traveloka.com) is ranked Indonesia's No. 1 flight search booking service, apart from the direct airline websites, by comScore, a marketing data and analytics firm based in the United States (Prabu, 2013). Traveloka's mobile application has been downloaded more than 20 million times, becoming one of the most popular travel booking applications in the region (Maulia, 2017). Total visits to its website on desktop and mobile in the first two quarters of 2017 amounted to 16.02 million (SimilarWeb, 2017).

Founded in 2012, Traveloka offers travellers hotel booking and transport options, such as flight and train services. It has since expanded its presence across Malaysia, the Philippines, Thailand, Singapore, and Viet Nam.

In July 2017, Traveloka obtained US$350 million from Expedia. This brought the amount it had raised to US$500 million over 2016 to continue its business

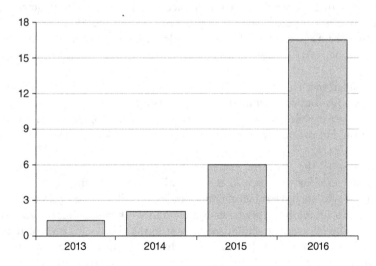

Figure 6.5 Items Sold per Month on Tokopedia (in Million US$)

Source: Freischlad (2016).

expansion. Expedia Group, the owner of Hotels.com and Trivago, expects the partnership with Traveloka to strengthen its presence in Asia.

5. Concluding remarks

With around 140 million digital natives, or 58.4 percent of its population, Indonesia is a promising market for global and cross-border e-commerce. This young generation, aged 12–32 years old, was born during the Internet era. They interact intensively through social media. The number of middle-class and affluent consumers in 2013 was 74 million, and is projected to become 141 million by 2020 (Victor, 2017). Middle class is defined using Asian Development Bank criteria as the segment of the population living with daily per capita expenditure of US$2–20 per day. These middle-class, Internet-intensive users are the potential engine of growth for e-commerce business.

Although still in its early phase, Indonesia's e-commerce is growing rapidly. With a business valuation of US$10 billion and projections that it will reach US$130 billion by 2020, Indonesia is on track to become the third largest e-commerce nation in the world, after China and India. The latest infrastructure and government policy development shows strong support for this objective. This progress has boosted investment decisions and significantly improved the confidence of e-commerce participants.

Indonesia should tackle issues that could hinder its ambition to become the biggest e-commerce nation in the region. Existing problems in Indonesia relate to e-commerce payment issues and the affordability of technology and service enablers, such as smartphones and data communication prices.

The penetration of banking services should provide consumers wider access to e-commerce. Despite the existence of many payment options for e-bills, only 36 percent of Indonesians had a bank account in 2015. The penetration of credit cards is 1.6 percent of the population, behind the Philippines and Viet Nam. According to the World Bank, only 26 percent of Indonesians hold debit cards (Shona, 2016). Most e-commerce payments are conducted via cash on delivery.

A popular way to pay for online purchases is via ATM direct transfer, but the ATM distribution is limited in the archipelago outside large cities. Online payments via mobile phones are also becoming more popular for the younger generation, but the penetration of smartphones as enablers of this method is low, at 24 percent.

Considering the potential demographic bonus from its huge population, Indonesia certainly possesses all the potential to become the digital energy of Asia. However, the government, communities and all stakeholders should move in synergy to develop the digital ecosystem and work hard to make this a vision a reality. The government should be present in the ecosystem, and create policy and regulation that favour the ecosystem while others collaborate and contribute their parts to support the ecosystem.

Notes

1 Digital divide is a term that refers to the gap between regions which have good access to modern information and communications technology, and those that do not or have restricted access.
2 Technopreneur can be defined as new age entrepreneur who makes use of technology to come up with something new or to produce innovation.
3 Regency is an administrative division ranking below a province in Indonesia.
4 The Internet Assigned Numbers Authority issued '.id' as the international code for Indonesia based on ISO 3166–1.
5 OTT is the term used for the delivery of multimedia contents such as network games, film, and TV via the Internet, without requiring users to subscribe to a particular telecommunication multimedia service, or traditional cable or satellite pay-TV service.
6 This plan has triggered heated debate among law experts, national data centre and cloud companies, Internet communities, and academics, as well as related ministries and law enforcement bodies.

Bibliography

Agarwal, M. (2017), 'Indonesia All Set for the Digital Push, Govt. Issues Much Awaited Ecommerce Roadmap'. Available at https://inc42.com/indonesia/indonesia-ecommerce-roadmap-digital/

APJII (2016), 'Penetrasi & Perilaku Pengguna Internet Indonesia,' Survey 2016, November. Available at https://apjii.or.id/downfile/file/surveipenetrasiinternet2016.pdf

Asian Development Bank (ADB) (2016), 'Indonesia: Economy'. Available at www.adb.org/countries/indonesia/economy

Coordinating Ministry for Economic Affairs (2017), 'Pertumbuhan dan Pemerataan: Mengisi Kemerdekaan Melalui Kawasan Ekonomi Khusus'. Available at http://supplychainindonesia.com/new/download/1012/

Cosseboom, L. (2015), 'Why Traveloka Could Be Indonesia's First Startup Unicorn', *Tech in Asia*, 5 May. Available at www.techinasia.com/indonesia-traveloka-unicorn-market-analysis

Freischlad, N. (2016), 'Tokopedia Says It Hit the 1 Million Merchants Mark', *Tech in Asia*, 18 August. Available at www.techinasia.com/tokopedia-hit-1-million-merchants-mark

Google-Temasek (2017), 'E-conomy SEA Spotlight 2017: Unprecedented Growth for Southeast Asia's $50B Internet Economy'. Available at www.blog.google/documents/16/Google-Temasek_e-Conomy_SEA_Spotlight_2017.pdf

Indonesia Investments (2012), 'Masterplan Percepatan dan Perluasan Pembangunan Ekonomi Indonesia (MP3EI)'. Available at www.indonesia-investments.com/id/proyek/rencana-pembangunan-pemerintah/masterplan-percepatan-dan-perluasan-pembangunan-ekonomi-indonesia-mp3ei/item306

Indonesia Investments (2018), 'Economy of Indonesia: 5.07% GDP Growth in Full-Year 2017'. Available at www.indonesia-investments.com/news/news-columns/economy-of-indonesia-5.07-gdp-growth-in-full-year-2017/item8566

Investor Relations Unit of the Republic of Indonesia (2017), 'Republic of Indonesia: A Resilient and Progressive Economy'. Available at www.bi.go.id/en/iru/

presentation/red/Documents/Presentation%20Book%20IRU%20-%20June%20 2017.pdf

KKR & Co (2016), 'KKR, Warburg Pincus, Farallon and Capital Group Private Markets Make Substantial Investment in GO-JEK, Indonesia's Leading On-Demand Mobile Platform'. Available at https://media.kkr.com/news-releases/news-release-details/ kkr-warburg-pincus-farallon-and-capital-group-private-markets

Marware (2015), 'Download Gojek V.1.0.69 APK'. Available at http://marware. maribelajar.web.id/2015/12/download-gojek-v1069-apk.html

Maulia, E. (2017), 'Indonesia's Traveloka Raises $350m from Expedia,' *Nikkei Asian Review*, 28 July. Available at https://asia.nikkei.com/Markets/Capital-Markets/ Indonesia-s-Traveloka-raises-350m-from-Expedia

Ministry of Communication and Information Technology (2013), 'Mobile Broadband Policy in Indonesia: Implementation Challenges,' [Presentation] Broadband Workshop, Pretoria, South Africa, 11–12 November. Available at http:// slideplayer.com/slide/3450221/

Prabu, K. (2013), 'Indonesia Flight Booking Service Traveloka Raises Capital on Back of Strong First Year'. Available at www.tnooz.com/article/indonesia-flight-booking-service-traveloka-raises-capital-on-back-of-strong-first-year/

Rumata, V.M. and A.S. Sastrosubroto (2017), 'The Indonesian E-Commerce Governance Issues in Addressing the Global User Generated Commerce Platform Penetration', Proceedings of 2017 the International Conference on Computer, Control, Informatics and its Applications, Jakarta, October. Available at https:// ieeexplore.ieee.org/stamp/stamp.jsp?tp=&arnumber=8251731

Russell, J. (2016), 'Report: Southeast Asia's Internet Economy to Grow to $200B by 2025,' *TechCrunch*, 24 May. Available at https://techcrunch.com/2016/05/24/ report-southeast-asias-internet-economy-to-grow-to-200b-by-2025/

Secretary of the Cabinet (2014), 'Pemerintah Luncurkan Rencana Broadband Indonesia 2014–2019'. Available at http://setkab.go.id/pemerintah-luncurkan-rencana-broadband-indonesia-2014-2019/

Shona (2016), 'Debit and Credit Card Usage in Asia'. Available at www.demystifya sia.com/creditdebit-card-adoption-asia/

SimilarWeb (2017), 'Tokopedia: Overview'. Available at www.similarweb.com/ website/tokopedia.com

Statista (2018), 'eCommerce'. Available at www.statista.com/outlook/243/120/ e-Commerce/indonesia#

Suzuki, W. and E. Maulia (2017), 'Indonesia's Tokopedia gets top investment from Alibaba,' *Nikkei Asian Review*, 18 August. Available at https://asia.nikkei.com/ Business/Deals/Indonesia-s-Tokopedia-gets-top-investment-from-Alibaba

Tan, I. (2016), 'TRAVELOKA – The New Online Travel Booking Platform'. Available at www.isaactan.net/2016/04/traveloka-new-online-travel-booking-platform-malaysia.html

Tayyiba, M. (2015), 'Broadband as National Strategy: Case Indonesia'. Available at https://www.google.com/url?sa=t&source=web&rct=j&url=https://www.itu. int/en/ITU-D/Regional-Presence/AsiaPacific/Documents/Events/2015/Sep-WABA/Presentations/Indonesia%2520Broadband%2520Plan%2520(ITU%2520J akarta,%2520090915).pdf&ved=2ahUKEwij4bWV3q3gAhWOWX0KHT6vChQ QFjAAegQIAhAB&usg=AOvVaw1UwnJ5i_kGKTUxMBsTwFSP

Vanston, M. (2013), 'Asia Pacific Telecommunity (APT) 700 MHz (Whitepaper)', Melbourne: Telstra. Available at www.gsma.com/newsroom/wp-content/

uploads/2013/09/Telstra-_-Asia-Pacific-Telecommunity-APT-700-MHz-White
paper-FINAL.pdf

Victor, T. (2017), 'Will Indonesia Fail into Middle-Income Trap?' *The Jakarta Post*,
27 April. Available at www.thejakartapost.com/academia/2017/04/27/will-
indonesia-fall-into-middle-income-trap.html

Wu, K. and J. Zhu (2017), 'China's Tencent invests in Indonesia's Go-Jek amid
SE Asia push: Sources', *Reuters*, 4 July. Available at www.reuters.com/article/
us-gojek-m-a-tencent-idUSKBN19P17N

7 E-commerce adoption by ASEAN SMEs and its domestic challenges

Evidence from Malaysia

Noor Azina Ismail and
Muhammad Mehedi Masud

1. Introduction

The emergence of e-commerce has changed the global economy, significantly impacting the development of small and medium-sized enterprises (SMEs). This has created a new paradigm for SMEs, in which they must be more productive and efficient. SMEs aim to become sufficiently competitive to integrate into global value chains through cross-border links between trade and investment. For example, in the Organisation for Economic Co-operation and Development (OECD) countries, over 95 percent of firms are SMEs and microenterprises, accounting for 55 percent of gross domestic product (GDP) (OECD, 2004). A similar report based on 670 Asian organisations concluded that 50 percent of SMEs expect significant future growth, as they can innovate quickly and have strong customer relationships (Qureshi and Herani, 2011). It is important to support SMEs' participation in e-commerce through government intervention such as regulation, technical assistance, and cross-border cooperation among Association of Southeast Asian Nations (ASEAN) countries.

SMEs are important drivers of a country's economic growth, so e-commerce adoption by SMEs can improve their operational efficiency, effectiveness, and productivity. This can also promote long-term economic growth. E-commerce adoption among SMEs faces challenges which have received considerable attention, not only in Malaysia but also in other ASEAN countries.

Historically, SMEs have prompted a transition from agriculture-led economies towards industries and services that integrate small and large firms, attract foreign investment, and ensure stable terms of trade. This has occurred in East Asia and other industrialised economies (e.g. China, Republic of Korea [henceforth Korea], and Japan), but many ASEAN economies (e.g. Indonesia, Malaysia, Viet Nam, and Thailand) are behind this trend. Including SMEs in e-commerce will increase employment opportunities, reduce poverty, and boost economic growth (Dhungana, 2003).

On the other hand, e-commerce can provide efficient functioning for SMEs, but insufficient empirical research has been undertaken in this area. Few attempts have been made to unpack the relationship between e-commerce and SMEs, employment and poverty reduction, and the overall impact on GDP growth. SMEs face barriers in many ASEAN countries. The difficulty of determining correlative relationships between SMEs and their impact on employment and poverty reduction may also contribute to the insufficiency of research to date.

Numerous studies have shown that firms, especially large corporations, play a significant role in generating employment within the ASEAN region. However, the literature has not provided much support to demonstrate how they can work together to develop a good set of practices that can enable SMEs in ASEAN countries to overcome major issues. To date, the literature has made some important contributions which highlight the challenges faced by SMEs, such as globalisation, liberalisation of trade, and organisational, institutional, and technological changes. Nonetheless, it has not been able to offer insights for SMEs to overcome such challenges.

This chapter focuses on the issues related to domestic e-commerce adoption and international challenges, as well as barriers associated with e-commerce adoption by Malaysian SMEs. The rest of chapter is organised as follows: Section 2 presents SMEs' contribution to economic growth in Malaysia. Section 3 discusses SMEs' development and challenges in e-commerce adoption, while Section 4 overviews the initiatives and actions by the Malaysian government to promote e-commerce. Section 5 presents insights learnt from face-to-face interviews with Malaysian SMEs. Section 6 provides policy suggestions.

2. SMEs' contribution to economic growth in Malaysia

The New Economic Policy of 1971 recognised the importance of SMEs to economic development. This policy was targeted at improving peoples' well-being and restructuring economic imbalances (Saleh and Ndubisi, 2006). SMEs are the mainstay of Malaysian economy (Radam et al., 2008). SMEs operate in all industries and sectors of the economy, so their contributions to the Malaysian economy has been significant, particularly in manufacturing (Abdullah, 2002; Khalique et al., 2011). According to Economic Census 2011 and 2016 published by the Department of Statistics, Malaysia (DOSM, 2016), 907,065 SMEs operated in 2015 – a rise of 40.6 percent from 645,136 establishments in 2011. This growth is due to the support by Malaysian government through the SME Masterplan 2012–2020, which includes a structured framework to drive SME development. Of this total, about 76.5 percent were classified as micro, around 21.2 percent were small, and the rest (2.3 percent) were medium-sized businesses. The services sector had the highest number of SMEs (89.2 percent), followed by manufacturing (5.3 percent); construction (4.3 percent); and agriculture, mining, and quarrying (1.2 percent) (DOSM, 2016).

The contribution of SMEs to GDP increased from 29.6 percent in 2005 to 36.6 percent in 2016 (DOSM, 2016). SME GDP grew moderately by 5.2 percent in 2016 compared with the 6.1 percent recorded in 2015 (DOSM) (Figure 7.1). The country's annual growth of 5.8 percent in 2017 was better than expected. Unfortunately, the annual growth forecast for small businesses

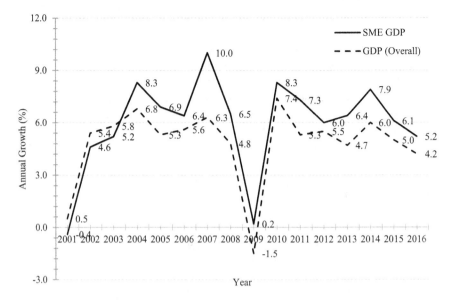

Figure 7.1 SME GDP and Overall GDP Growth (%)
Source: DOSM (2016) and SME Corporation, Malaysia (2016).

decreased to 2.2 percent from 3.7 percent forecasted earlier by the Retail Group Malaysia (RGM).

In 2015, SME employment grew by 5.6 percent to 6.6 million workers compared with 3.4 percent employment growth in large firms. However, the SME employment growth rate was lower than in 2014, when numbers were inflated by the redefinition of SMEs, which caused about 8,000 firms that were previously considered large firms to be recategorised as SMEs (DOSM, 2016). The higher employment growth of SMEs versus large firms caused the percentage share of employment by SMEs to total employment to increase from 57.5 percent in 2013 to 65.5 percent in 2015, as shown in Figure 7.2 (DOSM, 2016; SME Corporation, Malaysia, 2016).

Despite the high percentage share of employment and their huge number, the export contribution of Malaysian SMEs is still low. The DOSM (2016) showed that the share of SME exports to total exports increased very gradually from 16.4 percent in 2010 to 17.8 percent in 2014 before declining to 17.6 percent in 201,5 as shown in Figure 7.3. The shares in the agriculture and manufacturing sectors are almost stagnant. The only sector that showed a significant increase is the service sector, where the share of exports increased from 7.8 percent in 2010 to 8.8 percent in 2015.

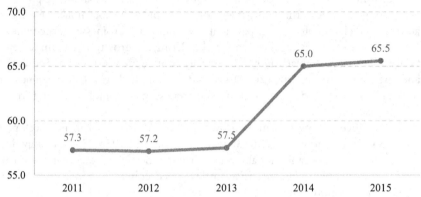

Figure 7.2 Employment of SMEs as the Share of Total Employment
Source: DOSM (2016) and SME Corporation, Malaysia (2016).

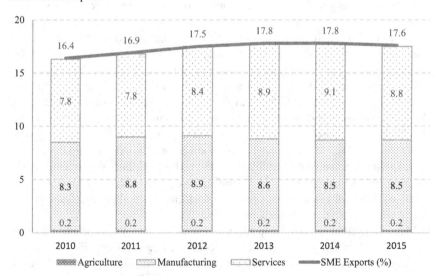

Figure 7.3 Share of SME Exports by Economic Sector (%)
Source: DOSM (2016) and SME Corporation, Malaysia (2016).

3. Development and challenges

Frost and Sullivan (2016) recognised several key factors impeding the growth of e-commerce activities. These include low credit card ownership, which is below 7 percent in all markets in Southeast Asia, except for Malaysia and Singapore. In some countries, more than 50 percent of the population does not have a bank account, which complicates the payment of e-commerce businesses in the region. Logistics inefficiency is another problem hindering the growth of e-commerce in Southeast Asia, particularly in geographically complex regions such as Indonesia and the Philippines. Coroş (2012) pointed out the high risk of exterminating SMEs if they do not increase their competitiveness in the rapidly changing world of globalisation.

E-commerce adoption is much slower in ASEAN SMEs than in developed countries (Janita and Chong, 2013; Molla and Licker, 2005). This is mainly due to administrative, organisational, and environmental restrictions that are more typical in developing countries than in developed countries (Molla and Licker, 2005). Furthermore, emerging markets often face many challenges, including lack of e-commerce policies and regulations, as well as inadequate infrastructure, confidence, and security. In most Asian developing countries, the penetration of personal computers (PCs) is not well dispersed. For example, by the end of 2014, 88 percent households in Singapore had personal computers (PCs), while in Indonesia, only 18 percent households had PCs (Statista 2018). Moreover, in some parts of Indonesia, the telecommunications infrastructure is still in poor condition, with only 0.2 percent households having fixed telephone lines (Janita and Chong, 2013). It is worth noting that for emerging countries, insufficient telecommunications infrastructure and expensive Internet access could inhibit companies from participating in e-commerce (Janita and Chong, 2013).

E-commerce also offers an electronic path for business dealings between buyers and sellers, which could be complicated in emerging countries because of the lack of policies and regulations to control online transactions (Shakir et al., 2007). The low rate of e-commerce adoption in ASEAN SMEs is caused by concerns about privacy, security, and taxed income, as well as lack of regulation, trade laws, and legal protection for businesses. Thus, the ASEAN region is confronting common problems in terms of e-commerce adoption. Governments should be aware of these problems while preparing and improving their strategies for the adoption of e-commerce in their countries.

Major barriers to e-commerce adoption in SMEs are (i) insufficient resources and knowledge, (ii) lack of trust in the online marketplace, (iii) inadequate e-commerce readiness, (iv) high costs of adoption, and (v) apprehension regarding the realisable benefits (Ongori and Migiro, 2010; Lewis and Cockrill, 2002). SMEs which have overcome these obstacles and embarked on the path of online business often make full use of the electronic marketplace. The adoption of e-commerce technologies allows SMEs to access larger markets without developing their physical presence (Quaddus and Hofmeyer, 2007). E-commerce technologies appeal strongly to SME retailers because e-commerce can transcend geographical distance and time (Premkumar and Roberts, 1999). However, e-commerce implementation in the business processes of ASEAN SMEs has been slow (Noor and Hussain, 2005) because of the negative social, economic, technological, and political situations prevailing in numerous emerging nations (Kurnia et al., 2015).

In Malaysia, the use of information and communication technology (ICT) by SMEs has increased in 2011–2015 (SME Corporation, Malaysia, 2016). Zakaria and Hashim (2003) found that only 15 percent of Malaysian SMEs used the Internet for business development. This increased to 20 percent of SMEs using IT in their daily operations in 2009 (Alam and Noor, 2009) before surging from 27 percent in 2010 to 89.1 percent in 2015. However, the percentage of establishments involved in online transactions is still small, as only around 20 percent used e-commerce to reach out to customers. Ahmad et al. (2015) indicated that e-commerce adoption among SMEs remains low despite government efforts to encourage the use of ICT. Furthermore, SMEs involved in online business were in the service and manufacturing sectors (DOSM, 2016; SME Corporation, Malaysia, 2016). The high cost of acquiring e-commerce infrastructure, continuous changes in e-commerce technology, and varying needs of local and global businesses could be reasons for the low adoption of e-commerce among SMEs (Jones et al., 2011).

4. Government initiatives and support to promote e-commerce

Malaysia has taken steps in spurring the growth of e-commerce. As one of the countries with an open trade policy, Malaysia had envisaged vast opportunities for doing business online. Through the Malaysia Digital Economy Corporation (MDEC), an agency with more than 20 years of experience in advising the Malaysian government on legislation, policies, and standards for ICT and multimedia operations, Malaysia hopes to play a leading role in the global digital revolution. In its 2018 budget, the Malaysian government announced five initiatives that would help to stimulate the growth of e-commerce. A total of US$19.7 million was allocated to construct the first phase of the Digital Free Trade Zone (DFTZ) which was launched by Dato' Seri Mohd Najib Tun Abdul Razak, the former Prime Minister of Malaysia, together with Jack Ma, the founder and executive chairman of the Alibaba Group on 22 March 2017. The DFTZ is Malaysia's first initiative towards capitalising on the confluence and exponential growth of the digital economy and cross-border e-commerce activities. The e-services platform provided by the DFTZ will digitally connect users with the government and other business providers in supporting cross-border trade. Furthermore, the DFTZ will facilitate a seamless cross-border trade that will enable SMEs, marketplaces, and mono brands to export their goods with a priority for e-commerce. The DFTZ was expected to contribute to RM211 billion (US$48 billion) by year 2020, and the Malaysian SMEs' goods export via the DFTZ is expected to be double the growth rate by 2025 (MDEC 2017).

In order to help the SMEs get involved in the online business, the MDEC and the SME Corp, a central coordinating agency that formulates policies and strategies for SMEs, developed an online platform called the *Go E-Commerce*. This platform serves as an active learning platform and hub; it provides a comprehensive guide to all SMEs that are keen to explore and build their businesses via e-commerce. The aim of *Go E-commerce* is to enable and empower the SMEs to channel or diversify their businesses digitally. *Go E-commerce* also comes with a specially made SME Readiness Tool feature. Through the platform, members are able to obtain information and find out which level they are at in an instant. *Go E-commerce* is also programmed to assist the SMEs in choosing the best solution by tailoring to the needs of each company. The launch of the National E-Commerce Strategic Roadmap in October 2016 proves that the Malaysian government is very serious in driving the national e-commerce agenda as it strives to double the Malaysian e-commerce growth rate from the current 10.8 percent to 20.8 percent by 2020, and to elevate the e-commerce GDP contribution of more than RM170 billion by 2020.

The MDEC (2016) outlines the government's intervention in six thrust areas. To prepare the SMEs in Malaysia for their participation in e-commerce, one of the thrusts focusses on efforts to accelerate the sellers' adoption of e-commerce. This thrust will help the sellers to increase the availability and range of their products through online channels. The second thrust aims to increase the adoption of e-procurement by businesses since majority of the transaction values are from business-to-business (B2B) e-commerce. The third thrust of the National E-Commerce Strategic Roadmap is the lifting of non-tariff barriers. This includes efforts to increase the adoption of e-payment, intensify the level of maturity in the national e-fulfilment sector, augment mass awareness of consumer protection and facilitate the cross-border e-commerce movement of goods. One of the important thrusts is the re-alignment of existing economic incentives which will ensure and motivate effective product delivery to areas with higher possible multiplier benefits. The last two thrusts involve making strategic investments in selected e-commerce players and promoting national brands to boost cross-border e-commerce. The thrust offers support to domestic companies operating in strategic sectors so as to fully capture the enormous opportunities available in the region and the world through e-commerce. The six thrust areas of the National Strategic Roadmap will allow buyers, sellers, government agencies, platform providers, payment providers, and logistics and fulfilment providers to contribute to the growth of e-commerce.

In order to ensure that the digital economy is inclusive for all levels of society, the Malaysian Government, through the MDEC, has introduced a few programmes such as eUsahawan and eRezeki. The eUsahawan programme was launched in 2015; it is aimed at encouraging the use of digital economy among micro, small, and medium entrepreneurs. The eRezeki, on the other hand, is a training course programme which aims to assist low-income households by connecting them to the digital income opportunities. The programme will also match individuals to suitable available tasks or work. The MDEC is also pushing the integration of digital entrepreneurship knowledge into the curricula of higher education institutions.

In terms of the e-commerce regulation, Malaysia is the first ASEAN member country to pass the privacy legislation with the introduction of the Personal Data Protection Act 2010. Previous acts, including the Electronic Commerce Act 2006 and the Electronic Government Activities Act 2007, became the sources for formulating the e-commerce regulation. Malaysia further introduced the Digital Signature Act 1997 to cover regulations for the use of digital signatures. To protect the consumers against unfair practices and the right to minimum product standards which cover electronic commerce transactions and general safety requirements, consumers can refer to the Consumer Protection Act which was amended for the third time in 2010.

5. Interviews with Malaysian SMEs

5.1. Methodology

This study collected data from face-to-face interviews with entrepreneurs from 12 SMEs in Kuala Lumpur that include e-commerce as part of their businesses. Kuala Lumpur was selected because it is the business centre of Malaysia and home to around 15 percent of Malaysia's SMEs (DOSM, 2016). These SMEs involved in several types of businesses such as boutiques, financials, toys and games, electronic goods, computer hardware, and mobile telecommunication. The interviewees were managers, planners, or directors of the companies. The interview questions were mainly developed considering one main theme, such as exploring domestic and international challenges in Malaysian SMEs stemming from the cross-border trade agreement in the ASEAN region. Data were then organised and analysed based on a descriptive thematic analysis. The targeted participants consisted of managers, planners, and directors levels of the following industry as shown in Annex 7.1.

5.2. Results and discussions

5.2.1. Major factors causing e-commerce adoption to lag behind

E-commerce is flourishing in East Asia and other industrialised economies, while it is growing more slowly in ASEAN economies. One possible cause of this seems to be the low Internet penetration across regions in ASEAN countries, as well as the low purchasing power of people in the countries concerned. This study asked participants the following question: 'Why are ASEAN SMEs lagging behind in the adoption of e-commerce?' The responses are recorded in Table 7.1.

These responses show that several factors cause e-commerce adoption to lag behind. Lack of general and technical knowledge of e-commerce are the main factors preventing businesses from adopting e-commerce. Participants cited insufficient technical experience, weak familiarity with e-commerce, inadequate

Table 7.1 Major Factors Causing E-commerce Adoption to Lag Behind

Knowledge	Technical	Constraints	Entrepreneurship	Infrastructure
i. Lack of experience	i. Have insufficient technical experience	i. Lack of awareness of the importance of e-commerce	i. Weak entrepreneurial spirit among youth	i. Inadequate facility
ii. Weak familiarity	ii. To use e-commerce, training needed	ii. Low perceptions of the benefits of buying products online		ii. Technology in Malaysia is not advanced
iii. Lack of knowledge		iii. Low perceptions of the advantages of e-commerce		
iv. Lack of information				
v. No clear role models, unlike China (e.g. Taobao, Alibaba)				

Source: The authors. Based on the interviews.

knowledge of e-commerce applications, lack of a clear role model (e.g. Taobao and Alibaba in China) to provide guidance, and lack of consumer information as reasons for not using e-commerce. Others admitted that lack of technical knowledge and the need for training are reasons for not adopting e-commerce. Low perception of the benefits of using e-commerce is another reason for not adopting e-commerce noted by participants in this study. Other causes cited are the lack of entrepreneurial spirit among Malaysian youth and lack of infrastructure.

These responses are consistent with the results obtained by Shakir et al. (2007), Ongori and Migiro (2010), Zulkiffli (2009) and Saleh and Ndubisi (2006). Their findings are also consistent with the information provided by the SME Corporation, Malaysia (2015). SME Corp chief executive director H. Hafsah said that:

> SMEs face various challenges including challenges in retaining their competitive edge, limited access to finance, lack of entrepreneurial spirit and management skills, low innovation and technology adoption, lack of information, limited access to markets, lack of conducive business environment and inadequate capacity to comply with standards and certification.
>
> (http://smecorp.gov.my/index)

However, the e-commerce market in ASEAN has a bright future, and regional integration among member countries may offer new opportunities for SMEs to expand and grow as they adopt e-commerce. SMEs can also harness market potential in other countries as well as increased cross-border trade and investment via e-commerce. Despite this huge potential for SMEs in the ASEAN region to adopt e-commerce, gaps exist between the ASEAN-6 (Indonesia, Malaysia, Thailand, Philippines, and Viet Nam) and the CLMV countries (Cambodia, Lao PDR, Myanmar, and Viet Nam). These gaps are traced to lack of an institutional framework, technology and technology transfer, access to finance, promotion of entrepreneurial education, cheaper and faster start-up and better regulations, access to support services, international market expansion, and stronger representation of SMEs' interests (ERIA, 2012).

Other factors include administrative, organisational, and environmental restrictions, which may be more common in developing countries (Janita and Chong, 2013; Molla and Licker, 2005). This makes the adoption of e-commerce in ASEAN SMEs much slower than in developed countries. Moreover, emerging markets may experience challenges in the form of inadequate e-commerce policies and regulations, as well as poor infrastructure and low confidence and security. These will prevent companies from participating in e-commerce.

Since e-commerce is transacted electronically, business dealings between buyers and sellers are only possible if policies and regulations are in place to control online transactions. Lack of a regulatory framework can also hamper e-commerce adoption by developing countries (Shakir et al., 2007). The low rate of e-commerce adoption by ASEAN SMEs can be traced to their concerns about privacy, security, and taxed income. The ASEAN region is likely to face similar problems when adopting e-commerce trade and business. Therefore, ASEAN SMEs may need to apply more caution while preparing and improving their strategies for e-commerce adoption in their respective countries.

5.2.2. *Challenges from cross-border e-commerce for domestic business*

To understand the kind of challenges or competition that SMEs face when adopting cross-border e-commerce with dominant online retailers like Alibaba, it was necessary to conduct interviews. The responses of some of the 12 participants are provided in Table 7.2 to highlight the key findings of the discussion.

The findings reveal positive and negative responses. A few participants stated that cross-border trade would have a positive impact on Malaysian SMEs. They asserted that cross-border e-commerce would bring multiple benefits in terms of (i) increasing computing capabilities, (ii) cross-functional communications, and (iii) cooperation within organisations. Online customers also have the opportunity to enter global markets. To compete with international dominant online retailers like Alibaba and Amazon, participants suggested that Malaysia needs to improve its logistics and delivery services. They also mentioned that collaboration between both parties (international and regional) is necessary. The challenge is how domestic e-commerce can absorb the best practice of regional and international e-commerce firms, so that both parties can get inside each other's market. Participants also said that Malaysians have an edge over international competitors in domestic e-commerce, since they know their co-nationals better than foreign firms.

Table 7.2 Key Findings on Challenges or Competition Faced by Domestic SMEs in Cross-Border E-commerce with Dominant Online Retailers Like Alibaba and Amazon

Items	Key Findings
Positive impact	Increase in computing capability, emergence of globalisation, cross-functional communication, and cooperation within organisation.
	Online customers have opportunities to enter global markets.
Update logistics services	Need to update logistic services.
	Need to improve quick delivery service.
Collaboration with dominant online retailers	International dominant online retailers are not our competitors; they are more like our partners.
	The leading foreign e-commerce platforms, i.e. Alibaba and Amazon, help solve e-commerce problems in Malaysia, but at the same time pose challenge for Malaysia. These foreign e-commerce platforms will have to work with local/regional companies to embrace the business as a whole.
Values	To instil the values and characteristics of each international and regional player.
	Malaysian SMEs have a local advantage, as they know the market and consumers well.
Regulations and technical barriers	Uncertainty of security of online financial transactions and privacy.
	The lack of e-commerce technology skills, professionals, and government regulations.
Developing innovative ideas	Too many e-commerce platforms.
	Problems with product and innovation ideas.
Payment Methods	Lacking an efficient e-payment gateway.
	Lagging behind in e-payment supporting logistics.

Source: The authors. Based on the interviews.

Participants noted the huge potential for SMEs in Malaysia to compete in the e-commerce market, but stated that regulations and technical barriers pose challenges to the adoption of e-commerce. For example, uncertainty regarding the security of online financial transactions, privacy of online transactions, lack of skilled professionals in e-commerce technology, and government regulations were among the reasons cited for the slow adoption of e-commerce in the region. It was also noted that cross-border trade may highlight cultural barriers, and cross-border trade involves different e-commerce platforms, incentives, and packages; therefore, it may be difficult to choose the most effective model to apply. Locally, Malaysia deals with Lazada, Shoppie, Mudah, and other marketplaces. To compete with dominant online retailers in the international market, the most important challenge for Malaysia's SMEs is their lack of innovative ideas and products. Finally, participants emphasised that Malaysian SMEs may face two key problems: lack of an efficient e-payment gateways, and the lag-behind in e-payment supporting logistics.

These outputs show that Malaysian SMEs that will adopt e-commerce need to consider two perspectives: the benefits and the challenges. Cross-border trade will benefit Malaysian SMEs in terms of an increase in computing capabilities, a taste of globalisation, and exposure to cross-functional communication and cooperation, as well as offering online customers a vast and diverse choice for online purchases. However, to access these benefits, it is important for Malaysian SMEs to improve their logistics services, provide an effective payment gateway, and develop innovative ideas and products for their customers. Through this strategy, they can remain competitive with international dominant online retailers like Alibaba and Amazon.

The government of Malaysia should consider collaborations with other ASEAN countries to link the e-commerce payment gateway, creating a regional logistics centre for global market trading. This will allow Malaysia to increase its Internet economy through innovations, boosting inward investment. The government already considered cooperation with Alibaba or Amazon to benefit from their knowledge and experience. This goal has been partly achieved through the establishment of the Digital Free Trade Zone between Malaysia and China in conjunction with Alibaba in November 2018.

5.2.3 Considering e-commerce in RCEP

To broaden the internal market and promote economic growth, agreements such as the Trans-Pacific Partnership (TPP) and Regional Comprehensive Economic Partnership (RCEP) play an important role for the development of SMEs among the member countries. Particularly, the RCEP agreement could facilitate development of SMEs in Malaysia, to be internationalised through trade and participation in global value chains, which will help create a large economy, expand the market, create jobs and improve well-being. It will be easy to find skilled employment and encourage innovation and technological progress.

E-commerce has substantial potential to accelerate SME growth in developed and developing countries, but the adoption of e-commerce by SMEs in developing countries faces many challenges which should be surmounted by their own domestic abilities. However, the fundamental question here is: if Malaysia has an agreement with the RCEP, what would be Malaysia's ability to commit to the e-commerce chapter?

The RCEP is a proposed free trade agreement between ASEAN's ten member states and six Asia-Pacific countries (Australia, China, India, Japan, Korea, and New Zealand). The ASEAN agreement on E-commerce and the E-commerce chapter in RCEP were drafted in parallel. But by the end of 2018, only the former has been concluded; the latter was still under negotiation. Our interview also collected the participants' opinions on the implication of the potential RCEP agreement on cross-border trade. Main viewpoints are summarised in Table 7.3.

The RCEP would create a regional free trade market of 3.4 billion population and US$49.5 trillion in terms of GDP. To many Malaysian SMEs, this means a vast exporting market for them to get access to. But this is not risk-free. An imminent challenge that many Malaysian SMEs need to face is how to compete

Table 7.3 RCEP in the Eyes of the Malaysian Business Sector

Response	Key Findings
Positive impacts	i. Have better benefits in getting high quality raw materials from other parts of the world at a lower price to compete in this trade.
	ii. RCEP will become the world's largest market.
	iii. RCEP will improve standards of living in Malaysia and throughout ASEAN region.
Negative impacts	RCEP may discourage innovation and creativity among SMEs in Malaysia because of low-cost manufacturing in China and India.

Source: The authors. Based on the interviews.

directly with low-cost, low-priced goods and services from China and India. For example, a wardrobe that costs RM100 in Malaysia sells for CNY100 (about RM63) in China, leading price-conscious consumers to prefer Chinese goods. If Malaysian SMEs can overcome these challenges, e-commerce in the domestic market will mature and can boost the nation's economy.

Even before the start of RCEP negotiations, China's largest e-commerce platform, Alibaba, entered a partnership with the government of Malaysia to facilitate cross-border e-commerce between China and Malaysia. This agreement allows Malaysian SMEs to access global commerce through e-commerce and gain consumer confidence beside the implementation of the RCEP. E-commerce will help Malaysian SMEs achieve a greater market share, but they could be at a disadvantage in a more competitive market with cheaper foreign-made goods unless the competition is for Malaysian products only. To protect Malaysian SMEs, the government may need to emphasise locally produced products such as Sabah tea, Cameron highlands tea, and handcrafts; and improve their quality and packaging, if necessary. Therefore, the government should be well prepared with full capacity of e-commerce adoption before the establishment of RCEP.

The government believes that Malaysian SMEs' use of e-commerce will accelerate growth and drive the GDP contribution of e-commerce to surpass RM170 billion by 2020. The responses of survey participants endorse this view. Malaysia needs its economy to expand more rapidly. The development and expansion of local SMEs through e-commerce adoption can be used to help eradicate poverty in Malaysia and the rest of Asia before 2030. It is also hoped that this can increase Malaysia's Human Development Index ranking, gross national income, and GDP.

Malaysia needs to improve its ability to adopt e-commerce and compete with cross-border trading partners. The government has provided significant support in recent years, including the Economic Transformation Programme, which introduced and expanded on several key industries including e-commerce such as 'virtual mall' project. The government's effort, through the Performance Management and Delivery Unit, also created better broadband services and access to more advanced mobile devices as a result of its aim to develop the Internet-based retail market by taking advantage of the higher disposable income of the Malaysian population. The National E-commerce Strategic Roadmap reflects this inventiveness in its six main objectives: (i) accelerate the adoption of e-commerce by sellers, (ii) increase the adoption of e-procurement by businesses, (iii) eliminate non-tariff barriers (e-processing at the national level, cross-border e-commerce, e-payment, and consumer protection), (iv) realign economic incentives, (v) make strategic investments in key businesses, and (vi) promote Malaysian businesses to increase cross-border e-commerce.

6. Policy implications

First of all, incentives, laws, and policies could promote confidence and trust among e-commerce participants. The issue of lack of trust between buyers and unknown suppliers in e-commerce needs to be overcome. For instance, the government could provide guidelines for SMEs in developing a system of collaborative ratings. That is, customers could rate and comment on suppliers in terms of the quality of products or services and the speed of delivery. To minimise fraud, safeguard mechanisms should be built into the rating system. This would promote confidence and trust between e-commerce participants. The government should also establish a legal framework that provides standards and requirements that transmit transparency of e-commerce services. The government could also assign the authority to ensure the security of e-commerce transactions. For example, the government could verify the identity of buyers and sellers and review transactions with security procedures to ensure they are transparent.

Second, SMEs' performance and economic contribution to a nation depend on the competence and quality of their skilled labour force. Upgrading the skill of the labour force can be accomplished through training programs for SME managers and employees, emphasising technical and managerial skills. Through cooperation with business organisations, training institutions, and commercial training services, such training can improve the service quality of the industry and increase entrepreneurs' confidence and performance. ASEAN countries should encourage SME development by maximising the benefits of e-commerce policy initiatives, such as using each other's resources to develop a solid and coordinated effort for enhancing managerial skills and training between large firms and SMEs. The adoption of e-commerce will strengthen global participation and easy access to global information.

Moreover, lack of IT knowledge can make SMEs too cautious about the associated costs and the potential risks, and therefore affect their willingness to adopt digitalisation. To overcome these challenges and barriers, the government and the private sector can develop a partnership to raise awareness about e-commerce adoption. For example, the Ministry of Entrepreneur and Cooperative Development or other agencies could conduct awareness campaigns to stimulate interest among SMEs. They could also provide some evidence of lack IT and e-commerce adoption to SMEs with insufficient knowledge of IT and e-commerce adoption to increase their confidence. Based on the opinions of participants in this study, many SMEs appear to lack IT expertise, which is a significant challenge for the adoption of e-commerce.

To make the campaigns more attractive and successful, the government should provide free e-commerce adoption workshops and training courses, including award programs, security and privacy training, and information centres to assist SMEs. That lack of ICT support and capital are among the main obstacles to SME growth. Aiming to help SMEs overcome these challenges, the government has introduced the Soft Loans for ICT (SLICT) program under the Eighth Malaysia Plan to encourage SMEs to purchase ICT hardware and software. However, the government still needs to increase the coverage of the program to benefit more SMEs. Meanwhile, the government could also encourage individuals to enter digital business by providing preferential tax treatment, lowering rental rates, or expanding their credit facilities.

Third, government agencies should be more proactive in providing microfinance soft loans without collateral, at minimum interest rates, for start-up micro business. The amount of capital provided must be enough for the start-up of the proposed businesses to encourage low-income earners to get involved in microenterprises. Microfinance loans could be bundled to incorporate financing, skills training, links with SMEs, advancement and marketing facilities, consultation services, and monitoring activities. Existing efforts in this area could be expanded to encompass the process from hatching out start-ups to providing an eco-system for them grow faster. Private agencies should play a greater role in this process, and business-to-business partnerships – especially between large companies and SMEs – will be very useful.

Last, regional cooperation – via either inter-governmental collaboration or public-private partnership – could help promote e-commerce. This is particularly useful when developing the regional e-commerce payment gateway to facilitate seamless connectivity for business. In the case of Malaysia, the government has already started the cooperation with Alibaba. This partnership is supposed to create a win-win situation, as it opened a gateway for small businesses in both countries to share each other's market potential, thereby enhancing bilateral economic ties.

Bibliography

Abdullah, M.A. (2002), 'An Overview of the Macroeconomic Contribution of Small and Medium Enterprises in Malaysia', in C. Harvie and B-C. Lee (eds.), *The Role of SMEs in National Economies in East Asia*. Cheltenham: Edward Elgar, pp. 181–200.

Ahmad, S.Z., A.R. Abu Bakar, T.M. Faziharudean and K.A. Mohamad Zaki (2015), 'An Empirical Study of Factors Affecting E-Commerce Adoption among Small- and Medium-Sized Enterprises in a Developing Country: Evidence from Malaysia', *Information Technology for Development*, 21(4): 555–572.

Alam, S.S. and M.K.M. Noor (2009), 'ICT Adoption in Small and Medium Enterprises: An Empirical Evidence of Service Sectors in Malaysia', *International Journal of Business and Management*, 4(2): 112–125.

Brown, R.C. (2017), 'A New Leader in Asian Free Trade Agreements: Chinese Style Global Trade: New Rules, No Labor Protections', *UCLA Pacific Basin Law Journal*, 35: 1.

Coroş, M.M. (2012), 'The Development of Romanian SMEs since the Beginning of the 20th Century', *Studia Universitatis Babes-Bolyai, Negotia*, 57(1): 75–93.

Department of Statistics, Malaysia (2012), *Economic Census 2011: Profile of Small and Medium Enterprise*. Kuala Lumpur: Department of Statistics, the Government of Malaysia.

Department of Statistics, Malaysia (DOSM) (2016), 'Small & Medium Enterprises'. Available at www.dosm.gov.my/v1/index.php?r=column/cone&menu_id=bWl2a DJzM2ZieGJFTENHTWtxYUhMQT09

Dhungana, B.P. (2003), 'Strengthening the Competitiveness of Small and Medium Enterprises in the Globalization Process: Prospects and Challenges', in *Investment Promotion and Enterprise Development Bulletin for Asia and the Pacific*. Bangkok: United Nations Economic and Social Commission for Asia and the Pacific, vol. 1, pp. 1–32.

ERIA SME Research Working Group (2012), 'ASEAN SME Policy Index 2014: Towards Competitive and Innovative ASEAN SMEs', *ERIA Research Project Report*, No. 8, Jakarta: ERIA.

Frost and Sullivan (2016), 'Analysis of Southeast Asian E-Commerce Market'. Available at www.frost.com/sublib/display-report.do?id=P8F7-01-00-0000&bdata= aHR0cHM6Ly93d3cuZ29vZ2xlLmNvbS9AfkBCYWNrQH5AMTUzODMxMT QyOTEwOA%3D%3D

Janita, I. and W.K. Chong (2013), 'Barriers of B2B e-Business Adoption in Indonesian SMEs: A Literature Analysis', *Procedia Computer Science*, 17: 571–578.

Jones, P., G. Packha, P. Beynon-Davies and D. Pickernell (2011), 'False Promises: E-Business Deployment in Wales' SME Community', *Journal of Systems and Information Technology*, 13(2): 163–178.

Khalique, M., A.H.B.M. Isa, N. Shaari, J. Abdul and A. Ageel (2011), 'Challenges Faced by the Small and Medium Enterprises (SMEs) in Malaysia: An Intellectual Capital Perspective', *International Journal of Current Research*, 3(6): 398–401.

Kurnia, S., J. Choudrie, R.M. Mahbubur and B. Alzougool (2015), 'E-Commerce Technology Adoption: A Malaysian Grocery SME Retail Sector Study', *Journal of Business Research*, 68(9): 1906–1918.

Lewis, R. and A. Cockrill (2002), 'Going Global – Remaining Local: The Impact of E-Commerce on Small Retail Firms in Wales', *International Journal of Information Management*, 22(3): 195–209.

Malaysia Digital Economy Corporation (MDEC) (2016), 'National Ecommerce Strategic Roadmap'. Available at mdec.my/digital-innovation-ecosystem/ecommerce/nesr

Malaysia Digital Economy Corporation (MDEC) (2018), 'Malaysia Launches World's First Digital Free Trade Zone'. Available at mdec.my/news/malaysia-launches-worlds-first-digital-free-trade-zone

Molla, A. and P.S. Licker (2005), 'E-Commerce Adoption in Developing Countries: A Model and Instrument', *Information and Management*, 42(6): 877–899.

Noor, A. and S.F. Hussain (2005), 'Risk Factors Associated with Development of Ventilator Associated Pneumonia', *Journal of the College of Physicians and Surgeons Pakistan*, 15(2): 92–95.

OECD (2004), *Women Entrepreneurship: Issues and Policies*, 2nd OECD Conference of Ministers Responsible for Small and Medium Sized Enterprises (SMEs), 3–5 June. Istanbul, Turkey.

Ongori, H. and S.O. Migiro (2010), 'Information and Communication Technologies Adoption in SMEs: Literature Review', *Journal of Chinese Entrepreneurship*, 2(1): 93–104.

Premkumar, G. and M. Roberts (1999), 'Adoption of New Information Technologies in Rural Small Businesses', *Omega*, 27(4): 467–484.

Quaddus, M. and G. Hofmeyer (2007), 'An Investigation into the Factors Influencing the Adoption of B2B Trading Exchanges in Small Businesses', *European Journal of Information Systems*, 16(3): 202–215.

Qureshi, J. and G.M. Herani (2011), 'The Role of Small and Medium-Size Enterprises (SMEs) in the Socio-Economic Stability of Karachi', *Indus Journal of Management & Social Sciences*, 4(2): 30–44, Spring.

Radam, A., M.L. Abu and A.M. Abdullah (2008), 'Technical Efficiency of Small and Medium Enterprise in Malaysia: A Stochastic Frontier Production Model', *International Journal of Economics and Management*, 2(2): 395–408.

Saleh, A.S. and N.O. Ndubisi (2006), 'An Evaluation of SME Development in Malaysia', *International Review of Business Research Papers*, 2(1): 1–14.

Shakir, M., G.R. Smith and E. Gulec (2007), 'E-Procurement: Reaching Out to Small and Medium Businesses', *MIS Quarterly Executive*, 6(4): 225–238.

SME Corporation, Malaysia (2016), 'SME Annual Report 2015/2016'. Available at www.smecorp.gov.my/index.php/en/sme-annual-report-2015-16

Statista (2018), 'Household PC Ownership Share by Country 2014'. Available at www.statista.com/statistics/551760/worldwide-selected-countries-personal-computers-as-percentage-households/#0

Zakaria, M. and M.K. Hashim (2003), *Malaysian SMEs Perceptions of E-Business: Some Empirical Evidence*. Proceedings of the National Seminar on E-commerce, Kuala Lumpur, October.

Zulkiffli, S. (2009), 'A Literature Analysis on the Supply Chain Operational Capabilities in Malaysian Small and Medium Enterprises (SMEs)', in *3rd International Conference on Operations and Supply Chain Management*. Malaysia: International Society of Management Science and Engineering Management (ISMSEM), pp. 1–13.

Annex 7.1

Table 7A.1 Demographic Profile of Participating Companies

Participants	Sector	Type of Business	Size
1	Consumer goods	Boutiques	Small
2	Banks	Financials	Micro
3	Telecommunications	Mobile telecommunications	Medium
4	Consumer goods	Boutiques	Medium
5	Manufacturing	Electronic goods	Medium
6	Consumer goods	Toys and games	Small
7	Consumer goods	Toys and games	Micro
8	Banks	Financials	Micro
9	Manufacturing	Electronic goods	Medium
10	Technology	Computer hardware	Small
11	Telecommunications	Mobile telecommunications	Medium
12	Telecommunications	Mobile telecommunications	Medium

Source: The authors.

8 E-commerce development and Internet banking adoption in Cambodia

Reth Soeng, Ludo Cuyvers, and Morarith Soeung

1. Introduction

E-commerce contributes to a dramatic trade cost reduction in sending goods and services to different destinations. Its advantages include reduced time of sending and receiving goods and services, reduced prices and costs, increased sales, higher profits, and expanded market reach (Rahayu and Day, 2017). This has made e-commerce and its applications increasingly popular among many businesses, including those in Cambodia. The use of Internet or online banking services in the country has been rising, thanks to the Government of Cambodia's policy to promote the information and communication technology (ICT) sector and the reasonably fast Internet available at a low cost.[1]

Despite the advantages of e-commerce technology, research suggests that e-commerce adoption still faces many challenges, especially in developing economies where legal frameworks, law enforcement and implementation, and the quality of institutions are still relatively weak and Internet security is a major concern when it comes to financial information (Rahayu and Day, 2017). Therefore, customers must be convinced that online transactions are sufficiently safeguarded.

Factors inhibiting the adoption of e-commerce include customers' lack of trust, security concerns and risks, lack of information technology (IT) knowledge and resources, privacy issues, and lack of understanding of e-commerce. Salwani et al. (2009) listed some reasons why businesses were reluctant to adopt e-commerce technology. These include lack of success stories, not having e-commerce knowledge, low Internet access among consumers, lack of knowledge of e-commerce potential, and lack of information about the impact of e-commerce on performance. A good understanding of consumers' perceptions and intentions regarding the applications of e-commerce is important for developing and formulating strategies to increase the use of online or Internet banking services, which are considered important soft infrastructure to promote regional connectivity.

This chapter contributes to the understanding of ICT development and e-commerce activities in Cambodia and to the literature on e-commerce technology adoption in several ways. First, e-commerce implementation in Cambodia is in its infancy. Cambodia's population is largely unbanked (United

Nations Conference on Trade and Development [UNCTAD], 2017), but the acceptance of banking services and use of Internet banking have increased. Second, to the best of our knowledge, no research has been conducted on its importance for Cambodia, especially on the adoption of Internet or mobile banking services, despite Internet banking being increasingly popular among local consumers. Third, the findings of the current study are expected to serve as important inputs for promoting e-commerce activities, policy formulation, and implementation in Cambodia, as well as listing some implications for Cambodia and countries with similar economic development.

The remainder of the chapter is organized as follows. Section 2 briefly presents Cambodia's ICT development. Section 3 reviews the ICT-related legal framework, policy, and challenges faced by the ICT sector. Section 4 provides some stylized facts on e-commerce in Cambodia. Section 5 present a case study of Internet banking adoption in Cambodia, and Section 6 is the conclusion.

2. ICT development in Cambodia

Cambodia is a highly open economy. Since the 1993 election, it has adopted an open policy towards foreign direct investment (FDI) and trade with the rest of the world. The investment law, drafted and approved in 1994, was amended in 2003 to simplify investment application procedures and make approved investment projects eligible for generous incentives on a non-discriminatory basis. Cambodia received about US$1.58 billion of FDI in 2000, increasing to US$6.2 billion in 2010 and US$18.3 billion by the second quarter of 2017.[2]

The distribution of FDI in Cambodia was uneven during 1994–2017. Labour-intensive manufacturing was the most popular sector, attracting 24 percent of total FDI stocks, followed by the financial sector (21 percent). Over the same period, FDI in telecommunications remained small, at about 3 percent of total FDI stocks. This may pose challenges for the development of ICT and other ICT-related sectors, including electronic commerce (e-commerce), in Cambodia. With the inflows of foreign capital and wide-ranging reforms initiated in the 1990s, Cambodia has made remarkable achievements through impressive economic growth and rapid economic development. It has maintained high economic growth rates[3] and enjoyed prosperity and unprecedented peace since late 1998. Despite these successes, Cambodia has faced several challenges, especially the quality of institutions, which are largely shaped by its history (Hill and Menon, 2013).[4]

E-commerce in Cambodia is in its infancy but has significant development potential (UNCTAD, 2017). This is mainly because of the emergence of a middle class in urban areas, a large pool of young people with a strong desire for IT, the availability and adoption of smartphones and other electronic devices, a 4G network, the latest LTE technologies, and low-cost mobile data in prepaid contracts. The Internet can be easily accessed at an affordable cost through smartphones, tablets, and other devices. Measures to promote e-commerce are included in Cambodia's National Strategic Development Plan 2014–2018 (Royal Government of Cambodia, 2014) and the Rectangular Strategy Phase III (Royal Government of Cambodia, 2013).

According to the Ministry of Posts and Telecommunications (MPTC), Cambodia had 20,402 Internet subscribers in 2000, increasing exponentially to 320,190 in 2010, 6.80 million in 2015, and 7.57 million in 2016 (Figure 8.1). This sharp increase in Internet use correlates with the rise in mobile cellular subscriptions from 4,810 in 1993 to 8.15 million in 2010 and 20.85 million in 2015, although this dropped slightly to 19.92 million in 2016 and 18.6 million in 2017 (MPTC, 2018; World Bank, 2018). Most of them are using their smartphones to access to the Internet. Cambodia's Telecommunications and ICT Development Policy 2020 estimates that 70 percent of the population will have regular Internet access by 2020.

Cambodia has 37 Internet service providers and 19 other Internet-related voice over Internet protocol services (VoIPs) in operation (MPTC, 2018). Three large operators – Cambodia Fiber Optic Communication Network (CFOCN), Viettel Cambodia, and Telecom Cambodia – have established fibre-optic backbone routes with a combined total length of 29,800 kilometres. In addition, submarine cables have been granted to Telcotech, Chuan Wei Cambodia, and CFOCN. Telcotech's submarine cable has been in operation since March 2017, connecting Cambodia, Malaysia, and Thailand. CFOCN's cable has been operated since late

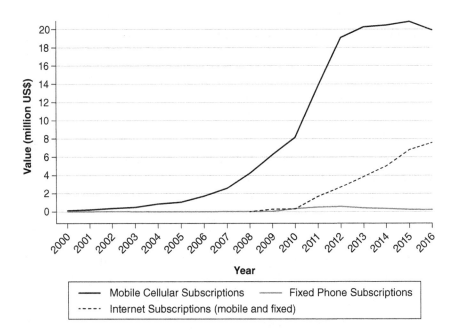

Figure 8.1 Subscription by Service, 2000–2016

Source: MPTC (2018), World Bank (2018).

2017 and connects Cambodia to the Asia-Africa-Europe 1 submarine networks. This could help transform Cambodia into a digital economy, although the level of digitization lags behind other advanced Association of Southeast Asian Nations (ASEAN) member states.

3. ICT-related legal framework and policy in Cambodia

3.1 Institutions responsible for ICT development

Several key public organizations are responsible for building telecommunications infrastructure to promote the digital economy, in particular e-commerce and online business transactions. These include the MPTC, the Telecommunications Regulator of Cambodia (TRC), and the National ICT Development Agency (NiDA), which was integrated into the MPTC in 2013.

The MPTC, responsible for the postal service in Cambodia, proposes legislation to be approved by the legislative body, leads and oversees the telecommunications and ICT sector, and formulates relevant ICT policies for online transactions and activities. To promote e-commerce activities, a supporting postal system has been established and streamlined. In its Cambodia Rapid e-Trade Readiness Assessment, UNCTAD (2017) indicated that an increasing number of people acknowledges electronic banking and related services. The World Bank (2017) reported that 22.2 percent of Cambodians had bank accounts in 2014, up from 3.66 percent in 2011. Electronic banking transactions now exceed over-the-counter dealings. ICT technology has also been introduced in the tourism sector.

NiDA was established in 2000 to promote ICT technology. Originally under the Office of the Council of Ministers with the Prime Minister serving as chair, it was integrated into the MPTC in 2013 to improve public service delivery, efficiency, and effectiveness as their ICT policy responsibilities overlapped.

The TRC was created in late 2012 to formulate telecommunications policy and regulations. It (i) monitors telecommunications services; (ii) proposes legal instruments; (iii) sets standards for the use of telecommunications infrastructure and networks; (iv) promotes competition; grants, alters, suspends, transfers, and withdraws permits, certificates, or licenses; and (v) acts as a regulatory body and resolves disputes relating to the telecommunications sector.

State-owned Telecom Cambodia, under the supervision of the MPTC and the Ministry of Economy and Finance, is responsible for telecommunications and ICT infrastructure. This includes landlines, international gateways, and connections to mobile phone service providers.

The Ministry of Commerce oversees small and medium-sized enterprise development, trade regulations and promotion, intellectual property, and development of e-commerce. It is finalizing the law on e-commerce to promote electronic transactions, protect consumers and their personal information and data, enhance online content regulations, protect consumers against cybercrime, and strengthen cybersecurity.

3.2 Legal framework

Legal frameworks often offer confidence to businesses and the public as to the reliability, integrity, and enforceability of their electronic transactions. ICT-specific laws, decrees, and related legal frameworks are needed to secure digital activities in which electronic documents are protected. Cambodia's ICT-related laws have been initiated to build basic infrastructure for the ICT-related sectors; some have been enacted and others, including the e-commerce law, are in draft form pending review by relevant executive authorities before being submitted for approval by the legislative bodies.

3.2.1 Law on Telecommunications

The Law on Telecommunications was drafted by the MPTC and enacted in 2015. It has two main purposes: (i) ensuring that the utilization and provision of telecommunications infrastructure, networks, and services are made in an effective, reliable, and affordable manner, to support the country's sustainable socio-economic development needs, and (ii) encouraging active participation by the private sector in the development of the telecommunications industry and ensuring fair competition in the industry.

The Law on Telecommunications covers many issues related to telecommunications and development of the sector, including infrastructure and networks; quality of telecommunications services; service obligations; capacity building, research, and development; competition in the telecommunications sector; dispute settlement; telecommunications inspection; and universal service obligation and penalties. The sub-decree on the implementation of universal service obligation was issued on 21 July 2017 to establish a mechanism to execute it effectively. Under the legislation, the MPTC is tasked with formulating the legal framework and policy, strategic plan development, telecommunications infrastructure, inspection, capacity building, and research and development. The law also provides detailed procedures for resolving deputes that may arise among telecommunications operators and/or subscribers, with the TRC playing a mediation role. In addition, it details provisions on penalties for violating the communications practices and law, ranging from monetary fines to heavy prison sentences.

3.2.2 Law on e-commerce

The draft law on e-commerce has been developed to promote trade flows, as well as in response to its ASEAN membership and the e-ASEAN initiative, and increasing online transactions in Cambodia. An inter-ministerial working group on e-commerce law, comprising the Ministry of Commerce, MPTC, and the Ministry of Justice, has been established to draft the e-commerce legislation.[5] The new regulations governance e-commerce eventually got approved by the Office of the Council of Ministers and was set to come into force as of 1 January 2019. It contains provisions on electronic payments, consumer protection in online transactions, data protection, and cybercrime.

The 2018 version of the draft legislation has been made available after several rounds of revisions. With 11 sections and 59 articles, it is comprehensive and covers a wide range of e-commerce-related issues, including general provisions, the validity of electronic communications, communication processes, electronic signatures, e-commerce service providers, consumer protection, government activities and transactions, electronic evidence, e-payments and electronic funds transfers, and offenses against information systems and data.

The draft e-commerce law covers the security of online transactions, such as online consumer protection, data protection, and protection against offenses such as unlawful interference with and interception of data, as well as malware and invasion of privacy. An inter-ministerial committee will be established to implement the legislation after its approval.

The draft e-commerce law also includes elements such as a digital signature framework, which are critical building blocks for the government's ICT development programs (World Bank, 2010). It provides guidance on how to put in place national laws and policies relating to e-commerce transactions based on international norms; facilitate the establishment of mutual recognition of digital signature frameworks; facilitate secure regional electronic transactions, payments, and settlements through mechanisms such as electronic gateways; adopt measures to protect intellectual property rights arising from e-commerce activities; take measures to promote personal data protection and consumer privacy; and encourage the use of alternative dispute resolution mechanisms for online transactions.

3.2.3 Electronic signature

The electronic signature law is a necessary legal instrument to legitimize the electronic signature on an electronic document. In 2017, Cambodia made available a sub-decree that is intended to formalize the use of electronic signatures to facilitate electronic communications and promote e-commerce through efficiency gains and cost reduction. The electronic signature sub-decree gives electronic documents the same legal standing as physical documents. It consists of 41 articles and covers sections on dispute resolutions and specific offenses that are punishable and subject to fines.

3.2.4 Intellectual property law

In Cambodia, the Law on Copyright and Related Rights was enacted in 2003 to provide authors and performers with rights with respect to their works and to protect works of literature, cultural performance, etc. in order to secure a just and legitimate exploitation of those cultural products.[6] The copyrights law grants authors exclusive both moral and economic rights to their works, which is enforceable against all persons.[7] The author's moral right is perpetual and inalienable. As for economic right, authors are given the exclusive right to exploit their own work through the authorization of reproduction, communication to the public, and creation of derivative work.[8] The copyright holder is authorized to bring legal action against parties that violate the law. Remedies include compensation for damages, the redress of moral injury, the return of the disputed materials or equipment, and the return of any benefits deriving from that illegal act.[9] The protection of the economic right starts from the date of the creation of a work and lasts for 50 years after the death of the author.

Cambodia also has a Law on Marks, Trade Names and Acts of Unfair Competition (trademark law) which was promulgated in 2002. Its patent law was enacted in 2003 and a sub-decree was issued in 2006 to implement the trademark law. The legislation gives legal protection to trademarks, service marks, collective marks, and trade names. Under the trademark law, a trademark owner can attack infringement in three different ways: (i) sue for monetary damages and/or specific relief in civil court, (ii) request the customs authorities to suspend the clearance of imported infringing goods, and (iii) seek criminal prosecution and/or fines (BNP Legal, 2012). The patent law aims to encourage innovations and scientific and technological research and development, stimulate and promote trade and investment, promote the transfer of technology, and provide protection over industrial property rights and combat their infringement and other illegal business practices.[10]

Some other important laws – including the consumer protection law, the cybercrime law, and the competition law – are being drafted or are under review by relevant government institutions. They are expected to be promulgated in the near future. A survey by UNCTAD (2017) shows that legal frameworks are very important for e-commerce uptake, since they provide legal protection for consumers, intellectual property, and data and privacy.

3.3 ICT-related policy

ICT is a driving force for many aspects of the national economy, through promoting competitiveness, sustainable economic growth, and development in the age of digitalization. Countries with more developed ICT tend to enjoy an advantage over their competitors and achieve higher economic prosperity through cost advantages, faster business communication, and round-the-clock commercial transactions.

To sustain the country's socio-economic development, in 2016 the government implemented its Telecommunications and ICT Development Policy 2020 (Royal Government of Cambodia, 2016) to serve as a roadmap and mechanism for successful development of the ICT sector. With this policy, Cambodia could continue to sustain high economic growth and equitable economic development in the digital age.

Based on its ICT policy, Cambodia envisages becoming a competitive information-based society that can provide ICT-based solutions for transforming the country into a knowledge-based economy to enhance economic growth and development. To achieve this, the government is committed to achieving the following targets by 2020. First, it is improving and expanding the telecommunications infrastructure and use of sector services by expanding broadband service coverage in urban and rural areas, as well as increasing the Internet penetration rate. By 2020, the government targets increasing broadband service coverage in urban areas to 100 percent, broadband service coverage in rural areas to 70 percent, the mobile penetration rate to 100 percent, the Internet penetration rate to 80 percent, the broadband Internet penetration rate to 70 percent, the percentage of households with Internet access to 30 percent, and the percentage of households with a computer to 30 percent.

Second, the government is developing human resources and capacity in ICT skills by setting a target for 2020 to increase the percentage of government officials with basic ICT skills to 95 percent, the percentage of subnational government officials with basic ICT skills to 75 percent, and the percentage of high school graduates with basic ICT skills to 100 percent. Third, the government is committed to encouraging expansion of the ICT industry and promoting ICT applications in all public institutions. It welcomes more investment in ICT and telecommunications, as well as ICT-related companies. It encourages the intensive use of e-mail and the development of websites in all public institutions.

To achieve the 2020 targets, the government formulated three broad strategies. The first strategy is strengthening the development of the telecommunications and ICT-related sector. The government will develop legal and regulatory frameworks, and formulate policies on broadband, the ICT-related strategic plan, and other ICT-related issues. A sub-decree on digital signatures was issued in late 2017, cybercrime legislation is being prepared, and e-commerce legislation is in final draft form. In addition, telecommunications and ICT infrastructure investment has to be intensified, including the promotion of investment in submarine cable, satellite, and broadband network infrastructure; building and expanding Internet exchange points and the national data centre; and encouraging digital broadcasting. The digital divide is to be narrowed through ICT content and applications in the national language (Khmer), promoting ICT for community development, making available assistive technology for people with disabilities, and equipping women with ICT skills to provide them with greater opportunities for employment. ICT literacy and research and development (R&D) are to be enhanced by improving telecommunications and ICT curricula, establishing an ICT literacy plan, raising public awareness of the benefits of ICT, and promoting public-private partnerships for ICT innovations. A sub-decree on the management of capacity building and telecommunications and ICT R&D was issued on 21 July 2017 to implement the capacity building and telecommunications and ICT R&D plan in an efficient, effective, and transparent manner.

The second strategy is enhancing ICT security. Security is a serious concern among online users, as they are worried that their information and data provided online may leak out to others, as a result of hacking. To address these issues, the government has made efforts to develop and implement ICT security standards, national technical frameworks on ICT security, and best practices; establish the digital forensic laboratory and mechanism to protect information; enhance the security of websites; and increase international cooperation on ICT security.

The third strategy is promoting ICT applications. ICT applications, including e-commerce and e-government, play an important role in enhancing work efficiency and productivity. Because of these benefits, the government has made efforts to introduce, among others, e-government, e-commerce, e-education, e-tourism, and the use of ICT applications for environment-related issues such as environmental protection, climate change adoption and mitigation, and disaster management.

3.4 Challenges

Cambodia was 'reborn' on 7 January 1979 when the country was liberated from the Khmer Rouge regime during which almost 2 million people perished, including the highly educated. Years of wars, a genocidal regime, and internal conflicts destroyed Cambodia's basic infrastructure, educational system, health care, human resources, basic institutions, financial system, judicial system, and telecommunications system. Given this tragic history, the sector has developed rapidly, although the level of ICT development is lower than in some neighbouring countries (Unger and Robinson, 2008). The relatively slow development of the ICT sector may be due to the following factors.

3.4.1 Electricity

Electric power supply continues to be problematic, especially in rural areas where infrastructure lags far behind urban areas, even though the government in 2015 intensified efforts to bridge the divide. The electricity supply is often unstable, which results in frequent blackouts. Electricity cost is much higher in Cambodia than in its neighbouring countries, and even higher in rural areas where the national grid is not available. Pan and Chriv (2009) reported that a large proportion of the population in rural areas did not have access to electricity, and power was supplied by rechargeable batteries. A study by Richardson (2011) suggested that lack of electricity was a major challenge in adopting ICT in education.

3.4.2 Human resources in ICT

High-quality human resources, especially in ICT, are vitally important for the ICT sector in terms of sector development and the use of ICT applications. Enrolment in IT academic programs in higher educational institutions, universities, and colleges has increased noticeably, with many degree holders in IT. However, employers complain that many IT graduates are not employable and lack adequate skills and knowledge for employment in the ICT sector (Unger and Robinson, 2008). It is reported that on-the-job training is needed, which increases hiring costs. In addition, a serious challenge of the government-led development of ICT is high turnover of the government's highly skilled IT employees, who receive lower pay in the public sector than in the private sector.

3.4.3 Investment in the ICT sector

Investments in ICT have been largely made under projects funded by development partners. Donor-funded projects are one-time investments and are often short-lived. Lack of government investments in the ICT sector has a serious impact on the sustainability of the IT systems already created (World Bank, 2010). Thus, government investment in ICT needs to increase, while foreign direct investment into the sector should be encouraged.

3.4.4 Government policy

Government policy affects investment decisions in general and development of the ICT sector as well as e-commerce activities in particular. There has reportedly been a lack of official guidance on how ICT implementation is ensured (World Bank, 2010). However, a sub-decree on Telecommunications and ICT Development Policy 2020 was formally issued in April 2016, detailing many aspects of ICT development and implementation, to achieve the government-targeted level of ICT development in 2020. To be successful, the ICT policy pursues strategies in three main areas: (i) strengthening and expanding telecommunications infrastructure connectivity and services, (ii) human resources development in the ICT sector, and (iii) ICT industry development and ICT usage. With this policy in place, the ICT sector is expected to develop faster to support online transactions and related business activities.

3.4.5 Institutional and legal environment

Institutional and legal environments have been identified as a key driver of successful development of the ICT sector and e-commerce, as they offer legal protection for innovators and online transactions. The quality of domestic institutions – regulatory quality, control of corruption, rule of law, and political stability – have been found to promote the adoption and use of ICT (Martinez and Williams, 2010; Agarwal and Wu, 2015).

In general, the Cambodian government has devoted its meagre resources to improving good governance and institutions (Hughes and Un, 2011). Its commitments to institutions are also reflected in several policy agendas, including the Governance Action Plans and Rectangular Strategy updates. However, Hill and Menon (2013, 2014) have reported that Cambodia's formal institutions are weak. Figure 8.2 depicts the evolution of Cambodia's institutional quality, which is often used as a proxy for the quality of institutions, during 1996–2016. Since 1996, global governance indicators have been assessed

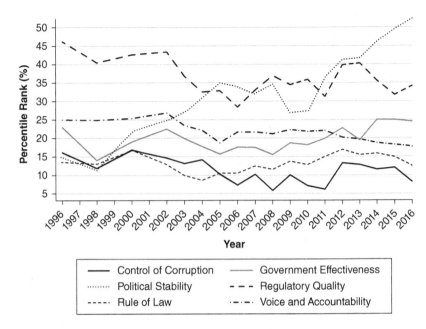

Figure 8.2 Evolution of Cambodia's Institution Quality, 1996–2016

Source: World Bank (2017)

for the World Bank's member countries, covering six aspects of governance: control of corruption, regulatory quality, government effectiveness, rule of law, political stability and absence of violence or terrorism, and voice and accountability. Each country is ranked, using percentiles, for each governance dimension.

On average, Cambodia scored below the 50th percentile rank for almost all dimensions over 1996–2016, except political stability at the 52nd percentile in 2016. Although Cambodia scored below the average for all aspects of governance indicators, it has performed better on some of the governance dimensions – political stability and government effectiveness – during 1996–2016. However, regulatory quality and control of corruption show downward trends during this period, with control of corruption being identified as the most problematic factor for doing business (Hill and Menon, 2013, 2014; WEF, 2016, 2017).

4. Some stylized facts of e-commerce in Cambodia

In its efforts to diversify Cambodia's narrow-based economy and sustain economic growth and development, the government is committed to promoting e-commerce and related online business activities. No definition of e-commerce has yet been established in the literature. Yet, for Cambodia, it is broadly defined as commercial activities via electronic communications (KOICA, 2014). E-commerce in Cambodia is at a nascent stage of development, but developing rapidly, although the country is still facing a lack of ICT infrastructure; legal tools, including e-commerce law and consumer protection legislation; and necessary policies to support secure functioning of these online activities. E-commerce offers both consumers and businesses selling goods and services many benefits, including round-the-clock transactions, ease of delivery, and product information at their fingertips.

Online commercial transactions such as online banking and shopping have become very popular, thanks to the availability of affordable smartphones, reduced prices of electronic devices, as well as shopping portals. Phong et al. (2016) conducted a survey on the uses of mobile phones and the Internet in Cambodia. Their results showed that the phone market in Cambodia is saturated, with over 96 percent of Cambodians owning a phone and almost 100 percent being reachable through some sort of phone. The proportion of people with more than one phone did not change (13 percent), while one in four phone owners used more than one mobile operator, mainly because of more expensive off-net calls.[11] The survey also suggested that 48 percent of Cambodians had at least one smartphone.

Almost half of the population (48 percent) has access to the Internet or Facebook, and five out of every six respondents have their own Facebook account (Phong et al., 2016). Some 85 percent of Facebook users accessed their Facebook through smartphones. In 2016, the Internet or Facebook became the most important information source. Almost one-third of Cambodians did their reading on the Internet.

The TRC (2018) reported that as of February 2018, it had issued telecommunications licenses to 82 ICT operators, of which 37 (more than 45 percent) are Internet service providers and 19 (23 percent) are VoIPs. VoIP service covers the 24 provinces and major cities of Cambodia. Nine mobile phone operators and eight fixed telephone operators are active in the Cambodian telecommunications market. In November 2016, Viettel (Cambodia) enjoyed a market share of almost 46 percent in the mobile cellular market, followed by Smart Axiata at 40 percent and CamGSM at 13 percent. Similarly, in the fixed telephone market, Viettel (Cambodia) captured a market share of 73 percent, leaving the remainder to be shared by Telecom Cambodia at 14 percent and others at 13 percent. In the Internet market, Smart Axiata had a mobile cellular Internet market share of about 60 percent, while Viettel (Cambodia) had 30 percent and CamGSM captured about 10 percent. For the fixed Internet market, Viettel was in the lead, enjoying a market share of more than 60 percent, followed by Cogetel (www. online.com.kh) at 10.31 percent, Telecom Cambodia at 7.60 percent, and Xinwei (Cambodia) Telecom at 6.18 percent.

The evolution and rapid growth of e-commerce in Cambodia is attributed to the rising Internet penetration rate and the prevalence of cheaper and seamless Internet connectivity options. Better Internet infrastructure, increasing use of credit cards made available by banks, and affordable Internet use on smartphones and other electronic devices are also facilitating factors explaining the growing e-commerce activities. The introduction of compatible mobile apps makes it easy for buyers to shop online, make electronic payments at a reduced price, and even get a ride in three-wheeled vehicles or taxis.

The National Bank of Cambodia (2017) reported that electronic payments have grown rapidly. The increase in e-payments is greatly facilitated by new payment systems introduced to enhance trading activities quickly and effectively. Fast and Secure Transfer (FAST), launched in mid-July 2016, is a retail payment system to provide funds to customers on a real-time basis. The National Bank of Cambodia is also developing a central shared switch system to facilitate interbank settlement transactions using debit cards with automated teller machines (ATMs) and point of sale (POS) machines. Cambodia had 1,260 ATMs and 11,761 POS machines in December 2016, but this is undoubtedly higher because of Cambodians' preference for electronic transactions, switching from cash to cashless transactions, and the rapid increase in the use of banking services. A total of 1.55 million debit cards and 55,402 credit cards were issued in 2016 by commercial and specialized banks that operate in Cambodia.

Although formal training in ICT and e-commerce business is lacking, an increasing number of local online shopping portals is available, such as Little-Fashion (www.l192.com), Khmer24 (www.khmer24.com), Khmersupermarket (www.khmersupermarket.com), Sabay (sabay.com), Phsar (www.phsar.net), and Real Estate (www.realestate.com.kh). There are also a number of e-commerce payment gateways, including ACLEDA Bank, Safe Pay Kit, CamboPay, PayWay, Wing, SmartLuy, SmartPay, eMoney, TrueMoney, PayGo, and Pi Pay. With the growing e-payment methods and portals, consumers – especially young people – shop more online (UNCTAD, 2017). These young people look for information about products and services via the Internet on their smartphones and other electronic devices.

5. Internet banking adoption: preliminary evidence for Cambodia

The increasing trend of online transactions presents great opportunities for commercial businesses, including Internet banking. This gives rise to the digital economy, which has reportedly played an increasingly important role and offers many benefits for sellers and consumers, who can exchange goods and services without boundaries. Banks and their consumers greatly benefit from Internet banking (Nath et al., 2001; Cheng et al., 2006). Banks can enjoy cost advantages from lower operating costs by offering Internet banking services and varied services efficiently, as fewer staff members and physical branches are required. They can also enjoy higher profitability through cost savings as a result of automating customer transactions, including funds transfers, payments, and account balance inquiries (Nath et al., 2001).

These value-added services allow banks to retain customers (particularly high-profit clients) and attract new clientele. Customers benefit from convenience, fast speed, and round-the-clock online services. Like their banks, they can also enjoy cost savings and other financial benefits from online banking. They can access and review account information, online transactions, fund transfers between accounts, bill payments, and bank statements (Nath et al., 2001).

Davis (1989) developed a paradigm known as the technology acceptance model (TAM) to explain how people accept or reject the use of IT. According to the TAM, a user's adoption of a particular technology depends on their intention to use the technology, which in turn depends on the perceived ease of use and the perceived usefulness of technology (Davis, 1989; Cheng et al., 2006). The two constructs – perceived usefulness and perceived ease of use – are determining factors for the use of IT in a business organization (Davis, 1989; Cheng et al., 2006) and provide better measures for predicting and explaining system use than other constructs. This makes the TAM a preferred model which has been widely employed to predict the acceptance and use of IT in many sectors, including Internet adoption in the banking sector.

The original TAM was refined several times and was updated by Venkatesh et al. (2003) with the aim of proposing a unified theory of acceptance and use of a technology system. Based on their statistical testing, they identified important predictors of technology adoption, including social influence.

Studies on the adoption of e-commerce have been carried out and are documented in the literature. Using augmented TAM, Cheng et al. (2006) found for Hong Kong that perceived usefulness had the greatest influence on the customer's intention to adopt Internet banking services. Yang (2005) examined the factors that may affect the adoption of mobile commerce in Singapore and found that perceived usefulness influenced the consumer's attitude toward adopting mobile commerce. His results also suggested that gender affected adoption behaviour. Male consumers were found to perceive mobile e-commerce more favourably than their female counterparts. Lee (2009) found that customers' intention to use online banking is positively affected by perceived benefit, attitude, and perceived usefulness, but it is negatively related to financial risk. Santouridis and Kyritsi (2014) reported for Greece that perceived usefulness, perceived credibility, and perceived ease of use were found to be significant determinants of behaviour intention to adopt Internet banking.

5.1. Research methodology

The current study intends to evaluate customers' intention to adopt Internet banking services in Cambodia. Following previous studies (Yang, 2005; Cheng et al., 2006; Lee, 2009; Santouridis and Kyritsi, 2014), we use the augmented TAM by incorporating other factors that may influence the users' adoption of Internet or mobile banking in Cambodia.

A questionnaire was designed by adapting the instruments used by Davis (1989), Salisbury et al. (2001) and Cheng et al. (2006), among others.

A total of 500 questionnaires was distributed to target respondents and Internet banking users in five large banks in Cambodia: Acleda Bank Plc., Advanced Bank of Asia Ltd., Canadia Bank Plc., Kookmin Bank Cambodia Plc., and Chief (Cambodia) Specialized Bank Plc. Since many questionnaires were unusable because of incomplete answers, only 399 have been taken into consideration.

To receive the most accurate responses possible, the questionnaire was translated into Khmer. The questionnaire contains information related to the demographic characteristics of the respondents as well as factors that may affect the consumer's Internet banking adoption, including perceived ease of use, perceived usefulness, attitude towards using Internet banking and social influence. Respondents were asked to respond to each item on a widely used seven-point Likert scale, ranging from 1 (strong disagreement) to 7 (strong agreement). Dependent and explanatory variables that are used in the current study are defined as follows.

The dependent variable is the customer's intention to use Internet banking, which is hypothesized to be influenced by (i) perceived ease of use, (ii) perceived usefulness, (iii) perceived web security, (iv) perceived benefit, (v) performance risk, (vi) financial risk, (vii) social influence, (viii) attitude, and (ix) demographic factors (see Annex 8.1 for details on the explanatory variables employed in the regressions).

The statistical analysis consists of descriptive statistics and other necessary statistical tests to report the best possible results. Reliability and consistency analysis, using Cronbach's alpha coefficient values, was carried out to test the internal consistency of each of the perception and expectation attributes. It is generally accepted that Cronbach's alpha coefficients should be 0.70 or higher to be internally consistent and reliable (Nunnally, 1967; Hair et al., 2010).

5.2. Results and discussion

Table 8.1 presents detailed descriptive statistics of the respondents' demographic characteristics and profile in our sample. Of the 399 usable responses, 52 percent of the respondents are male and 48 percent female, indicating a relatively dominant role of males in the digital economy. About 91 percent of the respondents are 20–40 years old. The distribution of our sample showed a high proportion of respondents with university or college education, with 66.5 percent of the individuals having a university-level education and 25.6 percent having a master's degree. This is consistent with our assumption that younger and well-educated individuals tend to be more familiar with IT and are more likely to adopt new innovations and new technology systems more easily.

Responses to statements on the use of Internet and Internet banking are provided in Table 8.2, which contains the rating of individuals relating to their experience in using the Internet and online banking services. More than 88 percent of respondents reported that they could easily have access to the Internet, and more than 78 percent indicated that the Internet speed was good. Almost 74 percent of the individuals in the sample stated that they used Internet banking frequently,

Table 8.1 Demographic Characteristics of Respondents

Demographic Characteristics	Items	Frequency	Percentage
Gender	Male	192	52.03
	Female	177	47.97
Age	< 20	13	4.15
	20–30	190	60.70
	31–40	94	30.03
	41–50	9	2.88
	> 50	7	2.24
Position	CEO	5	1.26
	Manager	27	6.80
	Company staff member	224	56.42
	Student	45	11.34
	Teacher/professor	26	6.55
	Government official	67	16.88
	Other	3	0.76
Education	Less than high school	7	1.85
	High school	16	4.22
	College/university	252	66.49
	Master's degree	97	25.59
	PhD	7	1.85

Source: The authors.

Table 8.2 Response to Statement on Usage of Internet and Internet Banking Service

Statement	Strongly Disagree	Disagree	Slightly Disagree	Neutral	Slightly Agree	Agree	Strongly Agree
I have easy access to the Internet	2 (0.50)	5 (1.25)	15 (3.76)	32 (8.02)	112 (28.07)	184 (46.12)	49 (12.28)
Internet speed is good	1 (0.25)	7 (1.76)	30 (7.56)	48 (12.09)	135 (34.01)	147 (37.03)	29 (7.30)
Internet fee is low	5 (1.31)	10 (2.61)	25 (6.53)	44 (11.49)	114 (29.77)	132 (34.46)	53 (13.84)
I use Internet banking frequently	7 (1.83)	19 (4.97)	27 (7.07)	47 (12.30)	124 (32.46)	123 (32.20)	35 (9.16)
I encounter problems frequently in using Internet banking	36 (9.09)	35 (8.84)	41 (10.35)	67 (16.92)	115 (29.04)	71 (17.93)	31 (7.83)
I use Internet banking service frequently as source of information	19 (4.77)	17 (4.27)	34 (8.54)	64 (16.08)	101 (25.38)	125 (31.41)	38 (9.55)
Besides Internet banking, I frequently use other banking channels (ATM, phone banking, etc.)	10 (2.52)	15 (3.78)	16 (4.03)	27 (6.80)	92 (23.17)	144 (36.27)	93 (23.43)

Source: The authors.

Note: The values are frequencies, and values in parentheses refer to percentages.

and 66 percent pointed out that they used Internet banking service frequently as a source of information. Almost 83 percent of the individuals reported that they also used other banking channels such as ATMs frequently, but 54 percent pointed out that they experienced problems frequently in using Internet banking. On average, the rating for almost all of the seven statements have a mean score of greater than 5 on the 7-point Likert scale.

Table 8.3 presents basic statistics, multicollinearity check, and reliability check for the included explanatory variables. Most constructs have a mean of well above 5 on the 7-point Likert scale, except social influence with an average rating of 4.85.

Cronbach's alpha values for all variables are very high, far exceeding the 0.7 cut-off recommended by Hair et al. (2010). As can be seen from Table 8.3, Cronbach's alpha estimated for perceived ease of use is 0.89, perceived usefulness is 0.92, attitude is 0.93, and social influence is 0.90. The constructs are therefore deemed to have adequate reliability. Based on estimated reliability coefficients, it is apparent that the scale for all constructs is highly reliable.

The problem of multicollinearity can be examined by the variance inflation factor (VIF). The VIF, which indicates the extent to which an explanatory variable can be explained by the other explanatory variables in the model, is widely used in the empirical literature to check whether multicollinearity is present in the regression equation. High multicollinearity masks the impact of the individual effect of each explanatory variable. Referring to Table 8.3, the VIF values for all independent variables are much less than 5, implying that multicollinearity issues are of no concern.

Table 8.4 reports the correlation between the dependent and explanatory variables. The correlation between the intention to use Internet banking and each explanatory variable is highly significant at the 1 percent level, except gender which is significant at 5 percent. Education is not statistically correlated with Internet banking usage.

We also performed regression analysis to show vigorously how each factor affects Internet banking adoption in Cambodia. The results of our regression analysis are provided in Table 8.5. Four of the eight factors – perceived ease of use, attitude of consumers, perceived benefit, and social influence – are found to be significant in predicting consumers' intention to adopt Internet banking in Cambodia.

Table 8.3 Statistical Description of Explanatory Variables

Variable Name	Mean	Standard Deviation	VIF	Cronbach's Alpha (α)
Perceived ease of use	5.29	1.03	2.98	0.89
Perceived usefulness	5.57	1.04	4.21	0.92
Attitude	5.65	1.03	4.21	0.93
Social influence	4.85	1.41	1.58	0.90

Source: The authors.

Table 8.4 Correlation Matrix

Variable Name	Intention to Use	Perceived Ease of Use	Perceived Usefulness	Attitude	Social Influence	Gender	Education
Intention to Use	1.00						
Perceived Ease of Use	0.65***	1.00					
Perceived Usefulness	0.68***	0.78***	1.00				
Attitude	0.72***	0.74***	0.80***	1.00			
Social Influence	0.39***	0.31***	0.34***	0.36***	1.00		
Gender	0.11#**	0.10*	0.15***	0.11**	2×10^{-3}	1.00	
Education	-0.01	-0.03	-0.04	-0.02	-0.15*	0.13**	1.00

Source: The authors.

Note: ***, ** and * refers to statistical significance at the level of 1%, 5%, and 10%, respectively.

Table 8.5 Estimation Results for Internet Banking Adoption in Cambodia

Variable Name	(1)	(2)
Perceived ease of use	0.141	0.155*
	(0.087)	(0.093)
Perceived usefulness	0.126	0.118
	(0.075)	(0.080)
Perceived web security	1.28×10^{-5}	-0.013
	(0.033)	(0.033)
Attitude	0.258***	0.259***
	(0.074)	(0.078)
Perceived benefit	0.247***	0.260***
	(0.070)	(0.076)
Performance risk	0.047	0.030
	(0.040)	(0.040)
Financial risk	-0.022	-0.013
	(0.032)	(0.031)
Social influence	0.099**	0.094**
	(0.033)	(0.032)
Gender	–	0.016
		(0.069)
Education	–	0.034
		(0.126)
R-squared	0.591	0.601
No. of observations	390	363

Source: The authors.

Notes:
1. Standard errors are heteroskedasticity robust standard errors in parentheses.
2. * denotes that the slope parameter estimates are statistically significant at the level of 10%, ** at 5%, and *** at 1%.

These results provide strong statistical support for the hypotheses that perceived benefit, attitude, and social influence are positively related to Internet banking adoption. Estimation results reveal that perceived benefit is a significant positive determinant, contributing most significantly to consumers' intention to adopt Internet banking in Cambodia. Several benefits are associated with the adoption of Internet banking services. Referring to the empirical results of the current study, it confirms that Internet banking is more advantageous than traditional banking, as it creates an instant link between customers and banking services. In comparison to traditional bricks and mortar, Internet banking provides more flexibility to carry out round-the-clock banking transactions because of time flexibility and convenience, as well as service provision, without boundaries. The results also suggest that people tend to be attracted to Internet banking, thanks to its ease of use. As expected, the attitude of consumers towards Internet banking is also found to have a significant positive impact on Internet banking adoption.

The coefficient of social influence is positive, as expected, and is significant at the 5 percent level, suggesting that social influence has a positive effect on Internet banking adoption in Cambodia. This implies that customers feel that the use of Internet banking brings them prestige and image in society. The experience of peers and friends regarding the advantages of Internet banking is clearly a motivating factor for individuals to adopt the new banking technology. The estimated coefficient of social influence is 0.094, which is economically small. The estimate of perceived benefit is 0.26, so perceived benefit is by far the largest contributor in predicting Internet banking adoption compared with the effect of social influence. The findings imply that customers' attraction to Internet banking is attributed more to perceived benefit felt by consumers than to social influence from peers and friends.

The current study also investigates if the demographic characteristics of the consumers – gender and education level – affect their intention to use Internet banking. No evidence is found with respect to the relationship between Internet banking adoption in Cambodia and gender and education.

6. Concluding remarks

We have taken stock of the development of ICT, which is important to develop e-commerce activities and other online business communications. as the development of ICT will allow to transform Cambodia's narrow-based economy into a knowledge-based or digital one, in order to sustain its high economic growth and achieve equitable economic development. ICT and its applications, such as e-commerce and other online businesses, have developed rapidly in Cambodia. Although in its infancy, ICT has been introduced in many sectors, including education, tourism, health, transportation, administration, and commercial activities. Government institutions now have their own websites, although some are under construction.

To support the ICT sector and applications, the government has made great efforts to build ICT infrastructure and ICT-related legal frameworks to safeguard intellectual property and promote ICT investments, provide protection for consumers' data and privacy, and bolster users' confidence. Concurrently, access to information has been streamlined through the government's policy to promote the ICT sector and ensure fair competition within the sector. Investment in telecommunications has been particularly encouraged. As a result, 82 ICT operators have invested in the sector. The country is home to nine mobile cellular operators and eight fixed telephone operators, which also provide mobile and fixed Internet services across Cambodia's 24 provinces and major cities.

The current study also presents a case study to examine the factors that may affect Internet banking adoption in Cambodia using the augmented TAM. Our findings, based on a data set of 399 observations, show that perceived benefit is the most influential factor in Internet banking adoption, followed by attitude and social influence. Relatively speaking, it is easier to persuade customers to use Internet banking by letting them become aware of the perceived benefit than doing so via enhancing the social influence from peers.

This study offers some further practical implications. First, since consumers find it beneficial to use Internet banking, this points to the additional advantage of Internet banking over other traditional banking services; therefore, it is crucial to design a marketing strategy to inform potential users and the public of the benefits of online banking, which will contribute to the promotion of Cambodia's digital economy. Second, banks may change the attitude of consumers by highlighting the benefits of Internet banking in their promotional and advertising activities. Third, bank customers are concerned with their social image and are influenced by their peers; thus, users of Internet banking can serve as promotors for further adoption of online banking. Fourth, efforts should be intensified to move forward with the draft e-commerce law and other relevant legislation such as consumer protection law, competition law, data protection law, and cybercrime law. The enactment of these important long-awaited laws is expected to boost the ICT development level to a new high, thereby enhancing e-commerce activities and many related sectors that depend on reliable access to ICT services. Challenges, including physical infrastructure, need to be addressed effectively to develop the ICT sector to sustain Cambodia's high economic growth and achieve equitable development.

Notes

1 The Internet industry in Cambodia is considered very competitive, having brought tariffs down significantly from between 15–28 cents in 2001 depending on depending on whether call is fixed to mobile, mobile to fixed or mobile to another mobile network (ITU, 2002) to 5–11 cents in 2010 (Vong et al., 2012).
2 The amounts are FDI stocks in Cambodia, based on the data made available by the National Bank of Cambodia (2017).
3 Since 1991, Cambodia recorded impressive growth of GDP of 7 percent per annum on average, graduating from the World Bank status of low-income country to lower middle-income country in 2016. If this rate of growth continues, Cambodia's income would double every 10 years. Based on this success, in 2016 the Asian Development Bank predicted that Cambodia would become the

new Asian Tiger economy. However, this high economic growth does not seem to benefit the poor much, especially those residing in rural areas, as economic development is uneven and over-concentrated in Phnom Penh and other urban areas (Cuyvers et al., 2009), encouraging the migration of workers from rural to urban areas. Urban-rural inequality appears to have been widened, which is also seen in many developing and advanced economies.

4 Efforts were made during the 1990s, when Cambodia was relatively at peace, to rebuild basic infrastructure and formal institutions abolished by the Khmer Rouge regime.

5 Reportedly, the e-commerce law has moved very slowly because it has to go through a number of review processes before the law can be submitted for approval by legislative bodies.

6 Article 1 of the Law on Copyright and Related Rights.

7 Article 18 of the Law on Copyright and Related Rights.

8 Article 21 of the Law on Copyright and Related Rights.

9 Article 57 of the Law on Copyright and Related Rights.

10 Article 2 of the Patent Law, Utility Models and Industrial Designs.

11 In Cambodia, it is more expansive when a call is made from one network to another. To avoid this, an increasing number of Cambodians own more than one cellular phone.

Bibliography

Agarwal, J. and T. Wu (2015), 'Factors Influencing Growth Potential of E-Commerce in Emerging Economies: An Institution-Based N-OLI Framework and Research Propositions', *Thunderbird International Business Review*, 57(3): 197–215.

BNP Legal (2012), *Trademark Law in Cambodia*. Phnom Penh: BNP Legal.

Cheng, T.C.E., D.Y.C. Lam and A.C.L. Yeung (2006), 'Adoption of Internet Banking: An Empirical Study in Hong Kong', *Decision Support Systems*, 42(3): 1558–1572.

Cuyvers, L., D. Van Den Bulcke and R. Soeng (2009), 'The Competitive Position of a Developing Economy: The Role of Foreign Direct Investment in Cambodia', in D. Van Den Bulcke, A. Verbeke and W. Yuan (eds.), *Handbook on Small Nations in the Global Economy: The Contribution of Multinational Enterprises to National Economic Success*, Cheltenham-Northampton: Edward Elgar Publ. Ltd, pp. 244–272.

Davis, F.D. (1989), 'Perceived Usefulness, Perceived Ease of Use, and User Acceptance of Information Technology', *MIS Quarterly*, 13(3): 319–340.

Davis, F.D., R. Bagozzi and P. Warshaw (1989), 'User Acceptance of Computer Technology: A Comparison of two Theoretical Models', *Management Science*, 35(8): 982–1003.

Hair, J.F, W.C. Black, B.J. Babin and R.E. Anderson (2010), *Multivariate Data Analysis: A Global Perspective*. Harlow, UK: Pearson.

Hill, H. and J. Menon (2013), 'Cambodia: Rapid Growth with Weak Institutions', *Asian Economic Policy Review*, 8(1): 46–65.

Hill, H. and J. Menon (2014), 'Cambodia: Rapid Growth in an Open, Post-conflict Economy', *The World Economy*, 37(12): 1649–1668.

Hughes, C. and K. Un (eds.) (2011), *Cambodia's Economic Transformation*. Copenhagen: NIAS Press.

ITU (2002), *Khmer Internet: Cambodia Case Study*. Geneva: International Telecommunication Union (ITU).

Iv Tek, T. (2017), 'Status on Digital Infrastructure in Cambodia', Presentation by Tram Iv Tek, Minister of Posts and Telecommunications at the 2017 Global ICT Leadership Forum.

KOICA (2014), 'Cambodian ICT Masterplan 2020', Phnom Penh.

Lee, M-C. (2009), 'Factors Influencing the Adoption of Internet Banking: An Integration of TAM and TPB with Perceived Risk and Perceived Benefit', *Electronic Commerce Research and Application*, 8(3): 130–141.

Martinez, C.A. and C. Williams (2010), 'National Institutions, Entrepreneurship and Global ICT Adoption: A Cross-Country Test of Competing Theories', *Journal of Electronic Commerce*, 11(1): 73–91.

Ministry of Posts and Telecommunications (2016), 'Telecommunication and ICT Development Policy 2020', Phnom Penh.

MPTC (2018), 'Monthly Report for February 2018', Phnom Penh.

Nath, R., P. Schrick and M. Parzinger (2001), 'Banker's Perspectives on Internet Banking', *E-Service Journal*, 1(1): 21–36.

National Bank of Cambodia (2017), 'Annual Report 2016', Phnom Penh.

Nunnally, J.C. (1967), *Psychometric Theory*. New York: McGraw-Hill.

Pan, S. and K. Chriv (2009), 'Cambodia', in S. Akhtar and P. Arinto (eds.), *Digital Review of Asia Pacific 2009–2010*. New Delhi: Orbicom and the International Development Research Centre, pp. 167–174.

Phong, K., L. Srou and J. Solá (2016), 'Mobile Phones and Internet Use in Cambodia 2016', Phnom Penh.

Rahayu, R. and J. Day (2017), 'E-Commerce Adoption by SMEs in Developing Countries: Evidence from Indonesia', *Eurasian Business Review*, 7(1): 25–41.

Richardson, J.W. (2011), 'Challenges of Adopting the Use of Technology in Less Developed Countries: The Case of Cambodia', *Comparative Education Review*, 55(1): 8–29.

Royal Government of Cambodia (2013), 'Rectangular Strategy Phase II', Phnom Penh.

Royal Government of Cambodia (2014), 'Cambodia's National Strategic Development Plan 2014–2018', Phnom Penh.

Royal Government of Cambodia (2015), 'Cambodia Industrial Development Policy 2015–2025', Phnom Penh.

Royal Government of Cambodia (2016), 'Sub-Decree on Implementation of Telecommunications and ICT Development Policy 2020', Phnom Penh.

Safeena, R., A. Kammani and H. Date (2014), 'Assessment of Internet Banking Adoption: An Empirical Analysis', *Arabian Journal for Science and Engineering*, 39(2): 837–849.

Salisbury, W.D., R.A. Pearson, A.W. Pearson and D.W. Miller (2001), 'Perceived Security and World Wide Web Purchase Intention', *Industrial Management and Data Systems*, 101(4): 165–177.

Salwani, M.I., G. Marthandan, M.D. Norzaidi and S.C. Chong (2009), 'E-Commerce Usage and Business Performance in the Malaysian Tourism Sector: Empirical Analysis', *Information Management and Computer Security*, 17(2): 166–185.

Santouridis, I. and M. Kyritsi (2014), 'Investigating the Determinants of Internet Banking Adoption in Greece', *Procedia Economics and Finance*, 9: 501–510.

Telecommunication Regulator of Cambodia (TRC) (2018), 'Type of Telecommunications Licenses'. Available at www.trc.gov.kh/licenses/

Unger, B. and N. Robinson (2008), 'Cambodia', in F. Librero (ed.), *Digital Review of Asia Pacific 2007–2008*. New Delhi: Orbicom and the International Development Research Centre, pp. 122–130.

United Nations Conference on Trade and Development (UNCTAD) (2017), *Cambodia: Rapid eTrade Readiness Assessment*. Geneva: United Nations.

Venkatesh, V., M.G. Morris, G.B. Davis and F.D. Davis (2003), 'User Acceptance of Information Technology: Toward a Unified View', *MIS Quarterly*, 27(3): 425–478.

Vong, S., D.H. Lee and G. Zo (2012), 'Cambodia Mobile Telecommunication Market: Opportunities and Challenges', Paper presented at the 19th ITS Biennial Conference 2012, Bangkok, Thailand.

World Bank (2010), *Cambodia: Review of Government Information and Communications Technologies (ICTs) Policies and Investments*. Washington, DC: World Bank.

World Bank (2017), *World Development Indicators 2016*. Washington, DC: World Bank.

World Bank (2018), *World Development Indicators 2017*. Washington, DC: World Bank.

World Economic Forum (WEF) (2016), *The Global Competitiveness Reports 2016*. Geneva: WEF.

World Economic Forum (WEF) (2017), *The Global Competitiveness Reports 2017*. Geneva: WEF.

Yang, K.C.C. (2005), 'Exploring Factors Affecting the Adoption of Mobile Commerce in Singapore', *Telematics and Informatics*, 22(3): 257–277.

Annex 8.1

Table 8A.1 List of Explanatory Variables

Variable	Notes
Perceived ease of use	The degree to which a person believes that using a technology system would be free of effort (Davis et al., 1989).
Perceived usefulness	The degree to which a person believes that using a technology system would enhance their job performance (Davis et al., 1989).
Perceived web security	The extent to which one believes that the Internet is secure for transmitting sensitive information (Cheng et al., 2006).
Perceived benefit	Customers benefit from a wider range of lower transaction fees and faster transaction speeds, resulting in low costs and time savings since online banking is paperless and requires much fewer personnel (Lee, 2009). Moreover, online banking allows customers to engage in transactions and monitor contractual performance continuously from anywhere.
Performance risk	Losses caused by deficiencies or malfunctions of online banking websites (Lee, 2009). This occurs because of a breakdown in system servers or disconnection from the Internet while conducting online transactions.
Financial risk	The potential for monetary losses due to transaction errors or bank account misuse (Lee, 2009). According to Lee (2009), customers are afraid of losing money while performing transactions or transferring money on the Internet. When errors occur, they usually face difficulties in obtaining compensation.
Social influence	The extent to which a consumer perceives that people who are important to him/her would believe that he/she should use the Internet banking system.
Attitude	The individual's positive or negative feelings about performing a particular behaviour (Cheng et al., 2006).
Demographic factors	Identified as determinants of the use and adoption of a technology system. Safeena et al. (2014) found that gender has affected Internet banking.

Source: The authors.

9 E-commerce in the Philippines

Gains and challenges

Ramon L. Clarete

1. Introduction

E-connectivity of countries in the region has the potential of opening up cross-border trade opportunities, particularly for small and medium-sized enterprises (SMEs) in global trade (APEC, 2017; ASEAN Secretariat, 2015). Kimura (2018) noted how information and communications technology (ICT) had facilitated the global fragmentation of production, which not only permitted countries to perform specific tasks in production based on their respective comparative advantages, but also accordingly expanded global trade significantly. However, further ICT development opened up the unbundling of tasks. Transaction costs are significantly lowered, giving way to faceless transactions in digital commerce. The use of digital platforms and increasingly efficient and dependable logistics systems give SMEs the opportunities to internationalise their businesses.

The Philippines has great potential to gain from the digital economy. However, when compared with its neighbours, the country seems to lag behind in e-commerce, despite its recent gains in technology-facilitated business process outsourcing. This chapter investigates how the Philippine market remains to be constrained by several factors but particularly in the poor quality of Internet access and payment system. The rest of chapter is organised as follows: Section 2 provides an overview of the development of e-commerce in the Philippines, based on which section 3 summarises the key features of the online market. Section 4 assesses the country's readiness for a digital economy, and Section 5 reviews the government's efforts in providing legal and institutional support to promote e-connectivity for e-commerce. Section 6 concludes.

2. E-commerce in the Philippines

The Organisation for Economic Co-operation and Development (2013) defines online commerce as using 'computer networks by methods designed for the purpose of receiving or placing of orders'. It is how the transaction or purchase is placed that separates online commerce from other retail markets. The transaction can be between businesses (B2B), with consumers (B2C), between consumers (C2C), and with governments (B2G).

2.1. Global e-commerce sales

Collection of e-commerce statistics is fairly recent, and generally has been undertaken by private entities of e-commerce stakeholders. It provides analysts with online commerce data that tends to be narrower in span and with shorter time frames, confining the number and quality of quantitative analyses on the determinants of e-commerce growth. Lemma (2017) noted that the lack of data on e-commerce prevents the measurement of the impacts on cross-border e-commerce of the proposals at the World Trade Organization (WTO) to liberalise and facilitate trade.

Based on existing data, global B2C retail sales reached US$2.3 trillion in 2017 and are projected to reach US$4.9 trillion in 2021 (Figure 9.1). Annual growth has been strong. Statista (2018) reported such sales at US$1.3 trillion in 2014. The compounded annual growth rate over the eight-year period is 17.6 percent.

North America had the largest share of total e-commerce sales in the world in 2012, claiming nearly 36 percent of the total. However, Asia-Pacific surpassed it in 2014, and in 2017 the region claimed nearly half of total B2C retail sales of the world, as Table 9.1 shows. The region's performance is largely due to the strong growth of China's economy and online market. The compounded annual growth rate (CAGR) of the region's online market from 2012–2017 was 23.2 percent, more than double that of North America of 9.7 percent. However, Asia-Pacific

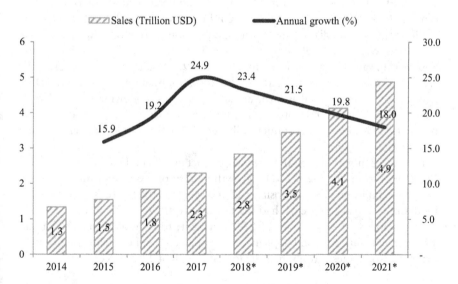

Figure 9.1 Global B2C E-commerce Sales and Growth, 2014–2021

Note:

* projected data

Source: The author. Based on Statista (2018).

Table 9.1 B2C E-commerce Sales Worldwide by Region, 2012–2017 (in Billion US$)

	2012	2013	2014	2015*	2016*	2017*
Asia-Pacific	301.2	383.9	525.2	681.2	855.7	1,052.9
North America	379.8	431	482.6	538.3	579.9	660.4
Western Europe	277.5	312	347.4	382.7	414.2	445
Central and Eastern Europe	41.5	49.5	58	64.4	68.9	73.1
Latin America	37.6	48.1	57.7	64.9	70.6	74.6
Middle East and Africa	20.6	26.9	33.7	39.5	63.4	51.4
Worldwide	1,058.2	1,251.4	1,504.6	1,771	2,052.7	2,357.4

Source: eMarketer.

Note: *Estimated data.

regional e-commerce has slowed in recent years. Statista (2018) estimated the CAGR of Asia's online market at only 11.7 percent from 2018 to 2022.

2.2. The Philippine online market

Figure 9.2 shows the e-commerce market of the Philippines from 2016–2022, growing at a rate of 17.2 percent a year. In 2016, the value of the B2C market was US$1.01 billion and projected to reach US$2.6 billion in 2022. The annual growth of online sales ranged from a low of 12.6 percent to a high of 31.3 percent in 2018. The CAGR is 17.23 percent between 2016 and 2022.

Electronic and media products made up the largest component of the market with their average annual sales in 2016 and 2017 reported at US$506.6 million, which was 47 percent of the total (Figure 9.3). Besides this group, the mix comprised food and personal care articles; toys, hobby, and do-it-yourself (DIY) items; and fashion, as well as furniture and appliances. Following the top largest were toys, hobby, and DIY products (18 percent). A close third were the fashion products (17%). Furniture products followed (10%), while food and personal care articles accounted for 8%.

Figure 9.4 shows the CAGRs of these product groups in the B2C market in the Philippines from 2016–2022. The growth pattern of the groups mirrored their relative standing in the composition of the online market. The smallest group, food and personal care items, had the fastest growth, at 28.35 percent. Fashion products followed with a rate of 23.14 percent; toys, hobby, and DIY items, 19.6 percent; furniture and appliances, 16.3 percent; and electronics and media items, the top largest group, had the lowest CAGR at 11.3 percent.

2.3. Philippines vs. selected ASEAN countries

Compared with the e-commerce markets of selected countries in the Association of Southeast Asian Nations (ASEAN), the market in the Philippines is the smallest. Table 9.2 compares the e-commerce markets of six ASEAN countries in

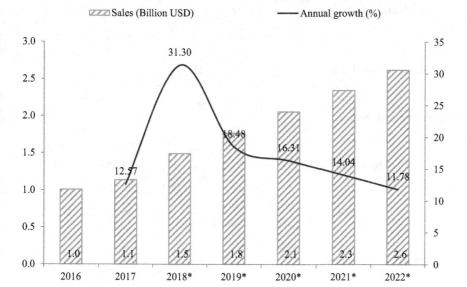

Figure 9.2 E-commerce Market in the Philippines, 2016–2022 (in Million US$)

Note:

* projected data

Source: The author. Based on Statista (2018).

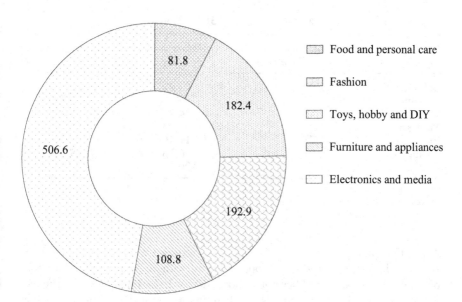

Figure 9.3 Product Mix of Online Market in the Philippines, Average 2016–2017 (in Billion US$)

Source: The author. Based on Statista (2018).

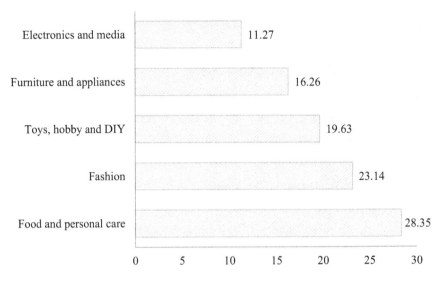

Figure 9.4 Average Growth Rate of Product Groups Purchased Online in the Philippines, 2016–2022 (%)

Source: The author. Based on Statista (2018).

Table 9.2 E-commerce Markets in Selected ASEAN Countries, 2016

Country	Sales (in Billion US$)	Share (in %)	Growth Rate (in %)
Indonesia	5.29	35.27	20.70
Thailand	2.89	19.27	16.70
Singapore	2.13	14.20	n.d.
Malaysia	1.97	13.13	23.70
Viet Nam	1.71	11.40	17.20
Philippines	1.01	6.73	18.30
Total	15	100	

n.d. = no data.
Source: Statista (2018)

2017. The Philippines had only 6.73 percent of the total regional market of the six countries in 2016. Indonesia topped the list with 35.27 percent, which may be explained by the size of her population. Although the Philippines has the second largest population in ASEAN, its share in the regional e-commerce market is significantly exceeded by the other four countries (Malaysia, Singapore, Thailand, and Viet Nam) with smaller populations (Table 9.2). However, it was the third fastest growing market – Malaysia's online commerce expanded the most in

2016, followed by that of Indonesia. The growth of the online markets of Viet Nam and Thailand were comparable to that of the Philippines.

3. Key features of the online market in the Philippines

The key features of the e-commerce environment in the Philippines are important to understand the market's performance. One factor is that the country's ICT infrastructure level and quality are inadequate for the potentially large market (Kinasih, 2016). The Philippines has the second slowest Internet connection among Asia-Pacific countries, and it is the lowest among ASEAN countries in terms of facilitating businesses.

The country has a relatively large population, with a comparatively high propensity for using the Internet and mobile phones. The Department of Trade and Industry (DTI, 2016) regards this as positive for the advancement of the market. It cited a survey result that Filipinos use the Internet an average of 6.3 hours every day. Mobile subscriptions in the Philippines exceeded its 101.1 million population by 13.5 million.

Second, the number of active Internet users in the country was 44.2 million, according to a survey conducted by We Are Social (2018). Of these users, 42 million used the Internet and mobile phones for social media. More users have already had online shopping experience. But in general, Filipinos still prefer instead to go to malls 'as it has become a part of their culture' (DTI, 2016).

Third, the degree of concentration of e-platforms is high, indicating less competition. Lazada, which Alibaba controls, is the leading platform for e-commerce in the country. The number of merchants participating in its platform has doubled to 4,000 compared to 2016. E-commerce platforms exhibit scale economies, being a disadvantage to late entrants, especially if these are inadequately capitalised. iTrue Mart, a Thai e-marketplace that operated locally, closed shop in less than a year. The major retailers in the Philippines, SM department store and Robinsons Appliances, have tested online retailing using Lazada's platform. Samsung is likewise using this online marketplace to sell its electronic products on the Internet.

Fourth, the C2C e-commerce market in the Philippines continues to thrive, with OLX providing the largest platform. About 100,000–200,000 sellers of varying supply capacities participate in C2C platforms. Filipinos give strong preference for variety. Branded imported products are in high demand. With the cross-border B2C market in the country still small, C2C markets continue to be vibrant. Under online C2C transactions, the intermediation cost is saved, giving both sellers and buyers their respective shares in the margins that would have gone to retailers in a B2C transaction.

The option for payment upon delivery makes C2C popular in the Philippines. The low degree of financial inclusion of the population could raise the cost of using online platforms, which require the use of credit cards or e-cash. Kinasih (2016) reported that only 3 percent of Filipinos use credit cards and 70 percent of the population is unbanked. Thus, the payment on delivery mitigates a disadvantage of C2C transactions, which is a risk either on the part of the seller of not being paid, or on the part of the buyer of not having any after-sales service or warranties.

This arrangement is not necessarily unique to C2C markets. There are B2C transactions which are consummated with payment upon delivery. With this, B2C sellers may stay competitive with C2C suppliers.

The next feature, however, gives an important boost to C2C transactions: the use of 'balikbayan' boxes. Overseas Filipinos returning to or visiting the country from abroad tend to bring with them presents for their immediate or extended family members, putting these in such boxes as accompanied luggage. The boxes are still used as such, but their use has diversified into use for commercial transactions. Brokerage firms engage in the business of door-to-door delivery of these boxes. They clear such boxes through customs, and arrange through a local logistics firm for their delivery to their intended addressees.

This facilitates C2C transactions. Through 'balikbayan' boxes, Filipinos in the Philippines may indirectly gain access to cross-border merchandise and purchase online from abroad. Through their relatives or friends, Filipinos can get access to merchandise from Amazon or other international marketplaces, especially in the United States. These virtual intermediaries, residents in the United States, place the online order for a B2C transaction, and with the goods delivered place the merchandise inside 'balikbayan' boxes to ship to the Philippines.

It is worth noting that compared to that of B2C, statistics of C2C e-commerce sales may be under-reported. For instance, although C2C transactions completed through digital platforms such as OLX can be documented, there are C2C sales that do not go through such platforms. These are transacted using the network of relatives and friends, which makes C2C transactions hard to document. 'Balikbayan' boxes are break bulk shipments, and it is difficult to determine if the boxes contain legitimate presents or products that may be purchased as B2C abroad and sold locally under a C2C arrangement.

Last, poor infrastructure, the archipelagic nature of the country, and high incidence of payment on delivery are enough to scare companies from offering delivery services to complete online transactions. International delivery companies find the country's processes complicated, which makes the online market in the Philippines unlike any in the rest of ASEAN, where foreign not local delivery companies dominate the logistics part of the supply chain.

Filipino logistics companies, such as LBC and 2GO, have expanded their networks all over the country to encompass delivery to the provinces. Other delivery companies operate only in Metro Manila.

4. Readiness for e-commerce development

Readiness indicators for e-commerce in the Philippines are presented and compared with those of five other ASEAN countries in Tables 9.3–9.7. These are grouped into five categories, namely: access to ICT infrastructure and services, trade logistics and trade facilitation, e-commerce skills indicators, access to financing, and payment options indicators.

4.1. Access to ICT infrastructure

Four indicators are presented in Table 9.3. They describe the level and quality of access of Filipinos to ICT infrastructure and services. The country is not in the bottom with regard to such access. However, it had the third or second lowest score in all indicators among the selected ASEAN countries between 2014 and 2015.

The Philippines ranked second lowest in terms of the number of Internet users per 100 people, second highest in Internet tariffs, the lowest in Internet subscriptions, and third lowest in mobile broadband subscriptions. Except for the tariffs, which is in units of currency, the numbers in the table are the number of subscribers or users per 100 people.

The country's Internet speed, as already noted, was one of the slowest in Asia-Pacific, according to a survey done for Akamai Technologies' Global State of the Internet Report (Barreiro, 2017). The country has an average interconnection speed of 5.5 Mbps, lower than the global average of 7.2 Mbps. In comparison with other ASEAN countries, Singapore, Thailand, Malaysia, Indonesia, and Viet Nam have speeds equal to 20.3, 16.0, 8.9, 7.2, and 9.5 Mbps, respectively. It should be pointed out, however, that the country's Internet speed improved from about 3.5 Mbps in 2015.

4.2. E-commerce skills

The Philippines topped the indicator of the proportion of firms using e-mail to interact with clients/suppliers (Table 9.4), with 80 percent of the enterprises

Table 9.3 Access to ICT Infrastructure and Services, 2014–2015

	Indonesia	Malaysia	Philippines	Singapore	Thailand	Viet Nam
Internet users (per 100 people) – ITU Database	22	71.1	40.7	82.1	39.3	52.7
Fixed broadband Internet tariffs, PPP US$/ month – ITU Database	25.1	55.4	51.6	33	40.14	7.1
Fixed broadband subscriptions per 100 inhabitants – ITU Database	1.1	9	3.4	26.5	9.2	8.1
Active mobile broadband subscriptions per 100 inhabitants – ITU Database	42	89.9	41.6	142.2	75.3	39

Source: The author. Raw data retrieved from ITU (2015).

Table 9.4 E-commerce Skills Indicators in Selected ASEAN Countries, 2015

	Indonesia	Malaysia	Philippines	Singapore	Thailand	Viet Nam
Percent of firms using e-mail to interact with clients/suppliers – Enterprise Survey	30.6	46.2	80.4	-	52.9	91.5
B2B ICT use	4.9	5.7	4.9	5.8	5	4.9
B2C Internet use	5.4	5.9	4.8	5.5	5.1	4.9
Firms' technology absorption	5.1	5.6	5.1	5.7	4.9	3.9

Source: The author. Raw data retrieved from WEF (2017).

using e-mail. However, it ranked low or average in three networked readiness indicators from a survey done by the World Economic Forum. The country's scores in each of these three indicators run from 1–7 (highest). In two indicators having to do with B2B or B2C e-commerce, the country scored the lowest. It scored average in the readiness of business firms to adopt new technologies.

4.3. *Trade logistics and facilitation*

Table 9.5 lists ten indicators on the support to e-commerce provided by the trade logistics and facilitation system in the country. Four of these are on the quality of the postal service in the country, another four are from the World Bank's logistics performance index (LPI), and the last two are about the quality of customs services. In all ten indicators, the country scored worst in eight. The LPI indicator scores range from 1 (lowest) to 5 (highest). The country scored lowest in two indicators, and was a close second lowest to Indonesia or Viet Nam in the other two. The Philippines had the worst customs service indicator; it takes 14.5 days for exports to clear customs control.

4.4. *Access to financing and payment options*

The country has weak access to financing compared to four other ASEAN countries. It had the lowest proportion of working capital financed by banks, 5.1 percent in 2015 (Table 9.6). The Philippines also had the lowest percentage of loans that require collateral, and was average in terms of percentage of firms citing access to finance as a major constraint, which was 10.5 percent in 2015.

Table 9.7 shows several payment options indicators. The country scored significantly below average in all of these indicators. In particular, it had the lowest proportion of the population 15 years old with a debit card – only 3.2 percent of the population cohort which had a credit card, but only 2.2 percent had used their credit card in the past year.

Table 9.5 Trade Logistics and Trade Facilitation Indicators, 2013–2016

	Indonesia	Malaysia	Philippines	Singapore	Thailand	Viet Nam
Percentage of population having mail delivered at home	80	95	85	100	96	80
Percentage of income linked to parcels and logistics services	23.2	42	3.5	–	48.9	16.1
Postal reliability index	65.6	84.3	48	98.2	90	70.3
Percentage of the population without postal services	0	0	0	0	0	0
LPI international shipments score	2.9	3.5	3	4	3.4	3.1
LPI logistics competence score	3	3.3	2.7	4.1	3.1	2.9
LPI tracing and tracking score	3.2	3.5	2.9	4	3.2	2.8
LPI timeliness score	3.5	3.7	3.3	4.4	3.6	3.5
Days to clear direct exports through customs – Enterprise Survey	8.3	6.3	14.5	–	1.9	6.9
Burden of customs procedures	3.9	5.2	3.5	6.2	3.7	3.6

Source: The author. Raw data retrieved from UPU (2018), the World Bank (2018a), and WEF (2017).

Table 9.6 Access to Financing, 2015

	Indonesia	Malaysia	Philippines	Thailand	Viet Nam
Percentage of firms identifying access to finance as a major constraint – Enterprise Survey	16.5	12.0	10.7	2.4	10.8
Percentage of loans requiring collateral – Enterprise Survey	80.4	64.7	51.0	93.4	91.0
Percentage of working capital financed by banks – Enterprise Survey	9.9	16.7	5.1	15.4	13.1

Source: The author. Raw data retrieved from WEF (2017).

Table 9.7 Options of E-commerce Payment in Selected ASEAN Countries, 2015

	Indonesia	Malaysia	Philippines	Singapore	Thailand	Viet Nam
Debit card (% age 15+) – Global Findex	25.9	41.2	20.5	89.4	54.8	26.5
Debit card used in the past year (% age 15+) – Global Findex	8.5	18.6	11.9	78.2	7.9	3.1
Credit card (% age 15+) – Global Findex	1.6	20.2	3.2	35.4	5.7	1.9
Credit card used in the past year (% age 15+) – Global Findex	1.1	16.9	2.2	31.3	3.7	1.2
Mobile account (% age 15+) – Global Findex	0.4	2.8	4.2	6.1	1.3	0.5
Used an account to make a transaction through a mobile phone (% age 15+) – Global Findex	1.5	7.8	2.5	16.0	3.8	2.7

Source: The author. Raw data retrieved from the World Bank (2018b).

Based on these indicators, World Integrated Trade Solution computed the e-commerce readiness index of the country using the United Nations Conference on Trade and Development (UNCTAD) index for B2C e-commerce. The country scored 35.7, comparable to Indonesia with the lowest score among the selected ASEAN countries. Singapore scored the highest with 75.8, followed by Malaysia, Thailand, and Viet Nam.

5. Legal and institutional support

The Philippines was relatively ahead in enacting an e-commerce law intended to advance e-commerce in the country. As early as 2000, the government enacted the Electronic Commerce Act (ECA) or Republic Act No. 8792, which legally recognised electronic forms of data messages, documents, signatures, transactions, and storage of information, providing penalties for access of data without consent, piracy, hacking, and other violations. The law further provided the DTI the authority to direct and supervise the promotion and development of e-commerce in the country with relevant government agencies.

The Philippines was relatively successful in creating a vibrant business process outsourcing (BPO) sector. The enactment of the e-commerce law partly contributed to attracting investments in the sector. In 2014, the information technology business process management (IT-BPM) sector recorded US$18.1 billion in revenues and had a year-to-year growth of 17 percent (DTI 2016).

5.1. ITECC, CICT, and CITO

Pursuant to the law, which gave the DTI the mandate to oversee the advancement of e-commerce, the government created the Information Technology and Electronic Commerce Council (ITECC) in 2000 through Presidential Executive Order No. 264. ITECC drafted the ECA's Implementing Rules and Regulations, which the DTI Secretary issued.

ITECC created an e-government fund to support the implementation of the e-commerce law and automation of government services. It funded government ICT projects, which were regarded as critical for the improvement of public service such as a national single window at the Bureau of Customs and improvements in the IT capabilities of the Bureau of Customs and the Bureau of Internal Revenue. Other government agencies also received funding. However, the government missed the opportunity to maximise the inter-operability of the various ICT capabilities of the government agencies.

The IT-BPO industry expanded, largely due the de-regulation of the telecommunications sector in the 1990s when mobile phones and other value-added services were introduced in the market. The reform ensured competition in the industry, lowered communication costs, and attracted investments into the industry. The downstream IT-BPO sector benefited from these reforms, which were complemented by the country's commitment under WTO to keep the trade of information and technology products free.

Several permutations of ITECC between 2000 and 2010 inadvertently made the council ineffective in passing additional laws and attracting support for e-commerce. In 2004, ITECC was renamed the Commission on Information and Communications Technology (CICT) and was transferred from the DTI to the Office of the President. The move was seen as a prelude to creating a 'Department of Information and Communications Technology'.

In another setback for e-commerce in 2010, the CICT was transferred again, this time to the Department of Science and Technology. A presidential order renamed the CICT the Information and Communications Technology Office (ICTO). The accomplishments of the ICTO included the following:

i Formulation of a national broadband plan as a segment of its Philippine Digital Masterplan that aims to improve the country's Internet infrastructure (e.g. speed, access, connectivity).

ii Formulation of the Integrated Government Philippines (iGovPhil) Project to establish, upgrade, and improve government ICT infrastructure, systems, and ICT-related procedures to allow for integrated government operations. The priority systems that would be integrated are the (i) Business Permits and Licensing System (BPLS), Real Property Tax System, eBayad (Payment)

System, and eSerbisyo System under the e-Government Portal; and (ii) systems under the Community eCenter (CeC) Project to also be integrated under this environment.

The iGovPhil Project requires the provision of seamless connectivity throughout the country from the national level down to the household level. It involves the creation of data centres and laying out of fibre-optic networks to interconnect government offices and provide high-speed communication and sharing of tasks and data.

5.2. National e-commerce office

Following the ECA, which mandated it to shepherd the development of e-commerce in the country, the DTI created its E-commerce Office in March 2009. With this office, the government addressed the immediate requirement for the advancement of the e-commerce industry. The Office was tasked with:

i   Formulation of policies and guidelines in support of e-commerce.
ii   Formulation and implementation of plans and programmes for further development and implementation of e-commerce in the country, in coordination with other DTI agencies, other government agencies, the private sector, and other stakeholders.
iii Monitoring and evaluation of the implementation of e-commerce policies, plans, and programmes.
iv   Active participation in local and international organisations related to e-commerce.

In 2012, the Data Privacy Act (Republic Act No. 10173) and Cybercrime Law (Republic Act No. 10175) were enacted, strengthening confidentiality and penalty provisions under the e-commerce law.

5.3. National e-commerce road map

Given these initiatives, as well as the strengths and weaknesses of the industry, the DTI issued a five-year industry road map for the development of e-commerce (2015–2020). Its primary goal is to increase the contribution of the industry to the country's economy from the then-current 10 percent to 25 percent in 2020. The 150-percent expansion is to be realised with the following six initiatives: infrastructure, investments, innovation, intellectual capital, information flow, and integration.

More specifically, inadequate payment systems for e-commerce and difficulties in Internet access are twin problems existing in many developing countries. In the case of the Philippines, the Bangko Sentral ng Pilipinas (BSP) has created the National Retail Payment System (NRPS), which was designed to progressively promote the use of electronic payment for retail transactions. It was initially implemented for transactions involving entities that the central bank regulates, such as banks and financial institutions. When Congress passed the Retail Payments Act, the NRPS was expected to roll out throughout the country to reduce the use of cash or cheques in paying for purchases. Until now, however, only 1 percent of transactions are paid electronically.

Poor Internet access, however, may be the more important obstacle in the Philippines. While the use of smartphones is expanding quickly, Internet speed needs to catch up. As pointed out earlier, the country has the slowest Internet among the six ASEAN countries studied, although the situation has been improved significantly.

Moreover, the cost to access the Internet is still relatively high. The DTI reported that Internet users accessing Philippines-hosted sites pass through sites in the United States before being routed back to the Philippines. The problem is prevalent with government websites, by not making their services easily accessible to stakeholders. On 15 April 2015, many taxpayers failed to meet the tax payment deadline due to this problem. The ICTO proposed offering a programme to provide free Wi-Fi nationwide for the citizens to access government services, though this proposal may not be sustainable. For example, importers have to pay a private sector value-added service provider to access the Bureau of Customs automated customs operational systems when getting their products cleared. If the ICTO's plan replaces that system, the government would have to pay the cost of Internet access.

Addressing these problems, the national e-commerce road map lists the following initiatives:

i   The National Broadband Masterplan comprising the rolling out of Internet infrastructure by various players committing to services, speed, and internationally competitive pricing; and the Philippine Internet Exchange for easy access of government-related websites, as well as to increase Internet speed and lower Internet subscription costs.
ii   Updated Telecommunications Law and Charter of the National Telecommunications Commission, to make these responsive to the market.
iii New telecommunications and value-added services investments (new players) to meet expanding industry demands.
iv   Implementation of Republic Act No. 10667 or the Philippine Competition Act.

There is no doubt the country needs to have a national broadband masterplan, but the difficulty is in realising it. There are various private sector investors, but all these potential entrants would be looking for the most lucrative parts of the Internet infrastructure to invest in, which may require measures such as bidding out the frequencies in the spectrum to be awarded.

5.4. Market competition

Lack of competition in the telecommunications industry is key to reversing the deteriorating quality of telecommunications and Internet services in the country.

Presently, there are only two players in the telecommunications industry. Both are not investing quickly enough to increase their respective capacities. Both companies are reportedly allocating most of their capacity primarily for the lucrative BPO market, and the remaining capacity is set aside for the rest of the market. This is reminiscent of the situation in the 1980s and earlier, when there was a monopoly in the industry. New users had to wait months before they were able to get their subscriptions due to lack of capacity.

Rigidity in the allocation of frequencies in the mobile spectrum contributes to the problem. Frequencies were awarded to existing players, two of which now dominate the telecommunications industry. Telephone companies had gained access from the government to use certain frequencies, but when these companies stopped operating the frequencies remained with the previous players or with other companies, which acquired them. This is seen as a move to block the entry of competitors in the industry.

Existing players may be dragging out the return of such unused frequencies, which causes delays to the auctioning of the frequencies and thus the entry of new players. Mirandilla-Santos (2018) reported that one dominant player was ordered by the National Telecommunications Commission (NTC) to return the frequency it controlled when it acquired the now-defunct telephone company, Digitel, in 2011. However, the company is requesting that the government pay 2.215 billion pesos to recover its cost for purchasing Digitel. The government refused to pay, but it can compel the company to return it. In another case, a large company, a newcomer which acquired smaller telephone companies with existing frequencies to go into the broadband business, also experienced failure to enter the market.

Telstra, an Australian company, was reported to have negotiated to form a joint venture with San Miguel Corporation and become the third player in the country's duopolistic telecommunications market. Mirandilla-Santos (2018) cited the benefits for the joint venture. Telstra owns Pacnet, which has an international submarine cable landing in the provinces of Cavite and Batangas, south of the National Capital Region. The planned joint venture could have jumped over the initial hurdle of a late entrant. It stood to offer competitively priced international bandwidth without the need to go through the two big companies, as San Miguel has access to the frequencies. Telstra was exploring the deployment of 4G, which only makes up 5 percent of the Philippine mobile broadband market. In the end, however, Telstra backed out from the plan because of restrictions on foreign direct investments. As a multinational company, Telstra is limited to only 40 percent of the company's equity, and it reportedly would be investing more if the design of the joint venture was to be followed. The market remains stuck with two dominant players.

On 7 November 2018, the NTC awarded a third permit to a consortium of a local company Udenna and China Telecom. The award was announced after a lengthy search based on the highest committed level of service through a point system scheme with criteria including population coverage, Internet speed, and capital investment for 5 years. The NTC accepted three applications; it dropped two for lack of a letter of credit in the case of one company and lack of a certificate of technical capability in the case of the other.

However, there are problems associated with the award, which one of the disqualified companies has questioned. The first is that the local company is not a telephone company. Udenna bought a telephone company, Mislatel, after it automatically lost its franchise as a telephone company when it failed to become a publicly listed company in 2003. Second, the restrictions on foreign direct investments may still apply. The defence offered by the government was that the restriction would be lifted with a proposed law updating the Public Services Act. The existing act requires foreign direct investments in utilities to be restricted, including telephone companies. Even the proposed bill, which the government cited, continues to include telephone companies. Congress can still change this, but with matters still unsettled, the question of why the bidding was not declared a failure has come up.

This has led to the criticism that the Office of the President had pressured the NTC to award the permit to the Udenna-China Telecom consortium. There is no evidence to the claim, but the optics for it exists. The owner of Udenna is a close friend of the President. The Office of the President had put pressure on having an award soon, which may have been legitimate to improve ICT and Internet services in the country. However, with questions arising about the qualification of the consortium given the provisional permit – and litigation likely to follow – the problems of slow Internet and high tariffs, and their implications on the future digital commerce in the country will likely persist.

6. Concluding remarks

There is a need to focus on strategic elements to drive the e-commerce industry in the Philippines forward. This chapter focussed on how the country can overcome its problem of poor Internet speed and the present preference of the population to use cash or cheques for retail payments. It is important to look at how competition in the past shook up the telephone monopoly of PLDT in the 1990s. Paradoxically, the two dominant firms in the industry providing connectivity services benefited from the competition. The lesson is that if there is no radical reorganisation in the industry, it will mimic the past monopoly in the telephone industry.

The government needs to find ways to quickly get away from the present lack of effective competition in connectivity. The road map is unclear about how it plans to attain its primary goal of improving the contribution of e-commerce to the economy in 2020. Clear measures need to be acted upon, as in the 1990s when the regulator declared that mobile phone technology was not covered by the franchise of the phone monopoly.

There have been improvements in the current industry. In the area of Internet access, between 2015 and 2017, the speed improved to 5.5 Mbps, but that is not good enough. The Philippines requires more investments on the part of existing players. If this does not happen, the country may be compelled to force competition in the industry.

Bibliography

APEC (2017), 'APEC Cross-Border E-Commerce Facilitation Framework'. Available at http://mddb.apec.org/Documents/2017/SOM/SOM3/17_som3_027 anx02.pdf

ASEAN Secretariat (2015), *ASEAN Economic Community Blueprint 2025*. Jakarta: ASEAN Secretariat.

Barreiro, V. (2017), 'PH Has Slowest Average Internet Speed in Asia Pacific'. Available at www.rappler.com/technology/news/171680-philippines-akamai-broadband-adoption-internet-speed-rankings

Department of Trade and Industry (DTI) (2016), 'The Philippine e-Commerce Roadmap 2015–2020', Sector Planning Bureau/E-Commerce Office, Department of Trade and Industry, January.

International Telecommunication Union (ITU) (2015), 'Measuring the Information Society Report 2015: Executive Summary'. Available at www.itu.int/dms_pub/itu-d/opb/ind/D-IND-ICTOI-2015-SUM-PDF-E.pdf

Kimura, F. (2018), ' "Unbundlings" and Development Strategies in ASEAN: Old Issues and New Challenges', *Journal of Southeast Asian Economies*, 35(1): 13–21.

Kinasih, R. (2016), 'Philippines' Ecommerce Landscape: 5 Key Takeaways from Philippines' Online Runway', *Ecommerceiq.Asia*, 16 November. Available at https://ecommerceiq.asia/philippines-ecommerce-landscape-ecommerceiq/

Lemma, A. (2017), *E-Commerce: The Implications of Current WTO Negotiations for Economic Transformation in Developing Countries*. London: Overseas Development Institute, December.

Mirandilla-Santos, G. (2018), 'The Perfect Telco'. Available at www.telecomasia.net/blog/content/perfect-telco

Organisation for Economic Cooperation and Development (OECD) (2013), 'Glossary of Statistical Terms'. Available at https://stats.oecd.org/glossary/detail.asp?ID=4721

Statista (2018), 'B2C E-Commerce Sales Data, Various Countries'. Available at www.statista.com/outlook/243/109/ecommerce/

The World Bank (2018a), 'World Development Indicator Database 2017'. Available at datatopics.worldbank.org/world-development-indicators/

The World Bank (2018b), 'The Global Findex Database 2017'. Available at globalfindex.worldbank.org

Universal Postal Union (UPU) (2018), 'UPU Database'. Available at www.upu.int/en/resources/postal-statistics/query-the-database.html

We Are Social (2018), 'Digital in 2018 in Southeast Asia'. Available at digitalreport.wearesocial.com/

World Economic Forum (WEF) (2017), 'The Global Competitiveness Report 2016–2017'. Available at https://www.weforum.org/reports/the-global-competitiveness-report-2016-2017-1

10 Measuring e-readiness of Thailand in ASEAN

Macro and micro e-commerce perspectives

Siriluck Rotchanakitumnuai

1. Introduction

The government of Thailand has set up the Thailand 4.0 initiative to increase the security, prosperity, and sustainability of the country. This is the vision to transform Thailand into an innovative digital economy. The government has recognized the need to improve telecommunication infrastructures across the country, and to adopt public private partnerships (PPPs) policy with many sectors such as business, education, and research intuitions. The strategic focus is to decrease the digital divide and push Thailand from the middle-income trap to a high-income economy (ETDA, 2018).

In the digital economy, it is indisputable that information and communications technology (ICT) plays an important role in communication and work. These capabilities also have an impact on the country, business, and societal development. As a result, governments in most countries identify strategies and policies to increase their readiness in information and communications technology (ICT readiness or e-readiness). This is even more critical for Association of Southeast Asian Nation (ASEAN) countries, since the ASEAN Economic Community (AEC) was established in 2015 to foster economic collaborations to gain competitiveness among ASEAN member states (Ministry of Science and Technology, 2011). The ASEAN Information Summit agreed on the e-ASEAN initiative to prepare the AEC for e-readiness for ASEAN cooperation in IT to benefit from the opportunities offered by the revolution in ICT and e-commerce. This initiative will also liberalize trade related to IT under the World Trade Organization framework. In 2000, government leaders signed the e-ASEAN framework agreement, which focuses on e-readiness in terms of IT infrastructure, e-commerce, e-society, and e-government (IBM, 2001).

E-readiness can be measured using several approaches. These include Bridges. org (2001, 2005), Bui et al. (2003), Dada (2006) and Vaezi and Bimar (2009), which share some dimensions such as ICT infrastructure and human capital. This research will specify the current e-readiness assessment framework, and analyse whether Thailand is more ready to be the leader of e-ASEAN than other ASEAN members. Thailand has announced policies to achieve Thailand 4.0 by formulating initiatives to an innovation-driven economy. One of the initiatives identified by the government is to advance the digital technology related to e-commerce and e-service. The development of digital technology should stimulate e-commerce in the business-to-consumer (B2C) segment to grow rapidly.

Consumers who buy goods via the Internet will obtain benefits including convenience, time savings, and a wider variety of goods than shopping at stores. Moreover, online shoppers prefer to buy products from popular online merchants through cross-border e-commerce, which can create significantly higher value added than domestic e-commerce, with reliability and lower prices, e.g. Amazon, eBay, or Alibaba. Thailand's cross-border e-commerce value is lower than other Asian countries such as China (Ecommerce Foundation, 2016). If barriers to cross-border e-commerce are reduced or removed, customer purchases will probably increase. The second objective of this study is to identify the obstacles and limitations on cross-border e-commerce in B2C from the perspective of Thai consumers.

The first objective of this research is to apply the e-readiness framework to assess Thailand's electronic readiness. This chapter aims to assess Thailand's e-readiness at the country level when compared to other ASEAN member states. At the micro level, e-readiness related to electronic commerce is assessed in terms of barriers to cross-border E-commerce from Thai consumers so that the results can provide substantive information to adjust the ICT policy of the Thai government. The rest of chapter is organized into four parts. Section 2 reviews the selected literature review and introduces the indexes used in the study. Sections 3 and 4, respectively, explain the employed methodology and discusses the main findings. Section 5 concludes.

2. Literature review

Several e-readiness assessment methodologies have been developed. E-readiness assessments used for analysing country-specific dimensions contribute to reaping the full benefits of IT investments. This readiness has an influence on social-economic development growth (Vaezi and Bimar, 2009).

2.1. *Networked readiness index*

The Networked Readiness Index (NRI), developed by the World Economic Forum (WEF), is a benchmarking study of readiness which assesses the political environment, marketing and infrastructure, and readiness of the business sector, government sector, and people, as well as ICT use. In 2016, the NRI was revised with four main indicators: environment related to a high-quality regulatory and business environment; ICT readiness measured by ICT affordability, skills, and infrastructure; government, business sector, and population's use of ICT; and impact of ICT on the economy and society (WEF, 2016).

2.2. *E-Government Development Index*

The United Nations (UN) E-Government Development Index (EGDI), conducted by the Department of Economic and Social Affairs, assesses the development of e-government at the national level. EGDI criteria include telecommunications infrastructure, human capital, and online service indices (United Nations Department of Economic and Social Affairs, 2016).

2.3. B2C e-commerce index

In B2C e-commerce, the UN Conference on Trade and Development (UNC-TAD) developed four indicators to measure B2C e-commerce readiness: Internet use penetration, B2C web presence, credit card penetration, and Universal Postal Union (UPU) postal reliability score (UNCTAD, 2016).

2.4. ICT Development Index

The International Telecommunication Union (ITU) developed the ICT Development Index (IDI) to assess three major indicators: ICT access, ICT use, and ICT skill (ITU, 2015). The index measures the development progression and potential levels, and the digital divide of ICT development, in each country.

2.5. Digital economy ranking

The Economist Intelligence Unit (EIU), which provides political, economic, and social research for The Economist Group, developed the e-readiness rankings (EIU, 2010). In 2010, the e-readiness rankings by EIU were renamed as the digital economy rankings. The rankings and weights have been revised to better reflect the digital era, which influences consumer and organizational behaviour. The assessment criteria for rankings are categorized into five factors: (i) connectivity and technology infrastructure, (ii) consumer and business adoption, (iii) business, (iv) social and cultural environment, and (v) government policy and vision.

2.6. E-ASEAN readiness

In ASEAN, an IT infrastructure framework has been developed to assess the e-ASEAN framework, which encourages ASEAN cooperation in digital libraries and facilitates regional Internet exchanges and gateways (IBM, 2001). Another dimension is e-commerce readiness, which includes e-commerce transactions, recognition of digital signatures, electronic payments (e-payments), intellectual property rights, and personal data protection. This covers e-society with which the workforce of ASEAN countries can enhance the ICT competitiveness. It aims to narrow the digital divide within the country and among member states, facilitate freer movement of workers with IT skills, and foster the use of IT to develop the ASEAN e-society. Related to this is e-government readiness to promote the use of ICT applications in the public sector in the delivery of government services and procurement of goods.

Many academic studies have proposed that an e-readiness assessment cover the IT infrastructure, economy and society, and public sector management (Bui et al., 2003; Dada, 2006; Molla and Licker, 2005; Vaezi and Bimar, 2009). The readiness assessment approaches overlap, depending on their objectives. These studies reviewed the readiness assessment frameworks for ICT from several sources. These criteria for rankings are summarized in Table 10.1.

2.7. Barriers to cross-border e-commerce

2.7.1. Logistics

Logistics is extremely important for goods purchased from abroad. Cross-border e-commerce customers expect speedy and safe delivery of products ordered. Some prefer to track their own goods in real time (Cho and Lee, 2017). Reasonable delivery costs are a major concern of customers who purchase products from online sellers from abroad (Duch-Brown and Martens, 2015; Hunter and Wilson, 2015; Okholm et al., 2013). An efficient logistics system is a key success factor of Amazon (Liu and Hong, 2016). Inefficient logistics cause delivery costs from cross-border online merchants (Kawa and Zdrenka, 2016). High delivery costs, lack of reliability, and unexpectedly long delivery times are major barriers to cross-border e-commerce (Cho and Lee, 2017; Liu et al., 2015; Marti, 2016).

2.7.2. Trust

Trust in global online merchants relates to benevolence, ability, and integrity (McKnight and Chervany, 2001, Rotchanakitumnuai and Speece, 2009; Pavlou, 2003). Online consumers need first of all to build up trust in cross-border merchants from other countries. Typically, they have concerns about whether the

Table 10.1 E-Readiness Assessment Framework for ICT

Indices	NRI	EGDI	B2C ECI	IDI	DER	E-ASEAN
Connectivity and technology infrastructure	✓	✓	✓	✓	✓	✓
Supporting environment	✓	✓			✓	✓
E-Society	✓	✓	✓	✓	✓	✓
E-Government	✓	✓			✓	✓
Consumer and business ICT use or ecommerce adoption	✓	✓	✓	✓	✓	✓

Source: The author. Raw data from EIU (2010), IBM (2001), ITU (2015), UNCTAD (2016), UNDESA (2016), WEF (2016).

Notes:
NRI = Network Readiness Index
EGDI = E-Government Development Index
B2C ECI = B2C E-Commerce Index
IDI = ICT Development Index
DER = Digital Economy Ranking
E-ASEAN = E-ASEAN Readiness

online sellers can provide fair treatment and are willing to respond adequately in case of poor performance (Gomez-Herrera et al., 2014). Liu and Hong (2016) found that trust is one of the success factors of cross-border e-commerce. Sellers' integrity, fast feedback on complaints, and benefits provided to consumers are very important concerns for online cross-border customers (Gibbs et al., 2003; Hunter and Wilson, 2015).

2.7.3. *Legislative protection*

Since cross-border e-commerce is a form of international trade, law enforcement from international trade will be different from consumer's country of origin. B2C cross-border e-commerce is affected by legislation designed to protect cross-border consumers (Gibbs et al., 2003; Kommerskollegium, 2012; Liu et al., 2015; Okholm et al., 2013). Customers have strong awareness of their rights (Hunter and Wilson, 2015). There may be different law enforcement and protection related to specific problems occurred from cross-border e-commerce (Marti, 2016). If problems are related to online commerce, the law in the seller's country is applied. The laws of different countries may be inadequate, however, and consumer protection codes for buyers from other countries may be weak.

2.7.4. *Product and sales policy*

Many shoppers would like to see the products before deciding to purchase. E-commerce fraud is a common problem highlighted in the literature on online trade. Consumers shopping online cannot touch or test the physical product. Purchase from cross-border e-commerce has significantly higher problems than local e-commerce vendors when consumers face problem related to product specification. Major issues are associated with product quality, fake goods, and return policies (Hunter and Wilson, 2015; Liu and Hong, 2016).

2.7.5. *E-payment*

Rotchanakitumnuai and Speece (2003) point out that although most payment gateways have data encryption to prevent financial fraud, many online customers still perceive risks and insecurity associated with e-payment. Many countries have legislation to regulate online payment methods to ensure payment security and consumer protection. Financial safeguards are important to build trust in consumers when they face online payment problems. Moreover, the online payment methods are often not suitable for the users. Considerable financial risks may create problems to hinder cross-border e-commerce, such as increased costs and unavailability of payment methods. (Gibbs et al., 2003; Liu and Hong, 2016).

3. Methodology

For the first research objective, the relevant literature was summarized to develop a detailed conceptual framework of e-readiness in the context of e-ASEAN. Secondary data and previous research on ASEAN member states were considered. Other recent data sets about e-readiness reported by several agencies, including the WEF, UN, ITU, and UNCTAD, were considered. The EIU and IBM have not published follow-ups to their 2010 reports so the data are substantially out of date. This study excluded data from these two sources. The ICT master plans of each country were also reviewed to develop a framework for analysing and assessing the e-readiness leadership of ASEAN countries in ICT.

For the second research objective, the results are based on empirical research (Rotchanakitumnuai, 2018). The barriers to cross-border B2C e-commerce were developed from past studies. An online survey was used to collect data on the barriers to cross-border e-commerce. This included: (i) trust in cross-border e-commerce merchants, (ii) logistics, (iii) legal protection, (iv) product and sales policy, and (v) e-payment measurement. The questions were measured using a Likert-type scale that has a range of answer to measure attitude from one extreme attitude to another. The measurement items of the questionnaire use a five-point of Likert scale ranging from 1 (strongly unimportant) to 5 (strongly important). Judgment sampling was used to choose Thai consumers that have experience in using the Internet or purchase goods from e-commerce. Some 250 questionnaires were sent out and 227 respondents replied, representing a 90 per-cent response rate.

The summary of sample characteristics is in Annex 10.1. About 60 percent of respondents are female, most respondents are aged 25–30 (49 percent), and the respondents' most common education level is undergraduate (68 percent). About 90 percent of respondents have purchased goods from local e-commerce and 52 percent from cross-border e-commerce merchants. The frequency of average Internet usage is 33 hours per week.[1]

4. Data analysis and discussion

Past rankings have placed Thailand lower than Malaysia and Singapore in every index of the e-readiness assessment. Analysis of the top three ASEAN countries – Malaysia, Singapore, and Thailand – shows that Thailand has the lowest ranking in almost all sub-indices (Table 10.2). The IDI of Thailand showed the most improvement in overall indices in Asia from 2010 (ITU, 2015). Thailand also showed good improvement in online service support of the e-government development index from the previous assessment in 2014. The percentage of individuals using the Internet is only 35 percent (UNDESA, 2014, 2016).

In addition, the WEF report indicated that skills readiness related to the quality of education of Thailand is not high when compared with Indonesia, Malaysia, the Philippines, and Singapore (Figure 10.1). The level of education and ICT skills in Thailand need to be improved to enhance ICT readiness.

Table 10.2 E-Readiness in Singapore, Malaysia, and Thailand

	Indices/Sub-Indices	Singapore	Malaysia	Thailand
IDI by ITU (Ranking)	ICT access	14	63	92
	ICT use	16	58	64
	ICT skill	59	101	64
EDGI by UN (Score 0–1)	Online service index	0.88	0.62	0.55
	Telecommunication infrastructure index	0.97	0.72	0.55
	Human capital index	0.84	0.44	0.41
NRI by WEF (Ranking)	Environment	1	21	54
	Political and regulatory environment	2	24	80
	Business and innovation environment	1	18	48
	Readiness	16	73	62
	Infrastructure	15	71	67
	Affordability	72	91	64
	Skill	1	46	73
	Usage	1	30	63
	Individual usage	12	47	64
	Business usage	14	26	51
	Government usage	1	6	69
	Impact	1	30	65
	Economic	5	30	74
	Social	1	28	57
B2C ECI by UNCTAD (% or Number)	Share of individuals using Internet	82%	68%	35%
	Credit card penetration	35%	20%	6%
	Secure Internet servers per 1 million people	88	69	58
	UPU postal reliability score (out of 100)	98	84	90

Source: The author. Raw data from ITU (2015), UNCTAD (2016), UNDESA (2016), WEF (2016).

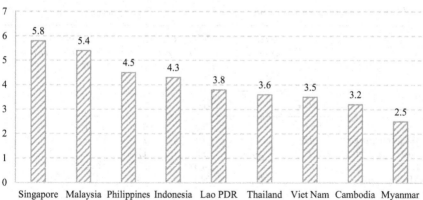

Figure 10.1 Quality of Education (Scale 1–7)

Source: The author. Based on WEF (2016).

Specific to e-commerce readiness, UNCTAD reported that Thailand has lower Internet and credit card penetration and fewer secure Internet servers than Singapore and Malaysia. Thailand was assessed to have good logistics for e-commerce delivery. In addition, the ITU reported that Thailand has improved significantly in the use of and access to mobile broadband usage rankings in the Asia-Pacific region (ITU, 2015), with a high level of online service of the government and business (UNDESA, 2016). Moreover, the WEF (2016) reported the readiness of business-to-consumer Internet use of individuals to be high, at 5.1 out of 7 (Figure 10.2). This is a good opportunity for Thailand to promote online services for local and cross-border e-commerce.

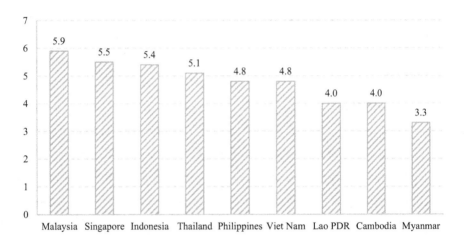

Figure 10.2 B2C Internet Use of Individuals (Scale 1–7)

Source: The author. Based on WEF (2016).

Table 10.3 B2C E-commerce and Cross-Border B2C E-commerce (in Billion US$)

	B2C e-commerce (Billion US$)		B2C cross-border e-commerce trade volume (Billion US$)		Contribution of global total incremental trade volume (%)
	2014	2020	2014	2020	
Asia Pacific	558	71	1525	476	53.6
Western Europe	402	73	674	216	18.9
North America	502	67	918	176	14.4
Latin America	61	6	140	53	6.2
Mideastern Europe	51	13	93	45	4.2
Middle East and Africa	15	5	43	26	2.7

Sources: The author. Based on Accenture (2016).

By 2020, Accenture (2016) forecasts that there will be 2 billion online shoppers – or 60 percent of the world's population – transacting 13.5 percent of their overall retail consumptions online. The global B2C market value will increase up to US$3.4 trillion from 2014 to 2020 (Table 10.3). In addition, cross-border e-commerce is an important growth to B2C trade value.

Forrester Research predicts that global B2C cross-border e-commerce will reach US$424 billion by 2021, comprising 15 percent of overall e-commerce (eMarketer Report, 2017). Particularly in Asia, Heel et al. (2014) predicted that Asia will have significant growth in cross-border e-commerce and generate about 40 percent of the total revenue of global cross-border e-commerce trading. China is the leader in cross-border e-commerce, with the accumulative value of US$1 trillion by 2016 (Mooney, 2016). In Thailand, the wider mobile Internet penetration is driving the online spending of Thai shoppers. In 2015, cross-border e-commerce purchases in Thailand increased to 31.5 percent from 20 percent in

Table 10.4 Descriptive Analysis of Barriers to B2C Cross-Border E-commerce

Factor/Measurement Item	Mean	Standard Deviation
1. Trust Factor	**4.32**	
Integrity of cross-border e-commerce merchants	4.36	.784
Rapid assistance when purchase problem occurs	4.32	.832
Fair consumer protection	4.29	.757
2. Product and Sales Policy Factor	**4.18**	
Inauthentic or fake goods	4.48	.776
Goods do not meet the specifications	4.36	.893
Delay in return process	4.16	.827
Inability to review goods before purchase	3.83	1.000
3. Logistics Factor	**4.08**	
Goods are damaged during transit	4.22	.823
Expensive logistic costs	4.11	.927
Goods delivery delays	3.97	.890
4. E-payment factor	**4.06**	
Payment errors	4.17	.912
Lack of security for online credit card payments	4.09	.928
Lack of online payment method	3.89	.970
5. Legislation Protection Factor	**4.05**	
Adequate legal protection for cross-border online purchases	4.19	.792
Fair consumer complaint policy	4.02	.824
The different payment protection laws in different countries	3.92	.891

Note: Scale from 1 (strongly unimportant) to 5 (strongly important).
Source: Rotchanakitumnuai (2018).

2011 and the value of online spending grew to 29.9 percent from 20 percent in 2011 (The Paypers, 2015).

Rotchanakitumnuai's (2018) study shows that barriers to B2C cross-border e-commerce of Thai consumers consist of five factors: product and sales policy, trust, logistics, legislation protection, and e-payment. Table 10.4 shows that trust in cross-border e-commerce merchants is important factor. The most important variable is 'integrity of cross-border e-commerce merchants' (4.36). 'Rapid assistance when purchase problem occurs' is rated 4.32, and 'Fair consumer protection' is rated 4.29.

The most important measure of the product and sales policy factor is 'Inauthentic or fake goods' with an average of 4.48 and 'Goods do not meet the specifications' with the mean score of 4.36. Thai consumers agree that 'Delay in return process' is a major barrier with a mean score of 4.16, but rated 'Inability to review goods before purchase' with lowest mean among all barriers measured (3.83).

Logistics factor is another major barrier, of which 'Goods are damaged during transit' (4.22) and 'Expensive logistics costs (4.11) received much more concerns compared to 'Goods delivery delays' (3.97) did. Related to e-payment, 'Payment errors' (4.17) and 'Lack of security for online credit card payments' (4.09) are major concerns. 'Lack of online payment method' was rated at 3.98. As for the barrier from legislation protection. 'Adequate legal protection for cross-border online purchases' (4.19) and 'Fair consumer complaint policy' (4.02) are considered important. 'The different payment protection laws in different countries' was rated at 3.92.

In general, the results show that Thai consumers are concerned about the efficiency and quality of cross-border e-commerce logistics. They worry about product quality and authenticity of products. In some countries, such as the Republic of Korea, the authorities inspect products to ensure that they meet the consumers' requirements and the relevant product specification. Legislation and policy are more important barriers for cross-border e-commerce than for local e-commerce. Consumers prefer to have strong legislation and a fair complaints policy. Thai consumers felt that being unable to see the goods before making a purchase order would not impede cross-border e-commerce. E-payment via credit card should be supported by secure infrastructure to ensure the security of cross-border e-commerce transactions.

Finally, Thailand is considered a country with very low political stability (The Global Economy, 2015). Because of this, Thailand is not ready to be leader in e-ASEAN, since political instability could influence the implementation of Thailand ICT master plan successfully.

5. Conclusion

The analysis shows that Thailand is unable to be the leader of e-readiness in ASEAN, but it has the potential to be in the top three ASEAN countries.

Singapore is the leader of e-readiness in ASEAN, and also the global leader. E-readiness requires the integration of ICT to promote social development, government leadership, and business and private sector initiatives and collaboration. In 2011, The Thailand Information and Communication Technology Policy Framework (2011–2020) was initiated to be the roadmap of Smart Thailand in 2020 (Ministry of Science and Technology, 2011). The fundamental components of Smart Thailand are ICT human resources and an ICT competent workforce, ICT infrastructure, and the ICT industry. These smart projects have not progressed because the current government has adopted a new digital economy policy framework, Thailand 4.0, to drive societal and business development. If Thailand achieves political stability, it could improve its e-readiness of ICT infrastructure, regulatory, and innovation environments for e-business and society usage through smart government.

Government leadership is important in enhancing the ICT infrastructure and regulating support for individual and business usage. The most important issues for e-readiness development are to support economic transformation, facilitate ICT infrastructure development, and bridge the digital divide with quality education and skills.

Thailand has improved significantly in the e-government development index in terms of online service support. The high growth in mobile penetration can improve e-society and e-commerce growth in Thailand. This relates to the forecast by PayPal (Thailand) that the number of online shoppers in Thailand reached 7.9 million in 2016, with 2 million purchasing goods from cross-border e-commerce (Leesa-Nguansuk, 2017). Thailand's cross-border e-commerce is not high compared with other Asian countries such as China, Japan, the Republic of Korea, and Singapore (Ecommerce Foundation, 2016). Thailand must improve the four important e-commerce readiness indices: Internet use penetration across the country, credit card penetration, security of e-commerce websites, and efficiency of logistics issues. Logistics and e-payment are major barriers to cross-border e-commerce adoption. Logistics are extremely important for goods purchased from abroad (DHL, 2017; Duch-Brown and Martens, 2015; Hunter and Wilson, 2015, Rotchanakitumnuai, 2018). Since cross-border e-commerce is an online international trade, the law enforcement will be different. Cross-border e-commerce is affected by rational legislation to protect cross-border consumers (Kommerskollegium, 2012).

If barriers to cross-border e-commerce are reduced or removed with the collaboration and support of related organizations (e.g. government, postal delivery, banks), cross-border purchases will probably increase as forecast, which can build long-term customer trust and loyalty in cross-border e-commerce merchants. Therefore, the macro e-readiness of Thailand could support the micro readiness of e-commerce or cross-border e-commerce growth in terms of ICT infrastructure, supporting environment and regulation, e-society and human competency, and e-government readiness. Finally, the implementation of the AEC can also assist in the creation of economic integration with a free flow of online trade through cross-border digitization among the members to enhance the e-commerce competitiveness of the ASEAN region.

Note

1 Annex 10.1 details the demographics of the survey respondents.

Bibliography

Accenture (2016), 'Cross-Border Ecommerce'. Available at www.scribd.com/document/332919657/Cross-Border-Ecommerce-Accenture

Baller, S., S. Dutta and B. Lanvin (eds.) (2016), *The Global Information Technology Report 2016: Innovating in the Digital Economy*. Geneva: WEF.

Bridges.org (2001), 'Comparison of E-Readiness Assessment Models'. Available at www.scirp.org/(S(351jmbntvnsjt1aadkposzje))/reference/ReferencesPapers.aspx?ReferenceID=1188159

Bridges.org (2005), 'Comparison E-Readiness Assessment Models and Tools'. Available at http://ictlogy.net/bibliography/reports/projects.php?idp=333

Bui, T., S. Sankaran and I.M. Sebastian (2003), 'A Framework for Measuring National E-Readiness', *International Journal of Electronic Business*, 1(1): 3–22.

Cho, H. and J. Lee (2017), 'Searching for Logistics and Regulatory Determinants Affecting Overseas Direct Purchase: An Empirical Cross-National Study', *The Asian Journal of Shipping and Logistics*, 33(1): 11–18.

Dada, D. (2006), 'E-Readiness for Developing Countries: Moving the Focus from the Environment to the Users', *Electronic Journal of Information Systems in Developing Countries*, 27(6): 1–14.

DHL (2017), 'The 21st Century Spice Trade: A Guide to the Cross-Border E-Commerce Opportunity'. Available at www.dhl.com/content/dam/downloads/g0/press/publication/g0_dhl_express_cross_border_ecommerce_21st_century_spice_trade.pdf

Duch-Brown, N. and B. Martens (2015), 'Barriers to Cross-Border eCommerce in the EU Digital Single Market', *Joint Research Centre Technical Reports: Institute for Prospective Technological Studies Digital Economy Working Paper*, No. 7. Available at https://ec.europa.eu/jrc/sites/jrcsh/files/JRC96872.pdf

Ecommerce Foundation (2016), 'Global B2C E-Commerce Report 2016 Facts, Figures, Infographic & Trends of 2015 and the 2016 Forecast of the Global B2C E-Commerce Market of Goods and Services'. Available at www.ecommercewiki.org/wikis/images/5/56/Global_B2C_Ecommerce_Report_2016.pdf

Economist Intelligence Unit (2010), 'Digital Economy Rankings 2010: Beyond E-Readiness'. Available at https://www-935.ibm.com/services/us/gbs/bus/pdf/eiu_digital-economy-rankings-2010_final_web.pdf

Electronics Transactions Development Agency (ETDA) (2018), 'Thailand Development Path Towards Digital Economy'. Available at https://unctad.org/meetings/en/Presentation/dtl_eWeek2018p18_ChantiraJimreivatVivatrat_en.pdf

eMarketer Report (2017), 'Cross-Border Ecommerce 2017: A Country-by-Country Look at Consumer Behavior and Trends'. Available at www.emarketer.com/Report/Cross-Border-Ecommerce-2017-Country-by-Country-Look-Consumer-Behavior-Trends/2001986

Gibbs, J., K.L. Kraemer and J. Dedrick (2003), 'Environment and Policy Factors Shaping Global E-Commerce Diffusion: A Cross-Country Comparison', *The Information Society*, 19(1): 5–18.

The Global Economy (2015), 'Political Stability – Country Rankings: Political stability index'. Available at www.theglobaleconomy.com/rankings/wb_political_stability/

Gomez-Herrera, M.E., B. Martens and G. Turlea (2014), 'The Drivers and Impediments for Cross-Border E-Commerce in the EU', *Information Economics and Policy*, 28: 83–96.

Heel, B. van, V. Lukic and E. Leeuwis (2014), 'Cross-Border E-Commerce Makes the World Flatter', Boston Consulting Group. Available at www.bcgperspectives. com/content/articles/transportation_travel_tourism_retail_cross_border_ ecommerce_makes_world_flatter/

Hunter, J. and M. Wilson (2015), *Cross-Border Online Shopping Within the EU: Learning from Consumer Experiences*. Brussels: ANEC. Available at www.anec.eu/ attachments/ANEC-RT-2015-SERV-005.pdf

IBM (2001), 'e-ASEAN Readiness Assessment'. Available at http://unpan1.un.org/ intradoc/groups/public/documents/APCITY/UNPAN007625.pdf

International Telecommunication Union (2015), 'Measuring the Information Society Report 2015: Executive Summary'. Available at www.itu.int/dms_pub/itu-d/ opb/ind/D-IND-ICTOI-2015-SUM-PDF-E.pdf

Kawa, A. and W. Zdrenka (2016), 'Conception of Integration in Cross-Border E-commerce', *Scientific Journal of Logistics*, 12(1): 63–73.

Kommerskollegium (National Board of Trade Sweden) (2012), *E-Commerce– New Opportunities, New Barriers: A Survey of E-Commerce Barriers in Countries Outside the EU*. Stockholm: Kommerskollegium.

Leesa-Nguansuk, S. (2017), 'Online Cross-Border Shopping Set to Surge 84%', *Bangkok Post*, 17 February. Available at www.bangkokpost.com/tech/local-news/ 1199921/online-cross-border-shopping-set-to-surge-84

Liu, C. and J. Hong (2016), 'Strategies and Service Innovations of Haitao Business in the Chinese Market: A Comparative Case Study of Amazon.cn vs Gmarket.co.kr', *Asia Pacific Journal of Innovation and Entrepreneurship*, 10(1): 101–121.

Liu, X., D. Chen and J. Cai (2015), 'The Operation of the Cross-Border E-Commerce Logistics in China', *International Journal of Intelligent Information Systems*, 4(2–2): 15–18.

Martin, R. (2016), *Understanding the Challenges in Cross-Border Ecommerce*. Stamford, CT: Pitney Bowes. Available at www.pitneybowes.com/us/global- ecommerce/case-studies/the-challenges-of-cross-border-ecommerce.html

McKnight, D.H. and N.L. Chervany (2001), 'What Trust Means in E-Commerce Customer Relationships: An Interdisciplinary Conceptual Typology', *International Journal of Electronic Commerce*, 6(2): 35–59.

Ministry of Science and Technology (2011), 'Thailand Information and Communication Technology Policy Framework (2011–2020)'. Available at http:// unpan1.un.org/intradoc/groups/public/documents/ungc/unpan048145~1.pdf

Molla, A. and P. Licker (2005), 'Perceived E-Readiness Factors in E-commerce Adoption: An Empirical Investigation in a Developing Country', *International Journal of Electronic Commerce*, 10(1): 83–110.

Mooney, T. (2016), 'E-Commerce, FTZ Buoy Tianjin Recovery', *The Journal of Commerce*, 15 April. Available at www.joc.com/port-news/asian-ports/ ecommerce-ftz-buoy-tianjin-recovery_20160415.html

Okholm, H.B., M.H. Thelle, A. Möller, B. Basalisco and S. Rølmer (2013), 'E-Commerce and Delivery: A Study of the State of Play of EU Parcel Markets with Particular Emphasis on E-Commerce'. Available at www.copenhageneconomics. com/dyn/resources/Publication/publicationPDF/8/238/0/E-commerce-and-delivery.pdf

Pavlou, P. (2003), 'Consumer Acceptance of Electronic Commerce: Integrating Trust and Risk with the Technology Acceptance Model', *International Journal of Electronic Commerce*, 7(3): 101–134.

The Paypers (2015), 'Cross-border Ecommerce Report Thailand'. Available at www. thepaypers.com/ecommerce-facts-and-figures/thailand/27

Reuters and E. Kim (2016), 'Amazon Just Leased 20 Cargo Planes to Build Its Own in House Delivery Network', *Business Insider*, 9 March. Available at www.businessin sider.com/amazon-leases-20-cargo-planes-to-build-delivery-network-2016-3

Rotchanakitumnuai, S. (2018), 'Impacts of Perceived Risk and Trust on Purchases via Cross-Border E-Commerce', *Chulalongkorn Business Review*, 40(157): 79–99.

Rotchanakitumnuai, S. and M. Speece (2003), 'Barriers to Internet Banking Adoption: A Qualitative Study Among Corporate Customers in Thailand', *International Journal of Bank Marketing*, 21(6–7): 312–323.

Rotchanakitumnuai, S. and M. Speece (2009), 'Modeling Electronic Service Acceptance of an E-Securities Trading System', *Industrial Management & Data Systems*, 109(8): 1069–1084.

United Nations Conference on Trade and Development (UNCTAD) (2016), *UNCTAD B2C E-Commerce Index 2016*. Geneva: UNCTAD.

United Nations, Department of Economic and Social Affairs (2014), *E-Government Survey 2014: E-Government for the Future We Want*. New York: United Nations. Available at https://publicadministration.un.org/egovkb/Portals/egovkb/Documents/un/2014-Survey/E-Gov_Complete_Survey-2014.pdf (accessed 19 April 2017)

United Nations, Department of Economic and Social Affairs (2016), *E-Government Survey 2016: E-Government in Support of Sustainable Development*. New York: United Nations. Available at workspace.unpan.org/sites/Internet/Documents/UNPAN97453.pdf

Vaezi, S.K. and H.S.I. Bimar (2009), 'Comparison of E-Readiness Assessment Models', *Scientific Research and Essays*, 4(5): 501–512.

World Economic Forum (WEF) (2016), *The Global Information Technology Report 2016: Innovating in the Digital Economy*. Geneva: WEF.

Annex 10.1

Table 10A.1 Demographic Characteristics of Sample

Question	Answers	Number	Share, %
Gender	Female	137	60.35
	Male	90	39.65
Age	Below 25	41	18.06
	25–30	112	49.34
	31–40	43	18.94
	41–50	15	6.61
	51+	16	6.61
Education	Below bachelor's degree	14	6.17
	Bachelor's degree	154	67.84
	Master's degree	55	24.23
	Doctorate	4	1.76
Domestic e-commerce purchase	Yes	204	89.87
	Never	23	10.13
Cross-border e-commerce purchase	Yes	117	51.54
	Never	110	48.46
Average of Internet usage per week (hours)		33	

Source: Rotchanakitumnuai (2018).

11 Internet services and the potential for market access for rural agricultural households in Myanmar and Viet Nam

John Walsh

1. Introduction

Research (e.g. Walsh, 2016) has shown that the Greater Mekong Subregion (GMS) has significant food insecurity problems. This occurs in urban and rural settings, as well as comparatively wealthy countries such as Thailand. Researchers also report that some local farmers have observed the emerging impacts of global climate change. Myanmar, for example, has seen an increase in the prevalence of drought events; an increase in the intensity and frequency of cyclones/strong winds; rainfall variability, including erratic and record-breaking intense rainfall events; an increase in the occurrence of flooding and storm surges; an increase in extreme high temperatures; and sea-level rise (Myanmar Climate Change Alliance, 2017).

Although urban areas face their own problems in this regard, the issues are more severe in rural areas because these tend to be poorer, farther away from government services, and have less educated people. Most people in rural areas of the GMS are in subsistence farming households. One way of improving their income-generating opportunities is to enable them to connect with regional markets. However, to do so, they need more skills, knowledge, and access to inputs and information about market access. Government extension services can be helpful in these cases, but in the GMS, government agencies have limited resources and technical capacity to meet these demands. In some cases, non-governmental organisations (NGOs) can help to address this need. However, governments in the GMS tend to mistrust NGOs for various reasons, and limit their activities. With the public and civil sectors unable to meet the demand for services, might it be possible for the private sector to take a role? This is already taking place to some extent in the form of contract agriculture, whereby the investor (an individual or company) makes a contract with individuals or groups of farmers that they will produce specific produce meeting various requirements within a definite time frame, for which they are paid a fee. This situation can work well when a transparent transaction takes place and both sides understand the situation and are willing to abide by the conditions specified. However, these conditions do not always apply in this region, since conditions vary beyond the control of the farmers, sudden shocks can require immediate access to cash, and a verbal contract might be disputed on either side.

An alternative means of involving the private sector is by encouraging those involved to help themselves through the adoption of technology. Mobile telephones have achieved very high rates of penetration in the region over the past decade. As more companies have been given permission to enter national markets, prices have declined and levels of service have increased. This has included the provision of Internet via smartphones and the extension of the network across more territory. As a result, people in urban and rural areas have achieved quite high levels of connectivity. In Viet Nam, for example, 90 percent of rural residents own a mobile telephone and half of these are smartphones; some 24 million rural residents use the Internet, which is the same as in urban areas (Nhung, 2017).

People use mobile telecommunications in a variety of ways. Prahalad (2006) observed that poor people quickly learned how to use telephones to obtain market information (e.g. prices at rival fish merchants for fresh catch) and were able to use this to increase their income. Other studies have also indicated a positive link between technology adoption and poverty eradication (e.g. Mendola, 2007; Cecchini and Scott, 2003). Mobile telephones can be used to give and receive information, and this can include family-based information, as well as social and leisure-based interactions. Is this happening in Myanmar and Viet Nam yet? If so, what is the role of technology in helping people to incorporate themselves into market-based activities and what problems and prospects are there? Attempting to answer these questions is the purpose of the research project reported on in this chapter. The project consisted of an empirical, quantitative survey conducted in different parts of two countries and used a self-developed questionnaire.

This chapter goes on in Section 2 to provide a literature review that is used to highlight gaps in knowledge and the creation of a research framework that has been used to address these gaps. This is followed by a discussion of the methodology used in the project in Section 3, and the findings are presented and discussed in Sections 4 and 5.

2. Literature review

Mobile telecommunications differ from fixed-line telecommunications as they use radio waves rather than wires to connect users (Gruber and Verhoven, 2004). Attempts to use wireless networks are almost a century old, but it is only in the past ten years that sophisticated use of the available frequencies was introduced. Contemporary smartphones are characterised by being data generators as much as data exchange systems, and for having an easily changeable suite of apps (software programmes customarily designed for a narrow range of uses) which are mostly selected by the user rather than the manufacturer (Bin Dhim and Trevena, 2015). The use of mobile telephones and smartphones has become endemic around the world. Users find that they provide psychological benefits and offer safety, belongingness, self-esteem, and self-actualisation (Kang and Jung, 2014). They are likely to choose services and apps which their friends, family members, and colleagues use and, hence, derive network externalities (Lin and Lu, 2011).

Numerous studies have been made on the impact of smartphones and attendant technology on various aspects of contemporary life.

2.1. The agrarian question

In the 'Eighteenth Brumaire of Louis Napoleon', Marx infamously considered peasants to be equivalent to 'a sack of potatoes' (Marx, 1999), with an inherently conservative nature and spatial dispersal that made political organisation problematic. He seems to have assumed that they would, as a class, wither away once revolutionary change takes place. Seeking to provide empirical support for this position, Kautsky (1988) noted the differentiation that existed within the diversity of peasant experiences and the fact that they seemed to persist above and beyond political logic. Although it might be expected that smallholdings would be amalgamated into larger units under capitalism, this did not take place, and Kautsky concluded that some forms of equilibrium would be established in which small and large farms would exist in a needful relationship with each other. Bello (2009) writes that numerous attempts have been made around the world to finish off the peasant farming household, which has nevertheless managed to cling on to survival. Given the risks inherent in seeking employment away from the farm, it is evident that holding on to such land as is available represents a prudent risk reduction strategy. As the states of the GMS enter the next phases of the Factory Asia paradigm of intensive, export-oriented, import-substituting, low-labour-cost manufacturing through the opening of special economic zones, the precarity of non-farm employment may, if anything, be intensified as a result (Walsh, 2017).

According to agrarian theory (e.g. Thein, 1997; Bojnec and Latruffe, 2011), farms should increase in size but decrease in number as time passes and income-generating opportunities increase. This is because larger land sizes represent opportunities for economies of scale and scope, and greater efficiencies in the adoption and deployment of new forms of technology. This phenomenon is witnessed across much of the developed world, particularly in countries such as the United States and Australia, where extensive flatlands make large, efficient pastoral or arable farms a logical response to conditions, particularly given the regime of incentives and subsidies available. However, this response does not apply to every type of landscape. After all, the collectivisation of agriculture, which relied on an ideology shaped by the broad open lands of Georgia and Ukraine, turned out to be disastrous when tried in the complex and variegated terrain of the GMS. In that case, the rhythms of rice-based agriculture had already led to the creation of a seasonal system of shared labour. In any case, GMS smallholders continue to operate and the anticipated change in size has not yet materialised. That is not to say that there has not been a change in landholding in the region. Some farmers have sold their land to corporate interests or outside farmers, if they no longer wished or were able to continue agriculture, especially when the land price increases significantly because of the announcement of new infrastructure in the event of the opening of a special economic zone (Na Srito and Walsh,

2012). However, some farmers have reportedly lost their money in the cities to which they moved and have to return to become paid labourers on the land they once owned. Although this phenomenon has not yet reached all parts of the GMS, farming in Thailand is increasingly becoming a grey activity as the country has become an ageing society and farming does not appeal to many younger people, except in emergency situations. Research has shown that, at times of financial crisis, many people with entrepreneurial skills and capabilities prefer to become part of the informal sector by, for example, street vending rather than facing the alternative of returning to rural under-employment (e.g. Maneepong and Walsh, 2013). It is worth noting that with consideration of poverty existing within agricultural sectors across the GMS, farming as a livelihood should not be romanticised.

2.2. Value chains

Value chains are the successive stages of production from raw inputs (upstream) to ultimate sale and consumption (downstream). For emerging markets, integrating domestic firms into value chains with foreign firms (and, in due course, through domestic firms) is an important developmental goal. This is one of the more significant reasons for foreign direct investment (FDI) and helps to counter many of its negative impacts. Accepting and encouraging FDI should be a transactional decision for a developing country government since it is far from being a panacea (Chang and Grabel, 2014). The domestic market can benefit from FDI through the following means:

i   Direct efforts. Inwards FDI is likely to produce a number of jobs, although these are not guaranteed to be high-value jobs and workplace relations might be problematic as a result of incentives that may have been provided as inducements to potential investors. Incoming investors will want to retain some leading positions for people from their home company, but the remaining positions might be subject to negotiation. In addition to income provided by job creation, those involved might be able to learn skills and competencies which might subsequently be redeployed to the home economy. A multiplier effect will occur, as incoming investors will need services such as accommodation, education, and health.

ii Technology transfer. Incoming firms are almost certain to have some competitive advantages that domestic firms do not have. Some of the technology that represents these competitive advantages will find its way into the domestic economy, either because understanding of it leaks out of the investing firm or because local firms are required to service it in some way. Not all forms of technology will be suitable for transfer or yield their full value, but some will.

iii Industrial deepening. This represents the development of relationships between the investing firm and domestic firms. Local firms, many of which will be small and medium-sized enterprises (SMEs), might provide services such as maintenance, market research, and public relations. Investing firms will wish to localise their supply chains for cost purposes, but also because it gives the investors a better profile in the local community. Many opportunities might arise from such relationships.

One problem that GMS countries face when seeking to establish relationships with investing firms is the 'missing middle', i.e. within the SME category (which varies by definition according to country), the great majority of firms are small in size and are very often in the micro SME scale. Such very small firms are less likely to be able to offer goods and services to investing firms with the quality and reliability that international best practice has come to expect. Although it is possible that some providers of FDI might be willing to develop potential local partners, this should not be assumed.

Becoming part of a value chain is a significant objective for a host economy. Although it is difficult, this can usually be achieved as a result of market mechanisms, but not always. Examples of where this has taken place include the following:

i   Farmers in Thailand have worked with the retail giant Tesco Lotus so that their produce can be placed in retail outlets and incorporated in products such as ready meals which might then contribute to the export market (Poupon, 2013).

ii Firms or entrepreneurs can work with local producers to assist them to achieve international standards of quality and become suitable candidates for local and international retail outlets. This has been achieved by Inca Inchi nuts (Sacha Inchi), Doi Chaang coffee (Pendergrast, 2015), and various dairy products in Myanmar.

iii Some firms have established linkages with their own branches across borders for different stages of production. Toyota, for example, operates the Thailand+1 strategy whereby some less advanced aspects of automobile construction (e.g. manufacturing and fitting car seat covers) may be conducted in neighbouring countries with lower labour costs, such as Cambodia or Viet Nam, after which the final product is completed in one of the well-established Thai industrial estates.

iv Opportunities exist for local companies providing logistics, catering, security, and other activities which the investing firm might prefer to outsource. Special economic zones in Lao PDR include restaurants for employees working there because of lack of appropriate alternatives.

v   Some clusters of agricultural products have been organised with government assistance in Lao PDR, and these have led to sales of organic rice and vegetables in the domestic market. A group of investors negotiated directly with producers of white charcoal (*bintochan*), which is now exported to barbecue restaurants in Japan and the Republic of Korea (cf. Southiseng, Vilaychur, and Walsh, 2016).

For farmers in Myanmar and Viet Nam to integrate in regional value chains, a first step that could be followed would be to work with a farming cooperative, or farmers' product group (FPG). The term FPG is preferable here, because cooperatives have become associated with various unfortunate episodes in history. The FPG might be used to provide help and support to individual households, and thus act as an intermediary when commercial interests come calling. In Thailand, some farmers now have the confidence to deal with large-scale potential customers directly, but such confidence takes a while to obtain. An FPG of sufficient size can also act as a market participant through cooperation, which is the case with some organic rice growers in Lao PDR. In any case, an FPG can act as a source of information and a means of communication.

The previous analysis yields the following propositions: (i) farmers with access to more information sources are more likely to be able to access good market opportunities, (ii) farming households will work together to obtain information, and (iii) information and market access are connected.

3. Methodology

3.1. Research strategy

Since models of market integration of rural areas and the adoption of new technologies already exist, it was determined that a quantitative methodology would be appropriate. The contribution to knowledge would reside principally in the fact that investigation of these issues had not yet taken place in Myanmar or Viet Nam.

The two countries were selected because, although they have similarities because of their mutual location in the GMS, they have significant differences in conditions in rural settings:

i   Viet Nam has had considerable attention from the government sector, with targeted provision of resources, and this has led to the effective elimination of the worst forms of food insecurity (Walsh, 2016). In Myanmar, many parts of the countryside were virtually ignored by the military government, and much of the country belongs to semiautonomous zones which are effectively beyond the reach of the current government.

ii Viet Nam has a long coast which contains many ports that can be used to export goods. It has a higher population and a better developed retail sector in which sales of agricultural goods can be made in the domestic sector. Viet Nam is now connected to China via a branch of the North-South Economic Corridor, and this represents another important market. By contrast, transportation infrastructure is much less developed in Myanmar, and this makes market integration much more difficult. People are more remote, and geographical and climatic conditions can be harsher, particularly in the north-central dry zone.

It was decided that these factors meant that comparison between the two countries would be instructive. To ensure a good level of consistency within the two samples, country researchers were asked to select two distinct locations and try to ensure an even amount of male and female respondents. The demographic details of the sample achieved are provided ahead. Within each location, researchers used a combination of convenience and purposive sampling techniques to obtain the required overall sample. The total sample size was reached by balancing a high level of confidence in the results received with issues of time and budget. Overall, the sample size was 400, with 200 questionnaires each completed in Myanmar and Viet Nam.

In terms of questionnaire design, several sources were used. After reviewing the literature, a scale of technology adoption which had been successfully used in India (Meera et al., 2004) was employed. This scale was adjusted after the pilot test, when a few of the items included were deleted as they were not relevant to the research site. In addition to this, questions were devised to try to capture the other information required. These questions were considered by the research team and refined accordingly. They are questions that have in very similar forms been used successfully in other projects involving research in GMS rural settings (e.g. Walsh, 2015). Since experienced and qualified country researchers were used, it was considered unnecessary to recheck with respondents.

Once the completed questionnaires were returned, they were coded and entered into PSPP. PSPP is a free, open-source statistical analysis package which almost replicates better known products such as SPSS, but which does not require the high licensing fee.

Once the questionnaires were entered into PSPP, they were checked for accuracy, and various statistical techniques were used to obtain the findings presented in the following section. The data will be made available on request, and additional analysis may be conducted by interested researchers.

3.2. Research issues

Previous research in rural areas of the GMS has indicated that various problems exist beyond the normal methodological issues related to quantitative research (e.g. Walsh, 2016). These include the following:

i   Low levels of education and life experience mean that many respondents find it difficult to understand questions, particularly when unfamiliar vocabulary is used.

ii   In Myanmar in particular, less-well-educated women are often reluctant to participate in any form of research, so there is a danger of non-response bias.

iii   Some respondents misunderstand the role of the interviewer and suspect they might be government agents of some sort in disguise. This persuades some people that if they can provide the 'correct' answers, they will receive some sort of reward (and they might be punished for the 'wrong' answers). Relations between government and people across the GMS have often been antagonistic, and this, too, can have a negative effect on the accuracy of responses given.

iv   Local dialects and terminology can vary to the extent that phenomena such as insects or plant disease can be referred to by different names in different villages, and, in some cases, the phenomena might not be documented at all. This makes interviewing particularly difficult with respect to technical issues.

v   In some cases, village leaders wish to act as gatekeepers to the villagers, and suitable access must be negotiated before interviewing can take place.

vi   Rural households are often located in terrain that is difficult to traverse, and finding an appropriate sample may become time-consuming and expensive.

All these precautions were taken, in addition to the provision of a pilot test for the project. The country researchers used the draft questionnaire with a convenience sample of 10–20 potential respondents. The purpose of the pilot test was to check that respondents would be able to understand and answer the questions, amid some concern expressed by country researchers regarding the ability of rural persons in their home countries to answer some questions. As a result of the pilot test, some changes were made to the questionnaire (which became subtly different in each country). However, the extent of the changes required was less than the country researchers had expected, and this could be a further indication of the rate of change in rural areas regarding the issues under consideration.

4. Main findings

The findings will be presented in two subsections, detailing the two country case studies, Myanmar and Viet Nam.

4.1. Myanmar

A total of 411 questionnaires was collected in two different and contrasting regions. Of these, 203 (49.4 percent) were collected in the Mandalay region and 208 (50.6 percent) were collected in the Ayeyarwady region. As in Viet Nam, the responses given in the two locations were often statistically significant and this factor is the most important in explaining different opinions.

4.1.1. Demographic characteristics

It was difficult for researchers to obtain female respondents because many were unwilling to be interviewed, perhaps because of embarrassment about their lower levels of education (Table 11.1). As a result, nearly 80 percent of the respondents were men. However, analysis shows that the impact of gender on responses was not very significant – especially when compared with location, which was of considerable importance in predicting responses.

The distribution of education showed that more men had achieved secondary and high school or university levels than women, who were more likely to have reached primary level or who were just literate. Myanmar faces all the difficulties of less developed countries in terms of education, particularly in rural areas, as well as lack of resources, poor infrastructure, and the need for parents to pay teachers. Girls are still being withdrawn early from school to work on the farm or provide domestic labour (Sar, 2016).

Table 11.1 Demographic Characteristics of Sample in Myanmar[i]

Question	Answers	Mandalay	Ayeyarwady	Overall
Gender	Male (%)	78.8	79.3	79.1
	Female (%)	21.2	20.7	20.8
Education Level	Can Read and Write (%)	19.7	17.3	18.5
	Primary (%)	24.6	14.9	19.7
	Secondary (%)	33.0	33.7	33.3
	High (%)	16.3	30.3	23.4
	University (%)	6.4	3.9	5.1
Age	Up to 30 (%)	7.4	3.4	5.4
	31–40 (%)	9.9	13	11.5
	41–50 (%)	25.2	33.2	29.2
	51–60 (%)	33.2	30.8	32
	61+ (%)	24.3	19.7	22
Household Size, Persons	Up to 3 (%)	9.9	15.4	12.7
	4–6 (%)	58.9	54.3	56.6
	7–9 (%)	23.3	24	23.7
	10+ (%)	7.9	6.3	7.1
Amount of Land, Acres[ii]	Up to 2 (%)	24.6	16.3	20.4
	2.1–5.0 (%)	45.8	32.7	39.2
	5.1–10.0 (%)	24.1	39.9	32.1
	10.1+ (%)	5.4	10.6	8.3
Length of Time Farming, Year	Up to 5 (%)	11.9	9.6	10.7
	5.1–10.0 (%)	10.4	6.3	8.3
	10.1–20.0 (%)	16.8	18.8	17.8
	20.1–40.0 (%)	42.1	51	46.6
	40.1+ (%)	18.8	14.4	16.5
Other Job	Yes (%)	26.1	12.5	19.2
	No (%)	73.9	87.5	80.8
Monthly Income, MK[iii]	0–499,999	95.6	97.6	96.6
	500,000–999,999	4.4	2.4	3.4
	1,000,000+	0	0	0

Notes:
i. N=411.
ii. In Myanmar, land size is measured in acres. 1 acre = 4,046.86 m^2.
iii. Myanmar's currency is the kyat (MK). MK1 ≅ US$0.00064 (at the end of 2018).

It is evident from these results that the age of the sample is much higher than the age of the population as a whole. This is likely to be because many younger people have moved away from rural areas to seek work in urban areas or overseas. Mandalay, for example, is rapidly accumulating a peri-urban sector of undocumented residences providing housing for migrants looking for work in the emerging industrial sector there. In general, agriculture has become less appealing to younger people who increasingly are able to make changes in their lives, so farming has become a greying occupation.

Concerning the number of people living in the household concerned, the results indicate that household sizes can be quite large, which reflects the persistence of traditional family structures in these rural regions. The results are similar in the two research sites, which suggests that lifestyle changes associated with globalisation and household structure have yet to reach rural Myanmar.

As for the amounts of land farmed, cross-country data from the Food and Agriculture Organization of the United Nations (2017) suggests that the average small farm size is 2 hectares, which is equal to about 5 acres. While more land is better for family income, productivity also depends on factors such as access to inputs, knowledge, and markets.

When asked whether respondents farmed land other than their own, 1.5 percent of Mandalay respondents and no Ayeyarwady respondents said they did. If they did farm other land, the average amount of land was 5.0 acres. Regarding the experience with farming, the sample yields a large amount of experience with agriculture. This is true for the respondents in both research sites. However, there is a significant difference between sites concerning occupations.

More respondents in Mandalay region have jobs in addition to farming, suggesting it better connected with the outside world (compared to Ayeyarwady), at least in terms of finding additional income.

Income levels are difficult to measure. But given that most respondents live in a household with an income of less than MK500,000 (about US$366) and bearing in mind the large household size, it is clear that a number of households are living close to or in poverty, which is generally defined as living on US$2 or less per person per day.

4.1.2. Livestock ownership

Questions and answers regarding the ownership of livestock farming are presented in Table 11.2. There are significant differences in farming practices between the two research sites, with livestock ownership being significantly more likely at the Mandalay sites than the Ayeyarwady sites.

The results indicate a comparatively low level of ownership of chickens in the sample, as well, both in the proportion of respondents owning chickens and the number of chickens involved, which is also low, especially in Mandalay. The mean size of chicken ownership in Ayeyarwady suggests that there are farmers there who are raising them for market. This is also suggested by the large proportion of respondents in Ayeyarwady who are raising ducks, since ducks are also associated

Table 11.2 Livestock Farming in Myanmar

Question	Answers	Mandalay	Ayeyarwady	Overall
Livestock Owners	Yes	93.1	58.2	75.4
	No	6.9	41.8	24.6
Type of Livestock Owned	Chickens	12.7	8.1	10.9
	Ducks	1.6	62.3	25.4
	Buffaloes	2.1	0.8	1.6
	Cattle	95.8	68.6	85.2
	Sheep	1.1	0	0.7
	Fish	0	0	0
	Pigs	20.1	11.6	16.8
Information Source of livestock farming	Family	58.2	100	74.5
	Friends/neighbours	68.3	95	78.7
	Newspapers/magazines	15.9	1.7	10.3
	Television	18	0.8	11.3
	Radio	12.2	1.7	8.1
	Government officers	22.2	1.7	14.2
	Cooperatives/FPGs	5.3	0.8	3.6
	NGO representatives	0.5	1.6	1
	Internet	4.8	0	2.9
	Livestock market	9	0	5.5
	Other	2.1	0	1.3
Information Source of rice farming	Family	56.7	100	78.6
	Friends/neighbours	74.9	99.5	87.4
	Newspapers/magazines	30.5	15.4	22.9
	Television	25.6	13.5	19.5
	Radio	27.6	10.6	19
	Government officers	49.8	13	31.1
	Cooperatives/FPGs	11.8	2.4	7.1
	NGO representatives	2	9.1	5.6
	Internet	9.4	1.9	5.6
	Livestock market	–	–	–
	Other	1	0	0.5

Notes:
i. FPG = farmers' production group. FPG is often preferred to 'cooperative' in mainland Southeast Asia and elsewhere where communism has lent that word a poor image.
ii. NGO = non-governmental organisation. NGOs are often active in promoting rural development in less developed countries such as Myanmar and Viet Nam.

with market-based sales. Many more respondents in Mandalay (95.8 percent) own cattle than in Ayeyarwady (68.6 percent). Cattle are used for transportation and farm labour, so it is possible that these are needed more in Mandalay than they are in Ayeyarwady, where other options are available. Fish ponds have been introduced to some parts of the GMS (see the Viet Nam case study) as a means of providing more market sales opportunities for farming households, but this has not yet reached the research sites.

Differences between the two research sites regarding the sources of information for farming are also very clear. Ayeyarwady respondents are much more likely to consult family members and friends and neighbours than Mandalay respondents, but much less likely to consult nearly all the other potential information sources. It is possible to interpret this through the greater level of social connectivity available in Mandalay compared with Ayeyarwady, where people must fall back on people close to them for lack of any alternative. It is also notable that respondents generally seek information more often when considering rice agriculture compared with livestock agriculture. This may be because of greater expertise and knowledge regarding rice agriculture, in addition to its importance to the household. Finally, the low level of importance of the Internet as an information source is noteworthy. Internet access is widely available, but people do not seem to consider it a useful and trustworthy source of information about local agricultural conditions.

4.1.3. Connectivity

The next section of the questionnaire consisted of several questions relating to different aspects of connectivity. The first of these related to the locations of markets for agricultural products produced by the household. It is notable that there are statistically significant distributions for three of the five categories concerned, and these are the most important ones in terms of numbers (Table 11.3). It seems that the Ayeyarwady respondents are much more closely locked into their local economy than the Mandalay respondents, who have more flexibility in their choices and can sell to brokers and regional markets through their own efforts. However, some respondents in Ayeyarwady can use regional markets and brokers, and this suggests that more opportunities are available for respondents if they are willing and able to take advantage of them.

The availability and accessibility of various modes of information and communication technology (ICT) seems to quite different between Mandalay and Ayeyarwady, as well. These relate particularly to the availability of online media, with much more availability being reported in Ayeyarwady than in Mandalay. The exception to this is e-mail, which is reported at a much lower rate than other online services and which seems to be almost entirely absent in Ayeyarwady. Respondents may have different conceptions of these services than in other areas. However, it is evident that there is widespread availability of online media in both research sites, so there is an opportunity to provide information using these media which is not currently being taken. More research would be required to determine appropriate ways of bridging this gap.

It is also clear that the mobile phone, television, and radio are the most available and preferred modes of communication. This suggests that people are not yet necessarily expecting an interactive experience, but this situation might change quite quickly.

Respondents were presented with a Likert-type five-point scale with answers ranging from 'most preferred' to 'least preferred'. The answers received have been converted into mean scores, with 5 the highest ('most preferred') and 1 the lowest ('least preferred'). As suggested earlier, mobile phones, television, and

Table 11.3 Connectivity in Agriculture in Myanmar

Question	Answers	Mandalay	Ayeyarwady	Overall
Location of Markets[i]	Neighbours (%)	4.4	1.9	3.2
	Village markets (%)	6.9	69.2	38.4
	Brokers (%)	67.5	21.2	44
	Regional markets (%)	62.6	42.8	52.6
	International market (%)	0.5	1	0.7
Modes of ICT Available and Accessible for Livestock Farming[i]	Mobile phones (%)	99	100	99.5
	Television (%)	99.5	100	99.8
	Radio (%)	99	99	99
	Internet (%)	64	91.4	77.9
	Social media (%)	63.6	94.7	79.3
	CD/DVD (%)	60.6	92.3	76.6
	Computer/laptop (%)	2	1.4	1.7
	E-mail (%)	31.5	1	16.1
	Satellite (%)	0	1	0.5
Modes of ICT Available and Accessible for Rice Farming[i]	Mobile phones (%)	100	99.5	99.8
	Television (%)	99.5	100	99.8
	Radio (%)	98.5	94.7	96.6
	Internet (%)	58.1	65.4	61.8
	Social media (%)	58.1	70.2	64.2
	CD/DVD (%)	50.7	87.5	69.3
	Computer/laptop (%)	2.5	1.9	2.2
	E-mail (%)	25.6	1.9	13.6
	Satellite (%)	1.5	0.5	1
Preferred Modes of Communication[i], Score (1–5)	Mobile phones (%)	3.33	3.03	3.28
	Television (%)	3.48	3.23	3.25
	Radio (%)	2.93	2.9	2.92
	Internet (%)	2.49	2.19	2.35
	Social media (%)	2.4	2.31	2.36
	CD/DVD (%)	2.27	2.4	2.33
	Computer/laptop (%)	2	1.7	1.85
	E-mail (%)	2.35	1.86	2.1
	Satellite (%)	1.98	1.67	1.82
Connectivity[i]	Have mobile phone(s) (%)	96.6	95.2	95.9
	Have Internet access (%)	37.9	35.6	36.7
	Use mobile phone to look for information on agriculture (%)	62.3	37.8	50.3
	Use mobile phone to look for information on livestock (%)[ii]	9.1	2.7	6
Type of Agricultural Information Sought[iii]	Market prices (%)	50	3.6	32.9
	Weather forecasting (%)	95.8	100	97.3
	Seed varieties (%)	16.7	0	10.5
	Post-harvest technology (%)	18.8	0	11.8
	General agricultural news (%)	62.5	42.9	55.5
	Early warning and management of agricultural diseases (%)	12.5	0	7.9
	Latest agricultural news (%)	39.6	14.3	30.3

Notes:
i. n = 411
ii. n = 151
iii. n = 76

radio are the most preferred modes of communication, with television being the most preferred means.

All these different means of communication have received statistically significant distributions and, in all but one case, there is a higher level of preference in the Mandalay sites than the Ayeyarwady sites. This may be the result of the greater level of information available in Ayeyarwady – although this would contradict the results described earlier about connectivity and information searching. Perhaps, despite having more access to online sources, respondents in Ayeyarwady have less interest in more information than those in Mandalay. The market development can help educate people about the value added and profitable uses of information. The most popular media should be used for this purpose.

When asked about the types of agricultural information for which people searched, the results show the same consistent pattern of respondents in Mandalay being more active in searching for information than respondents from Ayeyarwady, with the exception of weather forecasting, although that is not a statistically significant distribution. The difference between the two groups in terms of searching for information about market prices is particularly striking, and it is a reminder that the Ayeyarwady respondents are much more likely to sell their produce at local markets rather than at regional ones or to brokers, so they already know the prices. However, there is scope here to increase the use of information by farmers as a means of helping them to improve their situations.

More specific questions are addressed to the use of Internet in information collection. Table 11.4 presents the main results. First, fewer than half of the

Table 11.4 The Use of Internet in Agriculture in Myanmar

Question	Answers	Mandalay	Ayeyarwady	Overall
Trust in Internet	Yes	50.7	43.2	47
Information[i]	No	49.3	56.8	53
Longevity of	Less than 1 year (%)	25	50	34.2
Internet Access[ii]	1–2 years (%)	70.8	50	63.2
	3–5 years (%)	4.2	0	2.6
Frequency of	Once per day (%)	48.1	32.4	40.4
Internet Access[ii]	Once per week (%)	29.9	31.1	30.5
	2–3 times a month (%)	18.2	27	22.5
	Once per month (%)	3.9	9.5	6.6
Motivations	Ease of access	49.4	27	38.4
for Using the	Availability of relevant content	41.6	52.7	47
Internet[iii]	Quality of information	10.4	10.8	10.6
	Cost of obtaining information	9.1	6.8	8
	Communicate with relatives and friends	90.9	93.2	92.1

Notes:
i n = 149
ii n = 76
iii n = 151

respondents trust information found on the Internet. This could be interpreted as a positive result because it shows people exercising a sceptical approach to what they find, or a negative result because it shows that people cannot believe what they are told. Given the history of propaganda in Myanmar's recent history, it is not surprising that people are familiar with discounting some of the things that they are told. There is an opportunity for informing people about information sources which may be deemed trustworthy overall, whether they come from Myanmar or elsewhere.

Second, the penetration of rural Myanmar by mobile telephones and the Internet is a very recent phenomenon, since their availability was previously restricted by extremely high prices because of political reasons (i.e. limiting communication to inhibit the organisation of political movements). As a result, more than 95 percent of respondents have obtained Internet access in the preceding two years. Mandalay had slightly earlier access to mobile phones than Ayeyarwady, but coverage is rapidly being rolled out across the country.

Third, feedback from the respondents in Myanmar shows that fewer than half of the respondents accessed the Internet daily or more often. This is a significant difference from contemporary urban living, even in developing countries, where permanent access to the Internet is expected at home and outside. Coverage in rural areas is much more restricted. This has implications for the means of communicating with people in this category, since one single outreach will not find everyone.

Fourth, it is noticeable from these results that Mandalay respondents felt that access to the Internet was significantly easier than it was for the Ayeyarwady respondents. By contrast, the Ayeyarwady respondents were more likely to feel that relevant information was available on the Internet, although this was not a statistically significant result. In both research sites, the most important motivation for going online was to communicate with relatives and friends. Cost and quality of information do not appear to be considered important factors.

When asked about potential benefits for agriculture to be derived from online access, such as: (i) easy access to accurate and timely information, (ii) access to regional and international markets and products, (iii) cheaper and faster generation and dissemination of information, (iv) support of post-harvest techniques, and (v) better crop management, a series of statistically significant distributions was produced (Table 11.5). In general, the results for Ayeyarwady respondents are higher than those for the Mandalay respondents. This suggests that the former see more potential benefits in these areas that are not currently being obtained, while the Mandalay respondents, with a greater level of accessibility, have already been disabused of this notion. Whether this is the correct interpretation or not, it is certainly true that the two sets of respondents regularly demonstrate different opinions.

However, ambivalence about the value of the Internet persisted among the respondents. Overall, more than half of the respondents would not agree with the idea that the Internet brings value to their lives, although a clear proportion of respondents was in favour in Ayeyarwady (though no one there strongly agreed

Table 11.5 Benefits, Perceptions, and Barriers to Using the Internet

Question	Answers	Mandalay	Ayeyarwady	Overall
Easy access to accurate and timely information[i]	Highly agree (%)	52.6	16.8	34
	Maybe (%)	22.4	57.2	40.5
	Not sure (%)	25	26	25.5
Access to regional and international markets and products[i]	Highly agree (%)	1.6	0	0.8
	Maybe (%)	14.1	26.9	20.8
	Not sure (%)	84.4	73.1	78.5
Cheaper and faster generation and dissemination of information[i]	Highly agree (%)	7.3	4.8	6
	Maybe (%)	43.8	49	46.5
	Not sure (%)	49	46.2	47.5
Support of post-harvest techniques[i]	Highly agree (%)	2.6	0	1.3
	Maybe (%)	12	26.4	19.5
	Not sure (%)	85.4	73.6	79.3
Better crop management[i]	Highly agree (%)	2.1	0	1
	Maybe (%)	7.8	26.4	17.5
	Not sure (%)	90.1	73.6	81.5
Perceptions of the Value of Internet Access[ii]	Strongly agree (%)	0.5	0	0.2
	Agree (%)	28.1	66.8	47.7
	Neither agree nor disagree (%)	71.4	33.1	52.1
	Disagree (%)	0	0	0
Possible Barriers to Accessing the Internet[iii]	High cost of Internet service (%)	52.1	43.2	47.5
	Language barrier (%)	83	62.5	72.4
	Cannot afford to buy ICT tools (%)	72.7	32.2	51.7
	Lack of ICT knowledge (%)	76.8	91.8	84.6
	No interest in using ICT tools (%)	21.7	43.3	32.8
	Lack of technical skills (%)	87.6	97.1	92.5

Notes:
i. n = 400
ii. n = 402
iii. n = 411

with the proposition). People in the sample appear to be quite conservative and perhaps sceptical about the benefits of this aspect of globalisation. More research would be needed to find out if this is an aspect of natural reserve, or whether people have learned to be cautious about technology and change because of difficult lessons learned in the past.

Regarding the potential barriers to accessing the Internet, respondents from Mandalay considered the high cost of services, tools, and the language barrier much more important, while respondents from Ayeyarwady were much more likely to see problems in lack of knowledge, skills, and interest. Overall, the principal problems observed were the lack of skills and knowledge, and the language barrier. There seems to be scope for some educational outreach to help overcome these potential barriers.

Finally, respondents were asked if they thought the government should intervene in financing ICT services in terms of agriculture and livestock management. Respondents certainly did think so, with 99.8 percent agreeing that this should take place.

To summarise, 411 questionnaires were completed and collected in Myanmar, divided between two research sites in Mandalay and Ayeyarwady. It was found that penetration of these regions by mobile telephones and Internet access had been very rapid in the years before 2018. However, it was not clear that people who valued access to the Internet were using it in the most productive ways. The principal differences among respondents could be traced to their location. It was evident that respondents in Mandalay regularly had differences of opinion from people in Ayeyarwady, and some attempts have been made to try to explain these differences. It is argued that there are specific areas in which interventions could improve people's lives with respect to Internet usage.

4.2. Viet Nam

A total of 200 questionnaires were completed in Viet Nam, including 100 from Cam Lo in Quang Tri province and 100 from Hoa Vang in Da Nang province. Eighteen villages were used as research sites.

4.2.1. Demographic characteristics

The gender figures show, as in the case of the Myanmar sample, a preponderance of male respondents (Table 11.6). As in the case of Myanmar, there was a preponderance of male over female respondents in this sample. This was less the case in Da Nang than in Quang Tri, perhaps because more males have migrated for work in Da Nang, leaving more women in household leadership positions. As will be seen, significant differences in the results are common based on the location of the research site, and this is shown in this result.

As in the case of Myanmar, the age of the sample is higher than that of the population as a whole, which is again indicative of the greying of agriculture in the region, as younger people are more likely to migrate for work either elsewhere in the country or overseas.

In terms of education, a statistically significant difference is again notable between the two research sites, with much higher levels of education in Da Nang than in Quang Tri. Since education is a contributory factor to higher levels of labour migration, it is not surprising to see these results in the light of the gender distribution described earlier.

As for the household size, the results show generally lower household sizes in Viet Nam than in Myanmar. Household sizes appear to be larger overall in Da Nang than in Quang Tri, although the reason is not clear.

Table 11.6 Demographic Characteristics of Sample in Viet Nam[i]

Question	Answers	Quang Tri	Da Nang	Overall
Gender	Male (%)	79.0	58.0	68.5
	Female (%)	21.0	42.0	31.5
Age	Up to 30 (%)	6.0	4.0	5.0
	31–40 (%)	10.0	21.0	15.5
	41–50 (%)	24.0	25.0	24.5
	51–60 (%)	45.0	41.0	43.0
Education Level	Up to 3 years	4.0	2.2	3.1
	4–6 years	23.2	10.8	17.2
	7–9 years	39.4	24.7	32.3
	10–12 years	33.3	62.4	47.4
Household Size, persons	Up to 2 (%)	3.0	6.0	4.5
	3–5 (%)	71.0	57.0	64.0
	6+ (%)	26.0	37.0	31.5
Amount of Land, hectares [ii]	Up to 2 (%)	0	9.0	4.5
	2.1–5.0 (%)	0	24.0	12.1
	5.1–10.0 (%)	13.3	27.0	20.2
	10.1+ (%)	86.7	40.0	58.1
Length of Time Farming, year	Up to 5 (%)	11.9	9.6	10.7
	5.1–10.0 (%)	10.4	6.3	8.3
	10.1–20.0 (%)	16.8	18.8	17.8
	20.1–40.0 (%)	42.1	51	46.6
	40.1+ (%)	18.8	14.4	16.5
Farmed other people's land in addition to their own[iii]	Yes (%)	6.0	2.0	4.0
	No (%)	94.0	98.0	96.0
Other Job	Yes (%)	62.0	72.0	67.0
	No (%)	38.0	28.0	33.0

Notes:
i. n = 200.
ii. n = 198.
iii. n = 192.

Regarding the amount of land that they farm, the difference between the two research sites is again noticeable, with farmers in Quang Tri having significantly larger farms than those in Da Nang. It is possible that labour migration from Quang Tri is lower than in Da Nang partly because of better prospects from larger farms as much as issues such as better education in Da Nang.

Not many respondents said they farmed other people's land in addition to their own. The average amount of land for those who farmed other land was more than 10 hectares. But when asked if they had another occupation, 67 percent overall answered that they did, with 62 percent of respondents from Quang Tri saying this and 72 percent from Da Nang province.

4.2.2. Livestock management

In terms of livestock, 71.5 percent of respondents overall answered that they kept some livestock, with 98 percent from Quang Tri saying this and only 45 percent from Da Nang agreeing. This shows important differences in farming practices between the two sites, which could have impacts on household income and prospects.

In addition to being more likely to own different kinds of livestock in Quang Tri compared with Da Nang, farmers there also owned a larger number of each type of animal investigated (Table 11.7). The numbers of animals involved suggest that they are being raised for market. For example, the mean number of ducks in Quang Tri among those who have them is 503 and the mean number of fish is 4,125. Various projects in Viet Nam have been aimed at introducing integrated production schemes at the household or community level to promote environmental sustainability and enhance incomes. Fish are often involved in projects of this sort and are aimed at market transactions.

Table 11.7 Livestock Farming in Viet Nam

Question	Answers	Quang Tri	Da Nang	Overall
Livestock Owners[i]	Yes (%)	98.0	45.0	71.5
	No (%)	2.0	55.0	28.5
Type of Livestock Owned[ii]	Chickens (%)	98.0	33.0	65.5
	Ducks (%)	22.0	9.0	15.0
	Pigs (%)	73.0	20.0	46.5
	Cattle (%)	51.0	4.0	27.5
	Buffaloes (%)	12.0	1.0	6.5
	Fish (%)	8.0	0	4.0
	Other (%)	1.0	0	0.5
Information Source of Livestock Farming[ii]	Family (%)	99.0	33.1	78.4
	Friends/neighbours (%)	98.0	28.9	76.4
	Newspapers/magazines (%)	1.0	37.8	12.5
	Television (%)	100	64.4	88.9
	Radio (%)	1.0	33.3	11.1
	Government officers (%)	27.3	88.9	46.5
	NGO representatives (%)	1.0	2.2	1.4
	Cooperatives/FPGs (%)	83.8	6.7	59.7
	Internet (%)	92.9	26.6	73.4
	Other (%)	0	90	9.0
Information Source of Rice Farming[ii]	Family (%)	99.0	32.0	65.5
	Friends/neighbours (%)	98.0	21.0	59.5
	Newspapers/magazines (%)	1.0	36.0	18.5
	Television (%)	99.0	85.0	92.0
	Radio (%)	1.0	25.0	13.0
	Government officers (%)	29.0	75.0	52.0
	NGO representatives (%)	1.0	2.0	1.5
	Cooperatives/FPGs (%)	88.0	4.0	46.0
	Internet (%)	93.0	36.0	64.5
	Other (%)	0	24.0	12.0

Notes:
i. n = 200.
ii. n = 192.

About the sources of information, the results are quite striking in showing the significant differences between respondents at the two sites. Quang Tri respondents are much more likely to consult their families, friends, neighbours, and television in searching for information on both livestock management and rice farming. On the other hand, Da Nang respondents are much more likely to consult government officers and the radio, suggesting a closer relationship with the state and a higher level of trust in it. Cooperatives/FPGs and the Internet are more likely to be consulted in Quang Tri in both categories. Use of the Internet to search for information is much higher than in Myanmar, suggesting both higher levels of penetration there and willingness of people to believe in the information they find online.

4.2.3. Using the Internet

In Viet Nam, most of the respondents have had access to the Internet for more than three years. This is in accordance with various reports describing the penetration of Viet Nam by mobile telephones and the Internet mentioned previously. More of the respondents in Viet Nam had access to online services and had such access for longer than the Myanmar respondents (Table 11.8). In Da Nang, most respondents say they use Internet at least once per day, while most respondents from Quang Tri have Internet access once per week. The higher frequency of using Internet could be related to cost or education about what is available online.

When respondents were asked about the types of agricultural information they search for, there is a long series of statistically significant results in this battery of questions – and they nearly all indicate that respondents in Quang Tri are more likely to search for these types of information. Quang Tri respondents might be more aware of the information they might find, especially online, or they might perceive a greater need to search for information, while the Da Nang respondents are more relaxed about this need. Greater awareness is the more likely explanation. As in Myanmar, searching for information on weather forecasting is very high, but so too are searches for information on seeds varieties and breeds, input prices, disease, and land records, among others. The Vietnamese respondents seem to be bigger users of information about agriculture than the Myanmar respondents, and it seems likely that this will be reflected in their household income and prospects.

Among the four optional reasons for using the Internet, respondents from Da Nang chose ease of access and cost of obtaining information as the two most important factors, which suggests that Internet access is more convenient there than in the Quang Tri sites. On the other hand, in Quang Tri, it is the availability of relevant content that is more important. In this regard, capacity building, such as education in what is available online, might be useful in promoting using the Internet (Table 11.9).

Regarding the potential benefits of Internet access in terms of their own household, the Da Nang respondents clearly feel much more strongly than the Quang Tri respondents that the Internet brings them opportunities for better

Table 11.8 The Use of Internet in Agriculture in Viet Nam[i]

Question	Answers	Quang Tri	Da Nang	Overall
Longevity of Internet Access	Up to 1 year (%)	0	2.2	1.1
	1–2 years (%)	24.2	25.0	24.6
	3–5 years (%)	64.2	57.6	61.0
	5+ years (%)	11.6	15.2	13.4
Frequency of Internet Access	Once per day (%)	36.8	60.9	48.7
	Once per week (%)	57.9	21.7	40.1
	2–3 times a month (%)	4.2	12.0	8.0
	Once per month (%)	1.1	5.4	3.2
Types of Agricultural Information Searched on the Internet	Marketing information (%)	58.3	31.5	45.2
	Seed varieties and breeds (%)	100	53.3	77.1
	Question and answer service (%)	68.8	45.7	57.5
	Rural development programmes and subsidies (%)	77.1	30.4	54.3
	Weather forecasting (%)	96.9	88.0	92.6
	Latest best practices (%)	97.9	13.0	56.4
	Post-harvest technology (%)	21.9	5.4	13.8
	General agricultural news (%)	59.4	51.1	55.3
	Crop insurance (%)	6.3	6.5	6.4
	Farm business and management information (%)	17.7	3.3	10.6
	Input prices and availability (%)	95.8	7.6	52.7
	Early warning and management of diseases and pests (%)	94.8	42.4	69.2
	Marketing milk and milk products (%)	1.0	1.1	1.1
	Accounting and payment (%)	3.1	1.1	2.1
	Soil testing and soil sampling information (%)	24.9	2.2	13.3
	Access to land records (%)	97.9	28.3	63.3

Note:
i. n = 187.

Table 11.9 Reasons for Using the Internet and Possible Benefits in Viet Nam[i]

Question	Answers	Quang Tri	Da Nang	Overall
Reasons for Using Internet	Ease of access (%)	41.1	72.8	56.7
	Availability of relevant content (%)	96.8	37	67.4
	Quality of information (%)	10.5	15.2	12.8
	Cost of obtaining information (%)	6.3	43.5	24.6
Possible Benefits of Using Internet	Agricultural outputs and income improved (%)	48.4	7.6	28.3
	Family income/livelihood improved (%)	48.4	16.3	32.6
	Better education (%)	44.2	81.5	62.6
	Better entertainment (%)	2.1	45.7	23.5

Note:
i. n = 182

education and better entertainment. Meanwhile, Quang Tri respondents are much more likely to feel that Internet access contributes to better agricultural outputs and income, and that family prospects will be improved. These results suggest that one set of respondents has a deeper understanding of what the Internet can provide than does the other. Since Da Nang respondents have more experience with Internet services, it is reasonable to assume that they have a more mature understanding of the situation. Consequently, it is reasonable to assume that respondents think that Internet access is more related to education and entertainment than development opportunities.

4.3. Summary

Internet access has increased very rapidly in both countries, although it occurred a little earlier in Viet Nam than in Myanmar. However, use of the Internet for commercial purposes has not yet reached a mature phase, and there is scope to educate people in how it can be used more profitably. For instance, Myanmar respondents are unsure if they can trust the information found on the Internet, and are sceptical of the value of access. It will take some time before these issues can be overcome.

The results also show significant differences between Myanmar and Viet Nam, and between the two research sites in each country. For instance, although Internet usage supports livestock management in Viet Nam to a certain extent, it is used to a very limited extent in Myanmar. Given such variability, no single plan or strategy can promote connectivity through ICT and market access.

5. Concluding remarks

This research project aimed to determine whether a hypothesised link between take-up of mobile telecommunications and the Internet could be linked to greater engagement with regional, national, and international markets, and hence, with better household prospects in terms of income and opportunities. It has been found that this is taking place to a certain extent, but not on a consistent or wholly coherent basis. In Myanmar, this seems to be in part because of a justifiable suspicion of the provision of information and its value, but also, it is evident that there are numerous statistically significant distributions with respect to the two research sites in each country. This suggests that no single strategy would be successful in promoting the goals of greater information and market access. However, the variations in the use and nature of information suggest that interventions in specific places and for specific purposes might be useful. These interventions might be made by government agency of agricultural service or by representatives of NGOs. Community education might also prove beneficial.

As part of its attempts to reduce the vulnerability of rural regions to global climate change effects, the government of Viet Nam has been encouraging the spread of climate-smart agricultural systems which aim to ensure that integrated systems make the best use of resources on a sustainable basis. For example, there are gender-aware aquaculture systems combining tilapia, tiger shrimps, sea crabs, and seaweed, and the campaign for 'growing grass, raising cows, earthworms, pigs, fish, chickens, ducks, and growing vegetables' (Tung and Tuan, 2016). The figures indicate that more sophisticated combinations of livestock exist in the Vietnamese sample than in the Myanmar sample, and it is possible that government policies have had an impact here. It is notable that most Myanmar respondents who have livestock have cattle, and they reportedly use bullock carts for transportation. In Viet Nam, a number of respondents who kept pigs had only one or perhaps two, indicating that they were being kept for special occasions. Keeping fish is a comparatively recent phenomenon for farmers in GMS, which is tied to sale to a market system. The keeping of ducks is also associated with market-based activities. These activities could be spread across the region.

Bibliography

Bello, W. (2009), *The Food Wars*. London and New York, NY: Verso.

Bin Dhim, N.F., B. Freeman and L. Trevena (2014), 'Pro-Smoking Apps for Smartphones: The Latest Vehicle for the Tobacco Industry?' *Tobacco Control*, 23(1): e4.

Bin Dhim, N.F. and L. Trevena (2015), 'There's an App for That: A Guide for Healthcare Practitioners and Researchers on Smartphone Technology', *Online Journal of Public Health Informatics*, 7(2): e218.

Bojnec, S. and L. Latruffe (2011), 'Farm Size and Efficiency during Transition: Insights from Slovenian Farms', *Transformations in Business and Economics*, 10(3): 104–116.

Cecchini, S. and C. Scott (2003), 'Can Information and Communications Technology Applications Contribute to Poverty Reduction? Lessons from Rural India', *Information Technology for Development*, 10(2): 73–84.

Chang, H-J. and I. Grabel (2014), *Reclaiming Development: An Alternative Economic Policy Manual*. London: Zedbooks.

Food and Agriculture Organization of the United Nations (2017), 'Family Farming Knowledge Platform, Smallholders Data Portrait, Farm Size'. Available at www.fao.org/family-farming/data-sources/dataportrait/farm-size/en/

Gruber, H. and F. Verhoven (2004), 'The Evolution of Markets under Entry and Standards Regulation – The Case of Global Mobile Telecommunications', Research Report, No. 0104. Leuven: Katholieke Universiteit Leuven. Available at https://lirias.kuleuven.be/bitstream/123456789/223770/1/013_0104.pdf

Kang, S. and J. Jung (2014), 'Mobile Communications for Human Needs: A Comparison of Smartphone Use Between the US and Korea', *Computers in Human Behavior*, 35: 376–387.

Kautsky, K. (1988), *The Agrarian Question*, vol. 1. London: Zwan Publications.

Lin, K-Y. and H-P. Lu (2011), 'Why People Use Social Networking Sites: An Empirical Study Integrating Network Externalities and Motivation Theory', *Computers in Human Behavior*, 27(3): 1152–1161.

Maneepong, C. and J. Walsh (2013), 'A New Generation of Bangkok Street Vendors: Economic Crisis as Opportunity and Threat', *Cities*, 34: 37–43, http://dx.doi.org/10.1016/j.cities.2012.11.002 (accessed 1 September 2018)

Marx, K. (1999), 'Eighteenth Brumaire of Louis Napoleon'. Available at www.marxists.org/archive/marx/works/subject/hist-mat/18-brum/ch07.htm

Meera, S.N., A. Jhamtani and D.U.M. Rao (2004), 'Information and Communication Technology in Agricultural Development: A Comparative Analysis of Three Projects from India', Agricultural and Research Extension Network, *Network Paper*, No. 135. Available at www.odi.org/sites/odi.org.uk/files/odi-assets/publications-opinion-files/5186.pdf

Mendola, M. (2007), 'Agricultural Technology Adoption and Poverty Reduction: A Propensity-Score Matching Analysis for Rural Bangladesh', *Food Policy*, 32(3): 372–393.

Myanmar Climate Change Alliance (2017), 'Impact of Climate Change and the Case of Myanmar'. Available at myanmarccalliance.org/en/climate-change-basics/impact-of-climate-change-and-the-case-of-myanmar

Na Srito, P. and J. Walsh (2012), 'Nakhon Phanom, the Third Mekong Friendship Bridge and the ASEAN Economic Community', *Journal of Social and Development Studies*, 3(5): 172–179.

Nhung, H. (2017), 'Nielsen Busts Myths about Rural Consumers', *Vietnam Economic Times*, 13 July. Available at http://vneconomictimes.com/article/Vietnam-today/Nielsen-busts-myths-about-rural-consumers (accessed 1 September 2018)

Pendergrast, M. (2015), *Beyond Fair Trade: How One Small Coffee Company Helped Transform a Hillside Village in Thailand*. Vancouver: Greystone Books.

Poupon, R. (2013), *The Thai Food Complex: From the Rice Fields to Industrial and Organic Foods*. Bangkok: White Lotus Press.

Prahalad, C.K. (2006), *Fortune at the Bottom of the Pyramid: Eradicating Poverty Through Profits*. Upper Saddle River, NJ: Financial Times, Prentice Hall.

Sar, H. (2016), 'Long Walk to School', *Mizzima Weekly*, 5(10): 16–21, 10 March.

Southiseng, N., S. Vilaychour and J. Walsh (2016), 'Cluster Formation for Lao SMEs in Three Sectors', Economic Research Institute for Industry and Trade (ERIT) Research Report. Available at www.laomoic.org%2Feriit%2Findex.php%3Foption%3Dcom_phocadownload%26view%3Dcategory%26download%3D70%253Acluster-formation-for-lao-smes-in-three-sectors%26id%3D39%253Acluster-formation-for-lao-smes-in-three-sectors%26Itemid%3D59%26lang%3Den&usg=AOvVaw0Dc5Qv49FF2Thh8r3IDMTu

Thein, M. (1997), 'The Economics of Farm Size and Land Policy in the Transition to a Market Economy', *Sojourn: Journal of Social Issues in Southeast Asia*, 12(1): 124–134.

Tung, N.S. and B.Q. Tuan (2016), 'Development and Application of Climate-Smart Agriculture in the Mekong Sub-Region: A Case study of Vietnam', *Vietnam's Socio-Economic Development: A Social Science Review*, 87: 13–28.

Walsh, J. (2015), 'Gendered Decision-Making and Division of Labour in Cambodia and Thailand', *International Journal of Agricultural Resources, Governance and Ecology*, 11(3–4): 209–227.

Walsh, J. (2016), *The Food Insecurity Experience Survey in Lao PDR, Myanmar, Thailand and Vietnam*. Bangkok: SIU Research Centre.

Walsh, J. (2017), 'Thailand's Border Special Economic Zones and Precarious Life and Work', Paper presented at the International Workshop on Living in an Age of Precarity. Singapore: National University of Singapore.

Part IV
Conclusion

12 ASEAN in the digital era
Enabling cross-border e-commerce

Lurong Chen

1. Introduction

Cross-border business-to-business (B2B) e-commerce has been steadily growing since the 1990s. The growth has accelerated with the spread and deepening of global value chains (GVCs) in the 21st century. Until now, B2B still dominates cross-border e-commerce, but the 'e-related' changes could be disruptive. The radical growth of business-to-consumer (B2C) and consumer-to-consumer (C2C) e-commerce has attracted the public's attention to global e-commerce. UNCTAD (2016) shows that global B2C e-commerce has been growing faster than B2B transactions; and the e-commerce market in the Asia-Pacific region is now growing faster than in any other region in the world.

Digitalisation provides shoppers with diversified retail channels with more options. Consumers take advantage of individual company retail websites focussing on B2B and B2C, as well as online marketplaces that also provide C2C services, such as Amazon and eBay. The total number of digital shoppers worldwide grew by over 100 million between 2011 and 2012 – and kept on expanding afterward (Statista 2016). Accordingly, the share of online sales in total revenue has increased continuously. Moreover, new business models, such as the combination of an online market and a brick-and-mortar store, have also emerged and increasingly been adopted by sellers and buyers.

E-commerce sales have climbed steadily worldwide, with sustained growth in sight. The Ecommerce Foundation (2017) estimated the actual market turnover of B2C e-commerce at as much as US$2.3 trillion by the end of 2015, with Asia-Pacific experiencing the fastest growth in the world. The share of e-commerce in total global retail sales increased by 12 percent between 2015 and 2016. In particular, the B2C e-commerce markets in China and India have been booming rapidly. The Chinese market expanded by 27 percent and the Indian market by 75 percent. China has been the world's largest B2C e-commerce market. In 2016, Chinese annual B2C e-commerce turnover reached US$975 billion, equivalent to the combined market size of the United States (the second largest) and the United Kingdom (the third largest). Measured by global Internet reach, eight of the 13 largest global online retail and auction sites (by mid-2014) were Chinese companies. In 2015, the Indian market was equivalent only to around 70 percent of the Canadian market, but a year later, its market size reached US$44.7 billion and surpassed that of Canada.

Globally, revenue from cross-border e-commerce was projected to reach US$600 billion in 2018, twice as much as that in 2012. Overall, the scale of the digital economy in the Association of Southeast Asian Nations (ASEAN) is projected to increase 5.5 times by 2025 (Think with Google, 2017). Overall, the East and Southeast Asian market will account for nearly 40 percent of the world's total revenues generated by cross-border e-commerce, making Asia the global epicentre of e-commerce (BCG, 2014).

From the technical perspective, the combination of e-payment and smartphones have greatly facilitated online shopping. Smartphone access has accounted for more than half of retail website visits worldwide and around one-third of e-retail revenues. Companies specialised in cross-border e-commerce have experienced fast development in mobile business. For example, in the case of DHgate.com, website visits from mobile devices accounted for 42 percent of the platform's total visits in June 2014. The number of orders sent from mobile terminals has more than doubled each year. In the case of Alibaba.com, over 30 percent of the orders came from mobile devices (AliResearch, 2016).

The total annual revenue of the global mobile payment market has been booming, as well. The market is projected to expand by US$150 billion – 170 billion per year and by 2019 to break the US$1 trillion mark. Mobile and personal computer platforms will tend to interact further with each other, and mobile businesses have adopted multi-app strategies. In the next five years, an increasing share of the increment in private consumption will come from global e-commerce growth. Sustained growth of online shoppers provides a solid base for e-commerce consumption. Singapore, Malaysia, and Thailand have been among the world's top markets, with the highest online shopping penetration rates.

ASEAN's digital economy has great potential, and e-commerce could serve as a new engine of regional growth. However, to fully unleash its potential, ASEAN member states (AMS) still have serious 'homework' to complete. This chapter investigates some common challenges faced by ASEAN and its member states, and then provides policy suggestions from the regional perspective. The rest of the chapter is organised as follows: section 2 looks at the future of the e-commerce market and reviews the actions that have been taken at regional and national level. Section 3 draws attention to the challenges from connectivity, services, labour skills, and rules and regulations. Attempting to overcome these, section 4 suggests some policy options to be included in AMS 'to-do' lists. Section 5 concludes.

2. ASEAN's response to economic digitalisation

2.1. ASEAN e-commerce development

The scale of the global e-commerce market has been growing continuously since 2015 (Figure 12.1). The average annual growth rate of retail e-commerce sales

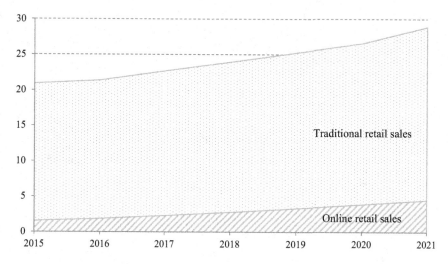

Figure 12.1 Retail E-commerce Sales Worldwide, 2014–2021 (in Trillion US$)
Source: The author. Raw data from Statista (2016).

until 2021 will reach at least 20 percent. This is much higher than the growth rate of traditional retail sales of 4 percent per year. The ratio between online and offline retail sales is projected to be 1:5 by 2021.

E-commerce in many emerging Asian markets has seen double-digit growth. According to Statista (2016), Malaysia and Indonesia are among the world's three fastest-growing retail e-commerce markets. The average compound annual growth rate (CAGR) of e-commerce in Malaysia and Indonesia between 2016 and 2021 is estimated to be 24 percent and 21 percent, respectively. The average CAGRs of other AMS, including those of the Philippines, Thailand, Viet Nam, and Singapore, are also impressive, ranging between 11 percent and 18 percent.

Accordingly, total regional e-commerce revenue is projected to increase from around US$12 billion in 2015 to US$34 billion in 2021 (Figure 12.2). In 2015, Indonesia was the leading market in ASEAN e-commerce. It contributed 38 percent of total regional revenue, followed by Singapore (22 percent). In five years' time, Indonesia will further consolidate its leading position and increase its regional market share to 43 percent. Malaysia will also increase its share from 6 percent to 8 percent during this period. Online business in Singapore will keep growing at a rate of more than 10 percent per year, but its relative share in regional revenue will decrease to 15 percent in 2021.

It is worth noting that China is the largest e-commerce market in the region and growing rapidly (17–18 percent annually). It is estimated that China's share in the world e-commerce market will increase from 30 percent in 2015 to nearly 40 percent in 2021. In comparison, ASEAN's combined share in the global market will increase from 1.2 percent to 1.6 percent. Therefore, when designing a

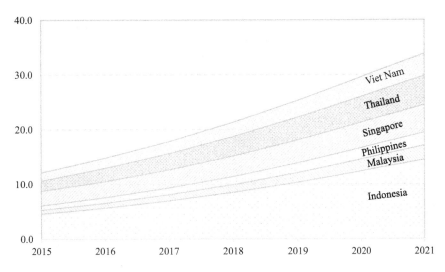

Figure 12.2 E-commerce Market Revenue in ASEAN, 2015–2021 (in Billion US$)
Source: The author. Raw data from Statista (2016).

digital economy strategic plan, AMS should not only consider their domestic market or the ASEAN market, but also think about wider coverage that includes the Chinese market and other big markets in the region.

2.2. *ASEAN's response*

Policy efforts have been underway to promote e-commerce in ASEAN, at both regional and national levels. Region-wide, ASEAN leaders initiated the e-ASEAN project in 1999. The 2000 e-ASEAN Framework Agreement aims to promote a productive ASEAN 'e-space' via (i) the enhancement of the information and communications technology (ICT) sector's competitiveness, (ii) reducing the digital divide within and among individual AMS, (iii) promoting partnership between the public and private sectors, and (iv) trade and investment liberalisation in ICT goods and services (ASEAN Secretariat, 2000). Facilitation of the growth of e-commerce is one of the six main areas[1] covered by the agreement. Moreover, there are joint actions with international trade facilitation measures, as well. For example, the region has already launched the AMS national single window and the ASEAN single window programmes. The 2008 meeting of the ASEAN Working Group on e-commerce and ICT Trade Facilitation gave birth to the ASEAN e-commerce database project to provide a vision of the development of e-commerce in the region.

In most countries, developing the digital economy and e-commerce has already been part of national strategy. By 2017, eight of 10 AMS had already published their broadband plans (Table 12.1). As for cross-border e-commerce, national

Table 12.1 National Broadband Plans in ASEAN

Country	Broadband Plans	Year
Brunei Darussalam	National Broadband Blueprint	2008
Cambodia	Cambodia ICT Development Strategy 2011–2015	2011
Indonesia	The Indonesia Broadband Plan 2014–2019	2013
Malaysia	National Broadband Implementation Strategy (National Broadband Initiative – NBI)	2010
Philippines	The Philippine Digital Strategy Transformation 2.0: Digitally Empowered Nation	2011
Singapore	Intelligent Nation 2015	2005
Thailand	National Broadband Policy	2010
Viet Nam	the Prime Minister's Decision No. 158/ QD-TTg and Decision No. 1755/QD-TTg to approve the national strategy to strengthen the information and communication technology sector in Viet Nam	2010

Sources: EIU (2014), Figure 2; Tayyiba (2015); ITU (2012).

actions normally combine with trade and investment facilitation, as well as measures of economic openness. For instance, in 2015, the Ministry of Industry and Information Technology in China announced that foreign investors were allowed to set up wholly foreign-owned e-commerce companies in the Shanghai Free Trade Zone. The new rules were to lift the 50 percent foreign ownership cap on e-commerce, to allow foreign companies a level playing field in the Chinese market. It also paved the way for expanding cross-border e-commerce and integrating China more with the global network.

In November 2018, ASEAN signed the ASEAN Agreement on E-commerce, which builds on Article 5 (Facilitation of the Growth of Electronic Commerce) of the e-ASEAN Framework Agreement and the e-commerce chapter of the ASEAN-Australia-New Zealand free trade agreement. The agreement incorporates elements in the fields of (i) cross-border information flow, (ii) location of computing facilities, and (iii) cybersecurity (ASEAN Secretariat, 2018). In parallel, ASEAN is also negotiating an e-commerce chapter within the ASEAN Plus Six framework with Japan, the Republic of Korea, China, Australia, New Zealand, and India.

3. Challenges

Challenges and opportunities of e-commerce come hand in hand. In many cases, there is no clear division between the two. Whether something is a challenge or opportunity depends on a country's economy, geography, politics, society, and culture, as well as its market reactions to the new trend of economic digitalisation. Proper actions can turn challenges into opportunities – and vice versa. Therefore, it is important to spot the areas for a country or region to strengthen competitiveness. Particularly, AMS need to pay more attention to (i) connectivity, (ii) services, (iii) rules and regulations, and (iv) labour skills. The following explains the challenges in view of the first three aspects. Labour skills are discussed together with corresponding policy suggestions in Section 4.5.

3.1. Connectivity

Connectivity is the cornerstone of e-commerce development. It consists of (i) the smooth exchange of data and information (information flow), (ii) the delivery of goods and services (logistics), (iii) the payment (cash flow), and (iv) the seamless links between the virtual and physical parts of the e-commerce network. In general, AMS face challenges from development gaps existing across different parts of the country, especially between metropolitan and remote/rural areas. The overall efficiency of connectivity is to some extent limited by those 'short slabs'.

First, the development of e-commerce demands a more stable and affordable Internet connection with higher speed. There are wide gaps in development, despite the countries' efforts in pushing ICT infrastructure. This is evident in the difference in Internet speeds across borders as well as within a country. The Akamai (2017) survey states that the quality of the Internet infrastructure in ASEAN looks satisfactory compared to the world average of peak speed of Internet connection. At the country level, the average Internet connection speeds in the region ranged from 20.3 Mbps in Singapore, ranked seventh globally, to 5.5 Mbps in the Philippines, ranked 100th. The peak Internet connection speeds in the region ranged from over 180 Mbps in Singapore, ranked first in the world, to 42 Mbps in the Philippines, ranked 97th.[2]

The picture is less optimistic when looking at broadband adoption. Not all AMS have met the world average level (Table 12.2). The gaps between the region and the front runners were wider at higher broadband speed tiers, showing that

Table 12.2 Internet Infrastructure in ASEAN

Country	Avg. Mbps	Peak Mbps	Broadband Adoption (IPv4)		
			% above 4 Mbps	% above 10 Mbps	% above 15 Mbps
Indonesia	7.2 (77)	66.1 (43)	76 (71)	18 (68)	5 (69)
Malaysia	8.9 (62)	64.1 (50)	72 (80)	32 (52)	14 (52)
Philippines	5.5 (100)	45 (88)	39 (107)	11 (78)	6.2 (63)
Singapore	20.3 (7)	184.5 (1)	94 (17)	72 (4)	51 (6)
Thailand	16 (21)	106.6 (8)	97 (4)	72 (5)	43 (13)
Viet Nam	9.5 (58)	59 (61)	86 (49)	37 (48)	11 (57)
World average	7.2	44.6	82	45	28

Source: The author. Raw data from Akamai (2017), Figure 23, 24, 25, 26, 27.

Note: Number in parentheses indicate the country's global ranking.

some AMS are still catching up in terms of pushing ICT infrastructure; within countries, the problems of uneven development of ICT infrastructure are quite significant.

Technically, fibre-optic cables are the most efficient media to 'carry' data, despite the rise of satellite use. Even when using mobile phones, the connection is only wireless between the device and the nearest cell phone towers. Data are carried over terrestrial and/or subsea fibre-optic cables. Fundamentally, fibre network building is a crucial part of the needed infrastructure of a digital economy. Compared to traditional fields of infrastructure, fibre technology is progressing rapidly. Building, maintenance, and upgrade of fibre networks require sustained input capital, technology, and managerial efforts. This poses similar challenges to all countries in the world, but many AMS are facing additional difficulties due to a highly dispersed geography and large population. Additionally, capital-scarce countries in particular commonly face budget problems.

Economically, factors such as broadband penetration, the utilisation of broadband infrastructure, and applications are likely to enhance national aggregate outputs (Ng et al., 2013). The development of ICT-related infrastructure in ASEAN is uneven. For instance, the entry-level broadband connection in Singapore is much faster than in Cambodia, Lao PDR, and Myanmar. The Internet Society (2015) categorises AMS in terms of three clusters of wired and wireless broadband. Relatively speaking, the gaps existing in wireless broadband are narrower than those in fixed-wired broadband, but the differences across countries are still quite significant. Region-wide development gaps in ICT infrastructure building may also imply high costs to connect the networks among countries (Table 12.3).

Second, while e-commerce allows people to do business online, delivery of the traded products still requires logistical arrangements. This covers not only trade costs, but also safety, security, reliability, transparency, flexibility, and efficiency. Indeed, e-commerce places higher demands on speed and transparency, posting additional challenges for storage, parcel delivery, and express postal services, thus demanding additional efforts from both physical connectivity

Table 12.3 Broadband Penetration in ASEAN

Types of Broadband	Cluster 1	Cluster 2	Cluster 3
	Majority Access	*Partial Access*	*Low Access*
Fixed-wired broadband	Singapore: 26% Brunei Darussalam: 6% Malaysia: 8%	Thailand: 7% Philippines: 3% Viet Nam: 6%	Indonesia: 1% Lao PDR: 0.1% Cambodia: 0.2% Myanmar: 0.2%
Wireless broadband	Singapore: 137% Brunei Darussalam: 7% Malaysia: 14%	Thailand: 53% Philippines: 27% Viet Nam: 22%	Indonesia: 36% Lao PDR: 2% Cambodia: 10% Myanmar: 1%

Source: The Internet Society (2015), Table 5.

and trade-supporting services. Typical obstacles include poor quality of roads, incomplete road and railway networks, inadequate ports, and problems in energy supply. Table 12.4 illustrates the uneven growth in ASEAN.

Third, e-payment is the vital bridge between the virtual and the physical parts of e-commerce. Its basic function is to provide technical solutions for buyers to pay for goods and services online, although the financial transaction could be either online of offline. Currently, various solutions are available in the market, including cash on delivery, prepaid, credit cards, debit cards, e-banking, mobile payment, smartcard, e-wallets, etc. The existence of various payment modes is a positive factor in promoting the growth of e-commerce, as the diversity gives consumers space to choose their preferred ways to pay for online business.

Ideally, e-commerce development looks for an e-payment system that can accommodate the available market solutions and remain open to new approaches in the future. Rather than being simply a network of payment, it should also be a service platform that can ensure secure transactions, trace credit records, and offer consumer protection. Security, privacy, creditability, reliability, and efficiency are among the factors to be considered. The project of building and maintaining

Table 12.4 Logistics Infrastructure in ASEAN

Country	Quality of Roads[a]	Quality of Railroad Infrastructure[b]	Quality of Air Transport Infrastructure[c]	Quality of Port Infrastructure[d]	Quality of Overall Infrastructure
Brunei Darussalam	4.70 (41)	2.07 (88)[e]	4.08 (84)	3.67 (87)	4.14 (67)
Cambodia	3.38 (93)	1.62 (98)	3.85 (99)	3.85 (76)	3.43 (95)
Indonesia	3.86 (75)	3.82 (39)	4.52 (62)	3.91 (75)	3.79 (80)
Lao PDR	3.42 (91)	n.a.	3.77 (100)	2.01 (132)	3.74 (81)
Malaysia	5.46 (20)	5.06 (15)	5.70 (20)	5.44 (17)	5.48 (19)
Myanmar[f]	2.33 (136)	1.79 (96)	2.62 (132)	2.62 (123)	2.42 (135)
Philippines	3.07 (107)	1.97 (89)	3.25 (116)	2.92 (113)	3.04 (112)
Singapore	6.28 (2)	5.74 (5)	6.85 (1)	6.66 (2)	6.39 (2)
Thailand	4.21 (60)	2.52 (77)	4.95 (42)	4.18 (65)	4.03 (72)
Viet Nam	3.47 (89)	3.15 (52)	4.06 (86)	3.84 (77)	3.63 (85)
World	4.05	3.38	4.41	4.04	4.06

Source: The author. Raw data from WEF (2017), Executive Opinion Survey 2016.

Notes:
n.a. = not available
a. Survey question, 'In your country, how do you assess the quality of the roads? [1 = not at all; 7 = to a great extent]'
b. Survey question, 'In your country, how would you assess the quality of the railroad system? [1 = not at all; 7 = to a great extent]'
c. Survey question, 'In your country, how do you assess the quality of air transport? [1 = not at all; 7 = to a great extent]'
d. Survey question, 'In your country, how do you assess the quality of seaports (for landlocked countries, assess access to seaports). [1 = not at all; 7 = to a great extent]'
e. Data of 2012–2013
f. Data of 2015–2016

an e-payment system is resource-intensive in terms of capital, technology, and human capital. This will be a big challenge to AMS whose domestic banking and financial sectors are still at the early stages of development.

Fourth, extra effort is required for e-commerce-supporting connectivity to smooth the connections between networks of different countries and coordinate the interactions between and among the three-layer networks (information, logistics, and cash flows) mentioned previously. Seamless links between the virtual and physical parts are vital to the functioning of the whole network. This calls for services sector development through multilayer cooperation, including public-private partnership, inter-institutional cooperation, subregional cooperation, and coordination among different government departments.

3.2. Service

Improving services is equally important as building physical infrastructure in every aspect of connectivity – from speed and accuracy to transparency and reliability. For instance, the existence of a reliable credit guarantee system has effectively stimulated cross-border B2B e-commerce. Online e-commerce platforms can collect and integrate information from various sources and provide user service packages. Both buyers and sellers may wish to share real transaction data with service providers, given that the latter have a reliable transaction credit system to help them gain trust and therefore better business opportunities. Extensively, with e-payment development, many financial institutions have found it profitable to provide fiduciary loans using Internet finance. E-commerce platforms such as eBay have started to launch cross-border insurance products to facilitate the transaction process.

From a logistics point of view, service is a key to the efficiency of distribution networks. Online consumers can be more demanding, particularly regarding information, with updates on shipment preparation and tracking delivery. They want to know when anything unexpected occurs – and the corresponding solutions. Indeed, a logistics network will not be optimised until it contains high-standard services, especially in critical facilities in supply chains, such as mega e-fulfilment centres, parcel sorting centres (hubs), local parcel distribution centres for last-mile supply chains, local city logistics depots, and returns centres.

Moreover, connectivity-derived service is also an area where e-commerce-supporting networks can generate extra value added. Services such as providing online credit information can generate value added to e-payment. In this regard, the development of e-commerce-supporting services could be self-enforced. A challenge will be market initiative – by triggering spring-up of services and making the whole industry and supporting facilities more comprehensive.

3.3. Rules and regulations

Cross-border e-commerce calls for new rules and regulations to improve trust, security, and facility in the online marketplace. Without appropriate regulations, there are risks that online business may lead to 'grey' zones of international trade associated with problems such as tax evasion, fake products, or violation of intellectual property rights (IPR).

Collaboration among governments is required, as well as private sector participation, to set up rules and regulations to strengthen global e-commerce governance. Given the status of the World Trade Organization (WTO) as the only international organisation that stipulates trade rules in a comprehensive manner and that can enforce the implementation using its dispute settlement mechanism, multilateral trade negotiation seems to provide an ideal platform for developing countries to participate in global rule setting on e-commerce. However, partially because of the stalemate in WTO negotiations,[3] most e-commerce issues are addressed in bilateral free trade agreements. Developed countries and big multinational companies are the main driving forces behind the process. Thus, challenges to developing countries in Asia are twofold. First, governments should be more active in negotiating and setting new international rules. Second, the voice from the private sector in developing countries should be considered equally to improve the inclusiveness of international agreement(s) on e-commerce.

Regulations on e-commerce will cover traditional trade issues (i.e. tariffs and non-tariff measures, trade facilitation, IPR protection, etc.), as well as new issues (i.e. cross-border information flow, privacy protection, data localisation, source code disclosure, etc.). Although many countries have agreed on trade facilitation issues, such as the acceptance of electronic authentication in commercial transactions and the use of customised electronic formats in paperless trade, reaching an agreement on some core e-commerce issues is not an easy task.

Rule setting in international information flow is a direct example. Information is the blood of e-commerce, with extensive effects on the economy, society, and even national security. It is, however, difficult to balance free data movement and privacy protection. While insufficient regulations lead to lack of market fairness and competition, excessive restrictions may generate negative impacts on free movement and accuracy of information.

Since cross-border e-commerce involves buyers and sellers located in different countries and governed by different laws and regulations, both international cooperation and domestic efforts are necessary to investigate, pursue, obtain, and, where appropriate, share relevant information and evidence, particularly on matters relating to cross-border fraudulent and deceptive commercial practices (OECD, 2016). Measures such as data localisation, privacy protection, and online censorship may have the potential to lower the volume of e-commerce trade in the short term. However, these measures are not necessarily trade barriers in the sense that they could help strengthen security, IPRs, and consumer protection, contribute to trust and legislation of online trade, and eventually promote e-commerce.

4. Policy recommendations

Opportunities and challenges of e-commerce are two sides of the same coin. In a nutshell, the market's actions determine whether and how to benefit from the new global economy trend of digitalisation. National strategic development plans and associated economic policies will also play a role. AMS all have included digital economy and e-commerce in their national plans. When implementing the plans, however, it is highly recommended that governments not directly intervene in the market. Alternatively, it will be more efficient for governments to help build up an 'e-commerce friendly' ecosystem and make it work for the development of digital economy, given the related economic, social, and cultural conditions.

4.1. ASEAN e-commerce-enabling ecosystem

E-commerce needs a suitable environment to grow. Although it is market mechanisms that should lead the transition, the role of policy intervention should not be neglected. Indeed, the market will appreciate the government's support in establishing and optimising such an environment, especially in areas where the market fails in allocating resources. The policy efforts, as far as they are in the right direction, can help the market cut down 'reaction' times to changes associated with economic digitalisation and promptly seize initiatives in global competition. This could be vital to success, because timing is critical to success in the digital age.

Value chains of e-commerce cover both the physical world and cyberspace. These two 'worlds' influence each other. For instance, the capacity and performance of fibre-optic cables determine the speed of data flow on the Internet, whereas major cyberattacks may lead to chaos in the real world. In this regard, a government's measures to improve connectivity include increasing the supply of public goods of infrastructure in both the physical world and cyberspace; establishing rules and regulations to ensure dynamics and competition of the online marketplaces; improving connectivity-derived services to generate more value added and job opportunities; and collaborating in building the region-wide e-commerce-friendly ecosystem.

Indeed, when e-commerce goes international, it is subjected to almost all issues that apply to other forms of trade. E-commerce in general and cross-border e-commerce are virtually the same concept, if obstacles holding back cross-border e-commerce are removed. That is, it no long matters whether a transaction occurs domestically or across borders. A top priority is to prevent data protectionism that damages cross-border free data flows, which is the core of cross-border e-commerce.

4.2. Improving connectivity

Connectivity is the key – and it covers multiple aspects. First of all, the public sector should lead in building infrastructure. Although it is less likely that improving connectivity can totally eliminate the digital divide, either among or within countries, at least it will contribute to reducing the divide by increasing the supply of public goods, in both quantity and quality.

A particular issue to highlight is capacity. To developing counties, obstacles normally come from capacity or/and resource limits, either capital or technology or both. Enhancing regional cooperation will provide a solution. In this regard, AMS should welcome the entry of Japanese and Chinese construction companies in the infrastructure sector. Governments of both countries are willing to provide low interest rate loans or other forms of financial assistance to host countries in support of infrastructure projects with their companies' participation. They have launched projects and raised funds to help develop Asian infrastructure via mechanisms such as the Asian Infrastructure Investment Bank, China's Belt and Road Initiative, and Japan's US$110 billion proposal for infrastructure in ASEAN.

Second, in addition to physical infrastructure that enables data and capital flow, the online marketplace needs rules and regulations to ensure the free movement and accuracy of information; fair access to information; protection of consumers and producers; security of payment, free trade, and investment; and therefore, market dynamics and competition. The related regulations will cover traditional trade issues and new issues (see Section 3.3 for details).

Third, improving services is equally important as building physical infrastructure in every aspect of connectivity – from speed and accuracy to security, transparency, and reliability. In general, user demand will motivate supply chain operations to create a greater focus on near-sourcing, omnichannel, and faster transport solutions (Inbound Logistics, 2014). Connectivity-derived service tends to have extensive implications on regional development as well. On the one hand, development of the services sector can create more jobs to absorb labour. On the other, service efficiency will decrease trade costs and increase reliability, and therefore promote e-commerce activities.

Fourth, Asian countries should focus on new technologies that can provide new solutions to improve regional connectivity. Two areas worth highlighting are (i) the smartphone economy, and (ii) innovation in e-payment and e-finance. The development of these areas deserves priority, since they could be the breakthroughs necessary for developing countries to achieve 'leap-forward development'.

4.2.1. Innovation in e-payment and e-finance

In many AMS, the development of domestic banking and the finance sector still lags behind their achievement in other aspects of economic growth. Problems in the financial area, such as the low coverage of the banking network, premature personal/household credit system, and lack of an efficient capital market, often hold back a country's economic development.

Following the traditional approach taken by developed countries to establish a modern banking system will take a longer time. E-commerce-deriving financial innovations, such as e-payment and Internet financing, can provide better (lower cost and easier to use) solutions to the market, either complementary or independent to the traditional banking and financial architecture. Indeed, these new tools and models have proved to be so efficient that even traditional financial service providers are eager to adopt them.

These innovations in e-payment and e-finance will be market changers and give AMS opportunities to achieve 'leap-forward development'. The process can be market driven and self-enforced as far as it does not encounter serious policy resistance. Policy efforts at the regional level, such as establishing industrial standards and harmonising regulations, could help the industry realise the scale of economy and support its development.

4.2.2. The smartphone economy

Smartphones and mobile applications (apps) provide a powerful new platform for e-commerce growth. The technical conditions for use of smartphones in e-commerce are mature – both in terms of functionality and affordability of phones, as well as the variety and reliability of applications to be installed and used. A smartphone today can replace many other devices and integrate their functions by simply installing an app. For example, it can work as a token for an e-signature, as a scanner to capture a product code, and as a credit card reader.

Market conditions are in favour, as well. Both the price of devices and the cost of mobile data use have been driven down dramatically. More people now use smartphones as their daily companion; not just as a phone, but a 'personal assistant in the pocket'. More than half of smartphone owners have already used their phones for online shopping and transaction (Think with Google, 2016).

In this regard, cross-border e-commerce based on smartphones and related mobile devices have huge potential. It is more user-friendly, more global in scope, and more open and promising to sustainable growth. To accelerate cross-border e-commerce, countries can consider prioritising smartphones and mobile apps. The following are some available policy options:

i Invest in the supporting infrastructure of smartphones, such as increasing wireless bandwidth and the number of Internet exchange points.
ii Keep driving down the cost of mobile data use, especially international roaming data use. In order to lower the price, governments may need to intervene in the Internet service market, which is normally monopolistic or oligopolistic.
iii Give consideration for low-income groups that cannot afford smartphones. Governments may consider providing a subsidy (or encouraging business donation) to help them obtain a device and offer necessary training to show how to use it.
iv Encourage creation and incremental innovation.

4.3. Encouraging value-added services

The development of the service sector can additionally increase government revenue, which will provide more resources to invest in infrastructure and capacity building to further improve connectivity. This helps the development of e-commerce-supporting services to be self-enforcing. Moreover, new emerging service intermediaries can lead structural changes in e-commerce. More broadly, E-commerce development generates more business opportunities for downstream companies in areas such as material suppliers, market investigation, software development, shipment and delivery, agency operation, search for keywords, and optimisation. As the production network clustering around the upstream core e-commerce actor(s) starts to deepen and spread, it leads to a finer division of labour – and therefore, a higher degree of specialisation. With more detailed market segmentation, demand is more precisely identified, and therefore, more service activities will find space for expansion. In this way, the growth of services can be market driven.

In particular, this generates opportunities for small and medium-sized enterprises (SMEs) to join GVCs. In Asia, SMEs account for over 95 percent of all enterprises in number and employ more than 80 percent of the workforce. Development of e-commerce and expansion of GVCs and related services help SMEs get involved in GVCs and benefit more from globalisation by enabling them to access more information, explore new markets, obtain better microfinance, and further enhance supplier-producer-consumer links.

4.4. Rule setting and regulatory harmonisation

The online marketplace needs rules and regulations to ensure free data flows as well as fair play, competition, and security. Internationally, cross-border e-commerce development is promoting the formation of global governance on digital trade. These new rules and regulations will then influence the development of e-commerce.

There is no doubt that cross-border e-commerce is a major development trend of international trade and globalisation in the 21st century. AMS may anchor their development to this global trend to reduce poverty, narrow inequality, or escape the middle-income trap. Accordingly, they should adopt policies in favour of globalisation and trade facilitation. Typically, cross-border e-commerce is hampered by difficulties in customs clearance, exchange settlement, and tax reimbursement,[4] especially for small-volume trade flows. The World Economic Forum (2017) estimates that lowering the supply chain barriers between countries, such as customs formalities, would increase cross-border e-commerce by 60–80 percent.

As for global trade governance, the current progress in multilateral trade negotiations can hardly catch up with the radical growth of e-commerce. It is reasonable to expect the 21st century free trade agreements – the ones that contain WTO-Plus and WTO extra provisions – to be pilots in new rule making, and the related global standards may be later established based on the related provisions existing in these agreements.

However, reaching agreement on some core issues about e-commerce will never be an easy task. It will be hard to balance the interests in economy, society, and national security, as well as the long-term gains and short-term costs. This again calls for collaboration among governments, as well as private sector participation in rule setting.

Indeed, the ASEAN leaders have been putting more effort into enhancing inter-governmental collaboration in these areas. It took less than 1.5 years to conclude the ASEAN Agreement on E-commerce. Implementing this agreement is expected to help ASEAN and AMS overcome the obstacles that hinder the e-commerce development. As the ASEAN Secretariat (2018) states, benefits are expected to come from improvements in (i) domestic regulatory framework; (ii) transparency; (iii) cooperation; (iv) facilitating electronic transaction and trading; (v) cross-border data and information flows, and location of computing facilities; (vi) logistics; (vii) consumer protection and privacy; and (viii) technology neutrality.

4.5. Improving human capital and labour skills

Most importantly, it is human capital and innovation that will be the key to the long-term success of e-commerce. The lack of skills has serious implications on e-commerce development in Asia. First, e-commerce is knowledge intensive. High-tech devices, software, and applications are widely used in production and business. Qualified labour must have sufficient technical skills to handle these tools proficiently, especially in real-world problem solving. Second, endorsed by ICT and services sector development, GVCs functioning behind e-commerce are much more sophisticated than ever before. The workforce will need high managerial skills to operate the network and monitor its functioning. Third, with the rapid growth of the B2C and C2C markets, e-commerce users will require the skills and knowledge that previously only experts had, such as knowledge about home and overseas markets, understanding different consumer habits, and learning about the trading rules. Fourth, human resources in e-commerce should be able to learn quickly about new technologies and business models that continuously emerge in the market. Fifth, innovation is a key to competitiveness. Reliance on homogenous products or services cannot lead to long-term success in e-commerce. The majority of value added in GVCs is generated by the most innovative elements or stages.

In ASEAN, the imminent challenges of developing a digital economy are twofold. First, it poses direct pressure on countries' education and training systems, both in terms of coverage and quality. That education lags behind compared to developed countries is not a problem specific to e-commerce. However, the rapid growth of e-commerce and the desire to grasp development opportunities associated with economic digitalisation urge developing countries to accelerate their pace in improving education, which is a long-term project in nature. It is critical to find a balance between expanding quantity and increasing quality, as well as between wide coverage and emphasis of growth.

Second, developing a digital economy also calls for region-wide service liberalisation and the free movement of skilled labour to help accelerate knowledge diffusion. Despite the progress and achievements in regional integration, cross-border labour mobility in ASEAN is still subject to barriers such as non-recognition of academic diplomas and professional certificates, lack of information about labour market opportunities, and domestic restrictions on work permits for foreigners.

5. Concluding remarks

Digitalisation and e-commerce are changing the world economic landscape. Opportunities and challenges coexist. To better grasp the opportunities for growth, ASEAN needs to make progress in connectivity, services, rules and regulations, and labour skills.

Policy intervention, as a supplement to market mechanisms, can help the market take the advantage of the information revolution and prevent potential market failure. First, policy efforts should establish an environment to enable e-commerce and support its growth. Second, governments need to continuously work on improving e-commerce-enabling connectivity. Third, the service sector deserves more policy attention as its development directly links to the dynamics of the e-commerce ecosystem. Fourth, cross-border e-commerce calls for new rules and regulations. Asian countries should actively participate in rule setting.

Speaking for ASEAN, in addition to individual national efforts, progress towards regional integration provides policymakers with an extra dimension to promote e-commerce development via deeper market integration and cooperation. The conclusion of the ASEAN Agreement on E-commerce is certainly a milestone achievement. Nevertheless, to what extent this can effectively benefit e-commerce development in ASEAN will still depend on how well the agreement will be implemented. At the time of writing, the e-commerce chapter of the Regional Comprehensive Economic Partnership is still under negotiation, but it is never too early to start thinking about the implementation of the commitments and the related policy packages, even before reaching an agreement.

Notes

1 The framework covers (i) ASEAN information infrastructure, (ii) electronic commerce, (iii) trade and investment liberalisation in ICT goods and services, (iv) trade facilitation in ICT products, (v) e-society, and (vi) e-government.
2 Data for Brunei Darussalam, Cambodia, Lao PDR, and Myanmar were not included in the original report by Akamai (2017).
3 In 1998, the WTO Ministerial Conference adopted the Declaration on Global Electronic Commerce aiming to establish a comprehensive work programme to examine all trade-related issues relating to global electronic commerce. There was, however, no substantive progress afterwards.
4 The lack of a Europe-wide value-added tax system is one of the big obstacles for cross-border e-commerce in Europe.

Bibliography

Akamai (2017), 'Q1 2017 State of the Internet Connectivity Report'. Available at www.akamai.com/us/en/about/our-thinking/state-of-the-Internet-report/
AliResearch (2016), 'China Cross-Border E-Commerce Report'. Available at http://download.dhgate.com/files/White%20Paper.pdf
ASEAN Secretariat (2000), '2000 e-ASEAN Framework Agreement'. Available at http://asean.org/?static_post=e-asean-framework-agreement
ASEAN Secretariat (2018), 'Factsheet on ASEAN Agreement on E-Commerce'. Available at www.asean2018.sg/Newsroom

Boston Consulting Group (BCG) (2014), 'Cross-Border E-Commerce Makes the World Flatter'. Available at www.bcg.com/perspectives/170622

Ecommerce Foundation (2017), 'The European Ecommerce Report 2017'. Available at https://ecommercenews.eu/ecommerce-europe-e602-billion-2017/

Economist Intelligence Unit (EIU) (2014), 'The Future of Broadband in South-East Asia'. Available at www.eiuperspectives.economist.com/sites/default/files/SE%20 Asia%20Huawei%20report%20Sep%2019.pdf

Economist Intelligence Unit (2017), 'The Inclusive Internet Index'. Available at https://theinclusiveinternet.eiu.com/

Inbound Logistics (2014), 'Adapting Your Supply Chain for the Future Now'. Available at www.inboundlogistics.com/cms/article/adapting-your-supply-chain-for-the-futurenow/

International Labour Organization (ILO) (2016), 'ASEAN in Transformation'. Available at www.ilo.org/public/english/dialogue/actemp/downloads/publica tions/2016/asean_in_transf_2016_r3_persp.pdf

International Telecommunication Union (ITU) (2012), *Wireless Broadband Masterplan until 2020 for the Socialist Republic of Viet Nam*. Geneva: ITU.

The Internet Society (2015), 'The Potential of the Internet for ASEAN Economies'. Available at www.internetsociety.org/sites/default/files/ASEAN_ISOC_Digital_ Economy_Report_Full_0.pdf

Ng, Tuan Hock, Chun Teck Lye and Ying San Lim (2013), 'Broadband Penetration and Economic Growth in ASEAN Countries: A Generalized Method of Moments Approach', *Applied Economics Letters*, 20(9): 857–862.

Organisation for Economic Co-operation and Development (OECD) (1998), OECD Ministerial Conference, 'A Borderless World: Realising the Potential of Global Electronic Commerce', Ottawa, 7–9 October, Conference Conclusions. Available at http://search.oecd.org/officialdocuments/displaydocumentpdf/?doclanguage= en&cote=sg/ec(98)14/final)

Organisation for Economic Co-operation and Development (OECD) (2016), *OECD Recommendation of the Council on Consumer Protection in E-Commerce*. Paris: OECD.

Statista (2016), 'Digital Market Outlook'. Available at www.statista.com/statistics/ 220177/b2c-commerce-sales-cagr-forecast-for-selected-countries/

Tayyiba, Mia (2015), 'Indonesia Broadband Plan: Lessons Learned'. Available at www. itu.int/en/ITU-D/Regional-Presence/AsiaPacific/Documents/Events/2015/ Sep-WABA/Presentations/Indonesia%2520Broadband%2520Plan%2520(ITU%2 520Jakarta%2C%2520090915).pdf

Think with Google (2016), 'How People Shop on Their Phones'. Available at www. google.com/url?sa=t&rct=j&q=&esrc=s&source=web&cd=1&cad=rja&uact=8& ved=0ahUKEwiKrpG38snVAhXEuI8KHZdRCfYQFgglMAA&url=https%3A%2F %2Fwww.thinkwithgoogle.com%2F_qs%2Fdocuments%2F322%2Fapp-marketing-mobile-shopping.pdf&usg=AFQjCNEJ5wt1Dm7MHC1_BKRxpzgAlCMsGw

Think with Google (2017), 'E-economy SEA, Unlocking the 200 Billion Digital Opportunity in Southeast Asia'. Available at http://apac.thinkwithgoogle.com/ research-studies/e-conomy-sea-unlocking-200b-digital-opportunity.html

United Nations Conference on Trade and Development (UNCTAD) (2016), 'UNCTAD B2C E-Commerce Index 2016'. *UNCTAD Technical Notes on ICT for Development*, No. 7. Geneva: UNCTAD.

World Economic Forum (2017), 'The Global Competitiveness Report 2016–2017'. Available at www.weforum.org/reports/the-global-competitiveness-report-2016-2017-1

Index

Note: **Boldface** page references indicate tables. *Italic* references indicate figures.

Printed in the United States
by Baker & Taylor Publisher Services